Sites Unseen

AMERICA AND THE LONG 19th CENTURY

General Editors: David Kazanjian,
Elizabeth McHenry, and Priscilla Wald

Black Frankenstein: The Making of an American Metaphor
Elizabeth Young

*Neither Fugitive nor Free: Atlantic Slavery, Freedom
Suits, and the Legal Culture of Travel*
Edlie L. Wong

*Shadowing the White Man's Burden: U.S. Imperialism
and the Problem of the Color Line*
Gretchen Murphy

Bodies of Reform: The Rhetoric of Character in Gilded-Age America
James B. Salazar

*Empire's Proxy: American Literature and U.S.
Imperialism in the Philippines*
Meg Wesling

Sites Unseen: Architecture, Race, and American Literature
William A. Gleason

Sites Unseen

Architecture, Race, and

American Literature

William A. Gleason

NEW YORK UNIVERSITY PRESS
New York and London

NEW YORK UNIVERSITY PRESS
New York and London
www.nyupress.org

References to Internet websites (URLs) were accurate at the time of writing.
Neither the author nor New York University Press is responsible for URLs
that may have expired or changed since the manuscript was prepared.

Library of Congress Cataloging-in-Publication Data
Gleason, William A.
Sites unseen : architecture, race, and American literature /
William A. Gleason.
p. cm. — (America and the long 19th century)
Includes bibliographical references and index.
ISBN 978–0–8147–3246–5 (cloth : acid-free paper) — ISBN 978–0–8147–3247–2
(pbk. : acid-free paper) — ISBN 978–0–8147–3248–9 (e-book)
1. American literature—19th century—History and criticism.
2. Architecture in literature. 3. Race in literature. 4. Architecture and
literature. 5. American literature—20th century—History and criticism.
I. Title.
PS217.A73G54   2011
810.9'357—dc22   2011007837

New York University Press books are printed on acid-free paper,
and their binding materials are chosen for strength and durability.
We strive to use environmentally responsible suppliers and materials
to the greatest extent possible in publishing our books.

Manufactured in the United States of America

c   10 9 8 7 6 5 4 3 2 1
p   10 9 8 7 6 5 4 3 2 1

This time, for Celia

Contents

List of Illustrations

Acknowledgments

Like my first book this one has been a long time in the making and has benefited from innumerable gestures of support, assistance, and encouragement. Special thanks must go again to Martha Banta, for showing me what it means to read and think and write with breadth and imagination and care; and to Eric Sundquist for (in this case) introducing me to the work of Charles Chesnutt. Once again I am also glad to thank the many colleagues, advisees, and friends who have read portions of the manuscript, talked with me about this project, or simply provided inspiration, including Oliver Arnold, Dave Ball, Peter Betjemann, Catherine Bishir, Christine Boyer, Daphne Brooks, Adrienne Brown, Eduardo Cadava, Anne Cheng, Judith Ferszt, Diana Fuss, Simon Gikandi, Dirk Hartog, Briallen Hopper, Greg Jackson, Claudia Johnson, Lois Leveen, Sarah Luria, Beth Machlan, Lee Mitchell, Jeff Nunokawa, Hollis Robbins, Valerie Smith, Vance Smith, Thorin Tritter, Sean Wilentz, and Michael Wood. I must also thank all the students in American Studies 201: American Places who for more than a decade have engaged me in such rich discussions about space and place.

I owe a particular debt to the staff of the Winterthur Research Fellowship Program at the Winterthur Library, where some of the most critical research for this book took place, particularly Gretchen Buggeln, Pat Elliott, and Gary Kulick, as well as the extraordinary group of research fellows and faculty who made me feel so welcome during my stay there: Peter Brownlee, Melissa Duffes, Stephanie Foote, Ritchie Garrison, Holly Heinzer, Bernard Herman, Arlette Klaric, Stephen Long, Ellen Menefee, Cynthia Munro, Mike Murphy, and Barbara Penner. I am grateful to the Environment and Culture Caucus of the American Studies Association for helping me find a home in what I like to call the "built environment wing" of the ECC, especially founding members Joni Adamson and Adam Sweeting. I also wish to thank the co-panelists and audience members who heard and commented on early versions of portions of this book at meetings of the American Studies Association; the Modern Language Association; the Winterthur Scholars Seminar; the Delaware Seminar in Art, History, and Material Culture; and the Princeton Society of Fellows.

Librarians, libraries, and societies near and far have helped me at every stage of this project. At Princeton I thank in particular the Princeton University Library (including Circulation, Interlibrary Loan, Graphic Arts, and Rare Books and Special Collections), the Architecture Library, and the Marquand Library of Art and Archaeology. At the Winterthur Library I thank Rich McKinstry, Helena Richardson, Jeanne Solensky, and especially Neville Thompson. I am also grateful to the research staffs at the Hagley Library and Archives and the El Paso Public Library for their assistance in helping me locate materials. I thank Nancy Carlisle of the Society for the Preservation of New England Antiquities for putting me in touch with Jane S. Tucker of Wicasset, Maine, and Jane S. Tucker for letting me spend time studying the veritable library of Vantine's artifacts to be found in Castle Tucker, her family home, in order better to understand their decorative use in situ. I also thank the several Vantine's collectors who graciously sent me photocopies of catalogs not available in the conventional archives.

At NYU Press I thank series editors Priscilla Wald, David Kazanjian, and Elizabeth McHenry; my editors, Eric Zinner, Ciara McLaughlin, and Despina Papazoglou Gimbel, and my copyeditor, Susan Ecklund; and especially the two anonymous readers whose detailed reports were so tremendously useful to me during the late phases of revision. For preparing the photographs of most of the images in this book I thank Princeton's ever-cheerful John Blazejewski.

Research and fellowship support for this project has been generously provided by Princeton University, including the Department of English; the George A. and Eliza Gardner Howard Foundation; and the National Endowment for the Humanities, which sponsored my semester at Winterthur. I thank each of these institutions in particular for their support of interdisciplinary work.

Portions of this study have appeared in print, and I am grateful for permission to reprint them here. An early version of chapter 2 appeared in *American Quarterly* 51 (1999), and an early version of chapter 1 appeared in Henry Louis Gates Jr. and Hollis Robbins, eds., *In Search of Hannah Crafts* (2004).

I must close by thanking those with whom I share my own house: my wife, Andrea, whose professional journals on planning and architecture have long helped train me in fields not originally my own; and my children, Celia and Jeffrey, two future writers who each day help make our space into a home. This book is dedicated in particular to Celia, for most of whose life-time I have been working on this study, and who in times of need lent me her own desk, on which much of this book was written.

Introduction
Race, Writing, Architecture

American Patterns

Architecture is fictional at a fundamental level. Yet its fictions are not just make-believe worlds, but rather the making of worlds, constitutive of our social being.

—K. Michael Hays, Catherine Ingraham, and
Alicia Kennedy, "On the House" (1994)

The idea for this book emerged from a deceptively simple question: Why are there so many porches in the conjure tales of Charles Chesnutt? Although Chesnutt's conjure stories center on often-fantastic transformations within a reimagined slave South, the contemporary frame settings of his late nineteenth-century tales can seem repetitious at best, almost always placing the same characters on the same porch of the same post-Reconstruction North Carolina mansion. Was this repetition a sign of a lack of narrative imagination? Or was Chesnutt's insistent return to the plantation porch instead a canny exploration of a powerfully resonant physical site and social space? And what did it mean in particular for an African American author writing at the so-called nadir of American race relations—and the peak of the Colonial Revival—to probe the socio-spatial legacy of the architecture of slavery? Why those porches, in this way, at that moment?

My pursuit of answers to these questions took me deep into Chesnutt's work and the state of late nineteenth-century American architecture before eventually leading to the chapters that make up *Sites Unseen*, a study of race, American literature, and the built environment. I soon found there were many sites like Chesnutt's porch in American writing: architectural representations, including but not limited to the built environment of slavery, that engage America's racial and spatial history in compelling ways, sites that had nonetheless largely been overlooked or ignored by scholars otherwise interested in the intersections between literature and architecture. Indeed, although race has been one of the most important analytic, theoretical, and historical categories in literary studies for more than a quarter century, it has played only a small role in the interdisciplinary study of architecture and literature—or, to borrow a phrase, the study of "buildings and books."[1] And although ideas about race and ideas about architecture turn out to be complexly intertwined in nineteenth- and early twentieth-century American culture, no major work has appeared on this subject. These are oversights this book aims to reverse. Foregrounding a series of often unexamined spaces, texts, and interactions while also returning to familiar forms with new questions, *Sites Unseen* seeks to make cultural and material practices that have heretofore gone largely unremarked—by literary critics and architectural theorists alike—visible and salient.[2]

In addition to reconstituting the interdisciplinary field of architecture and American literature to include a broader range of authors, this book thus investigates new narrative and physical territory. Rather than focus exclusively, for example, on the grand and the genteel, like so many previous studies—yet without ignoring what have traditionally been considered "white" spaces and texts—*Sites Unseen* interrogates a variety of equally expressive American vernacular forms, including (on the one hand) the dialect tale, the novel of empire, letters, and pulp stories, and (on the other) the plantation cabin, the West Indian cottage, the Latin American plaza, and the "Oriental" parlor. These are some of the overlooked plots and structures, I argue, that can and should inform a more comprehensive consideration of the literary and cultural meanings of American architecture from roughly 1850 to 1930, the period in which American architecture came of age as both a domestic profession and an international practice. Making sense of the complex relations between architecture, race, and American writing gives us a clearer view not only of this formative era but more broadly of what architectural historian Dell Upton has aptly termed the social experience of the built environment.[3]

Literature has a special role to play in the recovery and articulation of this experience. Stories rooted in specific places and housed in particular structures can tell us a great deal not only about past practices but also about meanings and ideologies, both shared and contested. But literature cannot do this job alone, and *Sites Unseen* thus draws crucially on important work by scholars in multiple additional fields, including history, urban planning, architecture, cultural geography, and material culture.[4] Indeed, it seeks to make these fields speak to each other in new ways. At stake are questions at once historical, material, literary, and philosophical. What are the specific relays between architecture and race in nineteenth- and early twentieth-century American culture and society? How are the racial dynamics of the built environment registered in the narratives of American writers? Whose stories, and what places, have we overlooked? Finally, how does the recovery of past meanings help us envision, design, or inhabit spaces today? Before turning to an account of the specific chapters in this study, I want first to place in view a few of the most important ways—and some of the most fascinating texts and objects—in which race, architecture, and representation have been inextricably linked in the U.S. in the nineteenth and early twentieth centuries.

Race and Architecture in the Pattern Book Era

A central premise of this book is that the built environment is always shaped in some way by race whether such shaping is explicitly acknowledged or understood. By this I mean that even structures appearing to have no racial inflection whatsoever cannot be understood apart from the racial circumstances that helped create them. Although contemporary scholars have only recently begun to pay close attention to the relationship between race and architecture, in the nineteenth century most American commentators understood built forms to have explicitly racial origins and connotations. Many of the very earliest American builders' guides, for example, dating from the late eighteenth century, included "Oriental" home designs—where "Oriental" could mean anything from Asian to East Indian to Middle Eastern—and even such imports as Italian and Gothic architecture were considered not merely national or regional styles but expressions of racial character.[5] As Scott Trafton has recently shown, the wide-ranging project of nineteenth-century American revivalism, which embraced such disparate yet overlapping modes as the Classical Revival and the Egyptian Revival, depended on an expressly racial understanding of architectural structures. "Much of the project of architectural revivalism was the construction of a set of essentialist connections between people and their buildings, and architectural styles were rendered with . . . ethnographic precision," Trafton observes. "Nineteenth-century revivalist architects were voracious in their considerations of nationalized or racialized styles of architecture, and the history of revivalism is characterized by continual comparisons between carefully delineated geographic—and what during this period were therefore ethnological—regions."[6]

By midcentury—the heyday of what we might call the pattern book era, when architectural publications were marketed directly to home buyers and not just builders and contractors[7]—such ideas were embedded not only in architectural publications but also in the broader culture, finding their way even into literature for children. N. W. Fiske's book, *A Rapid Tour around the World; or Young Peter's Remarks to His Cousins upon the Different Nations* (1846), for example, treats architecture as both sign and symptom of national and/or racial identity. Virtually all seventeen entries, ranging from "The Englishman" to "The Persian" to "The American," highlight architectural details in their snapshot descriptions, according built forms the same signifying power as clothing, food, religion, social mores, and forms of government. Several entries even feature built structures in their accompanying illustrations. The tour begins with the English, whom Young Peter accounts "generally a very well looking people."[8] Not surprisingly, the same can be said of their public buildings, which are described as "very costly and magnificent" (8–9). Even "the cottages of the poor are extremely neat; the walls being annually whitewashed; and the doors and windows overhung and festooned with honeysuckles and roses and other flowers" (9). In France, where "dress is a very important thing with every individual from the highest to the lowest," there are "many splendid public edifices . . . presenting the noblest forms of architecture" (17). The farther *A Rapid Tour* progresses, however, the less splendid the structures (and by implication the people) typically become. For instance, Young Peter is appalled at the disorderly domestic arrangements required by the servant-intensive homes of Russian nobility. "An enormous number of servants is sometimes attached to the establishment of a nobleman or grandee in Petersburgh; 400 or even 500, it is said," the book notes. At night "they are obliged to make their beds on the floors of the rooms and entries, of the kitchen and all the back apartments, which then present a motley crowd of human beings huddled together, under sheep-skins, great-coats, bed-covers and the like, in bad air, amid filth and vermin" (36). The phrase "it is said" in this passage suggests *A Rapid Tour* deals primarily in hearsay and stereotype, but that is partly my point. Texts like Fiske's generally consolidate rather than upend accepted beliefs about links between the built environment and national or racial character, making such sources useful as indices of the interpenetration of ideas about architecture and ideas about race.[9]

Outside Europe it takes a bit more to impress Young Peter. Although he notes that "Turkish cities have a splendid appearance," this is only the case when they are viewed "at a distance, on account of the towers, domes and minarets, which make an imposing show. But in the interior," Young Peter warns, "every thing is the reverse; the houses have neither elegance nor comfort; although there is sometimes much finery in the rooms" (69). Young

Figure 1. "The Chinaman," N. W. Fiske, *A Rapid Tour around the World; or Young Peter's Remarks to His Cousins upon the Different Nations* (1846), 92.

Peter is somewhat more taken by the "striking" and "peculiar" architectural signature of the Chinese, the pagoda, which was "supposed to have been formed originally after the model of a tent" (94). The accompanying illustration for "The Chinaman" duly models person and structure as parallel objects (Fig. 1). This conjunction is underscored by the text, which emphasizes the immense size not only of Chinese pagodas—"which sometimes rise to the height of nine stories" (96)—but also of Chinese bodies: "Their figure is rather large and corpulency is considered by them as becoming" (93). In the illustration the human figure mimics yet also dwarfs the work of architecture, as though the Chinese person depicted is merely the massive tower writ even larger. In its penultimate chapter, *A Rapid Tour* visits Africa, which it presents to its young readers as a collection of uncivilized tribes. "The native tribes are generally in the state of society which is denominated barbarian," Young Peter explains. Naturally, their architecture is just as primitive. "The houses are of very rude construction. The materials of the very best are merely stakes of wood plastered with earth; built in conical form like beehives. Many of them are designed chiefly for sleep at night or shelter from the showers" (104). The final chapter of *A Rapid Tour* introduces "The American" but demurs from illustrating him. "We have no picture for an American," Young Peter confesses. "We do not know how to draw him or describe him. The American, as he now is, seems to possess a combination of most of the good qualities of all other races of men, together with not a few of the bad ones" (107). The American's architectural accomplishments are similarly eclectic—and decidedly progressive. Much as he has developed in character and accomplishment beyond the more primitive native races of North America, the American builds better and with more variety. "In the place of the rude wigwam or hut of sticks and bark," Young Peter avers, "are houses of comfort and elegance, spacious mansions and temples, and villages and cities filling the land" (108–9).

A Rapid Tour's particular account of the material progress of "The American" suggests not merely a version of architectural manifest destiny but also a racial hierarchy of built forms. Other writers at midcentury would make this hierarchy even more explicit. Here it is helpful to examine the widely circulating pattern books that were exerting considerable cultural influence in the U.S. in the 1840s and 1850s. In *A Home for All: or a New, Cheap, Convenient, and Superior Mode of Building* (1848), for example, architectural innovator Orson Squire Fowler (who popularized the mid-nineteenth-century fad of the octagon-shaped house) theorized that human races, like animal species, build according to their innate physical and mental characteristics. "The residences of the various tribes of animals bear a close analogy to their characters," Fowler explains. "Thus, low-bred, coarse-grained inferior animals make inferior homes, of which worms, moths, etc., furnish examples. So, too, foxes, squirrels, ground-hogs, snakes, eels, etc., are low-minded and inferior, and creep or run upon the ground, and accordingly burrow in the earth. Yet their habitations, like their characters, far surpass those of animals below them, while the beaver, higher in the scale of mentality, builds him a better habitation." On and on this scale goes, until Fowler—who was also the midcentury's most famous phrenologist, and thus quite accustomed to reading character (and race) out of form—concludes: "Throughout all nature the abodes of all animals correspond perfectly with their characters, so that the latter can be safely predicated from the former." This is "equally true of man," Fowler insists. "The half-human, half-brute orang-outang constructs a rude hut of sticks and bushes, while the more advanced Bosjowan [Bushman] builds a habitation a little better, but of the lowest class of human architecture, as he is at the bottom of the ladder. The Hottentot, Carib, Indian, Malay, and Caucasian, build houses better, and still better, the higher the order of their mentality."[10]

Even midcentury pattern books that do not appear overly concerned with race turn out to be terraced by an array of racial assumptions. In his immensely influential volume *The Architecture of Country Houses* (1850), for example, Andrew Jackson Downing pauses to clarify his use of the term "English" in describing a certain building type:

> In saying that this is a farm-house in the English rural style, we do not mean that it is a copy of any building in England; but that in designing it we have seized upon that manifestation of rural and domestic beauty in architecture which the Anglo-Saxon race feels more powerfully and more instinctively than any other; and of which the English, who have had so much longer time than we have to work out these finer rural instincts, have given such admirable examples.

This is only one passage of many in Downing's writings that emphasizes the significance of America's Anglo-Saxon heritage and the importance of racial instinct in establishing a national architecture in the U.S.[11] In other texts of the period ideas about race and architecture at times emerge more defensively. In the final paragraph of his review of the history of ancient and modern architecture, for example, Oliver P. Smith in *The Domestic Architect* (1852) feels compelled to exclude the architectural practices of non-Western races from his discussion of the built environment of more civilized nations. "It might be proper to remark, before closing this article," observes Smith, "that there are many different forms or fashions of building prevailing in various countries, that have no strict conformity to the styles herein noticed, yet none possessing sufficient merit to take rank in the schools of architectural science." Smith could perfectly well stop here, but instead he names names: "The Chinese, the Turks, and people of other distinct political divisions of the earth, have each their fashions of building; yet they are possessed of little in the line of Architecture worthy of imitation in a country of common civilization." In this context "distinct" appears not simply to mean separate, but more pointedly different, in kind or type. (Similarly, the "domestic" of Smith's guide's title might be said to allude not merely to matters of the house but also to matters of the country, the national "home.") Indeed, given Smith's deep concern with the relationship between architecture and national morality—"Nothing has more to do with the morals, the civilization, and refinement of a nation," he insists in his preface, "than its prevailing Architecture"—his anxious exclusion of Chinese and Turkish "fashions" anticipates both the racial theories and the politics of those who would soon agitate for restrictions on foreign immigration to the U.S. In an ironic twist, despite Smith's antipathy for such "merit[less]" architecture, he includes in the very last plate of his book, without comment, designs for both a Turkish minaret and an "elevation in the Chinese style"—suggesting that even such nonconforming modes can, in the end, have some place in the domestic architecture of a nation "of common civilization."[12]

The socio-spatial complexities of American slavery presented a different set of challenges to pattern book writers. On the comparatively rare occasions that pattern books treat southern building forms—most texts of the era, typically published in the North, concentrate on structures for the northern and middle states—their authors generally avoid any direct mention of slavery.[13] But their circumlocutions betray an acute awareness that racial servitude both affects and is affected by the built environment. In Samuel Sloan's two-volume guide, *The Model Architect: A Series of Original Designs for Cottages, Villas, Suburban Residences, Etc.* (1852), the appearance of the first southern design (of only two) requires a preliminary account of regional differences. "There are many reasons why the principal features of the buildings North and South are and will be essentially different," explains Sloan. "Here, land is an object, and the architect is compelled to compress his plans into the smallest possible space; our climate requires a house that will prove equally habitable in the sultry days of June and July, and during the severe weather of December and January; and our habits need but one tenement,—kitchen, servants['] apartments and dwelling all being under the same roof." But northern constraints dissolve down South. "On the contrary," Sloan notes, "the southern gentleman is not circumscribed in the construction of his house, or the laying out of gardens and lawns, by the walls or fences of his neighbors, and the number of laborers at his command, the entire year, render him less chary in the indulgence of his tastes in these particulars, than he would be, if, to keep them in order, required a constant drain upon his purse."[14] It is not clear whether the phrase "to keep them in order" refers to the house, gardens, and lawns or to the euphemistic "laborers," but the effect is the same: for certain landowners in the south the availability of slave labor makes extravagant construction (and ongoing maintenance) a social rather than an economic issue. Indeed, as though in ignorance—or contorted denial—of the slave economy, Sloan's final price estimate for each southern house includes labor costs at the going rates for *Philadelphia* masons, carpenters, and bricklayers, as if one expected a southern slaveowner to hire northern workers to build his home. As we will see in chapter 1, this evasiveness about the economics of slavery will characterize other pattern books of the era, including Downing's.

At times the very language of the charged debate over the south's "peculiar institution"—as Senator John C. Calhoun of South Carolina famously characterized slavery in the late 1830s—seems to insinuate itself into pattern book descriptions of southern houses. *The Model Architect* is no exception. In his discussion of the second expressly southern design, for example, Sloan explains the dual rationale for the customary detached kitchen: not merely the southern climate (it is felt to be too hot to have the kitchen attached to the main house) but also "the *peculiarities* of construction required by the social and domestic habits prevailing in those sections of the country."[15] The frequent recurrence of this suggestive term in this particular context perhaps signifies not only the silent acknowledgment of slavery's distorting pressure on the southern built environment but also the pattern book authors' reluctance to call slavery by its real name. Treating slavery as merely a "social habit," virtually no pattern book will even mention the presence of black bodies in their accounts of southern landscapes, effectively erasing race from view much as nineteenth-century slaveowners increasingly sought to segregate their plantations into predominantly white and black spaces. When black bodies do appear, as in Gervase Wheeler's *Rural Homes; Or Sketches of Houses Suited to American Country Life with Original Plans, Designs, Etc.* (1851)—another text that lingers over the "peculiarities" of the southern kitchen and other servant spaces—they emerge not quite as occupants of space but, in Wheeler's case, as elements of the picturesque. In his chapter titled "Southern Homes," Wheeler declares: "The kitchen buildings must be much lighter, and more spacious than anything that would be contrived for a northern home;—in fact, the domestics require, as it were, a distinct house, and a separate establishment." Despite his own reliance on euphemisms for bondage ("domestics") and his use, like Smith's, of the term "distinct" to mark racial difference, here Wheeler almost grants slaves agency through inhabitation ("separate establishment"). But this possibility is quickly undercut by the next, and last, sentence of the paragraph. "Nothing could be made prettier," Wheeler concludes, "than a roomy block of kitchen buildings, with the little cots of the colored servants artistically grouped around."[16] And in truth, actual slaves still do not quite appear here. It is only the pretty little cots Wheeler wants in view, not their occupants.

Tell Us about These Pictures

One of the most fascinating architectural texts to emerge in the pattern book era, however—C. W. Elliott's *Cottages and Cottage Life* (1848)—actually takes a stand against slavery. Elliott's book is unusual for more than its politics. At first glance *Cottages and Cottage Life* looks like a conventional house pattern guide. Exhaustively subtitled, like so many of its genre (*Containing Plans for Country Houses, Adapted to the Means and Wants of the People of the United States; with Directions for Building and Improving; for the Laying Out and Embellishing of Grounds; with Some Sketches of Life in This Country*), Elliott's octavo volume contains ten lithographic plates of carefully drawn house elevations, each accompanied by floor plans, detailed descriptions, and, in most cases, an estimate of the cost to build. But as the last clause of the subtitle hints—"with Some Sketches of Life in This Country"—*Cottages and Cottage Life* is more than a pattern book: it is also a work of fiction. Indeed, setting aside the plates, a brief preface titled "Introductory Observations upon Building," and an illustrated appendix of "Particulars" on such topics as woodwork, flower beds, and fruit trees, by far the bulk of Elliott's 226-page text is devoted to a "continuous narrative" of one family's life "in the country."[17] Which is not to say the architectural and narrative elements are simply cobbled together. Instead, Elliott weaves the house patterns into the novel, turning many of them into homes that appear in the story. In fact the conceit of the narrative itself is that it answers a young boy's demand that his father "Tell us about these pictures," a "small portfolio" (1) of architectural drawings made years earlier by the young boy's grandfather and comprising the houses depicted in the book's ten plates.

As conceits go, this seems a surprisingly sophisticated twist for a genre still taking shape and whose most significant treatise—Downing's *Architecture of Country Houses*—would not appear for two more years. Elliott, who studied horticulture and landscape gardening with Downing in the late 1830s before moving to Cincinnati, where he wrote *Cottages and Cottage Life*, appears to have recognized early on the fundamental role of storytelling in the guidebook genre. After all, pattern books do not merely draw plans; they sketch ways of living. This was particularly true of the architectural advice manuals appearing in the 1840s and 1850s, which are fictional in the very best sense: they make new worlds imaginatively possible. In merging the technical with the fictional, *Cottages and Cottage Life* both understands and exploits the ways that, beneath all the builders' details, midcentury pattern books are profoundly interested in helping readers picture themselves not just in new homes but, as it were, in new situations. As Dell Upton notes, Downing in particular regarded the country house not merely as a living space but as a therapeutic site for the modern family, a place to restore the "moral values and psychic energy" weakened by the assaults of urbanism, capitalism, and industrialism.[18] Thereby, one might say, hangs a tale.

Contemporary reviewers found Elliott's approach appealing. Professional and general interest journals alike, including the *American Agriculturalist*, *Literary World*, *New Englander*, and *National Era*, as well as Downing's own *Horticulturist and Journal of Rural Art and Rural Taste*, praised the book's unique combination of science and story. The glowing review published by the *Merchants' Magazine and Commercial Review*, which pinpoints Elliott's multiple achievements, may serve as an example:

> Interspersed throughout this beautifully printed volume, which, by the way, would adorn the centre table of one of these tasty residences, we have a series of sketches of "life, love, and duty" in the cottage, evidently the product of a mind that not only understands the science of architecture, but the philosophy of home, and of all that makes home desirable and happy. In a word, the work combines the useful and the agreeable, the pleasant and the profitable; and is admirably well adapted to the tastes and habits of our people.[19]

At the same time, there is something a little odd about the "tasty" house plans in Elliott's book. Downing seems to note as much in his own review when he observes "the plan of the author, so far as we are able to gather it, . . . appears to have been rather to draw the attention of readers generally to the subject, than to furnish a careful or complete practical work on rural architecture."[20] Downing may simply have been preparing his readers for the far more encyclopedic volume he himself was in the midst of writing.[21] But by questioning how "careful" Elliott's designs are, Downing may also have been trying politely to signal the ways in which almost every one of the house plans in *Cottages and Cottage Life* has an unusual quirk.

The very first plan, for example, features a "bold and prominent" two-story tower with space for a bedroom and then also "an observatory, laboratory, or the like" above a dramatic arch that doubles as a carriageway. Even the description that accompanies the illustrative plate—which doubles as the frontispiece for the volume itself—allows that the arch, as pictured, may not be "sufficient to sustain the weight" (xiii). Similar idiosyncrasies appear in nearly every plan. Plate V is highlighted by an immense octagonal parlor. Plate III features a large book-lined alcove extruding from the living room. Plate VI includes a freestanding tower with two rooms arranged above a water closet. Plate X recommends enclosing a portion of one of its twin piazzas to make a bathroom.

Perhaps the most unusual plan in the book concerns the "snug" house in Plate II, which is almost entirely focused on a novel arrangement for the keeping of bees (Fig. 2). "In the corner of the living room," Elliott's description reads, "will be seen a place for bee-hives, separated from the room by a glass partition, which gives a view of their operations from within. Shutters should be provided for the outside to protect them from cold, heat, and storms" (13). But this is not just an arrangement for watching bees or protecting them. Rather, it is designed so the bees might at times share the living space with the human inhabitants. "In the winter," Elliott suggests, "they might be fed from within, and indeed be allowed to enter the room" (13). Although ideas about "bee space" and bee culture were undergoing significant revision in the mid-nineteenth century, there are no records of any such domestic beekeeping arrangement being attempted or even hypothesized in the U.S. in the 1840s. It is possible Elliott took inspiration from Scottish landscape architect J. C. Loudon's *Encyclopaedia of Gardening*, whose 1835 edition describes beekeepers on occasion inserting a hive into the wall of a cherry-house or a peach-house "so that the body of the hive may be half in the house and half in the wall, with two outlets for the bees" (613), but there is nothing even in Loudon's extensive work to suggest bringing bees into the parlor.[22]

Each of these unusual elements marks the degree to which Elliott's designs press against the limits of the genre—so much so that one wonders if Elliott is poking fun at the mania for "country cottage" advice manuals even as he purports to write one. Indeed, the description of the plan in Plate I hints as much. "This is the largest house in the collection," reports Elliott, "and one of a good deal of pretension. It can in no way be called a cottage" (xiii).

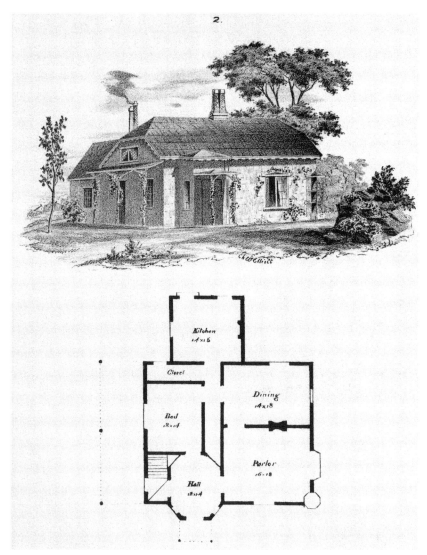

Figure 2. Plate II, C. W. Elliott, *Cottages and Cottage Life* (1848). Courtesy, The Winterthur Library: Printed Book and Periodical Collection.

Even more strikingly than the architectural idiosyncrasies sprinkled through his house designs, Elliott introduces into the chapters of his novel precisely the kinds of social and political tensions the pattern book genre tends studiously to avoid. At various points in the narrative the characters discuss, for example, slavery, religion, and class; marriage, domesticity, and gender roles; interest rates, tariffs, and stock speculation. There is a subplot about abduction and the threat of rape. An out-of-work laborer loses his health, his wife, his child, and his home before turning to robbery. There is a sense among many in the novel that there are multiple crises ahead. This is a far cry from the concerns of the typical "country cottage" handbook; yet what is so clear as the various plots of *Cottages and Cottage Life* unfold is that each potential crisis is connected in some way to the midcentury house. The cottages in Elliott's book are not simply safe refuges from the complexities of the modern world but are intricately linked to those selfsame complexities. This is not to say Elliott is fully in control of all these matters, either narratively or ideologically. As novels go, *Cottages and Cottage Life* is a pretty good design handbook. What is important here is Elliott's keen awareness that in the late 1840s discussions of domestic architecture and the built environment were not self-contained but inevitably touched on the most pressing social, political, and cultural issues in the U.S. That Elliott explored these points of contact in a hybrid genre of his own making, the pattern book novel, further suggests that, to at least one architectural practitioner, literature was a potentially provocative site for their exploration.

Living in Cincinnati during the turbulent 1840s surely influenced the development of *Cottages and Cottage Life* as well. As biographers of Harriet Beecher Stowe, who lived in Cincinnati from 1832 until 1850, have long noted, the proximity of the burgeoning "bordertown" city to the slave state of Kentucky—with, as Joan Hedrick observes, "its race riots, commercial trading, runaway slaves, disease, and death"—strongly affected Stowe's sense of social justice.[23] One suspects that living in Cincinnati may have had a similar effect on Elliott, whose only publication before *Cottages and Cottage Life* (as best the record shows) was a catalog of fruit trees. In fact Elliott's life in Cincinnati overlapped considerably with Stowe's. They lived, for example, in the same part of the city, Walnut Hills, where Elliott likely pursued his career as a horticulturist and landscape gardener. Elliott was also a member of the Semi-Colon Club, the elite literary society to which Stowe belonged and in whose company she had produced her first writings. These connections have to do with more than mere proximity or serendipity, for Elliott and Stowe, I have determined, were also related by marriage: Elliott was the younger brother of Elizabeth Elliott Foote, the wife of Stowe's favorite uncle, Samuel, in whose Walnut Hills mansion the Semi-Colon Club held its meetings. (Stowe would likely have known Charles Elliott even without this connection, for Elliott's other sister, Sarah, had married James Handasyd Perkins, another Semi-Colon Club member, to whom Stowe was attracted early in her days in Cincinnati.)²⁴ Reading the socially and politically aware "sketches of life" that constitute Elliot's novel, with their attentiveness to the intricacies of domestic life as well as the stain of slavery, the constraints of gender, and the stratifications of class, one cannot help suppose they may have first been shared with and perhaps even shaped by Stowe, Foote, Perkins, and such other members of the club as antislavery activist and politician Salmon P. Chase.

If *Cottages and Cottage Life* does not in the end assemble as thorough a commentary on race and the built environment as the one Stowe would offer only a few years later in *Uncle Tom's Cabin*, Elliott's text nonetheless shares Stowe's understanding that architecture has social and political dimensions. In Elliott's story, a city family, newly wealthy, seeks life "in the country; expecting there the happiness and repose which the town could not yield" (4). Although the narrative promises these country sketches "will, beyond all question, prove dull and uneventful—taking their hue from the life which is common there" (4)—country life turns out to be rather unsettling for "Uncle Tom" Ellison, his brother "Uncle John," his daughter Grace, and his nephew Ned. (Although the head of the family shares the same name as the man who would become Stowe's title character, the Ellisons are white and free, not black and in bondage.) None of the local builders, for example, is impressed with the plan for the Ellisons' new house, which happens to be modeled on the pretentious structure in Plate I of Elliott's book. Grace is alternately perplexed by a new kitchen servant's rural ways and besieged by an eligible bachelor who turns out to be a kidnapper and possibly a rapist. Ned, perhaps a stand-in for Elliott himself, flounders professionally until he finally decides to study landscape gardening with a man who may be a fictional version of Downing. Politics, both national and local, repeatedly intrude on the story. Casual conversations quickly turn to taxes, the right to vote, and "the bankin' system" (131). An ambitious lawyer, father to the bachelor-kidnapper, persuades Uncle Tom to run for county office, then undermines him in order to grab the position, and its possibilities for graft, for himself. Uncle John shows the others how the countryside is plagued by the same "social evils" (139), such as poverty, that they thought they had left behind in the city. Of the four main plotlines—will Uncle Tom build his house? will he be elected to office? will Grace marry? will Ned figure out his life's work?—none comes to fruition until the novel's epilogue, and even then some still fail. The principal narrative concludes with Uncle Tom not merely usurped by the deceitful lawyer but swindled by his broker and dead from a stroke. After her father's death Grace is unhinged by grief and insists on leaving the countryside. Although she eventually marries Ned—who has finally decided to become a landscape gardener—in the frame tale Ned is presented to readers as a widower, suggesting Grace has died sometime after their third child is born. Perhaps "happiness and repose" is not the fate of cottage life after all.

The debate over slavery erupts in the middle of a chapter in which Uncle Tom, Uncle John, Ned, and two neighbors discuss the myriad frustrations of house building and politics—and indeed helps propel the text toward an analysis of race and architecture. Exasperated by the resistance of the local building trade to his house plan, Uncle Tom is even more exasperated by rumors threatening his budding political candidacy. Asked by John whether what he has heard is true—that Uncle Tom has declared himself in favor of slavery—Tom responds with a vehement denial: "I never thought it,—never said it,—and never will!" (155). Apparently the ambitious lawyer who first recruited Tom has been twisting his words. "What did you say?" asks Uncle John.

> "I don't think of any thing, unless it was, 'that, were I living in a slave-holding country, under some circumstances, I should not hesitate to own slaves.' No, sir, if I had a thousand slaves, I would make use of my influence among my neighbors, and preach and pray that they might be led to unite with me in measures for the extinction of the practice, upon the face of this earth,—that I said, and will say any where." (156)

Uncle John is as vehement an opponent of slavery as his brother. "It is curious and incomprehensible, the tenacity with which [southern politicians] hang on to what they all know to be the greatest of moral, social, and political evils. They are monomaniacs" (156). When one of the Ellisons' neighbors wonders why the debate produces so much fuss—"why [can't] they . . . be left alone" (156)—John's answer shows a clear understanding of the way race structures the built environment. It also cuts to the heart of what, to John, it means to "build" a nation. "You have not been on the Ohio river?" he replies. "Well, sir, it is almost literally true, that from Wheeling to Cairo,—from its source to its mouth,—the one bank is bursting with life, vigor, and hope; the other, attenuated with weakness and wilderness. The one marches (good or evil as you may think) onward to wealth and power—the other sinks into decay and death" (156–57). John predicts Kentucky will thrive without slavery once the politicians are swept out, in the process helping to push the "great West" into the forefront of American economics and politics. "The west is becoming, or has become," John asserts, "the ruling power in this country."

Cincinnati, in particular, "is the center of the west,—therefore, the center of the world; and you had better calculate your longitude accordingly" (158). If it is not entirely clear whether Elliott's sketches are actually set in the West (the fact that John has to describe the banks of the Ohio River to his neighbors makes it clear the novel does not take place in Cincinnati, for example), it is passages like these that give *Cottages and Cottage Life* a political explicitness—and a desire, like Uncle Tom, to speak its politics "any where"—wholly absent from the architectural advice book genre. (John's politics are even more radical than Tom's. In this same chapter he expresses a proto-Marxist hope that one day the "producing classes" will "take their position in the front rank" at the expense of owners and other "factors.") If, as certain textual details suggest, Elliott's sketches are actually set in the East—perhaps even along Downing's own Hudson River—then *Cottages and Cottage Life* serves notice from the heart of pattern book country that the genre's silence on the racial politics of architecture could be ignored no longer.[25]

Where Will You Reside Next?

Although Elliott's hybrid text inspired no direct imitators—*Cottages and Cottage Life* remains the only American pattern book novel—in the years following its appearance the racial politics of architecture would become a more frequent, and more compelling, topic for American writers. Elliott's Cincinnati neighbor and in-law Stowe, for example, as we shall see in more detail in chapter 1, sparked an often rancorous debate about the built environment of slavery with the publication in 1852 of *Uncle Tom's Cabin*—a book whose very title foregrounds the buildingscape of bondage. Many of the responses to Stowe's novel, both fictional and otherwise, pointedly depict a more benevolent physical environment than the one Stowe imagines, for example, at Legree's plantation. In the mid-1850s Harriet Jacobs would begin work on *Incidents in the Life of a Slave Girl* (1861), a narrative that not only provocatively repurposes what Valerie Smith has aptly called slavery's "architectural close places," such as Jacobs's secret garret, but also, as Ann Gelder has shown, conspicuously revises the pastoral cottage ideology of the mid-century domestic architecture reform movement as epitomized by Downing.[26] And as I will discuss in more detail in chapter 1, during this same decade escaped slave Hannah Crafts would demonstrate a highly sophisticated awareness of the racial politics of antebellum space in the manuscript of her novel, *The Bondwoman's Narrative*.

Figure 3. Anthony W. Smith, "Smith's Pictorial Parlor Oracle" (1869). Courtesy, The Winterthur Library: Joseph Downs Collection of Manuscripts and Printed Ephemera.

As literary interest in exploring the relays between race and architecture deepened in the U.S., so too did cultural assumptions about the relationship between selves and structures. A brief look at two intriguing artifacts of late nineteenth-century material culture, both with links to the pattern book genre, helps make the depth of those assumptions more clear. In the first of these artifacts, a late 1860s board game, for example, one finds human faces—several of which appear to represent different racial and/or ethnic types—suggestively paired with distinct forms of architecture. Manufactured in Pittsburgh and "designed to supply a want long felt, of an innocent, highly entertaining and instructive amusement for the young of both sexes in the home circle, at social parties, picnics, &c," Smith's Pictorial Parlor Oracle consists of a square board with a metal spinner. On the board are six concentric rings, each ring representing a different game (Fig. 3). Although the directions do not specify the order of play, players may well have started at the outermost ring (a simple number game) and then worked their way toward the center. The second, third, and fourth rings, which feature small lithographed images in each of their squares, pretend to provide information about the person at the spinner. The second ring, for example, asks: "What is a prominent trait in your character?" and offers twenty-four possibilities, each a comparison to an animal—"wise as a serpent," "vain as a peacock," "harmless as a dove," and so on. The third ring then depicts an array of architectural structures as possible answers to the question "Where will you reside next?" Many of the images in this third ring resemble the architectural elevations typical of Downing's *Architecture of Country Houses* and other pattern books, from their picturesque, tree-accented frames to their tiny foregrounded human figures.

Part of the game's thrill, of course, is seeing what the Oracle predicts for you. Will you reside in a Farm House? The White House? A Log Cabin? Under a Cart? And while there is no necessary link between this ring and the fourth—which depicts twelve different male faces in answer to the question "What is your ideal of beauty?"—game players would very likely make the link between these two rings themselves, as the layout of the board matches one face with each structure. A dapper gentleman with a stylish mustache, for example, appears directly below the square "City Residence." A long-haired, piratical-looking figure is matched with the sailing ship depicted in "Ocean." The man depicted below the square, "Under a Cart," with his round face, low forehead, and dull expression, mimics popular physiognomic representations of an imbecile. Thus when someone spins to discover where he will "reside next," the joy or disappointment of landing on a particular type of architecture is doubled by the Oracle's implicit claim that if you reside in this space you are also probably this kind of person. In fact, the overall effect of the juxtaposition of these two rings is an uncanny merger of pattern book representations with the face studies common to phrenology. (Although Orson Fowler—the phrenologist/architect/comparative race theorist behind *A Home for All*—did not invent this game, he certainly would have understood it.) And while none of the faces depicted is African American, there are unmistakable racial and/or ethnic typologies invoked in many of the images. The face below the "R R Shanty," for example, resembles common nineteenth-century caricatures of Irish immigrant railway laborers, from the figure's bulbous nose, to his dark skin, to his cartoonishly bestial fea-

Figure 4. Detail, "Smith's Pictorial Parlor Oracle," showing figures for "Hotel," "White House," and "R R Shanty." Courtesy, The Winterthur Library: Joseph Downs Collection of Manuscripts and Printed Ephemera.

tures (Fig. 4). The face linked to the structure "Hotel" has what appears to be the stereotypically hooked nose and fleshy features of a German Jew and seems to wear a form of skullcap. The figure beneath the "White House," on the other hand—situated directly between the Jewish figure and the Irishman—has the blond curls and delicate features of a stereotypical white American.

If Smith's Pictorial Parlor Oracle depicts architecture as a racial trait, a second popular artifact, the late-century phenomenon known as the scrapbook house (also called house albums, collage albums, or paper doll houses) suggests ways that even the creation of imaginary houses often depended on ingrained ideas about racialized space. Flourishing between 1875 and 1920, the scrapbook house, which was part of the broader late nineteenth-century scrapbooking craze, represents the broad impact of the pattern book as a cultural form, especially in the postwar years as mass-market American women's periodicals such as *Godey's Ladies Book* began to include more and more house plans as regular features for their readers. (One historian estimates that *Godey's* published "some 450 house designs" between 1846 and 1892.)[27] Scrapbook house makers used clippings from trade catalogs and magazines, including *Godey's*, along with a variety of supplemental craft materials such as tissue paper and doily strips, to turn empty account books, ledgers, or scrap albums into miniature homes, typically by decorating each page (or double-page spread) as a single room. Although their decorative details might differ, certain features tend to remain consistent from house to house. Most scrapbook houses were made by women, often by mothers for daughters, or by mothers and daughters together, and were usually intended as backdrops for paper doll play, although in many cases images of people can also be found glued directly onto the pages. Most of the houses unfold in a common pattern, moving first through the relatively public spaces of the home—front halls, parlors, libraries, dining rooms—before reaching the more private recesses of bedrooms, dressing rooms, and bathrooms. Scrapbook houses also tend to imagine rather grand homes, often in excess of twenty or more rooms. The dominant decorative ethic similarly tilts toward profusion. Since decorative clutter was by no means unusual in middle-class Victorian homes, rooms like these are at once representations of and fantasies about late-century abundance, consumption, and collection.[28]

They are of course also representations of, and fantasies about, the ways race relations are inscribed within the built environment. Much like the midcentury pattern book, race is marked in the scrapbook house, in most instances, by its apparent absence. The homes on display are presumptively white spaces, at least as far as the human occupants are concerned. Many of the physical objects in various rooms, on the other hand, particularly those of "Oriental" or "Turkish" provenance, following the Victorian fashion for racially themed interior decoration, have racial codes attached to them. When explicitly raced figures do appear in scrapbook houses—an Irish maid in the parlor, say, or a black cook in the kitchen—they almost always do so in the spaces (and the roles) to which they are stereotypically confined. This convention was apparently so common that when in the early 1900s, trying to capitalize on the popularity of the homemade scrapbook house, publishers began marketing prepackaged commercial scrapbook houses to children, many of these homes came already supplied with a precut "mammy" figure to paste into the kitchen along with the pots and pans.[29] As Beverly Gordon has noted, the racist assumptions of the prevailing culture "were fully embedded" in scrapbook houses.[30]

A closer look at one handmade scrapbook house, however, suggests that some individual house makers (and/or users) may have had more complicated relationships to these implicitly raced homes. An elaborate house by an unknown maker in the holdings of the Winterthur Library designated as Folio 252, for example, does indeed have a black cook in its kitchen (Fig. 5).[31] At first glance her image appears to reinforce persistent racial stereotypes. Wearing an apron and standing to the left of a central stove, she is smiling broadly and appears to be gesturing—though precisely to what is not clear: the pots on the stove? the table set with food? the shelf of neatly arrayed

Figure 5. Image of kitchen, collage album, Folio 252 (ca. 1880–ca.1900). Courtesy, The Winterthur Library: Joseph Downs Collection of Manuscripts and Printed Ephemera.

dishes?—with her arms out and her palms up. Her round face, exaggerated lips, and headscarf trade eagerly on debasing minstrel representations. The very color scheme of the room—in which the bright orange window shades match the orange in the cook's dress and also the tablecloth—seems to identify her more as just another object in the kitchen than as an individualized human being. (In fact, upon closer inspection, the cook's dress and the tablecloth are not simply the same color but appear to be made out of the same material.) At the same time, other details give the cook a potential for agency and individuation rarely accorded scrapbook house servants. Unlike a different domestic worker who appears two pages earlier in the house, for example—a white servant flipping pancakes in a small walk-in "China Closet" just off the dining room—the cook in the kitchen is not depicted in the act of laboring but perhaps instead in the moment just before she sits down to eat her own dinner. Indeed, despite the minstrel-like exaggerations of her face, in the context of this otherwise empty kitchen her smiling gesture may be performed for no one's satisfaction but her own. The cook certainly occupies a more prominent position in this room than do most scrapbook house servants, who usually appear off to one side, arms folded or quietly engaged in domestic work, subordinated visually and spatially to the other objects and people in the room.

Unlike many of the images pasted into scrapbook houses, it is possible to identify the exact source of the cook's picture: she has been cut out of a late nineteenth-century trade card for stove polish (Fig. 6). In fact this trade card, which advertised the popular Rising Sun brand, is the source not only for the cook but also for the table set with food and the stove in the middle of the page. The trade card makes the cook's gesture more clear: in the original image she is welcoming another character, the black male figure leaning in at the door, into the room, for *his* dinner. "Come in Ephraim!" the cook says in stereotypical black dialect. "Ise not mad with you dis time, case yer sent me de genuine RISING SUN STOVE BLACKING; an' it shines de stove in good shape. An' here's yer dinner all ready." As the cook's words suggest—"Ise not mad with you dis time"—this trade card is actually the second in a sequence. In the first card of the series (which this house maker has not used), the cook is livid with Ephraim for bringing her an inferior brand of polish. Subtitled "No Dinner?" the first card's caption reads: "Look yere, old man! What kind o' stove blacking you call dat? Ise been rubbin' on dat stove all mornin' an' it don't gib it a polish worth a cent. You jest git de RISING SUN STOVE POLISH right away, or dar'l be trouble. You think I got time to 'speriment with such mud?" (In this first card the kitchen table stands empty, since the cook has had no time to

Come In, Ephraim! Ise not mad with you dis time, case yer sent me de genuine RISING SUN STOVE BLACKING; an' it shines de stove in good shape. An' here's yer dinner all ready. Somethin' agin yer? No, deed I haven't; yer tink Ise an anjul to get along without good Stove Polish?

Figure 6. Morse Brothers, trade card for Rising Sun Stove Polish, Canton, Massachusetts (ca. 1880). Courtesy, The Winterthur Library: Joseph Downs Collection of Manuscripts and Printed Ephemera.

prepare any food.) In its original context the image of the black cook is thus unmistakably racist, from her minstrel features and dialect to the demeaning way in which the Rising Sun brand metaphorically links her blackness with the blackness of the stove and the polish itself. And yet can the act of removing the image from its original source—not just cutting it out of the trade card but then pasting it into an imaginary home as this scrapbook house maker has done—reconfigure the meaning of the image as well as the narratives in which it might operate?

According to Ellen Gruber Garvey, it just might. In her work on Victorian trade card culture, Garvey suggests that clipping images out of trade cards and rearranging them in albums according to the designs of the maker rather than the advertiser can indeed shape new meanings, allowing one to "move characters almost magically from their original relationships and old frames into new narratives." In this case we might then imagine that the process of being moved from her original context to her new location in Folio 252's kitchen made the cook available to her assembler for story lines other than those in which the trade card advertisement rigidly constrained her. And yet as Garvey notes, even as relocated images "take on an independent existence," they "nonetheless [continue] to refer to the original advertising source."[32] And so perhaps Folio 252's black cook, despite being resituated, has not necessarily been rescued or reimagined, particularly if her mockingly humorous commercial origins are inevitably called up for the user of the scrapbook house. The frame of this new kitchen, in other words, may be just as disempowering or demeaning as the original trade card.

And yet given the context of Folio 252 as a whole, one cannot help but sense some more particular interest, on the part of this house maker, this book "author," one might even say, in exploring—in however limited a way—the texture of the lives of the help of the house. More so than many other examples in the genre, Folio 252 appears quite interested in domestic help. Not simply because maids and cooks appear in the book itself (there are actually fewer domestic workers in Folio 252 than in some other scrapbook houses, which Gordon notes sometimes include a "battery of servants"),[33] but because this house maker devotes considerable space to rooms in which servants might not merely work but also live, including several maid's rooms, a separate servants' dining room, and a seamstress's room. Not all of these rooms are complete, and some appear to be missing—including pages torn out—or belatedly transformed. One room labeled "Maid's Room," for example (the name of each room is usually written on the overleaf of the previous page), is actually finished as a sumptuous artist's studio. The room labeled

"Servants Dining Room" is actually finished as a bedroom. And while it is impossible to know what decisions guided the final composition of the book, it seems useful to think not only about the images contained within its pages but also about the possible relationship of the house maker (or recipient) toward its contents. In *A Sense of Things: The Object Matter of American Literature*, Bill Brown provocatively suggests that in interpreting material culture we might pay more attention to the ways "objects mediate relations between subjects" and "subjects mediate the relations between objects." "How," in other words, Brown asks, "are things and thingness used to think about the self?"[34] Along these lines, we might consider the ways that Folio 252's maker or recipient, through the construction of and/or play with the album, might have negotiated either a lived or an imaginary relationship to the particular persons and positions represented in the house, recognizing that these dollhouse figures are in some sense both objects and subjects. What kinds of stories might have played out on these pages, in these rooms, in this house? Could the artist's studio actually have been intended as a maid's room? What kind of maid would that be? (Or, in the kitchen, what might the cook now be saying?) Through its particular design, Folio 252 at least raises the possibility of an imaginative, even potentially empathetic inquiry on the part of the scrapbook house maker into the lives, needs, and narratives of the house's domestic laborers—a possibility generally foreclosed by the commercial versions marketed to children in the early 1900s, which tended to instruct the purchaser exactly where to place, and thus also how to use, each numbered object and person.[35] Indeed, although we can often only guess at the stories that handmade scrapbook houses were used to tell, they remain provocative artifacts in the study of race, architecture, and writing precisely to the extent to which they function as sites for the page-by-page unfolding of narratives that both employ and at times seem to push against cultural assumptions about race and the built environment.

A Floor Plan

In the chapters that follow I highlight a series of equally provocative texts and contexts to explore the ways in which American writing between roughly 1850 and 1930 concerned itself, often intensely, with the racial implications of architectural space, primarily but not exclusively through domestic architecture. As the foregoing sections have argued, race has been a central component of the concept and practice of all branches of architecture—by which I mean the creation, disposition, and also representation and imagination of the built environment—since at least the dawn of the pattern book era if not before. By focusing my chapters on the years 1850–1930, I mean to situate this book during the period not only in which architecture came of age professionally in the U.S.[36] but also in which ideas about architecture became a prominent part of broader conversations about American culture, American history, American politics, and (although we have not always understood this clearly) American race relations. Each chapter, moreover, takes as its primary context a critical stage in this history: the rise of the midcentury "cottage design" pattern book (chapter 1); the powerful nostalgia of the late nineteenth-century Colonial Revival (chapter 2); the turn-of-the-century explosion of the bungalow as both domestic icon and profitable export (chapter 3); and the early twentieth-century embrace by American middle-class households of "Oriental" decorative furnishings (chapter 4). This study thus not only takes seriously but indeed concretizes Dell Upton's trenchant observation that "architecture is an art of social storytelling, a means for shaping American society and culture and for 'annotating' social action by creating appropriate settings for it." *Sites Unseen* argues not only that literature can "shape" and "annotate" culture in similar ways but that literary texts—precisely for their ability to bring stories and structures alive—are particularly good sources for examining what we might call, after Craig E. Barton, the "complex social and cultural geography" of the always already raced American architectural imagination.[37]

In highlighting the overlapping relationship between literature and architecture as sites for social storytelling, I am thus also adapting for this study the approach of Diana Fuss, who in her recent study of architecture, writing, and interiority usefully challenges the "too easy bifurcation between literal and figurative spaces" found in most studies of architecture and literature. Where Fuss examines the ways that "architecture and literature work in tandem for the writer to create a rich and evolving sense of the interior," *Sites Unseen* explores the social and cultural geographies that narrative and architectural spaces, in equally provocative conjunction, can also make visible.[38] In the chapters ahead we will thus frequently attend not only to the narrative features of architectural space—the ways a floor plan, for example, can encode, as in the plot of a novel, the unfolding of a particular temporal and spatial experience—but also to the architectural features of narrative space. Chesnutt's conjure stories, in which the frame tale of almost every narrative not only *depicts* the porch of a plantation-era mansion but also *functions* as the "porch" of the story itself—a highly controlled and mediated social space where the inside and the outside of the story (and the house) meet—

offer only one example (chapter 2). In other chapters, different homologies between narrative and architectural form emerge, from Hannah Crafts's reconfiguration of the midcentury pattern book into a template for her own narrative reorientations (chapter 1), to Olga Beatriz Torres's insertion of English words into the linguistic landscape of her Spanish letters as though in imitation of the striking buildings that orient her to American society (chapter 3), to the ways the design of a Frank Lloyd Wright interior may uncannily resemble the plot of a mystery novel (chapter 4).

Another recurring concern in this study is domestic space. Although in this book I largely follow Upton's methodology in defining "architecture" broadly rather than narrowly—"I use 'architecture,'" Upton writes, "to stand for the entire cultural landscape, including so-called designed landscapes, urban spaces, and human modifications of natural spaces"[39]—the chapters that follow take many of their most important measurements in and around the nineteenth- and early twentieth-century American home. There are many reasons for this focus, including the presence of a large body of critical and historical literature that has helped make this space so powerfully visible for analysis. At the same time, I return to the home with new questions and in the process discern new forms and practices. This is particularly true in the second half of the book, in which, drawing on models provided by such critics as Amy Kaplan and Kirsten Silva Gruesz, and such historians as Kristin L. Hoganson and Mari Yoshihara, I trace a range of international and transhemispheric influences on American building practices that demonstrably shaped both the built and affective environments of American houses while also calling into question the very ways we presume to distinguish the domestic from the foreign.

If *Sites Unseen* does not prioritize gender in the same way many studies of American domesticity do, this is in part because I hope to show that race is as central to our understanding of nineteenth- and early twentieth-century spaces and structures as gender has already proven to be. Nonetheless, this study identifies multiple sites at which the intersection of race and architecture is also provocatively crossed and complicated by gender, from the sexual violations that so often structured the spaces of slavery to the not infrequently feminized "embrace" of "the East" through architectural and decorative tropes and practices. Though the profession of architecture in the U.S. came to be dominated by men, American women, particularly during this formative period, played critical roles in the discussion and dissemination of architectural designs as well as the theories of home space those designs sought to articulate. As noted earlier, *Godey's Ladies Book* and other mass-circulation women's periodicals were among the most important sources for the distribution of house plans in the nineteenth century. Women were thus shapers as well as consumers of pattern book ideology, especially in the absence of a national architectural press, which would not fully emerge until later in the century.[40] As putative superintendents of domestic space, moreover, women (particularly middle-class white women) often had the responsibility of regulating the home's implicitly racialized zones of labor and access, tasks eased (or complicated) not just by floor plans but also, as we shall see, by region. Women of color, on the other hand, particularly during slavery, often sought to claim the spatial rights—both inside and outside the house—typically denied them by their social, legal, or economic position.

One additional category of analysis about which this study has tried to think carefully, both in the layout of the plan of chapters and in the local arguments within each section, is geographic location. I have sought, for example, to distribute my texts and contexts widely, both within and outside the boundaries of the U.S., from the South, to the Gulf, to the Far West, and finally to Hawaii. While recognizing that there remain regions (and races) this study does not adequately address, my hope is that the chapters that follow will help not only to identify but also to open for further examination new spaces in this extraordinarily rich interdisciplinary field.

Chapter 1, "Cottage Desire: *The Bondwoman's Narrative* and the Politics of Antebellum Space," investigates the sustained engagement of escaped slave Hannah Crafts's 1850s novel with the socio-architectural philosophy of the dean of the midcentury pattern book genre, Andrew Jackson Downing. At once claiming and revising Downing's conception of the ideal cottage as her own desired domestic space, Crafts narrates—through an ingenious literary repurposing of the pattern book's model of architectural construction—a search for black homeownership that is inextricably linked to self-ownership. This chapter attends not just to Downing, whose evasiveness about slavery in a text like *The Architecture of Country Houses* betrays itself in often surprising ways, but also to Charles Dickens, whose depiction of Esther Summerson's housekeeper-to-homeowner happiness in *Bleak House* provides an alternative model for Crafts's narrator's personal and spatial self-reclamation.

Chapter 2, "Piazza Tales: Architecture, Race, and Memory in Charles Chesnutt's Conjure Stories," considers the late nineteenth-century African American writer's obsessive return to the plantation porch as a meditation on the failed racial and spatial politics of the post-Reconstruction South. Attending in particular to the largely ignored middle phase of Chesnutt's conjure tale production, I argue that Chesnutt's carefully framed stories index an acute understanding of the ways social relations are shaped by (and leave their impress on) the built environment. This chapter uncovers a revisionist historicism in which Chesnutt appears to dare readers to discover that the plantation piazza—perhaps the chief architectural marker of southern white racial superiority—is actually a creolized form whose polycultural origins owe as much to West African and Caribbean vernacular traditions as they do to the white colonnades of classical antiquity. If African Americans were often excluded from public spaces and "white" buildings at the turn of the century, Chesnutt shows powerfully how those same Americans have been claiming ground, in their own ways, since the days of slavery.

Where the first two chapters share a focus on the built environments of slavery and segregation, both actual and remembered, the last two chapters bring into relief equally evocative examples of race, architecture, and American writing in explicitly hemispheric and international turn-of-the-century contexts. Chapter 3, "Imperial Bungalow: Structures of Empire in Richard Harding Davis and Olga Beatriz Torres," examines three texts that together interrogate the buildingscape of empire: Davis's travelogue *Three Gringos in Venezuela and Central America* (1896), his popular romance *Soldiers of Fortune* (1897), and *Memorias de mi viaje (Recollections of My Trip)*, the little-known 1918 epistolary memoir of Torres, who emigrated to the U.S. in 1914 during the upheaval of the Mexican Revolution. All three books share a specific interest in the bungalow form, which though typically celebrated, particularly in the U.S., as the material incarnation of democratic ideals, actually emerges from within a far more complex narrative of global invention and appropriation, which these works help lay bare. Proposing a new reading of these texts as "Gulf" narratives—as concerned less with specific national demarcations than with the more fluid political and cultural geography of the hemispheric Gulf region—this chapter highlights not only the points of contrast between Davis and Torres but also the unexpected moments in which they find common ground. One of my goals through this comparison is to bring a multivoiced and specifically material context to Caroline Levander and Robert Levine's broad call for a hemispheric American studies committed to "excavating the intricate and complex politics, histories, and discourses of spatial encounter occurring throughout the hemisphere" that have generally been obscured in more nation-based U.S. inquiries.[41]

The fourth and final chapter, "Keyless Rooms: Frank Lloyd Wright and Charlie Chan," explores two strikingly different uses of "Oriental" space (and Asian decorative otherness) in the late nineteenth and early twentieth centuries. In the mid-1890s, still fascinated by the Ho-o-den, the half-scale replica of an Asian temple he had seen mounted on the Chicago World's Fair's Wooded Isle, Wright began designing homes with the horizontal lines and open floor plans characteristic of Japanese architecture. By 1905 Wright himself would travel to Japan, whose twinned aesthetic of openness and simplicity he continued to incorporate into his own work. "No dark pockets" is how one architectural historian has described Wright's sense of what he had learned from Asia.[42] In stark contrast to Wright's aesthetic, however, lay popular representations of "Oriental" space; one thinks, for example, of Sax Rohmer's Fu-Manchu stories or the "Oriental" tales of pulp fiction magazines. In these depictions, "Oriental" spaces are confining rather than open, "inscrutable" rather than simple; "all dark pockets" is how one might describe the mainstream American sense of Asian interiors. Possible exceptions to this general rule, however, are Earl Derr Biggers's Hawaii tales of Charlie Chan. In the very first Chan novel, *The House without a Key* (1925), Biggers tries to imagine "Oriental" settings that reveal secrets rather than conceal them. Enlisting metaphors of crumbling walls and expansive gardens, Biggers counters stereotypes of Asian space and décor (even as he creates others of Asian character) in stories that owe more to Wright's blueprints—and less to Rohmer's—than one might expect.

Sites Unseen then concludes with a brief coda, "Black Cabin, White House." After analyzing the bizarre appearance of two dilapidated slave cabins in a late nineteenth-century pattern book—offered as a "contrast" to the more modern (read: white) Queen Anne specimens that follow—I close with a compact history of our nation's *whitest* house, currently home to the first African American president and his family. An apt site with which to close this study, the story of the White House overlaps provocatively with nearly all the salient histories in this book, from its mode of construction, to the implicit (and sometimes explicit) racialization of its social spaces, to the stories that have used it as a potent site for their own imaginings. Taking us back in time to the early 1800s, and then ahead to the present moment, this concluding discussion thus also helps point to new terrain while offering new ideas for producing future sociocultural analyses of the built environment informed by questions of race and writing.

It bears repeating, at the close of this introduction, that the chapters in this study take up authors, texts, and sites that for the most part lie outside the typical investigations of architecture and literature. I have done this deliberately, in order to highlight the need for fresh perspectives in this interdisciplinary field. This does not mean that the terms and topics of this study are themselves marginal. Quite the contrary: I believe they are not only central to the field but that our having overlooked them for so long has contributed to the general myopia about the importance of race to American literary representations of the built environment. At the same time, I do not mean to suggest that the writers and texts in this study are the only ones to which we might turn in order to develop a more productive investigation of race, architecture, and American writing. Indeed, much work remains to be done, both "inside" and "outside" the traditional spaces and canons of American writing, and I hope this study will help spur more investigations into a variety of materials and periods.[43] The chapters presented here are intended as illustrative examples of what such investigations might look like, not as an exhaustive survey. Offered at a moment in our own history in which, on the one hand, some have declared the architectural profession to be undergoing a racial "crisis"[44] and, on the other hand, a nation watches as the first African American family settles into the White House, not as servants but as occupants, *Sites Unseen* ultimately underscores the need to make race itself a more salient factor in our studies—now and in the future—of the powerful contact points among architecture, culture, and American society.

1

Cottage Desire

The Bondwoman's Narrative *and* the Politics of Antebellum Space

> I learned to see freedom as always and intimately linked to the issue of transforming space.
> —bell hooks, "House, 20 June 1994"

Near the end of Hannah Crafts's novel *The Bondwoman's Narrative*, on the run from the North Carolina plantation of her final owners, the escaped slave narrator Hannah seeks a night's rest in the deep woods. For two weeks she has moved slowly north, seeking shelter and sustenance where she can find it, always anxious she will be discovered and reenslaved: "In every shadow I beheld, as in every voice I heard a pursuer." Although she has spent some of her fugitive nights in the houses of "kind and hospitable" people touched by her cover story—dressed as a young man, she is passing as a destitute orphan seeking relatives in the North—on this particular night, having learned that a paper describing her "exact size and figure" (albeit in female apparel) is circulating the countryside, Hannah avoids "the habitations of men." She finally "compose[s]" herself to sleep "in the friendly shelter of a small thicket," feeling "almost happy in the consciousness of perfect security." In the middle of the night, however, Hannah is awakened by the sound of voices. Peering through a gap in the thicket, she sees two other people—also fugitive slaves—making beds of dry leaves not far from her own temporary shelter. They, too, have sought security in the woods. "We will rest here," says one; "I think we can do so in perfect safety." What had been a private shelter, it would seem, is now a fugitive neighborhood. The distinction the novel makes between habitations that threaten and those that protect is heightened by an uncanny dream Hannah has later that night. Having watched the newcomers prepare themselves for sleep, Hannah herself begins to drowse. "Presently my thoughts became confused, with that pleasing bewilderment which precedes slumber," she relates. But bewilderment quickly turns to hallucination: "I began to lose consciousness of my identity, and the recollection of where I was. Now it seemed that Lindendale rose before me, then it was the jail, and anon the white towers of Washington, and—but the scene all faded; for I slept."[1]

On one level Hannah's hallucinatory tableau signals the tremendous anxiety that the presence of two strangers near her hideaway might produce. Even though the couple do not appear to pose an immediate threat—one is deliriously ill, the other preoccupied with making his companion comfortable—Hannah's watchfulness suggests that the sense of "perfect security" engendered by her temporary abode has indeed been breached, until in her drowsy state she imagines she is no longer safe in her "friendly shelter" at all but in a succession of built spaces patrolled by whites. These decidedly unfriendly (and, for Hannah, unfree) spaces—plantation, prison, metropolis—rise before her like specters, ghostly architectural hauntings from her enslaved past. To be returned to one of them at this point in the narrative would likely mean reenslavement instead of freedom, which is why Hannah experiences her momentary dissolution of identity (who am I?) in spatial terms (where am I?). On another level, this tableau also signals the text's deep interest in the shaping power of architectural form and epitomizes what one might call the broader architectural consciousness of the novel. The succession of spaces that rises in Hannah's confused imagination recapitulates, in the order in which they appear, the locations anchoring three of the main stages of the text: the plantation from which she first escapes; the jail in which she is imprisoned after her recapture; and the cityscape to which she is removed by her final owner. Hannah's hallucinatory tableau, that is, can be read not merely as a sign of one character's anxiety but also as a partial map of the novel's larger fascination with the uses and meanings of physical space under the system of chattel slavery.[2] For *The Bondwoman's Narrative*, as this episode makes clear, is a text not only concerned with, but in many ways structured by, the architectural forms of both bondage and freedom.

An examination of the role of these forms in the novel will shed light on specific authorial tactics as well as more general mid-nineteenth-century cultural practices. It will be instructive to consider the text's use of built forms not only in the context of midcentury architectural and landscape theory but also in relation to the ideological uses to which representations of architecture were frequently put in contemporary debates over slavery. For as we shall see, *The Bondwoman's Narrative* is attentive not only to architecture as fact (to actual examples of and physical developments within American building practice) but to architecture as a powerful literary trope—and even, in the end, as a narrative mode. Of particular interest to me is this novel's sophisticated awareness of the intricate relays between race and the built environment in antebellum America, relays often unarticulated by other prominent shapers of ideas about mid-nineteenth-century domestic space. I will propose a reading of *The Bondwoman's Narrative* as an implicit engagement with—and transformation of—the architectural imaginations of such disparate writers as Andrew Jackson Downing and Charles Dickens, from whose works *The Bondwoman's Narrative* liberally borrows (and, in Downing's case, also sharply critiques). Following bell hooks, who has observed that "many [black] narratives of struggle and resistance, from the time of slavery to the present, share an obsession with the politics of space, particularly the need to construct and build houses,"[3] I will trace in particular the persistence in Crafts's text of what one might call "cottage desire": a powerful yearning for independent black homeownership that is activated in the novel's earliest scenes, reaffirmed in fleeting moments throughout the text (including the temporary abode Hannah builds for herself in the woods and the possibilities for "neighborhood" suggested by the arrival of the newcomers), but only finally realized in the closing pages. I will also note how Hannah's gender, here deliberately masked by her cross-dressed disguise, also shapes her experience of the built environment within slavery. Whoever penned this text—"Hannah Crafts" herself, a different escaped slave, or yet another figure[4]—*The Bondwoman's Narrative* emerges today as a fresh and frank examination of the highly charged politics of space at once shaped and navigated by both black and white Americans in the decade preceding the Civil War.

Splendid Cottage, Lowly Mansion

The Bondwoman's Narrative signals its interest in architectural space long before Hannah's hallucination in the woods. Indeed, the novel's opening chapter, in which Hannah describes her childhood in slavery, makes extensive use of architectural spaces and metaphors as Crafts sets the scene for the story to follow. After explaining that her labors as a slave are "about the house" (6) rather than in the field, Hannah frames the story of her early years between two starkly contrasting structures whose interiors dominate the opening chapter. The first of these is "the little cottage just around the foot of the hill" to which as a young girl Hannah is invited for clandestine reading lessons by Aunt Hetty, an elderly northern woman who has noticed Hannah "ponder[ing] over the pages of some old book" (7) while the other slave children are at play. Hannah has never been in a cottage home before. She reflects: "I was surprised at the smallness yet perfect neatness of her dwelling, at the quiet and orderly repose that reigned in through all its appointments; it was in such pleasing contrast to our great house with its bustle, confusion, and troops of servants of all ages and colors" (8). In time Hannah discovers that Aunt Hetty and her husband had once lived in a great house of their own before being reduced to narrower means. "Wealth had been theirs, with all the appliances of luxury, and they became poor through a series of misfortunes," Hannah explains. "Yet as they had borne riches with virtuous moderation they conformed to poverty with subdued content, and readily exchanged the splendid mansion for the lowly cottage" (9).

The careful counterweighting in this last sentence, in which the sound pattern of "they had borne" is echoed in the partnered clause, "they conformed," and the phrase "virtuous moderation" is balanced by the chiastically meritorious "subdued content," heightens the ironic nobility of the house exchange described in the final line. For as the narrator suggests, the aged couple's "lowly" cottage, enriched by simplicity, moral goodness, and the invitation to literacy, is a more truly "splendid" space than that of any mansion in the text—certainly more so than the plantation estate owned by Hannah's master, the second principal structure framing the story of her childhood. Built in the colonial period by Sir Clifford De Vincent, the paternal ancestor of Hannah's current master, the "ancient mansion of Lindendale" (13) has been expanded by subsequent generations until there are multiple wings in this grand estate. Despite the mansion's size, Hannah and the other slaves "whispered though no one seemed to know" that Lindendale had become "impoverished" (13). This is not literally true, at least not in the material sense. As the slaves discover when preparing the house for the master's new bride, those portions of the mansion previously off-limits to servants conceal considerable luxuries ("what a variety of beautiful rooms, all splendid yet so different," marvels Hannah [14]). And yet in another sense Lindendale of course *is* impoverished, bankrupted morally by its successive masters' ongoing abuses of power, epitomized, as Hannah will make clear in the next chapter, by the original Sir Clifford's brutal punishment of the elderly slave Rose and her dog, whom he suspends without food or water from the branches of a giant linden tree until they die gruesomely from exposure.

Hannah considers this legacy of abuse—and has a presentiment of its present incarnation—in a lengthy interior scene that closes the first chapter. Asked by the housekeeper to shut some windows in a distant apartment of the mansion the night before the new bride's arrival, Hannah (now several years older than at the beginning of the chapter) "thread[s] the long galleries" of the house on her way to the "southern turret," which formerly housed the De Vincents' drawing room.[5] In a tradition begun by Sir Clifford, this room is "adorned with a long succession of family portraits ranged against the walls in due order of age and ancestral dignity" (15). Every Lindendale master since Sir Clifford has hung paired paintings of himself and his wife in this gallery, with the sole exception of Hannah's bachelor owner, who in defiance of his ancestor's wishes has displayed, prematurely, only his own portrait. Hannah interrupts her housekeeping duties to examine this pictorial mausoleum:

> Memories of the dead give at any time a haunting air to a silent room. How much more this becomes the case when standing face to face with their pictured resemblances and looking into the stony eyes motionless and void of expression as those of an exhumed corpse. But even as I gazed the golden light of sunset penetrating through the open windows in an oblique direction set each rigid feature in a glow. Movements like those of life came over the line of stolid faces as the shadows of a linden played there. (16)

To Hannah's surprise, in their lifelike movements the faces in the portraits assume expressions they "never wore in life" (16), appearing kind, gracious, relaxed. All, that is, except Hannah's master, who undergoes a contradictory transformation. In place of his "usually kind and placid expression," Mr. Vincent's face becomes wrathful and gloomy, "the calm brow . . . wrinkled with passion, the lips turgid with malevolence" (17). This puzzling change reinforces the splendid/lowly architectural inversion at the heart of the chapter: just at the moment Hannah is most impressed by her owner's material prestige ("we thought our master must be a very great man to have so much wealth at his command" [14]), he is flashed forth as a gilded criminal. "It never occurred to us to inquire whose sweat and blood and unpaid labor had contributed to produce [this splendor]," Hannah had pointedly observed at the beginning of the scene (14). The disturbing intimation of her master's hidden malevolence at scene's end betokens Hannah's rising awareness of the base corruptions that underwrite mansion glory.

If this reinforcement of the splendid/lowly inversion were all that the portrait scene accomplished in the novel, one might be tempted to write it off as a kind of gothic trick, or simply an allusion to Nathaniel Hawthorne's manipulations of the ancestral portrait of Colonel Pyncheon that hangs in his own architectural fiction, *The House of the Seven Gables* (1851). But Crafts further complicates the cottage/mansion dichotomy. Despite the looming presence of the ancient masters and the room's presentiment of "tragedy" (17), the enslavers' gallery helps Hannah feel oddly free, making this space unexpectedly consonant with the cottage home in which she had learned to read. Rather than flee the portrait hall, she lingers. "I was not a slave with these pictured memorials of the past," she explains. "They could not enforce drudgery, or condemn me on account of my color to a life of servitude. As their companion I could think and speculate. In their presence my mind seemed to run riotous and exult in its freedom as a rational being, and one destined for something higher and better than this world can afford" (17). Such feelings recall Hannah's awakening in the cottage: "I felt like a being to whom a new world with all its mysteries and marvels was opening" (8). Other unexpected similarities connect the plantation gallery to the cottage home. Both, for example, are figured as quiet retreats. Much as Hannah finds pleasure in escaping the "bustle" and "confusion" (8) of the big house when she steals away to the cottage, Mr. Vincent, she notes, withdraws to the southern turret when he is tired of the "noise and bustle and turmoil" (15) of the plantation estate. It is as though the drawing room, in its "retired situation" (15), is itself a kind of "cottage" space.

I will have more to say in the next section about the specific interest of *The Bondwoman's Narrative* in mid-nineteenth-century cottage or "country house" architecture. But let me close here by describing one more example of Crafts's pervasive use of architecture in the opening chapter, in this case a subtle counterpointing that centers on the misactivation of an architectural metaphor. Having discovered that other slaves, particularly children, trust and confide in her, Hannah wishes to instruct them as the aged couple has instructed her. Hannah expresses this desire in an apt, even routine, architectural metaphor: "How I longed to become their teacher and *open the door of knowledge* to their minds by instructing them to read" (12; my emphasis). Two paragraphs (if some few months) later, however, it is the literal yet *undesired* opening of a door that shatters this dream:

> The door [to the cottage] suddenly opened without warning, and the over-seer of my master's estate walked into the house. My horror, and grief, and astonishment were indescribable. I felt Oh how much more than I tell. He addressed me rudely, and bade me begone home on the instant. I durst not disobey, but retreating through the doorway I glanced back at the calm sedate countenances of the aged couple, who were all unmoved by the torrent of threats and invectives he poured out against them. (12)

Her surreptitious studies exposed, Hannah must retreat through the very doorway whose sudden opening, ironically, brings to a close her halcyon days in the cottage. It is with much additional irony that the overseer bids Hannah "begone *home*," when it is the cottage, not the mansion, that has become her true home.[6] Indeed, after this expulsion from the cottage Hannah will spend much of the novel searching in vain for other authentic "cottage" spaces. Not until she has escaped slavery altogether will she rediscover the structure she yearns for, and with it—by starting "a school for colored children" (237)—reopen the door that the overseer had metaphorically slammed shut.

To Elevate and Purify

Before the middle of the nineteenth century, for any American, slave or free, to yearn for a cottage would have been decidedly perverse. The term itself scarcely registers in the American architectural vocabulary before 1800, particularly in the South, and when "cottage" was used it tended to designate substandard housing.[7] By the 1850s, however, cottage structures were one of the most popular topics in American architectural treatises and pattern books. No longer chiefly suggestive of inadequate means, cottages had become respectable, even desirable, rural housing.

A motive force behind this radical reimagining of cottage space in the U.S.—for it was not so much the literal buildings that changed as the ideas behind them—was American landscape architect Andrew Jackson Downing. Strongly influenced by British models (in England, a similar transformation had occurred a generation earlier), Downing popularized for American audiences the new cottage ideal. After devoting his first book, *A Treatise on the Theory and Practice of Landscape Gardening* (1841), primarily to landscape design, Downing turned more fully in his 1842 volume, *Cottage Residences*, to domestic architecture. In the preface to *Cottage Residences* Downing objected that contemporary American dwellings were too often "carelessly and ill-contrived," resulting in "clumsy" and "unpleasing" structures.[8] His remedy for these ills was to nurture a more thorough appreciation for beauty in even the most humble of houses, particularly the rural cottage. "So closely are the Beautiful and the True allied," he wrote, "that we shall find, if we become sincere lovers of the grace, the harmony, and the loveliness with which rural homes and rural life are capable of being invested, that we are silently opening our hearts to an influence which is higher and deeper than the mere *symbol*" (iii; original emphasis). In practical terms, Downing called for "compact, convenient, and comfortable" (ii) homes based on "simple modifications of architectural styles" (32) appropriate to domestic life. The first edition of *Cottage Residences* provided ten specific house plans and site designs, ranging from a simple "suburban" cottage to more elaborate villas; later editions would add even more models. Though not all the plans were within the means of working-class laborers, each cottage conformed to what Downing termed the three leading principles of architecture: fitness, or the beauty of utility; purpose, or the beauty of propriety; and style, or the beauty of form and sentiment. Every home, so arranged and appointed, he argued, would "breathe forth to us, in true earnest tones, a domestic feeling, that at once purifies the heart, and binds us more closely to our fellow beings" (iv).

Both the *Treatise* and *Cottage Residences* were so well received that they quickly solidified Downing's position as the chief American authority on domestic architecture and landscape design. His influence was truly national. Though based in New York's Hudson Valley, Downing found appreciative audiences in both the North and the South and openly spoke of influencing the "national taste." (*Cottage Residences* is even listed among the books of the man believed to be Crafts's final owner, John Hill Wheeler, in an 1850 catalog of his library.)[9] In 1850, at the height of his fame, Downing received a presidential commission to plan the Public Grounds in Washington, D.C. That same year he published *The Architecture of Country Houses*, a return to the terrain of *Cottage Residences* but in far more extensive detail. Describing model cottages, farmhouses, and villas from their orderly architectural blueprints to their tasteful decorative furnishings, *The Architecture of Country Houses* further clarified the moral, social, and aesthetic stakes of refined home building. The opening paragraph of the opening section—"The Meaning of Architecture"—cuts right to the chase:

> Certainly the national taste is not a matter of little moment. Whether another planet shall be discovered beyond Le Verrier's [Neptune, identified in 1846] may or may not affect the happiness of a whole country; but whether a young and progressive people shall develope [*sic*] ideas of beauty, harmony, and moral significance in their daily lives; whether the arts shall be so understood and cultivated as to elevate and dignify the character; whether the country homes of a whole people shall embody such ideas of beauty and truth as shall elevate and purify its feelings; these are questions of no mean or trifling importance.[10]

Downing's shocking death in a spectacular steamboat fire on the Hudson River in July 1852 only enhanced his reputation as the midcentury's leading "apostle" of elevated and purified taste.[11] New printings and sometimes revised and enlarged editions of all his books continued to be issued after his death, including a much-praised "cheap" edition of *Cottage Residences* in 1853. That same year, George P. Putnam also brought out *Rural Essays*, a 557-page posthumous compilation of Downing's monthly editorial contributions to the *Horticulturist*, his widely circulating journal. Downing's theories saturated America in the 1850s, even in his physical absence.[12]

Composed during this decade, *The Bondwoman's Narrative* bears deeply the impress of Downing's ideas, beginning with Hannah's attraction as a young girl to the simple moral beauty of Aunt Hetty's plain yet dignified cottage. Like Downing, Hannah is drawn to the modest rather than the ornate, to neatness over disorder. Even under the duress of captivity she is awake to the beauty of rural forms. "Had we been less confused and troubled our ride probably would have been pleasant," Hannah remarks in chapter 7 while being conveyed in chains through the countryside, manacled to her former mistress—also a fugitive—after a foiled escape attempt. (Having fled Lindendale rather than be exposed as a slave passing for white, Hannah's mistress—her master's new bride—is finally caught, along with Hannah, after several months on the run.) "The sharp frosty air was clear and bracing, and the sunshine had a warm summer time look, really delightful," Hannah remarks. "Then, too, the country through which we passed has such a cheerful appearance with rickyards, milestones, farm houses, wagons, swinging signs, horse troughs, trees, fields, fences, and the thousand other things that make a country landscape" (90).

And yet throughout the novel even the most Downingesque buildings and landscapes almost inevitably betray rather than uphold Downing's rural ideal. Near the end of their manacled ride through this "delightful" scene, for example, Hannah and her mistress catch "a glimpse of a white house . . . on the top of a hill," which their driver informs them is their "journey's end." Not knowing where they are being conveyed, they look toward the house with great anticipation: "Presently we lost the house, presently we saw it, lost it again and again saw it; then turned into an avenue of cedar, and drew up before a fine cottage residence" (91). Everything about this description seems to call up Downing: not just the allusion to his own volume ("cottage residence") but also the curving approach to the house (Downing always recommended a curving path, with trees planted in loose groupings alongside) and even the adjective "fine" (one of Downing's most-used terms of praise). When someone comes out of the house to meet them, Hannah and her mistress are overcome with excitement—"Our hearts beat wildly, tumultuously as an old man came hobbling out on a crutch toward the wagon. Age sits beautifully on some ~~and the least farm~~. The frame bent with years, and the dark locks frosted with silver give the possessor a more interesting appearance, than all the flush of youth and beauty"—until they realize that this old man is bald, ugly, and "ogreish" (92). Once they are brought inside, they quickly discover that the "fine" residence is but a fancier prison than the temporary jail they have just left, and the old man their new jailer. The doors to their rooms are locked from the outside; the windows are shuttered tight. "We were amazed at the deep and utter silence that prevailed," Hannah reports (93).

This not so fine cottage residence, Hannah eventually learns, belongs to Mr. Trappe, a villainous lawyer and slave speculator whose threat to expose the racial secret of Hannah's mistress had precipitated their flight from Lindendale in the first place, and who now owns both women and plans to sell them back into slavery for profit. The evil Trappe, who has been hunting them down, is also at the center of an even more disturbing betrayal of Downingesque architectural space that takes place a few chapters earlier in the novel. While still on the run from Lindendale, Hannah and her mistress seek shelter in a modest farmhouse "in the outskirts of the village" (58–59). Having already sidestepped one house that looks inhospitable, the fugitives are on alert for architectural signs of welcome. To Hannah, the farmhouse's face, as it were, seems very promising:

> It was a happy-looking rural, contented spot, wanting, indeed, in the appearance of wealth and luxury, but evidently the abode of competence and peace. I felt that the possessors of such a place must be hospitable people, that they would have a care for two weak weary wandering women, and so exhorting my mistress to be of good cheer and strong in hope, we entered the gate, and advanced by a neatly graveled walk towards the dwelling. Everything seemed imbued with a quiet air of domestic happiness. Even the little dog came ~~running wagging~~ to meet us wagging his tail and frisking as if we were old acquaintances. (59)

Once inside the house, Hannah finds her initial judgment ecstatically confirmed. Soon she is ventriloquizing Downing: "It was the sanctuary of sweet home influences, a holy and blessed spot, so light and warm and with such an abiding air of comfort that one felt ~~so~~ how pure and elevated must be the character of its inmates" (60). It is Aunt Hetty's cottage all over again, complete with a kindly old woman and her husband. "Slavery dwelt not there," Hannah concludes firmly. "A thing so utterly dark and gloomy could not have remained in such a place for a day" (60). And yet Hannah is spectacularly wrong. The kindly old woman will turn out to be none other than Trappe's sister. Trappe himself will turn out not only to maintain a room in the house but to be present that very night. This *is* the house of slavery, not sanctuary, after all.

While the coincidental appearance of Trappe in the "happy-looking" farmhouse may seem a sloppy narrative contrivance, his menace unfolds with a precise spatial terror that meticulously dismantles the Downing ideal. Unaware that Trappe is in the house (they know only that the old woman's unnamed brother, a lawyer "retired in his habits," has arrived and gone to his room, unseen), Hannah and her mistress get ready for bed in a room "more secluded and retired than the former ones" (61). Though nervous about the unnamed brother—a lawyer "retired in his habits" sounds to Hannah suspiciously like Trappe—she pauses to provide a detailed inventory of the room: "It contained a bed very white and sweet, some chairs nicely cushioned, a small bureau, a very little stand, and a table. There was one window, only one, and that was low, little, and curtained by whispering leaves" (62). Perhaps Hannah's fears about the brother are misplaced after all, for this is a room whose simple furnishings Downing would admire, right down to the leafy curtains. (Downing regarded vines as the sine qua non of cottage decoration because they "always express domesticity and the presence of heart" [*Architecture of Country Houses*, 79].) But rather than offer safety, later that night the room exposes its inmates to Trappe's surveillant eye, which penetrates the lone window in a harrowing violation of Downingesque space. "The leafy curtaining of our window was slightly rustled, yet there was no breeze," Hannah recounts.

> Again there was a slight rustle, and I distinctly saw a human hand cautiously parting and pushing aside the leaves. The large white fingers were certainly those of a man. No less certainly was it a man's face that appeared there in another moment, the keen black eyes taking in the room and us at a glance. A keen black eye, and sharp angular features, though I obtained only a glimpse of them—but such an eye, only one person in the world possessed it, and that was Mr Trappe. (63)

Terrorized but giving no sign, Hannah and her mistress pretend to retire in the hope that Trappe will leave them until morning. Hours later, when all is still, they "[push] aside the leaves" (64) and creep through the window to flee the house.

This, too, is Aunt Hetty's cottage all over again: the site of apparent refuge violated by the hand of slavery, although this time, symbolized by the penetration of eyes and hands through a bedroom window, the violation carries an implicit sexual threat as well. (In fact, this threat may not only be implicit. Openly desiring Hannah's mistress, earlier in the novel Trappe had already threatened to possess her "on [his] own terms" [40] if she refuses to pay him to keep silent about her race.) Just as Hannah had earlier been forced to leave Aunt Hetty's cottage through the door flung open by the overseer, so must she and her mistress now squeeze through the space parted by Trappe. In this later scene, Crafts has Hannah reflect on the particularly vexed relation between bondwomen and built space in the South. "Were we ever again to sleep in peace?" she asks. "It seemed not. We must fly again. That very night we must set forth. We must leave the hospitable cottage and its inmates without thanks or ceremony" (63). Fleeing the cottage means avoiding sexual violation and recapture, but it also leaves Hannah and her mistress radically unhoused and thus ultimately, Crafts suggests, unfree. "Under the broad heaven, with the free air, the free leaves, the free beauties of nature about us, we could breathe freer than there," Hannah admits, "but could we hope to escape?" (63). Crafts suggests that a true escape from slavery—particularly for women—requires more than freedom from incarceration; it demands a free and safe habitation. Complete self-ownership, in other words, requires homeownership. This necessity makes the paradox of the novel's next episode more clear. After fleeing the farmhouse, Hannah and her mistress find shelter in a frightful structure, an uninhabited cabin that has been the scene of murder. The cabin's contents render it almost the precise opposite of the bedroom Hannah and her mistress have just fled: "There was neither floor, door nor window, an old bench, of which one leg was broken, a broken iron pot, and some pieces of broken crockery were scattered about. In one corner was a heap of damp mouldy straw that had probably served as a bed" (65). And yet this horrific space (the straw is later found to be matted with blood) protects the women for months, nearly the entire summer. It is their longest interval of safety since leaving Lindendale; moreover, it is the only space they can be said to "own" in the course of their flight.[13] "True, a more lonely and desolate place could not be imagined," Hannah notes, "but loneliness was what we sought; in that was our security" (66). The stay in the cabin is by no means a summer's idyll. Hannah's mistress becomes increasingly deranged, and the women cannot possibly survive the winter. They will eventually be caught, taken to jail, and turned over to Trappe. And yet this bloody cabin, despite representing in both design and decoration the antithesis of Downing's rural ideal, will prove, if not a terminus, nonetheless an unexpected and important model for Hannah, and for Crafts, in the narrative's quest to imagine the contours of successful black homeownership.

The Slave in the Archway

As we saw in the previous chapter, although antebellum pattern books typically shied away from direct discussions of race and slavery even when specifically addressing southern forms, many midcentury commentators—Orson Fowler and Andrew Jackson Downing prominent among them—hewed to a racialized theory of architectural design consonant with contemporary views about the hierarchical abilities of different races. We also noted the implicit racialization of *The Architecture of Country Houses*, in which Downing emphasizes the importance of Anglo-Saxon racial instinct in establishing a national architecture in the U.S., even though his volume pays no overt attention to American race relations. And yet because Downing includes plans for houses that are specifically identified as appropriate for "Southern States," *The Architecture of Country Houses* inadvertently introduces the topic of slavery even as it tries, through a range of euphemistic circumlocutions, to keep the subject at arm's length. When we look closely at Downing's discussions of southern houses, as well as the drawings and floor plans that accompany them, we will see how slavery begins to complicate Downing's architectural ideology in ways that he cannot quite admit—or even, in most cases, articulate. At the same time, we will also identify in his writings the precepts that would have spoken powerfully to midcentury African Americans seeking homes of their own, even if Downing never explicitly discusses black homeownership in his writings.[14]

Two of the house patterns in *The Architecture of Country Houses* are explicitly southern: Design XXVI, "A small Country-House for the Southern States," and Design XXXII, "A Villa in the Romanesque Style, for the Middle or Southern States."[15] As the first of the two southern examples, Design XXVI—"a simple, rational, convenient and economical dwelling for the southern part of the Union" (312)—receives more detailed attention for its regional idiosyncrasies. Downing singles out two features that distinguish this dwelling as southern: an extended veranda, "so indispensable to all dwellings in a Southern climate," and a detached kitchen, "a peculiar feature in all Southern country-houses" (313). Slavery enters the text indirectly during Downing's discussion of the kitchen. "This kitchen contains servants' bed-rooms on its second floor,—only such servants sleeping in the dwelling as are personal attendants on the family. For this reason there is not so much room required for servants in the Southern country-house itself—but, as many more servants are kept there than at the north, a good deal more accommodation is provided in the detached kitchen or other negro houses" (313–14). By using the word "servants" instead of "slaves," Downing partially camouflages the nature of slave labor, suggesting that slaves are semantically indistinguishable from domestic employees in the North. At the same time, however inadvertently, he offers a closer look than the pattern book genre usually provides into the hierarchies of domestic space that structure slave life. Not so much the well-known split between house slaves and field hands (here alluded to in the vague mention of "other negro houses") but the division between slaves who are "personal attendants on the family"—who sleep inside the family dwelling—and those other house slaves who labor more anonymously in the kitchen and apparently sleep above it.[16]

Since Downing's interest lies primarily in the master's house—he does not include a floor plan for either the kitchen or its upstairs bedrooms—he leaves any further account of slave accommodations vague. But this is not the last mention of servants. Two paragraphs later Downing must explain yet another peculiar spatial configuration required by the peculiar institution:

> In the rear of the hall is a back porch—which is a part of the veranda—that may be left open. Adjoining it is an entry or passage-way, five feet wide, for the servants to pass from the dining-room to the detached kitchen, without the necessity of entering the back porch or hall. Alongside of this entry is a large store-room (which is also part of the enclosed veranda), 10 by 10 feet. This is the larder and pastry-room, under the care of the mistress of the house; and adjoining it and the dining-room is a pantry or china-closet. (314)

Here the spatial divisions are unmistakable. The floor plan is constructed in such a way that the slaves from the detached kitchen have direct passage into the dining room (to conduct meal service, one assumes) but are carefully kept away from the back porch and the hall, where not only the master's family but also his guests might circulate. Control of space, shaped by both race and gender, is articulated here as well: the interior larder is "under the care of the mistress of the house," while the detached kitchen, presumably, is in the control of her (mostly female) slaves. Although Downing favored plans segregating domestic servants from homeowners in his designs for northern dwellings as well—including advocating the use of technological devices such as rising cup-

Figure 7. Andrew Jackson Downing, fig. 139, "Small Southern Country House," *The Architecture of Country Houses* (1850), 312. Courtesy Sinclair Hamilton Collection, Graphic Arts Division, Department of Rare Books and Special Collections, Princeton University Library.

boards and speaking tubes that would permit families, as Adam Sweeting notes, to "communicate their wants to the kitchen staff without so much as seeing the servants who performed the requested task"—nowhere in pattern book literature is the effect of slavery on building design and the movement of bodies more clear than in Design XXVI, whether that was Downing's intention or not.[17]

It seems all the more noteworthy, then, that the engraving (Fig. 7) and floor plan (Fig. 8) for this house—each of which shows the passageway to the kitchen in a *different* position—introduce a measure of confusion rather than clarity regarding the final home design, a confusion Downing must hasten to dispel. Returning to the detached kitchen yet a third time, he explains:

> We have shown the covered passage to the kitchen, and part of the kitchen itself, in our sketch of the *front* elevation, merely to convey an idea of their effect; though the position of those on the plan is in the rear, and not on the side of the house. This, however, is a mere matter of locality, as the kitchen and other outbuildings will, of course, be placed on the side offering the greatest facilities for their uses, and, at the same time, keeping them most in the back-ground. (315; original emphasis)

Downing's obsessive return, every few paragraphs, to the "detached" and thus ostensibly unseen labors of the southern slave is fantastically amplified by the presence of a most unusual figure in the engraving of the house itself. Framed in the archway of the passage connecting kitchen to villa is a female slave, in all likelihood carrying food to the main house (Fig. 9). A startling rarity in pattern book engravings, the slave is presumably there to illustrate, as though it were not clear enough from the text, the purpose of the passageway. Ironically, this places her not "in the back-ground," as Downing's text would relegate her, but very much in the foreground, a position inadvertently accentuated by her perfect centering in the arch's frame and the absence of any white figures in the drawing. The only other person depicted is yet another slave, framed neatly in the window to the right of the arch, who appears to be returning from the main house to the kitchen. The one figure kept in the background

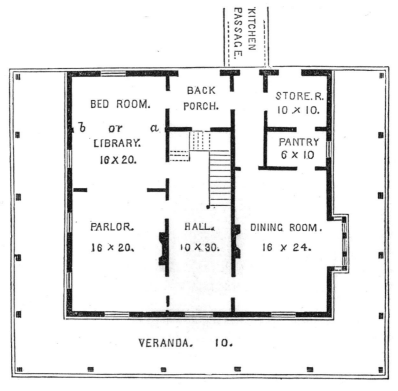

Figure 8. Andrew Jackson Downing, fig. 140, "Principal Floor," *The Architecture of Country Houses* (1850), 313. Courtesy Sinclair Hamilton Collection, Graphic Arts Division, Department of Rare Books and Special Collections, Princeton University Library.

Figure 9. Detail, Andrew Jackson Downing, fig. 139, "Small Southern Country House." *The Architecture of Country Houses* (1850), 312. Courtesy Sinclair Hamilton Collection, Graphic Arts Division, Department of Rare Books and Special Collections, Princeton University Library.

in this illustration, one might say, is the master, who is presumably inside the house receiving the food being ferried from the kitchen. The master remains hidden from view, however, only until the next engraving, a "variation" on the main design in which a planter can clearly be seen standing on the veranda, looking out over his plantation (Fig. 10). In this drawing, it is finally the kitchen and its labors that are put out of view.[18]

This compulsion simultaneously to depict and to screen the workings of slavery affects nearly every aspect of Downing's discussion of this southern country house, including (as was the case in Samuel Sloan's *Model Architect*, as we saw in the introduction) his closing estimate of its costs. While for other plans Downing provides exact estimates for materials and labor, in this design slavery's fuzzy math makes such precision impossible. Without fingering this cause explicitly, Downing euphemistically explains that the cost of the house will differ depending on "the locality where it is built" and on "the price of lumber, labor, etc., *which varies largely at the South*" (317; my emphasis).

Figure 10. Andrew Jackson Downing, fig. 142, "Exterior of Southern Country-House." *The Architecture of Country Houses* (1850), 316. Courtesy Sinclair Hamilton Collection, Graphic Arts Division, Department of Rare Books and Special Collections, Princeton University Library.

Downing's participation in the general evasiveness about slavery common to the pattern book genre, I am suggesting, is made even more apparent by his particular obsession with the detached southern kitchen. Another possible reason for Downing's evasiveness about slavery, however—although here I am only speculating—might have been an unacknowledged or even unconscious recognition on his part of the threat that human bondage posed to his conception of an independent citizenry that depends on individual home-ownership. For despite Downing's insistence in *The Architecture of Country Houses* on a racial hierarchy of architectural feeling, he also professed to believe in a "free and manly" republicanism that leveled old-world distinctions of class, hearth by humble hearth. "But the true home still remains to us," Downing asserted. "Not, indeed, the feudal castle, not the baronial hall, but the home of the individual man—the home of that family of equal rights, which continually separates and continually reforms itself in the new world—the republican home, built by no robbery of the property of another class, maintained by no infringement of a brother's rights" (269).

If Downing's language here veers, however unintentionally, toward an abolitionist rhetoric of "equal rights," it is of course little different in that regard from many other mid-nineteenth-century antiaristocratic pronouncements never intended to apply to slaves. In other words, I am not suggesting Downing was a closet abolitionist; he was not even in any conventional sense a social leveler when it came to whites. As Dell Upton has argued, Downing privileged distinctions of class even as he professed that in an ideal democracy they should not exist.[19] And yet so apparently invested was Downing in an equal opportunity and antihereditary politics of homeownership, one wonders whether he might have implicitly recognized that talking too much about slavery in a book about houses—especially in a text completed in 1850, amid intensifying sectional animosity—would have required paying more attention not just to the contradictions of the American system of bondage, but to those within his own rhetoric.

Even as Downing continued to evade these particular matters, he still spoke frequently in terms that on their face might have justified far more radical social action than he ever countenanced. Let one last example suffice. On a trip to England in June 1850, shortly after sending *The Architecture of Country Houses* to his publisher, Downing warmed once again to the topic of the gulf between haves and have-nots—and articulated the special responsibility of Americans to see this gulf eradicated. On "the top of the highest tower" of Warwick Castle, from which vantage point he "command[s] the whole panorama of feudal castle, tributary town, and lovely landscape," Downing reflects: "To England, the country of my ancestors, it had been given to show the growth of man in his highest development of class." But to America, he concludes, "has been reserved the greater blessing of solving for the world the true problem of all humanity—that of the abolition of all castes, and the recognition of the divine right of every human soul."[20]

To the extent that Downing's words—minus the whiff of Anglo-Saxon superiority—were heard by African Americans, they must have resonated deeply with long-standing black yearnings not just for the recognition of shared humanity but also for permanence of place through the possession of a home. In this light, Crafts's interest in putting pressure on Downing's ideology by imagining a succession of pattern book cottages violated by the hand of slavery seems designed not so much to expose that ideology's evasiveness or hypocrisy as to capture its promise for blacks, to activate its tropes and ideals for its excluded audience. Through its simultaneous critique and recuperation of antebellum architectural discourse, *The Bondwoman's Narrative* implicitly encourages its readers to reconsider Downing's theories from the point of view of the slave in the archway.

I would argue that this is the case even where such concerns about space and slavery seem least pressing in the text. Consider, for example, the pages Hannah spends describing the house owned by the Henrys, the "amiable family" (121) that offers her shelter after the midnovel accident that nearly kills her. (After Hannah and her mistress are recaptured and returned to Trappe, the evil lawyer sells Hannah to a slave trader. En route to his home, the trader's horse bolts, sending their wagon over an embankment. Hannah survives the crash; the trader does not.) At first glance, Hannah's detailed description of the architectural and decorative features of the Henry house— called Forget-me-not—might seem charmingly incidental to the novel's larger plot and thus unconnected to its racial politics. After all, the description of Forget-me-not interrupts the forward movement of the story for nearly three pages and consists largely of a room-by-room account of the house's aesthetic charms. Yet this detailed description not only is germane to the novel's larger escape plot; through subtle allusions to Downing, Crafts further explores the meaning—and what eventually becomes the *un*meaning—of the Henry house to a slave like Hannah.

The first allusion appears in the introductory frame of the extraordinary description that opens chapter 10 of *The Bondwoman's Narrative*:

> Every house with its surroundings possesses an air of individuality. In some it is more strongly developed than in others, yet it appertains to all in a greater or less degree. "Forget me not" as this dwelling had been beautifully and not inappropriately named was one of those dear old houses rich in panel work and fresco, and whose construction from first to last bespeaks an association with the past. Who does not find a charm about these ancient houses, with their delightfully irregular apartments, embellished with quaint carvings and mouldings, brown with age, and awaking in the mind a thousand reminiscen[c]es of olden times and fashions. (121)

When the narrator asserts that "every house . . . possesses an air of individuality," her words echo Downing's pronouncement in *The Architecture of*

Country Houses that "the country house should, above all things, manifest individuality" (262). In the section in which Downing makes this assertion, "What a Country House or Villa Should Be," he compares homes built by different types of men: men of "common sense" (262), men of "sentiment" (263), men of "imagination" (263), and men of "the past" (265). "Forget me not"—which Hannah describes lovingly as "one of those dear old houses . . . whose construction from first to last bespeaks an association with the past" (121)—belongs emphatically in this final group. The material details that anchor Forget-me-not to the past make the house seem appealingly quaint. "It was furnished in a style and manner that corresponded exactly with itself," Hannah informs the reader. "The furniture was not old, but rather old-fashioned" (122). In the early days of her stay, Hannah is delighted by these details. "Such houses were built rather for solid utility than for show, consequently the materials are durable and the timbers massy," she explains, "but there is likewise a great deal of variety, taste, and elaborate ornament-ing" (121).

In Downing's assessment, however, houses that look back instead of for-ward risk being out of touch with the currents of the day. "In every age and country are born some persons who belong rather to the past than the pres-ent—men to whom memory is dearer than hope," Downing explains. "It is not for these men . . . to understand and appreciate the value of an archi-tecture significant of the present time" (265). However full of meaning for "these men," Downing suggests, an architecture of the past is "unmeaning for the many, and especially for all those who more truly belong to our own time and century" (266).

Crafts encourages readers to recognize the dangers of Forget-me-not's backward glance by exposing the ways its owner is not just old-fashioned but cruelly out of touch. Hannah's room-by-room inventory conveys the appeal of Forget-me-not not only as a space of pleasing variety and taste but as one of potential domestic sanctuary. Its "home-bred air of genial quiet and repose [*sic*]" (198)—almost precisely recalling the "quiet and repose" (8) of Aunt Hetty's cottage—so appeals to Hannah that when she learns she is about to be claimed as property by a relative of the dead trader she begs Mrs. Henry to purchase her as her own slave. "You can save me from this," Han-nah tells Mrs. Henry, offering to perform any labor on the estate if only she will permit Hannah to stay. "All I ask," Hannah pleads, "is to feel, and know of certainty that I have a home" (125). But Mrs. Henry has made a promise to her dead father—"never on any occasion to buy or sell a servant" (127)—that prevents her even from considering Hannah's request, despite the fact that her action would prevent, not increase, Hannah's misery. Bound to the past by a vow intended to keep her morally clean, Mrs. Henry refuses to grant, despite her ability to do so, "the greatest favor that a mild kind hearted man or woman can bestow on members of the outcast servile race" (127). Hannah, however, recognizes the fundamental immorality of Mrs. Henry's insistence on following the letter rather than the principle of her father's deathbed wish.

To use Downing's terms, this is the moment in the novel in which "memory" cruelly trumps "hope." It is thus also the moment in which the architectural loveliness of the Henry house becomes "unmeaning" for Hannah. "Just at that moment I felt that it mattered little where I went, or what became of me. I was disappointed, without hope in this world, and half-forgetful of my trust in the next" (128). Given these reflections, Hannah's earlier observation that the "dear old" Henry house is "not inappropriately named" gains a sharp bite of irony. Why? Because it is now clear that Forget-me-not stands for something far darker than the "thousand reminiscen[c]es" prompted by the "many interesting objects surrounding the house" (121). It also stands for the iron mandate—*Forget me not*—of Mrs. Henry's dead father. After this moment, Hannah feels only "harassing anxiety" (133) within the house's walls. When she finally leaves this place, delivered by Mrs. Henry into the duplicitous slave-owning grip of her next owner, Mrs. Wheeler, Hannah treats the reader to no last encomiums on the house, no tearful (or even stoic) farewell. For her, this unmeaning frame—this house of the past—has lost its spell.

Borrowed Places

If the pattern books dodged the question of slavery, where might an interested reader (or author) turn for a discussion of race and architecture in the 1850s? To the very front lines of the ideological battle over bondage. By middecade, representations of built space had become indispensable features of the literature of slavery in both the North and the South, as each side deployed architectural imagery to buttress sectional claims. Journalistic accounts by northerners of their tours through the South, for example, often included detailed descriptions (and sometimes illustrations) of plantation housing, slave and free.[21] Slave narratives, for example, had long dissected the physical contours of segregation and in the 1850s were paying special attention to intrusions on African American domestic space. (Harriet Jacobs's *Incidents in the Life of a Slave Girl* [1861], in its depiction of Jacobs's paradoxically liberating self-confinement in her garret, provides one of the most incisive spatial commentaries of the decade.)[22] The catalytic text in this

Figure 11. "A View of Selma," frontispiece to J. W. Page, *Uncle Robin in His Cabin in Virginia, and Tom without One in Boston* (1853).

development was Harriet Beecher Stowe's *Uncle Tom's Cabin* (1852). Stowe not only gave dramatic fictional form to the slave cabin but chose to let that "lowly" space carry the titular weight of her critique. Stowe also animated, usually with trenchant irony, the grander structures of slavery, from the "well-furnished dining parlor" in which Mr. Shelby arranges Tom's sale, to the Moorish excess of the St. Clare mansion, to the decaying estates of the vicious Legree.[23]

The surest sign that Stowe's architectural representations had hit their mark is the vehemence and consistency with which her southern debunkers sought to reverse her tropes. Nearly every response to *Uncle Tom's Cabin* stages, early in the text, a socio-architectural rebuttal of Stowe's depictions. In these books, planters' mansions are always tasteful and refined, slave quarters clean and comfortable. No crumbling Legree plantations or fetid slave huts here, no ma'am—only the honest and open forms of a benevolent institution. Architectural challenges to Stowe and the slave narratives were so central to this genre that they sometimes took visual form, as in the frontispiece to J. W. Page's 1853 novel, *Uncle Robin in His Cabin in Virginia, and Tom without One in Boston*, "A View of Selma" (Fig. 11). This illustration draws on the visual idiom of the pattern books not simply to prove the inherent comfort of the enslaved but, one might say, to model it. Save for the presence of the slave cabins themselves, this elevation would not be out of place in one of Downing's texts, right down to the pair of tiny figures conversing in the left margin.

In its own architectural depictions, *The Bondwoman's Narrative* borrows much not only from Stowe but also, surprisingly, from her southern rebutters. The traces of Stowe's spatial imagination are evident throughout Crafts's text, from its invocation through Forget-me-not of Rachel Halliday's peaceful Quaker settlement to its use of a tripartite plantation structure very similar to Stowe's.[24] And yet there are also passages in *The Bondwoman's Narrative* that draw uncannily on southern tropes. Compare, for example, these two descriptions of visits to slave quarters, the first from Mary H. Eastman's *Aunt Phillis's Cabin; or, Southern Life as It Is* (1852), the second from one of the Forget-me-not chapters of *The Bondwoman's Narrative*:

> It was just sundown, but the servants were all at home after their day's work, and they too were enjoying the pleasant evening time. Some were seated at the door of their cabins, others lounging on the grass, all at ease, and without care. Many of their comfortable cabins had been recently whitewashed, and were adorned with little gardens in front; over the one nearest the house a multiflora rose was creeping in full bloom. Singularly musical voices were heard at intervals, singing snatches of songs, of a style in which the servants of the South especially delight. (*Aunt Phillis's Cabin*, 29)

> After the evening repast I attended Mrs Henry in a very pleasant walk among the ~~various~~ negro lodges, and in looking over their little truck patches and gardens, all of which gave evidence of being neatly attended in the absence of weeds and the appearance of thrifty growth in the various plants, vegetables, and flowers, designed for use and ornament. Various groups of persons, young and old, all of whom seemed impressed with a ~~feeling of reverence of the day~~ reverential feeling of the sanctity of the day, and of regard for their mistress, were seated on little low benches at their doors, quiet[l]y enjoying the beauty of the evening. (*The Bondwoman's Narrative*, 138)

The slave cabin tour is a stock device of pro-slavery texts. Sometimes it is rendered by the narrator, as in the preceding example from *Aunt Phillis's Cabin*. In other texts, the tour is dramatized in the plot, as when a northern visitor takes his or her first peek into the cabins, usually to declare with great surprise (as does the planter's Pennsylvania bride in *Uncle Robin in His Cabin in Virginia*) something like, "My dear husband, how very comfortable and neat they all seem to be!"[25] Hannah's peculiar status at the Henry plantation, where she is acknowledged as a slave but not as the Henrys' slave, coupled with her experiential divide from field hands (she has only ever worked in the house), help place Hannah in the outsider's position in this scene. Ultimately, however, Hannah's tour registers less surprise than appreciation, not only for Mrs. Henry's benevolence but also for the slaves' self-sufficiency. Whereas *Aunt Phillis's Cabin* works to obscure slave agency—when Eastman's narrator says that "many of [the slaves'] comfortable cabins had been recently whitewashed, and were adorned with little gardens in front," the credit for these conditions appears to fall to the magnanimous planter—Crafts's description foregrounds more active slave caretaking: "[All] the little truck patches and gardens . . . gave evidence of being neatly attended." Indeed, like the decrepit old cabin in the woods, these lodges provide a partial model for the neat, independent cottage Hannah herself will eventually own.[26]

If, as I have been suggesting, *The Bondwoman's Narrative* is deeply attuned to literary representations of built space, then the "architectural" text with which Crafts's novel indicates its closest familiarity, intriguingly, is Charles Dickens's *Bleak House*. As Hollis Robbins has shown, in addition to its widespread popularity in the U.S., *Bleak House* was a touchstone in abolitionist circles, in part on the strength of Dickens's empathetic representations of the miseries of poverty. (The novel even appeared in serial form in *Frederick Douglass's Paper*.)[27] The three-page description of the individual rooms of Forget-me-not, the most extensive and explicit architectural allusion in Crafts's text, is adapted from chapter 6 of Dickens's novel, "Quite at Home," in which Esther Summerson describes Bleak House itself for the first time. Here is the opening sentence of Dickens's description, followed by a corresponding excerpt from Crafts's text:

> It was one of those delightfully irregular houses where you go up and down steps out of one room into another, and where you come upon more rooms when you think you have seen all there are, and where there is a bountiful provision of little halls and passages, and where you find still older cottage-rooms in unexpected places, with lattice windows and green growth pressing through them. (*Bleak House*)[28]

Who does not find a charm about these ancient houses, with their delightfully irregular apartments. . . . [Y]ou pass from one room into another, and go up and down steps, and note a bountiful supply of little halls, entries, and passages leading you cannot tell where. Then every room seems a wonder in itself, with its old-fashioned fire place, and little windows, surrounded by lattice work with the luxuriant growth of honey-suckle and jasmine pressing through it. (*The Bondwoman's Narrative*, 121–22)

Both the directness of Crafts's borrowing and her alterations of the source text are evident here. Key descriptions and actions jump unchanged from Dickens to Crafts, such as "delightfully irregular" and "go up and down steps." Other phrases are slightly revised: "bountiful provision" becomes "bountiful supply"; "little halls and passages" becomes "little halls, entries, and passages"; "lattice windows" become "little windows, surrounded by lattice work." The ellipsis in the passage from *The Bondwoman's Narrative*, which marks my omission of seven additional lines of text, indicates the extent to which Crafts reworked her Dickens source material to propel, rather than merely puff out, her narrative.

As Robbins has argued, Crafts's extensive borrowings from Dickens are alchemic rather than plagiaristic; her copies transform their models instead of simply replicating them.[29] A continued side-by-side comparison of the descriptions of Bleak House and Forget-me-not would demonstrate Crafts's use of compression and dilation in adapting the Dickens passage to its new narrative context. In the detailed cataloging of individual rooms that follows the introductory lines quoted earlier, for example, Crafts excises a number of material details that stamp the Bleak House description as particularly British.[30] She also carries the description of Forget-me-not outside the house to include the rest of the plantation estate, making the American setting clear. "In the lodges of the servants, and every thing pertaining to the establishment the same variety was observable," Hannah notes. "Method and regularity likewise prevailed over the estate. The overseer was gentle and kind, and the slaves were industrious and obedient" (123).

Why so much, so carefully transplanted, from *Bleak House*? I would argue that the identification of Forget-me-not with Bleak House helps Crafts activate a trope of self-ownership through homeownership that is unavailable through her other sources; that this activation, and the role of the *Bleak House* borrowing in it, become fully clear only at the end of Crafts's novel through the introduction of yet another, more subtle, allusion to Dickens; and finally that the very extensiveness of her allusions—to one of the most widely known imaginary houses in British or American culture in the 1850s—suggests that Crafts wanted the parallels to Dickens understood rather than overlooked. To test these claims, we will need to move to the end of *The Bondwoman's Narrative*, where Hannah's journey completes the arc of desire initiated in Aunt Hetty's quiet, tidy house. But first, like Hannah, we have to pass through the hands (and increasingly bleak houses) of Mrs. Wheeler, her new mistress.

Black House

Not long after Hannah's fruitless discussion with Mrs. Henry about purchasing either her services or her freedom, Hannah's absentee owner agrees to sell her to the Wheelers, distant relatives of the Henrys who have come for a summer visit. Mrs. Henry gives her blessing to this transfer of title, believing, incorrectly, that the Wheelers are "kind and humane to their slaves" (128). They are in fact careless and cruel masters, intent primarily on improving their social position in Washington, D.C., where until recently Mr. Wheeler had held "a high official position" (150). Hannah has little to say about the "splendid mansion" (170) to which they remove her, but of course Crafts has already made clear that in this narrative "splendid" is a term of deflation, not admiration, particularly when it comes to slaveowners' mansions. Hannah actually spends most of the chapters set in the Federal City hearing stories about another splendid but morally bankrupt mansion: her former home Lindendale. Through a chance meeting with Lizzy, who had once been waiting maid to the mistress with whom Hannah fled Lindendale in the first place, Hannah learns of "strange doings at the old place" (172)—tales of concubinage, infant murder, suicide, and rape—that highlight what Augusta Rohrbach has aptly termed Crafts's "scathing critique of female vulnerability." Lindendale's new master, Mr. Cosgrove, taking literal advantage of the peculiarities of the mansion's architecture, particularly its "rambling style, that precluded the occupant of one part from knowing anything of the other" (173), has hidden from his unsuspecting wife multiple slave mistresses (and their children by him) within the house itself.[31] When Mrs. Cosgrove finally discovers their existence and insists they be sold, one of the slaves stabs her own child and then herself before falling dead at the master's feet, "bathing them in her blood" (177). Even these horrors are not enough to persuade the master to change his ways. Only pretending to sell his concubines, he not only continues to hide a new favorite in a secret room inside the mansion but also purchases a small country retreat in which to reestablish his slave "haram [*sic*]" (172).

Crafts's inclusion of this retreat, called Rock Glen, provides one last example in the novel of the ongoing betrayal of Downingesque architectural space under the system of slavery. "'Rock Glen,'" Mrs. Cosgrove thinks to herself when she hears it whispered from the overseer to her husband; "the name was romantic, the place was doubtless picturesque. Where could it be?" (187). In a charming mountain setting, as Mrs. Cosgrove eventually learns from an old beggar woman:

> The old woman then directed her what road to follow, where to turn to the right, and where to turn to the left, where there was a brook to ~~cross,~~ ~~a meadow to pass over~~ pass over, a meadow to cross, and a fence to leap, where there was a tavern and a store a blacksmith's shop, and an undertaker, where we might see negroes working in a field of tobacco, and just catch the glimpse of a habitation nestled beneath an overhanging crag, that looked as if it would fall every moment, though the wear and tear of centuries had failed to displace it. "And that crag" she continued ["] and that little habitation beneath it is called Rock Glen." (188–89)

Picturesque indeed—yet also shadowed by death. If "nestled" embodies the ideal Downingesque context, "glimpse" the preferred mode of viewing, and "little" (a word Downing used even more often than "fine") the optimal size for a snug cottage, then the "undertaker" and the crag poised like a Damoclean sword make plain Crafts's view of the true character (and deserved fate) of Mr. Cosgrove's love nest. The misery this "romantic" structure encodes redoubles first upon the master's wife (who in falling from her horse on her way to expose her husband's deceit suffers fatal internal injuries), then upon the master himself, who wastes away from remorse for his wife's death. The concubines and their children, of course, have suffered all along.

Crafts conspicuously spares Hannah the fate of Cosgrove's mistresses; sexual violence in this novel always happens to someone else, although Hannah is by no means exempt from the threat of rape as long as she remains a slave, or indeed a free woman without a safe home. Crafts finally brings Hannah face-to-face with this threat—and at last propels her toward her own cottage—when the disgraced Wheelers leave Washington to return to North Carolina. Like nearly all the plantation estates in the novel, the Wheelers' is lovely on the outside yet cancered within. Their "fine plantation," Hannah reports, still awake to the aesthetics of built form, "was altogether one of the most beautiful places I had ever seen" (198). Lacking the "stately majesty" of Lindendale or the hominess of Forget-me-not, the Wheeler estate possesses "a luxurious abundance of vines, and fruits, and flowers, and song-birds, and every thing wore such an aspect of maturity and ripeness" that Hannah was "fairly charmed" (198). All the plantation's labor, however, is expended in either picking cotton or tending the master's vines. No care whatsoever is expended on the cabins that house the slaves, which are not simply built "with far less reference to neatness and convenience than those in Virginia" (199) but express the most degraded forms of human habitation:

> Is it a stretch of imagination to say that by night they contained a swarm of misery, that crowds of foul existence crawled in out of gaps in walls and boards, or coiled themselves to sleep on ~~nauseous~~ nauseous heaps of straw fetid with human perspiration and where the rain drips in, ~~and the mid-night dew imparts some~~ and the damp airs of midnight fatch [fetch] and carry malignant fevers.
>
> They said that many of these huts were old and ruinous with decay, that occasionally a crash, and a crowd of dust would be perceived among them, and that each time it was occasioned by the fall of one. But lodgings are found among the rubbish, and all goes on as before. (199–200)

These paragraphs constitute yet another careful transplant from *Bleak House*. As Robbins has shown, Crafts here recomposes Dickens's account of a decaying London slum into a snapshot of slavery's "malignant" built environment.[32] Crafts also appends a further indictment: "Many of these huts," Hannah reports, "were even older than the nation" (200).

After accusing Hannah of having made her a local laughingstock by retailing the story of her disgrace in Washington, Mrs. Cosgrove banishes her from the house to the fields where she is to pick cotton and live in one of these ruinous huts. Not just live, but make a home: "You can herd with them," Mrs. Cosgrove sneers. "Bill, who comes here sometimes has seen and admires you. In fact he asked you of Mr Wheeler for his wife, and his wife you shall be" (205). Hannah spends a day in the fields but recoils that night from her leering, abusive "husband" and the rape or beating he has planned for her. "Frightened and anxious" (209), she flees his filthy hut, concocts a plan to escape the plantation, and runs into the darkness for her life—and, finally, toward her own cottage.

Hannah's route from fetid slave hut to comfortable free cottage takes her through the same deep woods with which we opened this chapter and in which we saw her hallucinate being pursued not by bloodhounds but by architectural symbols of her enslavement. Plagued in the novel's closing pages by the question of shelter—where to find it, how to know it is safe—Hannah abruptly arrives at the place she may be said to have begun: Aunt Hetty's "neat little cottage" (229). This is not the cottage next to Lindendale. Hetty and her husband had been evicted and jailed after Mr. Vincent's overseer caught them teaching Hannah to read; but upon gaining their freedom they were helped into a new house by an old friend. In another sense, however, it *is* the cottage next to Lindendale. "Tidy and comfortable, with a bright fire glowing on the hearth" (229), Aunt Hetty's new cottage not only restores Hannah to her "former self" but guides her to her own long-desired shelter. "I dwell now in a neat little Cottage," Hannah announces in the novel's final chapter, "and keep a school for colored children" (237). The unusual capitalization of "Cottage" (its only occurrence in the text) elevates this structure to the Downingesque ideal while simultaneously alluding to the end of *Bleak House*, which converges on a nearly identical, but easily overlooked, space: Esther Summerson's cottage. This is the "rustic," "lovely place" (797) given to Esther by her guardian, Mr. Jarndyce, as a physical gesture of his freeing Esther—his former housekeeper—to marry her true love, Allan Woodcourt, instead of Jarndyce himself. Fitted out by Jarndyce exactly according to Esther's taste, the cottage both anticipates Esther's future bliss and affirms her proprietorship, even though Esther does not yet realize the cottage is to be hers:

> As we went through the pretty rooms, out at the little rustic verandah doors, and underneath the tiny wooden colonnades, garlanded with woodbine, jasmine, and honey-suckle, I saw, in the papering of the walls, in the colours of the furniture, in the arrangement of all the pretty objects, *my* little tastes and fancies, *my* little methods and inventions which they used to laugh at while they praised them, my odd ways everywhere. (797)

Of all the ways that *Bleak House* matters to *The Bondwoman's Narrative*, this is perhaps the most important. Like Esther, Hannah Crafts ends her tale not as housekeeper but as homeowner, happily ensconced in an independent cottage, loving husband by her side. Lest the point be missed, Crafts gives Hannah's cottage a twin in the novel's final paragraph. "I must not omit telling who are my neighbors," Hannah interjects. "Charlotte, Mrs Henry's favorite, and her husband. From the window where I sit, a tiny white cottage half-shaded in summer by rose-vines and honeysuckle appears at the foot of a sloping green. ~~Before it is now~~ In front there is such an exquisite flower-garden, and behind such a dainty orchard of choice fruits"—Esther's cottage is surrounded by a similar garden and similar orchard—"that it does one good to think of it. It is theirs" (239). *It does one good to think of it.* At the end of this novel the idea of African American proprietorship, of the free black home, compels. *It is theirs.* No other literary text whose influence on Crafts's narrative we have been tracing provides a similar image. For Harriet Jacobs the lack of such a structure in *Incidents in the Life of a Slave Girl* casts a shadow over her very freedom. "The dream of my life is not yet realized," she admits. "I do not sit with my children in a home of my own. I still long for a hearthstone of my own, however humble" (302). The depth of Jacobs's lament accentuates the importance of Hannah's success.[33]

In trying to image forth black homeownership, the author of *The Bondwoman's Narrative* pursues in fiction a sociopolitical strategy that black activists like Frederick Douglass pressed outside the text. As Sarah Luria has shown, Douglass "urged African Americans to acquire homes of their own." The reasons, Luria explains, were multiple:

> A home provided a second skin by which African Americans could define themselves by class, taste, and morality rather than by their skin color. A respectable home did more than any speech or law to establish one's social equality. If blacks could acquire middle-class homes, then the chances for social contact with one's white neighbors would be improved greatly and so too the chances for lasting social change. . . . Further, private property offered African Americans the one spot in American life where they might exert significant control.[34]

As we have noted, Douglass, like Crafts, admired Dickens's *Bleak House.* In the 1880s Douglass even went so far as to dub the one-room, cabinlike structure that he erected as a study behind his Cedar Hill home in Washington, D.C., his "Growlery," after Mr. Jarndyce's home office of the same name in Dickens's text. According to Luria, Douglass's unusual study—a cross between a slave cabin and a rustic cottage—was one of several ways Douglass deliberately sought to challenge "conventional definitions of race" in his postbellum Washington home.[35] In the end, Crafts's antebellum transformation of Esther's modest cottage into a powerful image of black homeownership—of Bleak House into a *black* house, we might say—functions analogously. Much as Douglass would choose a hilltop with a prominent view of the federal capital to deliver his architectural message, Crafts selects one of the most prominent literary texts of the decade to provide the ground for her own.

New Patterns

There is yet a final, fitting way we might think about Crafts's architectural borrowings from Dickens. By selecting from *Bleak House* those passages most applicable to her own story and then reworking them in a fresh context, Crafts treats Dickens's text much the way midcentury builders treated pattern books. As Dell Upton has shown, although the architects who wrote pattern books typically prescribed every measurement and relation—offering integrated designs that stood as "cohesive artistic productions"—the builders who were hired to translate those designs into actual physical structures used the pattern books far more selectively. Builders tended to add to existing structures, borrowing and adapting what elements they needed to complete a job, rather than building exactly according to an architect's plan. Crafts, in other words, is not trying to copy *Bleak House*, either sneakily or sloppily. She is borrowing selectively from Dickens (and other writers), adapting familiar passages to new ends while demonstrating her literary knowledge and transformative skill. Indeed, in a significant sense all of Crafts's larger systems of narrative borrowing—including her gleanings not just from the pattern book genre but also from the range of other genres her text has been shown strategically to incorporate[36]—might be understood as a way of transforming the principle of the pattern book itself into a narrative mode.

In the case of Esther Summerson, we might say, Crafts borrows Dickens's original narrative design—the housekeeper turned homeowner—in order to fit out her own depiction of the independent black home. If Esther's cottage, moreover, is made visible at the end of *The Bondwoman's Narrative* only by the sheer copiousness of the borrowings in the earlier Forget-me-not description—which puts Bleak House as a structure in the mind of an alert midcentury reader—then it seems appropriate the very last scenes of Crafts's novel point back to the Forget-me-not episode a final time. They do so literally, of course, by having Charlotte and William, Forget-me-not's original fugitives, resurface unharmed. But these scenes also return to Forget-me-not metaphorically, in the surprising advent of Hannah's mother. In narrating this unlooked-for plot twist—all Hannah has ever said about her parents is that "no one ever spoke of my father or mother" (5)—Hannah explains that even though she was sold from Lindendale when she was an infant, her mother "*never forgot me* nor certain marks on my body, by which I might be identified in after years" (237; my emphasis). Here Crafts confers an even richer significance on the name Forget-me-not: where Mrs. Henry's refusal to forget punishes Hannah, Hannah's mother's refusal to forget ultimately rewards her long-lost daughter.

As though to drive home this reversal, Crafts reprises, then revises, the emotional heart of Hannah's pleading interview with Mrs. Henry. In that earlier scene, after Hannah begs Mrs. Henry to purchase her—"You have no idea how good I will be, or how exactly I will conform myself to all your wishes" (126)—Mrs. Henry lifts Hannah from the floor, embraces her, and "compassionate[s]" over her. "She wept," Hannah relates, "and our tears were mingled together" (126). In the novel's final chapter, however, Hannah and her mother share tears of wild joy when their true relation is discovered. "I was then resting for the first time on my mother's bosom—my mother for whom my heart had yearned, and my spirit gone out in intense longing many many times," marvels Hannah.

> And we had been brought together by such strange and devious ways. With our arms clasped around each other, our heads bowed together, and our tears mingling we went down on our knees, and returned thanks to Him, who had watched over us for good, and whose merciful power we recognized in this the greatest blessing of our lives. (238)

In terms of narrative design, the "strange and devious ways" by which Hannah and her mother are brought together seem as much Crafts's as any higher power's. Having thwarted Hannah's desire to live at Forget-me-not, in the end Crafts gives her all she wishes and more: her own freedom, her own husband, her own mother, all neatly packaged in her own home. Not even the orphaned Esther Summerson can claim quite as much.

Indeed, the intensity of desire expressed in the final chapter of Crafts's novel, "In Freedom," surpasses any emotive language the text has earlier offered, and encompasses both people and place. "Can you guess who lives with me?" Hannah asks in the first paragraph. "You never could—my own dear mother, aged and venerable, yet so smart and lively and active, and Oh: so fond of me" (237). The conjunctive rush of "ands" that propels this sentence comes to a sudden and powerful pause at Hannah's "Oh," and in the space between the colon and the final phrase ("so fond of me") one senses the depth of pleasure made possible by the mother-daughter reunion.[37] If this pleasure remains nearly inarticulable—"And then I—but I cannot tell what I did, I was so crazy with delight" (238), avers Hannah—it nonetheless permeates the final image of "undeviating happiness" that Hannah feels in "the society of my mother, my husband, and my friends" (239), cottaged side by side in self-owned freedom—indeed, in a true neighborhood. "I will let the reader picture it all to his imagination," Hannah concludes, "and say farewell" (239).

Of course Crafts's imagined reader never had that opportunity. Nor have we yet uncovered enough information about Crafts to gauge the degrees of fact and fantasy involved in Hannah's final transformation. Whatever discoveries lurk, one wonders what kind of effect the completed circuit of cottage desire in *The Bondwoman's Narrative* might have had on African American readers had the manuscript found a publisher. Perhaps Crafts's careful reworkings of Downing and Dickens would have offered black writers new patterns to use in shaping their own spatial imaginaries, whether in the crucible of the Civil War, or of Reconstruction, or of Jim Crow. Indeed, in the following chapter we will examine the work of a late-century African American author, equally concerned with the relationship between race and the built environment, who would likely have found Crafts's story a rich resource for his own had he only known of its existence.

2

Piazza Tales

Architecture, Race, and Memory in
Charles Chesnutt's Conjure Stories

Architecture is not simply a mechanical contrivance but an
essay in the art of communication, a complex web of memories
and messages.
——J. Mordaunt Crook, *The Dilemma of Style* (1987)

When Charles W. Chesnutt surveyed his literary prospects in the
fall of 1889, he had every reason to be optimistic. In the previous two years
Chesnutt had placed three of his conjure (or "Uncle Julius") tales in the
Atlantic Monthly, becoming the first African American fiction writer to be
published by such an influential arbiter of national taste. During the same
period, he had struck up fruitful correspondences with Albion Tourgée and
George Washington Cable, prominent white authors and social reform-
ers who read and commented favorably on Chesnutt's work. New stories,
including the beginning of a first novel, were flowing from Chesnutt's pen,
and a fourth conjure tale was about to appear in the *Overland Monthly*.
Feeling sure of his talent and connections—but also ambivalent about the
imaginative and professional constraints that continuing in the Uncle Julius
"plantation school" vein might impose—Chesnutt plotted the next steps of
his career. First, he would publish a collection of his stories, gathering the
Atlantic tales together with a selection of his nondialect work to make a
book. Then he would stop writing conjure tales altogether and concentrate
instead on more up-to-date representations of the American color line. As
Chesnutt explained to Tourgée that September, "I think I have about used
up the old Negro who serves as a mouthpiece, and I shall drop him in
future stories, as well as much of the dialect."[1]

Uncle Julius would thus help facilitate Chesnutt's arrival as a book
author—and then disappear. But the book that Chesnutt proposed never

materialized. As critics like Richard Brodhead have shown, in the wake of that optimistic fall of 1889, Chesnutt encountered a period of "literary blockage," not consolidated success, as white editors—even at Houghton Mifflin, the parent house of the *Atlantic*—rejected not only Chesnutt's proposed collection but more signally (and despite multiple revisions) the new color line story into which he poured much of his post-1889 energy, "Rena Walden."[2] It was not until 1898, nearly ten years later, that Chesnutt would finally strike his "entering wedge" into the literary world, although not in precisely the fashion he had imagined. For after reading through yet another of Chesnutt's story collections, *Atlantic* editor Walter Hines Page decided in March 1898 to commission more "'cunjure' stories" to fill out a possible book of North Carolina dialect tales. Chesnutt quickly complied, hammering out six tales in seven weeks, four of which Page then matched with Chesnutt's original *Atlantic* stories to make *The Conjure Woman*, which would appear to strong reviews in 1899. The irony here, of course, as Brodhead has aptly remarked, is that Chesnutt's success would come only through a return to the same plantation genre—and its "preferred fictions of racial life"—that he had earlier sought to leave behind.[3] Chesnutt would have his collection, but he would have to resurrect Uncle Julius to do so.

But in fact Chesnutt had not stopped writing Julius tales at all. Three times during his "blocked" decade—and well before Page's commission—Chesnutt turned of his own accord back to the plantation tale, to dialect, and to Uncle Julius. Why would the calculating author revisit a supposedly "used up" genre? Not, as one might imagine, in anticipatory deference to a proposition like Page's. Chesnutt did so, I argue, in order to explore in more detail what he found he had not "used up" in the earlier Julius stories: what we might call (following Dell Upton) the "social experience" of American architecture.[4] For what we discover when we look closely at the second phase of Chesnutt's Uncle Julius stories—the three pieces written between his 1889 letter to Tourgée and the 1898 summons from Page—is that the meticulously framed conjure tales offered Chesnutt a surprisingly versatile form through which to elaborate a penetrating investigation into race, memory, and the built environment that, it turns out, he had been developing since his first published story. The contours of this investigation become clear only when we isolate each of the phases of Chesnutt's conjure production.[5] Doing so will shed light not only on the tales themselves, particularly the often overlooked stories of the second phase, but, more significantly, on the importance of the meanings of place to African American writers in the 1890s. An "architectural" reading of the three phases of the conjure tales, I will suggest, brings into relief the sustained and complex inquiry that Chesnutt, foremost among his contemporaries, undertook into the ways that social relations, as historian Rhys Isaac has put it, are "incised" upon a society's living space.[6]

This was an important—and risky—project to undertake in the 1890s. The closing decades of the nineteenth century witnessed a particularly rabid cycle of neocolonial enthusiasm that expressed itself not just in architectural forms but in broader social and cultural movements as well. Anti-immigrationism, for example, shared both a vocabulary and an ideology with Colonial Revivalism. So, too, did the popular genre of plantation fiction, which sought, through an equally purposeful recourse to the perceived ideals of the past, to fix its own definitions of the proper meanings of "place" for black Americans in the Jim Crow era. Chesnutt wrote in part in reaction to these movements, using his interest in the social experience of architecture to challenge their assumptions and expose their motives, often by literally and figuratively playing with their forms. As Frederick Douglass declared in 1888, "The colored people of this country are bound to keep the past in lively memory til justice shall be done them."[7] Through the vivid recollections of Uncle Julius, Chesnutt (who would become Douglass's biographer in 1899) campaigned for a just present by marshaling countermemories of an unjust past. Given the ideological climate of the decade, it is not surprising that the second phase of conjure stories failed to put Chesnutt back on the literary map.

I have called these Chesnutt's "piazza tales" because it is the southern piazza that becomes the central imaginative location in the conjure stories.[8] Much as nearly every conjure tale is framed in precisely the same way—with an outer story set in the present introducing an inner story, told by Julius, from the plantation past—so too is nearly every tale staged in some significant way on the deck of a piazza. Ten of the thirteen conjure tales feature piazzas, which always appear in the outer story and occasionally in the inner tale. Eight of the ten open on the front porch of the frame narrator, John, the white northerner who has moved to North Carolina with his wife, Annie, and bought Julius's former master's plantation. Eight of Julius's own tales are told on that same porch; a ninth begins away from the house but concludes on its back piazza. In two stories, piazzas mark important sites of action in Julius's tale itself. Robert Stepto, the only critic to consider these insistent and intriguing sitings in any detail, rightly suggests that the piazza is a "logical revision" of the log on which Julius, John, and Annie sit in the first tale, "The Goophered Grapevine." Stepto argues:

The movement from the log of the first story to the carriage of the second ["Po' Sandy"] to the piazza of the third ["The Conjurer's Revenge"] communicates that John and Annie are now fully in residence in the South and that a traditional context for storytelling has been constructed. Moreover, it suggests a didactic strategy expressed through the siting of storytelling which plays a major role in the education of John and Annie as listeners. More so than the log or carriage, the "reconstructed" piazza of a southern plantation Big House is a "charged field," full of reference to history and ritualized human behavior.[9]

Stepto's discerning account, however, only begins to describe the multiple relays to which Chesnutt's piazzas give access. For the story of the piazza in the conjure tales is embedded in an even denser web of American histories than Stepto's "charged field" model suggests, histories crucial to an understanding of the ways that memories of slavery and Reconstruction were being shaped in the 1880s and 1890s. These histories include the polycultural evolution of domestic architecture; the reproduction and racialization of the southern landscape; and the nostalgic yearnings of not just the Colonial Revival but also its early nineteenth-century counterpart, the Classical Revival. What is perhaps most intriguing in the conjure tales' engagement with these reconstructions of the past is the suggestion in "The Dumb Witness" (a second-phase story) that the cherished southern piazza, which in its grandest form becomes a conspicuous architectural marker of white power and prestige, may actually have its roots in the vernacular building traditions of West Africa, crossing the Atlantic in the minds and hands (and memories) of black slaves.

Thus in this chapter I argue that the second phase of Chesnutt's conjure tales is a crucial one, for it is there that Chesnutt shapes an aggressively revisionist historicism that marks his own striking contribution to what architectural historian Dolores Hayden has elsewhere termed "a politics of place construction."[10] I show how both the politics and the place in these stories emerge from Chesnutt's earlier fiction, particularly the first phase of conjure tales. Once we trace the evolution of the piazza as a central imaginative space for Chesnutt, we can then also measure more precisely the costs and capitulations exacted by his eventual return to the "preferred fictions" of the final phase of stories. And yet even amid that phase's revisions and retreats we will be able to spot the resistances still at work within those compromised tales, as well as the ongoing interest in the forms and meanings of architecture that would mark, in different degrees, Chesnutt's next major projects, the novels *The House behind the Cedars* and *The Marrow of Tradition.*

Reading the conjure tales in this way will do more than simply clarify the goals and achievements of their separate phases of composition. It will help establish Chesnutt as one of the late nineteenth century's most incisive interpreters of race and the built environment. To confirm that Chesnutt was writing at a time when such interpretations mattered, one need look no further than the 1893 World's Columbian Exposition in Chicago, whose monumental public modeling of space and social order—coupled with its organizers' refusal to permit meaningful African American self-representation—one might instructively juxtapose with Chesnutt's insistent entwining of race and architecture. In the face of the exclusion of blacks from the exposition, for example, Chesnutt's stories show how African Americans have been shaping, mapping, and indeed *claiming* ground in America since the days of slavery, whether white Americans understood those claims or not. As we shall see, the conjure tales thus commemorate what in many instances the broader culture either made little sense of—or wanted to forget. That the tales were meant to do so for a predominantly white, not black, audience further magnifies Chesnutt's interest in integrating what historians of cultural memory have heretofore seen as separate traditions. For if in response to their exclusion from the "mainstream of retrospective consciousness" in the late nineteenth century a majority of African Americans chose to perpetuate "their own distinctive traditions and memories" (as Michael Kammen has argued), Chesnutt tried instead to cure white amnesia by writing those very memories back into American cultural history.[11] Finally, and more generally, understanding Chesnutt's interest in what we might call the "legibility" of architecture—the capacity (indeed the necessity) of buildings and other architectural forms to be "read" and interpreted—will help deepen a field of interdisciplinary inquiry that has so far concentrated primarily on high cultural forms at the expense of equally expressive American vernaculars.[12]

From Uncle Peter to Uncle Julius

Chesnutt's exploration of the stories that buildings could tell—and the stories that he could tell through them—begins not in the conjure tales but in "Uncle Peter's House," which, though only Chesnutt's first publication (appearing in the *Cleveland News and Herald* in December 1885, nearly two years before "The Goophered Grapevine"), offers a mature reflection on the potentially explosive crossings of architecture, race, and memory. The time is Reconstruction. Peter is a freed slave in postwar North Carolina whose "dearest wish" is "to own a house." Not just any house, but a "great," "two-story white house," with "green Venetian blinds" and "broad piazzas." A replica of his master's house, in other words—which to Peter's young eyes had seemed "heaven" itself, and around which, as an adult, still "clustered the most vivid impressions of childhood, . . . fresh in his memory." Saving the funds proves hard, but Peter eventually buys property "just beyond the limits" of town, puts up a temporary cabin, and slowly starts to build. He is "perhaps two-thirds done" when "one dark night" a gang of "jolly young" Klansmen burns the structure down. Undaunted, Peter patiently rebuilds. After many more years, as the "Klan, like Peter's [first] house, became a thing of the past," the second house nears completion; but Peter falls off an unsteady scaffold, breaks an arm and a rib, and never recovers, dying a few days later from an "internal injury."[13]

A parable of reading and misreading, of replication and deferral, "Uncle Peter's House" astutely engages the legibility of architectural forms and the geographies of power. The jolly "Kluckers" stop at the "tall, unpainted frame" of Peter's house merely because "it suggested possibilities for more fun" (they "had no special program for the evening" [173]), but they burn it because of what they think they read between the boards. No matter that their first reading is wrong:

> "What are you building here, old man?" asked one.
> "Jes' a little house to lib in, marse," answered the trembling Peter. . . .
> "Now yer lyin', ain't yer?" said another; "It's a nigger school house, ain't it?"
> "No, Marse, I 'clare to de Lo'd it's jes' my own house." (173)

The realization that Peter is not lying prompts a new reading no more socially or politically welcome than the first. Sounding much like Twain's Pap Finn (who also appeared in print in 1885), the Klansmen sound off against the evils of "reconstruction":

> "The idee of a nigger livin' in a two-story house is jes' ridiculous," remarked a tall "Klucker" with some warmth.
> "Ownin' land, too," said another; "what with niggers runnin' the guv'ment, and niggers buyin' the lan', I'm durned if I see what's to become o' the white people."
> "It's chilly tonight," suggested a little fellow, . . . "let's have a fire." (173)

Chesnutt's insistently ironic tone complicates the narrative's own take on Peter's motives for building in the first place. At times the memory of his master's house seems to cast an almost religious spell on Peter. Even though the narrator observes, for example, that "after a little experience" Peter ceased to think of the whites in the great house as "angels" (169), his dying vision of heaven still takes the shape of the slaveowner's mansion ("I see dat hebbenly mansion—a big white mansion, wid green blin's on de winders, and broad piazzas all 'roun' it" [175]). One might well ask whether Chesnutt means to criticize Peter's yearning for his great white house as a form of self-destructive white-worship. It is, after all, virtually the house itself that kills him. When Peter falls off the scaffolding, his fatal wounds are delivered by the pile of bricks stacked for the chimney. But it is not the whiteness of the house that Peter yearns for; it is what the house, in situ, signifies. Like Thomas Sutpen in Faulkner's *Absalom, Absalom!*, Peter has a shrewd understanding of architectural metaphors of power. Though "too ignorant of letters to do more than spell out the simple chapters of the Bible" (174), Peter can read territory. "From his earliest childhood" he understood the big house as "the symbol" not of whiteness per se but of "power, prosperity, and happiness" (168). Peter's knowledge comes straight from the hierarchy of forms arranged upon the plantation landscape:

> From the little group of cabins which made up the slave quarters of the large plantation on which [Peter] was born could be seen, at a short distance, the large white house, surrounded by broad piazzas, upon which opened the long windows guarded by green Venetian blinds. Standing on the highest part of the plantation, in a grove of patriarchal elms, it was the most conspicuous object in the landscape. From it the eye of the little autocrat who ruled this broad domain could overlook the acres of cotton stretching out to the edge of the distant forest, and the dark-green masses of waving corn which covered the meadows, and toward it the ear of the tired slave was turned at evening, to listen for the sound of the horn which announced a few hours' respite from the hard toil which made up his daily life. (168)

In the design of social and economic space, perspective is everything, and Chesnutt moves us back and forth here expertly. First we look passively (it "could be seen") up from the quarters to the house, which stands "guarded" and "patriarchal." Then we look out from the house through "the eye of the little autocrat" over the cotton and corn, to the very edge of the plantation, only suddenly to swing back to the perspective from below, this time to the slave's ear in the fields cocked for a signal from on high. At the center of the description, and controlling the movement of each sentence, stands the house, an arrangement that replicates in prose what Rhys Isaac has identified as the invariable tripartite design of plantation space, in which "the elevation of a central unit by means of balanced, subordinated lateral elements" expresses a "strong sense of gradations of dominance and submission."[14] The house is both "the most conspicuous object in the landscape" and the locus of the plantation's ruling eye.

Plantations were not always arranged this way. Not until the eighteenth century, when planters first began to communicate their social and economic status "not only by sheer scale but also by means of elaborately contrived formal relations," Isaac observes, did this tripartite design become "invariable." Before this moment, in many areas, plantation spatial relations were less conspicuously hierarchical. As John Michael Vlach explains, until the late 1600s slaves and masters typically lived and worked in close proximity, like a family. But this "day-to-day intimacy" was "progressively replaced by a stricter regimen of racial segregation that was expressed by greater physical separation." Seeking clearer definitions of status, position, and authority, slaveholders gradually removed slaves and many of their functions from the main house, giving rise not only to separate slave quarters, for example, but also to the detached southern kitchens so often misperceived merely as capitulations to the sultry climate.[15] Not surprisingly, it was at this same moment that the piazza took hold in the South as well, making its insistent display of white leisure—not to mention its elevated platform of surveillance—an integral component of the architecture of segregation. When the narrator of "Uncle Peter's House" notes that the broad piazzas of the great house were but "a short distance" from the slave cabins, he clarifies not merely the size of the plantation but the necessary relationship between quarters and porches.[16]

Given this history, "Uncle Peter's House" can be said to narrate the failure of Reconstruction to dismantle the architecture of segregation. Raised on these forms, and comprehending their signs, Peter nevertheless not only replicates his master's house but—by first erecting a small cabin "a little to one side" (170)—reproduces, however unwittingly, the hierarchical buildingscape of slavery. When his first house burns, he builds another to the same specifications, with the little cabin—in which Peter finally dies—always present. But rather than blame Peter for perpetuating these forms, or lament the seeming inevitability of dominant social and political structures to reproduce themselves, Chesnutt's story foregrounds Peter's resolute struggle to cross from cabin to piazza to claim the power, prosperity, and happiness so long out of reach. Even at his moment of death, though he looks to heaven, Peter's last earthly wish is that his son "*finish dat house*, dat de good Lo'd didn' 'low me to finish" (175; my emphasis).[17] At the end of the story, however, after several more years "have elapsed," the house still stands unfinished, even though Peter's son "is now lathing the interior" (176). The shift to the present tense caustically indicts the promises of post-Reconstruction America as little more than endlessly deferred gestures of completion, houses grandly framed but profoundly empty. "Aunt Dinah is growing old," Chesnutt's narrator deadpans, "but is still hale and hearty, and may yet live to see the house finished. The grove of young elms which Peter planted is thriving and will probably shade the yard nicely by the time the house is painted and the green blinds hung" (176).[18]

The edgy tone of violence in "Uncle Peter's House" ("hung" is indeed its ominous last word) is markedly subdued in "The Goophered Grapevine," where, perhaps in the hope of duplicating the success of Joel Chandler Harris's Uncle Remus (whose tales Chesnutt read to his own children),[19] Chesnutt replaces the socially threatening Uncle Peter with the (superficially) more innocuous Uncle Julius and turns from rebuilding the master's house to exploring ways to dismantle it from within. Deploying the familiar moves of plantation fiction—if not always to expected ends—Chesnutt crafts his own series of Julius tales, whose reiterated sitings and recurring characters allow him to investigate, with increasing complexity, the markers that social relations leave on physical terrain.

The first four stories of the series move from architectural symbolism to more concrete imaginings of the oppressions and opportunities of the built environment. In the beginning of the original version of "The Goophered Grapevine," for example, John and Annie drive symbolically into an "open space" where "a dwelling house had once stood," a space in which the transplanted northerners will soon build their own house—and in which Chesnutt will compose his tales. The description of the house that follows ("nothing remained . . . except the brick pillars upon which the sills had rested") invokes Shelley's meditation in "Ozymandias" on the inevitable and ironic fate of monumental architecture, making this "fallen" house a metonym not only for the defeated South but also for the collapsed structures of slavery.[20] Chesnutt then seats his characters on a "shady though somewhat hard" pine log, laying the groundwork, as Stepto argues, for their eventual transposition to John and Annie's more comfortable piazza. But this transformation from log to porch is effected only through the story—and the body—of Sandy, the "escaped" slave-turned-tree in Chesnutt's second conjure tale who is accidentally milled for lumber and then used to build (and rebuild) prominent plantation outbuildings. There are echoes of "Uncle Peter's House" here, to be sure, and Eric Sundquist is right to read "Po' Sandy" as a revision of that tale, in which anxieties about building property become anxieties about *being* property.[21] If the move from the pine log to the piazza is a logical one, "Po' Sandy" reminds us that it is anything but benign, figuring as it does the historical emergence of a more strictly segregated and hierarchical chattel slavery. Chesnutt's tales move to the piazza only after acknowledging, in blood, the costs exacted by the redesign of plantation space. The memory of Sandy's violently "quartered" body can be said to haunt all of the built structures in the subsequent tales.

This is not to say that all the tales are similarly grim, but rather that the physical spaces they depict signify in multiple ways. In the last two stories of the first phase of tales, for example, Chesnutt uses John and Annie's front piazza to communicate Julius's changing status within the series. Whereas in "Po' Sandy" Julius appears in the role of the working coachman, in "The Conjurer's Revenge" he is on his own time, arriving in the story in his "Sunday clothes" and "advanc[ing]," according to John, "with a dignity of movement quite different from his week-day slouch."[22] This freedom and dignity, of course, do not put Julius on equal footing with his white employers, and he is at first reluctant to become too cozy with a white couple who in the space of two short tales have already rebuilt a plantation mansion, right down to the big front porch and the freshly detached kitchen. ("Reconstruction," as Chesnutt made plain in "Uncle Peter's House," can look frighteningly similar to "antebellum.") But Annie finally coaxes Julius onto the piazza, where he seats himself "somewhat awkwardly" (71) in the rocking chair from which he narrates his tale of theft and revenge. By the next story, "Dave's Neckliss," Julius seems much more at home on his employers' porch. It is another Sunday afternoon, and John and Annie are "just rising from the table when Julius [comes] up the lane, and, taking off his hat, [seats] himself on the piazza" (123). If the hat-doffing connotes a certain deference, there is little trace of Julius's former awkwardness as he sits down without needing to be asked. Indeed, after only "a momentary hesitation" (123), Julius even accepts Annie's offer of dinner, which he takes inside their home, while John and Annie adjourn to the piazza. When Julius is done eating, he rejoins them outside and begins his tale.

Chesnutt would appear to be using the piazza here not only as an economical marker of Julius's acceptance by (and of) John and Annie but also as a literal and symbolic meeting ground for black and white folk in the postbellum South. Typically, historians suggest, the half-private, half-public nature of the piazza encourages only "minimally committal" interactions between resident and guest.[23] But Julius's entry onto John and Annie's piazza from *within* their house in "Dave's Neckliss" gives him more intimate standing and may make their porch more bridge than buffer. Sue Bridwell Beckham has written of the power of porches to work this way. Using anthropologist Victor Turner's model of "liminal space," Beckham argues that for women in particular, porches can facilitate socially liberating moments of "communitas—the temporary but vital attachment that only people caught between cultural states can establish." On the porch, "betwixt and between absolute private and absolute public, relationships that would be impossible elsewhere can flourish for however brief a time."[24]

While it may be tempting to make such claims for Chesnutt's piazzas as well—particularly if we are thinking of the bonds forged between Julius and Annie in the *Conjure Woman* collection of 1899—the first phase of Julius stories complicates matters. In the original version of "The Conjurer's Revenge," for example, the piazza is the site of Annie's surprisingly "zealous" proselytization of Julius.[25] And in "Dave's Neckliss" it is in his cozy hammock on the piazza that John tries to put himself in Julius's place but fails. ("Whether [Julius] even realized, except in a vague, uncertain way, his own degradation, I do not know. I fear not," concludes the obtuse narrator [125].) In addition, although he tries to laugh it off, John is clearly not comfortable with Julius's presence inside the house. In an unsettling echo of Dave's tale (where Dave is punished for stealing a ham), John carefully notes the exact number of ham slices Julius consumes. There is no suggestion that John will stop Julius from eating his fill; "I kept count of them," John says, "from a lazy curiosity to see how much he *could* eat" (124). Yet rather than function as a zone of communitas here, the piazza is (once again) a site of ongoing surveillance of black by white—a surveillance not substantially different in form from that of Mars Dugal' or the overseer Walker watching the smokehouses and counting the hams in Julius's story.[26] Chesnutt even fiddles with the layout of a typical nineteenth-century "country" home to make this scrutiny possible. Most builders' plans of the era, for example, put the dining room (where Julius is said to sit) in the back of the house, where it would not be visible from a front piazza. (Indeed, it would be unusual for Julius, as the story claims, to be able to see the dinner table through the front door, even if John and Annie's dining room were in the front of the house, since in most floor plans the front door opens onto a central hallway.)[27] At the end of the story, as though to signal the limits to the piazza's powers of mediation, Julius's tale is met with "a short silence," after which Annie mumbles something about the weather, and John abruptly goes "into the house" (135).

So, too, figuratively speaking, does Chesnutt, who was determined to leave Julius and his dialect tales behind after this story. But as we know, Chesnutt gradually returned to Julius, to dialect, and to the piazza in a second set of conjure tales, well before Page's 1898 request for more stories like "The Goophered Grapevine." A close look at this second group of tales suggests that if Julius and dialect were "about used up," the social experience of architecture was not.

The Return of the Oppressed

Known to critics as the "non-conjure" conjure tales, Chesnutt's second phase of Julius stories has received relatively little discussion. The most that has been said in terms of their role in the development of the genre is that in the last of the group, "The Dumb Witness," Chesnutt daringly experiments with having John "tell and inevitably embellish a Julius story in his own 'literary' English."[28] If we are thinking of the stories as contributions to Chesnutt's ongoing examination of race, memory, and the built environment, however, they accomplish far more. For it is in these tales that Chesnutt provocatively explores the transgressive politics of location first imagined in "Po' Sandy," where a slave "escapes" by concealing himself on (or indeed *as*) his master's property. By focusing more on territory than on conjure—and in particular by examining not only the slaves' resistances to slavery but their often successful transformations of its very terrain—"A Deep Sleeper," "Lonesome Ben," and "The Dumb Witness" give voice to a revisionist historicism at times only thinly masked by what John Edgar Wideman has called Julius's "*sho nuff*" role play.[29]

In these tales Chesnutt broadens his territorial inquiry to include not just the planter's piazza but also the sites and spaces onto which it opens. In "A Deep Sleeper" (1893), for example, Chesnutt reexamines the seemingly contradictory notion of a slave's "home." The frame story alerts us to the significance of home by speaking, for the first time, of Julius's home. Following the lead of "Dave's Neckliss," in which Chesnutt made Julius a character in his own tale, thereby radically personalizing his account, in "A Deep Sleeper" John reveals that Julius not only "worked on my plantation" but "lived in a small house on the place, a few rods from my own residence" (137). We also discover that Julius is not alone: "His daughter was our cook," John explains, "and other members of his family served us in different capacities" (137). While these descriptions provide more information about Julius than the first four tales combined, they also tell us more about John's sense of spatial control. This is the first time, for example, that John has referred to his vineyard as his "plantation" (it is usually just "our place" [70] or "my vineyard" [44]), and while the change in terminology may simply indicate that John has more fully capitalized his property, the presence of Julius's family members as John and Annie's servants makes their work site more and more resemble its antebellum counterpart. And while Julius now has his own home, its proximity to John's house (only "a few rods" away) disconcertingly recalls the spatial relations between slave quarters and planter's mansion dramatized in "Uncle Peter's House."

And yet in this story the similarities between postbellum vineyard and prewar plantation usefully heighten the congruence of the inner and outer tales, for the inner story of "A Deep Sleeper," we discover, also concerns "homes." Recalling some of the plot elements of "Po' Sandy," slave lovers Skundus and Cindy are separated when their master loans Cindy to a neighboring planter. Formerly a field hand, Cindy is taken into "house-sarvice" (140), where her initial sadness over leaving Skundus is alleviated by being in such "a fine new house" (142). When Cindy realizes that these separations might be permanent, however, she stops eating and pines for home. (On his part, after Cindy leaves, Skundus disappears and is assumed to have run away.) Although she had become "kinder use' ter" her "noo home," Cindy is finally sent "back home" (142) when Marse Dugal' needs more slaves to pick cotton. In short order Skundus reappears as well, claiming not to have run away at all but merely to have been asleep in the barn. Dugal's sputtering anger is tempered by his relief at having his slave back, and the next day a pair of local doctors pronounce Skundus the victim of a trance. To prevent any such future "fits," Dugal' not only allows Cindy and Skundus to marry but gives them their own house, "a cabin er dey own" (144).

What the story's almost obsessive interest in homes and locations ironically helps make visible are the acts of black resistance to planter-defined space—what Vlach would call the slaves' "territorial appropriation"—on which the plot turns. When Cindy begins to lose her appetite, her new mistress sends her to the swamp to gather roots for a restorative tea. Gone for several hours, Cindy claims to have had trouble finding the roots, but we soon suspect that what she has found is Skundus, come a "hunderd mile" (139) to see her. To appropriate this part of the plantation for themselves, Cindy convinces her mistress to let her search the edge of the swamp "ev'y day" for "fresh roots," while Skundus poses as a swamp "ha'nt" (142) to frighten others away. Cindy and Skundus thus accomplish on the fringes of the plantation what many slaves were already doing in myriad ways even at its center: claiming ground. As Vlach explains, acts of landscape appropriation were not only "an important means of day-to-day resistance," as slaves "privately remapped the domains designed by planters," but were easier to accomplish than one might think, often right under the planter's nose. Much as slaves who stood up physically to their overseers often found that their beatings decreased, Vlach observes,

> slaves who claimed their masters' land as their own similarly found that it virtually *was* theirs. Acts of territorial appropriation were exceedingly clever because they were carried out, in the main, simply by occupying the spaces to which they were assigned. Slaves gradually identified these spaces as theirs through a routine of innumerable domestic acts [such as Cindy's daily root-gathering]. Once the quarters were identified as a black place, further claims were made to other spaces and buildings such as fields, barns, and workshops. Their owner was unlikely to resist these assertions because these outbuildings were spaces that the slaves were supposed to occupy anyway, at least during the daylight hours. (235; original emphasis)

Skundus's successful ruse about sleeping in the barn thus further reveals that Marse Dugal'—whose "bark uz wuss'n his bite" (143)—has yielded control of his outbuildings both day and night. That Dugal' cannot factually contradict Skundus's claim to have been in the barn for thirty days, coupled with his immediate sponsoring of the face-saving, pseudoscientific "explanation" for Skundus's absence, suggests that the slaveowner recognizes the limits to his "ownership" of plantation space. This is not to say by any means that Dugal's slaves are "free" but rather, as Vlach suggests, that they have—or at least Cindy and Skundus have—successfully "established defensible social boundaries . . . in both pragmatic and symbolic terms." They have, in short, claimed "their own sense of place."[30]

In the frame story Chesnutt suggests that these are claims and resistances that the narrator John does not yet understand. Although in earlier tales John has been suspicious of Julius's narrative motives, here he still cannot imagine all the ways that people might covertly disrupt, and even partially control, an institution as deeply oppressive as slavery. John's comments in the prologue assessing Julius's "profound contempt" for poor whites suggest the narrator's blindness: "[Julius] assumed that we shared this sentiment, while in fact our feeling toward this listless race was something entirely different. They were, like Julius himself, the product of a system which they had not created and which they did not know enough to resist" (137). John's misreading of the conditions for and potential forms of resistance by the disempowered guarantees that he will not recognize Julius's own challenge to his authority—indeed, Julius's own appropriation of his territory—until it is too late. Although it is Sunday and presumably Julius's day off, John, hot and bored on his piazza, asks Julius to tote a heavy watermelon up from the garden. Conspicuously dressed (again) in "Sunday clothes" (137), Julius proposes waiting until the next morning, but to no avail. He finally avoids the task by feigning a rheumatic knee spasm and arranging to have a younger relative (Skundus's grandson, it turns out) take his place, the delay permitting Julius to tell his story. By the time Skundus's grandson arrives with a wheelbarrow and he, John, Julius, Annie, and her sister Mabel march to the watermelon patch, the melon is gone. A heist arranged by Julius? Presumably. And yet the tale does not speculate. For the first time in the series Chesnutt ends a tale without John's ruminatory epilogue. No turning things over, no self-satisfied interpretation of Julius's motives. Only a "shallow concavity" where the "monarch of the patch" (145) had rested, parodying John's shallow understanding of resistance and underscoring the subversive potential of an aggressive politics of place.

Here again the story bears comparison to "Po' Sandy," in which Julius appropriated one of John's outbuildings for his own use. But Chesnutt intensifies the level of resistance by imagining, for the first time in the series, successful challenges to a planter's control over space in both the frame tale and the inner tale. This rare double success in "A Deep Sleeper" may reflect Chesnutt's growing interest in the 1890s in exploring the more active roles that American blacks, slave and free alike, had played and continued to play in claiming their own spaces and marking their own locations. One of the chief ironies of "A Deep Sleeper," however, is that Cindy and Skundus use their powers not to flee their plantation but to go back to it. But if we understand their return as expressing a desire to reestablish on their own terms the life they had created together—albeit within the space of slavery—then Cindy and Skundus become legible as fictional analogues of those ex-slaves who, once emancipated, chose to return to their former plantations. Julius himself, as Brodhead points out, is such a figure, returning to the McAdoo plantation to work it "to [his] own interests and in [his] own ways."[31] If the autonomy that such claims to ownership conferred often proved tenuous

(John's first act in the conjure tales is to buy the McAdoo plantation out from under Julius's squatter's claim), the impulse to return to territory one had not merely worked but *remapped* must have been great.

If there is family involved—as Chesnutt imagines in the next story, "Lonesome Ben"—then the impulse to claim "home" may be all the greater. Rejected by the *Atlantic* in February 1897, "Lonesome Ben" turns "A Deep Sleeper" inside out by detailing the crushing self-annihilation that the forfeiture of home can produce. The inner tale is told, fittingly, not on John and Annie's piazza but away from their home, as John, Annie, and Julius wait in the rockaway to intercept Annie's sister Mabel on (again, fittingly) her return home. In Julius's tale, when field hand Ben is discovered drinking whiskey, he decides to run away from his plantation rather than receive a whipping. Heading north, although with little idea of how long the journey might take and no navigational resources besides the North Star, Ben quickly becomes disoriented when the night sky turns cloudy. After a week of walking, "'spectin' ter git ter de No'th eve'y day" (151), he ends up back on his old plantation, and though he refuses to give himself up, he seems equally powerless to leave. Hiding out, eating clay to survive, he finally resolves to go, but not until he has seen his family, for whom he feels "monst'us lonesome" (152). But to his family Ben is literally unrecognizable. Turned "yaller" (153)—from his voracious clay-eating, the tale suggests—the formerly "black ez coal" (149) Ben only frightens his wife and son. Nor do the other slaves, nor even his master, recognize him, ridiculing his claims to be himself. Feeling "so lonesome" (154) that he cannot go on, Ben crumbles first emotionally (feeling "mo' lak a stranger 'n he did lak Ben"), and then physically, as a falling tree smashes his sun-baked body and grinds him "ter powder" (156).[32]

Sundquist makes a compelling case for reading "Lonesome Ben" as a meditation on race, specifically the often crushing alienation of living as a mixed-race American in the late nineteenth century.[33] But much as Chesnutt's story of "Rena Walden" in the 1890s was finding its imaginative location in a "house behind the cedars," "Lonesome Ben" explores the vexed status of mixed-race Americans through metaphors of place and figures of home. After Ben goes unrecognized by wife, son, friend, and master, he is not merely lonesome but explicitly "homesick" and briefly contemplates going "right up ter de house [i.e., the big house] an' gib hisse'f up an' take his medicine" (154). But his master's violent repudiation ("You git off'n my plantation, . . . er I'll hab yer sent ter jail an' whip'") leaves Ben without even that recourse. "He crep' back in de bushes an' laid down an' wep' lak a baby. He didn' hab no wife, no chile, no fren's, no marster" (154)—in short, no home. Ben's lamentation recalls Sandy's complaint in "Po' Sandy" about the ill effects of being sent all over the county to work: "'pears to me I ain' got no home, ner no marster, ner no mistiss, ner no nuffin" (47). But where Sandy's misfortune is that he has to go everywhere, Ben's dilemma is that he has "nowhar ter go" (155). Ben is not only homesick, he is homeless. In Chesnutt's tale the loss of racial identity is experienced as a profoundly dislocating loss of place. Thus even in a tale that includes few actual buildings (indeed, their relative absence or decay, like the brickyard in the frame tale that is "all growed ober wid weeds an' grass" [147], makes the story's sense of loss even more acute), Chesnutt is still investigating not only the social experience of space but its representational power.

Chesnutt's fullest exploration of this terrain occurs in "The Dumb Witness." Tentatively accepted by Page for the *Atlantic* in October 1897 but never actually published by Chesnutt as a separate story, "The Dumb Witness" brings to a powerful confluence Chesnutt's interests in architecture, race, and the American past. In it he folds a piazza tale within a piazza tale, making this space for the first time the site not only of Julius's telling (in his most intimate contact yet, Julius actually joins John and Annie on their porch for dessert) but also of crucial action in the inner tale. In the frame, Julius drives John to the "old Murchison place" (158) to buy some walnut timber. John's detailed description of the Murchison house is the most architecturally precise in the conjure tales:

> As we drew nearer, the house stood clearly revealed. It was apparently of more ancient date than any I had seen in the neighborhood. It was a large two-story frame house, built in the colonial style, with a low-pitched roof, and a broad piazza along the front, running the full length of both stories, and supported by huge round columns, and suggesting distantly, in its general effect, the portico of a Greek temple. (159)

John's careful anatomization locates the Murchison house not only in place and time but also in ideology. A colonial mansion with a Greek temple front, the house recalls (though itself may have predated) the flourishing of the early nineteenth-century Classical Revival, in which American builders invoked the values of republican virtue and democratic revolution by borrowing from classical forms. If the architectural grammar of the Classical Revival was intended to allude to the ancient ideals of liberty and democracy (recently reaffirmed, many Americans felt, by their own colonial and revolutionary history), it just as frequently—and perhaps more effectively—

invoked the rule of law. Templelike porches, which typically fronted monu-mental public buildings, were legible chiefly as symbols of order and author-ity. As Alan Gowans explains, by adding a porch "decked out in some more or less classical detail," one could turn even an ordinary dwelling into "an instant authority symbol." This particular gesture was especially popular in the South, where temple porch fronts remained "mansion signals" up until the Civil War.[34]

The signal that the old Murchison place sends to John, however, is of an entirely different order. Above its huge columns, "the roof had sunk on one side, and the shingles were old and cracked and moss-grown; while several of the windows in the upper part of the house were boarded up, and others filled with sash from which the glass had apparently long since been broken" (159). The grounds surrounding the house are barren and uneven. When John notes that the porch columns "distantly" suggest the portico of a Greek temple, his choice of words signals both his distance from the house (as he drives up the long lane) and the house's distance from its monumental past. One might be tempted to read these signals as rather conventional invoca-tions of the once-mighty southern elite brought low, were one not to dis-cover—as Chesnutt, who lived in Fayetteville from the age of nine until his midtwenties, surely knew—that such mansions were extremely rare in the North Carolina sandhills. Even at the height of the Classical Revival, reports Catherine Bishir, "remarkably few North Carolinians adopted the notion of building houses to resemble temples."[35] This is partly because the prime years of the Classical Revival (the 1830s) were not prosperous ones for North Caro-lina, which suffered from both economic decline and excessive out-migra-tion. But North Carolina's dangerous coastline and lack of capable ports had long made the state a poor cousin of its more prosperous neighbors Virginia and South Carolina. Where large plantation estates developed more quickly in these regions, for much of the eighteenth century North Carolina was a forest society, dominated by small farmsteads. Even after the population bursts and relative prosperity of the late eighteenth and early nineteenth cen-turies, North Carolina maintained a "pragmatic unpretentiousness shared by rich and poor alike." Thus, "throughout North Carolina architecture ran . . . a focus on practicality and profit, a distrust of unnecessary expenditure or pretension, and even a stubborn pride in the lack of ostentation—values that would prevail even when more money was available."[36] It is not surprising that Chesnutt's narrator John—an eminently practical and profit-minded man, as he reminds us in the first paragraph of "The Dumb Witness"—assimilates so quickly to the state.

But what this local history also means is that Chesnutt wants us to attend to the exceptional position of the Murchisons within his fictional territory. The family "had occupied their ancestral seat on the sandhills for a hundred years or more," John explains at the start of the inner tale, some of the "facts" of which he has obtained from Julius, the rest from his investigation into "other sources" (162). (We might say that it is John's research impulse that in part justifies our own.) "There were not many rich families in that part of North Carolina," John notes, "and this one, by reason of its wealth and other things, was easily the most conspicuous in several counties" (162). The founding Murchison was a Revolutionary War general and a delegate to the Philadelphia Constitutional Convention, his son a "distinguished jurist" (162). They embody the patriarchal authority of law and the state on both a national and a local level. And as one of the handful of families who decide to build an outsized mansion in a region leery of ostentation, the Murchisons do so not in deference to fashion but, like the actual North Carolinians Bishir describes, to deliver—locally—"powerful assertions of attainment and intent."[37]

It is precisely such assertions that Viney, the slave figure of the inner tale in "The Dumb Witness," devotes much of her adult life, even after emancipation—and even after her owner has mutilated her tongue—to undermining. Chesnutt's decision to make the Murchisons such an exceptional North Carolina family strategically heightens Viney's resistance to their mastery: an illiterate slave, she brings her owner, the would-be legatee of a signing partner to the Constitution (including its legal sanction of her own slavery) to his proverbial, and almost literal, knees. By interfering in Malcolm Murchison's pending marriage to a wealthy northern widow and then refusing to disclose the location of his dead uncle's will or the mortgages he held on neighboring plantations, Viney thwarts both the accumulation and the transmission of slaveholding capital, successfully countering the Murchisons' aims with her own powerful (and powerfully gendered) assertions of "intent." (By preventing the marriage, which Viney accomplishes by telling the widow, Martha Todd, "something . . . [that] no one but herself and the lady ever knew" [165]—likely that she had not only been Malcolm's slave mistress for more than a decade but was also a blood relative—Viney also blocks the reestablishment of a direct line of inheritance by narrating a tale of sexual violation, forcing the Murchison family tree to lurch once again from uncle to nephew.) Chesnutt stages this monumental battle of wills on the plantation's immense piazza, turning the space of white authority and repose into a fractious theater of interracial conflict. "Day after day" (170), for "yeahs an' yeahs" (161), Viney and Murchison face each other on opposite ends of the long porch. On his visit, John witnesses the latest iteration of this "curious drama" (161). Rising from his "massive arm-chair" (159) and crossing to Viney, Murchison entreats and threatens; sitting "bolt upright" (160) in her "splint-bottom chair" (170), Viney remains stiffly silent until, fired by his threats, she unleashes a "flood of sounds" that John cannot comprehend but which causes Murchison to "bend like a reed before a storm" (160). Rebuffed yet again, he hobbles off the porch and digs "furiously" in the yard, looking for his uncle's papers. On this occasion Viney leaves the piazza to go inside, but we are later told that she usually remains outside, "watching him" with "inscrutable eyes" (170). Her resistance thus finally reverses the expected southern tableau: from *her* seat on the imposing piazza the black female slave watches her white male owner labor endlessly in his own front yard.

The piazza is not merely the site and reward of Viney's resistance; it is also in fair measure her accomplice. If she is a calculatedly "dumb witness," refusing to name the location of the papers, so too is the porch, which turns out to be their very hiding place.[38] This symbolic complicity, moreover, has a material and cultural history that makes Chesnutt's focus on the piazza in this story all the more powerfully apt. For although the plantation piazza is ostensibly "white" space, its own origins are in fact complexly multicultural and owe more, in particular, to West African vernacular forms—translated to North America through the West Indies—than most Americans likely understood or acknowledged. As Jay Edwards has shown, "Plantation houses with Neoclassic colonnades and peristyles represent a reworking in renaissance idiom of Creole forms previously adopted by the colonial farmer and planter." The Classical Revivalists may have thought they were merely bringing a touch of Greece or Rome to the South when they built their imposing piazzas, but they were instead reaching back along the routes of trade (particularly the slave trade) connecting the Atlantic Coast, via the West Indies, to West Africa. It was West African vernacular architecture—particularly the indigenous domestic structures of the Guinea Coast—that mixed with native Antillean and imperial European forms in the polycultural cauldron of the Caribbean to create what Ruth Little-Stokes calls the "West Indian house," the one- or two-story structure "set on a high foundation with a long porch extending along one or more sides" that settlers from the region brought to coastal North America beginning in the late seventeenth century and which in time evolved into the magisterial plantation house.[39] (For a quick sketch of this evolution in the Carolina Tidewater, from the West African and West Indian vernacular prototypes to the increasingly ornate elaborations of the local planter class, see Figs. 12–17.)[40]

Figure 12. Early indigenous West African House. Drawing by Mary Lee Eggart. Courtesy Jay Edwards.

Figure 13. West Indian house, Ruth Little-Stokes, "The North Carolina Porch" (1978), 105.

Figure 14. King House, Bertie County (1763), Catherine W. Bishir, *North Carolina Architecture* (1990), 21. Courtesy The Historic Preservation Foundation of North Carolina.

Figure 15. Old Town Plantation House, Edgecombe County (1786), Catherine W. Bishir, *North Carolina Architecture* (1990), 21. Courtesy The Historic Preservation Foundation of North Carolina.

Figure 16. The Homestead, Edenton (late 18th century), Catherine W. Bishir, *North Carolina Architecture* (1990), 120. Courtesy The Historic Preservation Foundation of North Carolina.

Figure 17. Cove Grove, Perquimans County (ca. 1830), Catherine W. Bishir, *North Carolina Architecture* (1990), 200. Courtesy The Historic Preservation Foundation of North Carolina.

And yet as Vlach points out, if a wide veranda eventually became "the height of architectural elegance" in the U.S., particularly in the South, "this was only after almost two centuries of experimentation during which its origins were apparently forgotten." As with far too many African cultural forms in America, Vlach argues, "the impact of African architectural concepts has ironically been disguised because their influence has been so widespread; they have been invisible because they are so obvious."[41] The professionalization of architecture in the late nineteenth century helped institutionalize this invisibility, as prominent textbooks circulated genealogies of style that excluded African forms. One of the most popular of these texts, Fletcher and Fletcher's *History of Architecture on the Comparative Method*, soon codified these omissions for generations of readers in its striking frontispiece, "The Tree of Architecture," which first appeared in 1905 and was later revised to set an American skyscraper at its apex (see Fig. 18). Heavily weighted toward European forms, the tree—like Fletcher and Fletcher's text—nonetheless still included nearly every world region except sub-Saharan Africa.[42]

These origins and exclusions bear on "The Dumb Witness" in several ways. Viney's speech, for example, the "flood of sounds that were not words, and which yet seemed now and then vaguely to suggest words" (160), may mark the irruption of a non-European vernacular consciousness (perhaps African, perhaps American Indian) into a supposedly Euro-American space. So disconcerting is this irruption that John dismisses its representational value to the white mind, although he vaguely senses that it may be "a language or dialect" of other than "European origin" (160). But he still cannot "read" Viney and never suspects the role she actually plays in the "devolution of the Murchison estate."[43] The story, moreover, consistently mocks this sort of blindness to what is right under one's nose. Indeed, the "invisibility of the obvious" that Vlach attributes to African architectural influence in North America is also metaphorically resonant here: like Poe's famous purloined letter, Roger Murchison's papers are hidden virtually in plain sight, in the same massive armchair from which his nephew glowers at Viney. One almost suspects the elder Murchison of a perversely apt design. What more fitting place for the documents of power than the seat of power? Where else hide the papers that assert control over neighboring plantations than the piazza from which one might view those coveted lands?

Vlach's discussion of the late nineteenth-century amnesia regarding the impact of African architecture on American forms further reminds us that Chesnutt wrote "The Dumb Witness" right in the midst (if not in the teeth) of a national *Colonial* Revival that sought aggressively to commemorate—

Figure 18. "The Tree of Architecture," frontispiece to Banister Fletcher and Banister F. Fletcher, *A History of Architecture on the Comparative Method*, 6th ed. (1921).

and revivify—what it saw as distinctly "American" traditions. As Karal Ann Marling has demonstrated, although such revivals cycled through America for much of the nineteenth century (as they would continue to do in the twentieth), the one that flourished in the 1890s was more noisy and noxious than its predecessors, particularly in its architectural yearnings. Rejecting the untidy eccentricities of the Victorian era for the clean lines and uncluttered rooms of Washington's day, Colonial Revivalists championed a "new" aesthetic of simplicity and honesty that would (in theory) restore the virtues of a nobler age. Though the rubric "colonial" was "notoriously elastic," neocolonial architecture tended to favor structures that communicated "Puritan plainness" on the one hand (boxy shapes, simple ornaments) and "old-fashioned" comfort on the other—the latter almost invariably signaled by "broad, sheltering porches or verandahs" that betokened longed-for days of unhurried hospitality.[44]

But simple structures often house complex aims, and the architectural movement that first seized the national spotlight at the 1893 Chicago World's Fair was driven by more than a love of clapboards and columns. As much a reaction against the supposed ills of immigration and urbanization as against an architectural style, the Colonial Revival's call for a return to Washington's porch was simultaneously a cry against the cultural diversity of 1890s America. Down nostalgic, tree-lined streets neocolonialism walked hand in hand with anti-immigrationism, each eagerly offering up its "purer" ideals as "antidotes to the poison[s]" of a polyglot world. The vocabulary of the Revival encoded social, not strictly material, aims: its key nouns included "proportion," "sobriety," "fitness," "subtlety," "harmony," and "restraint." As the spiritual descendant of early nineteenth-century neoclassicism—whose stately forms the Colonial Revivalists appropriated freely—neocolonialism "answered the same instinctive need for order." Perhaps not surprisingly, by the early twentieth century the color white had become one of the "visual cues" for the colonial style.[45] Colonial Revivalists might indeed have been the least eager to discover—as "The Dumb Witness" seems to urge us to—that their cherished "white" porches were actually polygenous to the core.[46]

Chesnutt's story stages the revivalists' ideals of balance and order only repeatedly to disrupt them. Seated decorously on opposite ends of the piazza, in chairs straight off the neocolonial porch (good solid oak, old-fashioned splint-bottom), Malcolm Murchison and Viney stand up and squabble right in front of John and Julius, oblivious to their guests' observing presence, not to mention the expected gestures of welcome. In the unusual phrase that

John uses to describe Murchison's relation to Viney—sitting on the porch, he is her "*vis-à-vis*" (160)—Chesnutt encapsulates similar tensions. Strictly speaking, John means that Murchison is the person seated opposite Viney, "facing" her, a balance disrupted every time Murchison stalks off the porch in frustration. But as a phrase that originally meant a carriage in which two persons sit face-to-face and is often used to describe a dance partner, *vis-à-vis* also denotes the miscegenational and incestuous intimacy forced by Murchison on Viney—an intimacy whose violent renunciation will bring the well-ordered estate to near ruin.

As the narrator who painstakingly reassembles the pieces of this shattered history "in orderly sequence" (162), John resembles not only the Murchisons of his tale (both Malcolm, the expert manager, and young Roger, who at the end of the story has "reduced" the plantation "to some degree of order" [170]) but also the Colonial Revivalists themselves. John recognizes "colonial style" architecture, appraisingly admires Murchison's massive oak chair (which "looked as though it might be of ancient make, perhaps an heirloom" [161]), and takes the same interest in precise genealogy that motivated late nineteenth-century preservationists and the newly popular American hereditary societies. He might even have had his own southern home built in what would have been identified in the 1890s as the colonial style, depending on how literally we take Julius's comments about the younger Murchison's intentions at the end of the story. "He be'n ober ter yo' place lookin' 'roun'," Julius tells John, "an' he say he's gwineter hab his'n *lookin' lak yo'n* befo' de yeah's ober" (171; my emphasis).

If John is arguably complicit with many of the goals of the Colonial Revivalists, can the same be said of Viney? After all, although denying Malcolm Murchison access to the estate's legal documents for years, once he is dead she tells his nephew where they are, allowing Roger to put the plantation back in "order." Viney would appear to remain little more than a servant in her new master's home, her "victory" over Murchison seeming more a private act of vengeance than a public disruption of a system of oppression. But if one reads Viney's story in the context of one of the dominant motifs of the other two tales in this group—the return of the slave to the site of enslavement and the subsequent attempt to *claim* that territory as his or her own—then perhaps Viney, too, can be said to claim ground that is rightfully hers. Rather than say she is returned to servitude, one might say that she chooses to remain *on* Murchison property, instead of *as* Murchison property. What John naively reads as Viney's "home instinct" (170) we might see as a much more willful and complicated decision, especially for a female ex-slave. For

Viney's struggle all along had been, in part, to sit on the piazza, not merely to sweep it—to be the "house-*keeper*" in a very different sense from what her master had ever intended, or from what John, despite his own "digging" through her past, ever perceives.[47]

"Similar Enough and Yet Unlike Enough"

Page's 1898 request for more stories in the "cunjure" vein presented Chesnutt with an equally complicated decision regarding his own fictional terrain. However disappointed he must have been at Houghton Mifflin's desire to remand him to conjure—an imaginative territory he had left behind beginning with "Dave's Neckliss"—Chesnutt chose to reclaim that ground and make it his own. If it would take more conjure tales to make a book, he would write more conjure tales. Yet it remains to be seen how this decision compromised the revisionist historicism taking shape in the non-conjure Julius stories of the 1890s. If works like "A Deep Sleeper" and "The Dumb Witness" were out, how sharply would Chesnutt have to curtail his exploration of the social experience of the built environment? What new strategies would he have to develop to avoid complete capitulation to the preferred fictions of white American memory? As we shall see, the restrictions presented by Page's request will make the third phase of the Julius cycle much less adventuresome, on the whole, than the first two. There are serious costs to the return to conjure that are perhaps best measured in what eventually became the capstone story to *The Conjure Woman*, "Hot-Foot Hannibal." But this does not mean that Chesnutt simply surrendered. In the tales that he hoped were "similar enough and yet unlike enough, to make a book,"[48] there are still carefully coded if much subdued depictions of resistance to racial configurations of space—resistances that emerge from the experimentation of the second phase of tales much as that group took its lead from "Po' Sandy" and "Dave's Neckliss." If the age demanded a nostalgic simplicity, Chesnutt would try only partly—and purposefully—to provide it.

A good place to begin an account of Chesnutt's strategies in the commissioned tales is the updated version of "The Goophered Grapevine," the 1887 story that would now head up the new collection and whose revisions thus not only reflect but also help organize the spatial concerns of the third phase of tales. Most of the changes to "The Goophered Grapevine" occur in the opening frame and might superficially be described as providing more background detail for the collection. But this detail is of a kind: it gives more concrete shape to many of the larger social, economic, political, and *physical* contours that the plantation genre wants to forget.⁴⁹ The lengthy and precise description of "Patesville" (a fictional Fayetteville), for example, provides an unusually urban backdrop for a pastoral form:

> There was a red brick market-house in the public square, with a tall tower, which held a four-faced clock that struck the hours, and from which there pealed out a curfew at nine o'clock. There were two or three hotels, a court-house, a jail, stores, offices, and all the appurtenances of a county seat and a commercial emporium; for while Patesville numbered only four or five thousand inhabitants, of all shades and complexions, it was one of the principal towns in North Carolina, and had a considerable trade in cotton and naval stores. (32)

This is more than scene-setting; this is detail that links physical structures to the social and economic practices they embody—or, as in the case of the bell tower, enforce. More than merely a county seat, Patesville is a commercial hub whose primary function is to provide planters with a market for their goods. The "considerable trade in cotton and naval stores" comes straight from the rural plantations, and Chesnutt is reminding us (as we head off to visit those plantations in his stories) that they are sites for the production of raw materials that will someday pass through the red brick market-house—the same building whose tower still chimes curfew even though slavery is over. "This business activity was not immediately apparent to my unaccustomed eyes" (32), John observes, as Chesnutt slyly stresses the importance of paying attention to that very activity. Even though it never reappears in the tales, in subtle ways it is the "four-faced" market-house that broods over the third phase of stories, much as it dominates the landscape of Patesville.⁵⁰

The second major place marker that Chesnutt adds to "The Goophered Grapevine," ironically, has the initial effect of making his story more closely resemble the plantation reminiscences it strategically mimicked. Between what had been consecutive sentences in the 1887 version—"One day I went over with my wife, to show her the place. We drove between the decayed gate-posts"—Chesnutt inserts a detailed description of the transitional drive from town to country, providing a clearer sense of what it was like to approach these stately plantations along winding rural roads:

> We drove out of the town over a long wooden bridge . . . passed the long whitewashed fence surrounding the county fair-ground, and struck into a

road so sandy that the horse's feet sank to the fetlocks. Our route lay partly up hill and partly down, for we were in the sand-hill country; we drove past cultivated farms, and then by abandoned fields . . . and once or twice through the solemn aisles of the virgin forest, where the tall pines, well-nigh meeting over the narrow road, shut out the sun, and wrapped us in cloistral solitude. (33)

On one level this is Chesnutt the dutiful regionalist giving his readers a more richly imagined sense of "the sand-hill country." Thomas Nelson Page's "Marse Chan," the lead story to his own collection *In Ole Virginia* (1887), begins similarly: "One afternoon, in the autumn of 1872, I was riding leisurely down the sandy road that winds along the top of the water-shed between two of the smaller rivers of eastern Virginia." And Patty B. Semple's "Old Kentucky Home," a nostalgic account of an "old stone homestead" in "the heart of the Blue Grass Country" that appeared in the *Atlantic* in July 1887, just one month before "The Goophered Grapevine," could almost be Chesnutt's prototype:

We jolted along for a time through the streets; then the houses became fewer and meaner . . . and soon [we] were fairly on "the pike," making our way over the bulwark of hills that shut in the town. The ride was full of interest: we knew every farmhouse, every turning; we watched for the bridge. . . . Before long we escaped from the white glare of the turnpike, and the wheels rolled smoothly over the soft brown clay of shaded lanes.[51]

If these are stock gestures of southern regionalism, however, they are gestures with a meaning—and a history—that Chesnutt now exploits. For in the antebellum South the *approach* to a plantation was as significant an expression of power and standing as the big house itself. Setting their principal buildings back from the roads, down "shaded lanes" like Semple's, planters communicated their spatial dominance through a carefully staged series of "threshold devices": the "gates, drives, forecourts, steps, terraces, porches, [and] passageways . . . which were intended to make the house, and its owner, appear more impressive."[52] And as the Semple, Page, and Chesnutt stories show, one does not even arrive at the plantation gate without first passing along the open public roads that gradually give way to the privately bounded spaces of the planters. (Indeed, as Upton points out, planters even "felt free to alter the public road courses for their own convenience.") The whole trip matters, in other words, progressing as it does along a consciously "articulated" and "processional" landscape. As Upton explains, this is an expressly white landscape; it is the route of access that the planter wants his visitors to follow. But the slave's plantation landscape—although part of the same physical terrain—"took a different form." Not bound in the same way to protocol as white guests, slaves worked "to alter and even to undercut the intended effects of the processional landscape" by moving around the plantation via routes that literally circumvented the preferred approaches.[53] Chesnutt's revisions to "The Goophered Grapevine" work analogously. In the course of laying out this processional approach, for example, Chesnutt quietly refigures one of the genre's key threshold devices. Instead of meeting, as in Semple's story, a stereotypically enthusiastic group of "a dozen little negroes . . . tumbling over each other in their zeal to open" the plantation gate, John and Annie—lost in the unfamiliar southern landscape—have this solitary encounter: "At length a little negro girl appeared, walking straight as an arrow, with a piggin of water on her head. After a little patient investigation, necessary to overcome the child's shyness, we learned what we wished to know, and . . . reached our destination."[54] This is the last major addition to the revised version of "The Goophered Grapevine" and a signal reminder that in the tales to follow, despite constraints of form, Chesnutt will still be trying to reimagine the spatial and social givens of his narrative terrain.

One very subtle way that Chesnutt marks these reimaginings in the six Page-sponsored stories is literally by changing Julius's routes of access to John and Annie's house. Julius, who has heretofore approached their home from the front, in plain sight, and typically "up the lane" (123, 137)—that is, along the "approved" path—now varies his approach, as often as not arriving obliquely from "around the house" (173, 184). Small details, to be sure, but symbolic reminders that in these tales most of the successful acts of black resistance to white control now occur in the frames, not in the stories Julius tells. Call this an expected result of the return to conjure: reliance on magic as a way to advance plot leaves less room for slave agency. Seeking the aid of an Aunt Peggy (the local conjure woman) to resolve disputes or to improve conditions on the plantation is of course active, but markedly less so (and more easily explained away) than the unaided daring of a Skundus or a Viney.[55] Julius's stories now almost always coax a sought-for action out of John or Annie, a strategy that had worked in three of the four tales of the first phase, but only once in the second. One could argue that Julius's varieties of approach to the house merely signal his increased familiarity with the new plantation, but this is precisely my point: like the slaves who knew their white owners' property well enough to mark (and conceal) their own trails upon it, Julius moves about the plantation grounds largely as he pleases. Chesnutt may not deliberately have sought to disrupt John's "articulated" landscape, but it is not surprising that in tales where Julius frequently undermines John's management of his property the underminer would no longer walk straight "up the lane" into every story. Certainly Chesnutt's characters understand the uses of space to express (or hide) themselves; as we have seen, when John is discomfited by Julius's tales, for example, he quits the piazza and goes inside.

Chesnutt's more elaborate descriptions of the piazza itself, which appears as the site of narration in four of the six phase three tales and in either the opening or the closing frame of the other two, provide further evidence of his continued effort to analyze social relations in spatial terms. If now obligatory, John and Annie's piazza is by no means static. We learn more about its features and functions in these tales than in the first seven combined: it is a quiet place to smoke ("A Victim of Heredity"), to read ("The Gray Wolf's Ha'nt"), or just to sit ("Tobe's Tribulations"); it is "broad and dry" ("The Gray Wolf's Ha'nt," 94) and offers a pleasant view, albeit of "somewhat monotonous scenery" ("Sis' Becky's Pickaninny," 82). It is large—John is somewhat surprised in "Hot-Foot Hannibal" that his guest can clear it "in two strides" (108)—and abuts the parlor (whose presence confirms our suspicions about the size of John and Annie's house). And it is comfortably and decoratively appointed: in addition to the armchairs and hammock (where John now naps), there is a honeysuckle vine large enough to sit "behind" (174, 107). If John and Annie have become more comfortable on the piazza, however, Julius seems less so. Whereas in the earlier stories he progressed from the top step, to a rocking chair, then finally to a seat at the piazza dessert table, in the six new tales he sits on the top step, if at all, and only when asked. Although present on the piazza in four of the tales, Julius is never described as sitting in a chair, nor even sitting on the steps without permission. For all we know, he narrates "The Gray Wolf's Ha'nt" standing up.[56]

We can interpret these changes in several ways. Chesnutt may be trying in these commissioned tales to mime more closely the preferred fictions of his anticipated audience by finding ways to limit Julius's familiarity with his white employers. Caste hierarchies are more clearly preserved with Julius restricted to the porch steps. Or Chesnutt may simply be more interested in exploring the attitudes, responses, and even postures of his white characters, a move perhaps anticipated by his shift to John's narration in "The Dumb Witness." For his part, Julius projects a decidedly warier attitude toward the piazza, as suggested by the deceptively comic opening to "The Gray Wolf's

Ha'nt." Approaching the piazza in a rainstorm, Julius lowers his umbrella before climbing the steps, receiving "a good dash of the rain as he stepped up on the porch" (95). "Why in the world, Julius," asks John, "didn't you keep the umbrella up until you got under cover?" Julius's response could easily express Chesnutt's own more cautious approach in these tales: "It's bad luck, suh, ter raise a' umbrella in de house," he explains, "an w'iles I dunno wuther it's bad luck ter kyar one inter de piazzer er no, I 'lows it's alluz bes' ter be on de safe side" (95). It is possible that Julius's "safe" soaking is only another deliberately staged event, performed to convince John that Julius is merely a superstitious ex-slave. But it also suggests that Julius (like Chesnutt) has decided to treat the piazza as "white" space—and may even figure Chesnutt's wry acknowledgment that in so doing he himself is *writing* on the "safe side."[57]

The story in which one can read the costs of this safer writing most clearly is the one that Chesnutt felt would leave "a good taste in the mouth" in the final collection.[58] He was probably right: the North-South reconciliation embodied in the end-frame marriage of Annie's sister Mabel to a Carolina planter in "Hot-Foot Hannibal" would likely have pleased Chesnutt's largely white audience. But later readers, familiar with the brilliant explorations of race and architecture in the previous tales, particularly in "The Dumb Witness," might find the taste far more disappointing. Of all the new stories Chesnutt wrote for Page, "Hot-Foot Hannibal" ranges most energetically over the antebellum and postbellum plantation landscapes. For the first time since "The Dumb Witness," piazzas figure prominently in both the frame and Julius's tale. For the first time in all the stories Chesnutt's characters draw sharp social distinctions between house slaves and field slaves.[59] The spatial markers are in place for another probing critique of race and the built environment—yet it never comes. What develops instead is not only a reconciliatory tale but a disturbingly upbeat revision of "The Dumb Witness" in which Annie's sister marries a man named for the same Murchison who brutalized Viney. Chesnutt's pretty-picture ending to *The Conjure Woman* reawakens some pretty ugly memories, not to mention sexual politics.

At the beginning of "Hot-Foot Hannibal" it is John who is rudely awakened from a nap on his piazza. This is part of the story's promising start; not only does the scene signal John's decline from energetic "pioneer" (in "The Goophered Grapevine") to leisured capitalist, it dramatizes the disruption of John's newfound southern comfort, as the harshly recriminatory squabble between his sister-in-law and her fiancé spills out onto the front porch and threatens to undo what in John's words "had promised to be another link binding me to the kindly Southern people" (108). By reintroducing Mabel, the scene also explicitly links "Hot-Foot Hannibal" to "A Deep Sleeper" and "The Dumb Witness" (the only other stories in which Annie's "sweet young sister" [137] appears) and suggests that a similar treatment of plantation space may follow. But Chesnutt's decision to engage Mabel not to Roger Murchison—who, according to the careful genealogy of "The Dumb Witness," should be the surviving heir—but to *Malcolm* Murchison is the first signal that "Hot-Foot Hannibal" will itself undo the historical revisionism of the second phase of tales.

The inner tale in "Hot-Foot Hannibal" also begins promisingly. Field slave Chloe is tapped for service in the big house and works so capably that she soon "run[s] de house herse'f" (110). When Mars' Dugal' decides that he wants a "house boy"—the phrase concisely encapsulating the intimate relations between slaves, property, and space—he calls two slaves from the quarters for evaluation and, to Chloe's disappointment, selects Hannibal over her preference, Jeff. Julius's inside knowledge of the tale comes from his own position on Dugal's property: "I wuz a young boy den, en use' ter wuk 'bout de stables, so I knowed eve'ythin' dat wuz gwine on 'roun' de plantation" (110). Given this concentration of slaves in and around the big house, it seems not only fitting but potentially quite subversive to place the story's main goopher beneath Dugal's own home, as (per Aunt Peggy's directive) Chloe shows Jeff "how ter git unner de house" (112) to hide a conjure doll that will make Hannibal unfit for service. But the story fails to turn this infiltration of the master's home into either a critique of white privilege or an assertion of covert spatial control by the slaves. Even though the goopher briefly unsettles the lives of the Dugal' household (spilled food, a ruined garden, disturbed sleep), its ill effects are felt most severely by Hannibal, who is whipped and sent back to the quarters. When the doll is later forgotten and left under the house, its "monst'us powerful" spell rebounds only on Chloe and Jeff themselves, as Jeff is sold and commits suicide and Chloe dies of grief. The whites are not only untroubled, they are sought for succor: when Chloe believes she has seen Jeff hugging another woman (actually the disguised Hannibal), she rushes to tell Mars' Dugal' about the doll, hoping he will punish Jeff. As though to highlight the story's reluctance to challenge white control of plantation space, Chesnutt stages this crucial scene on Dugal's front piazza, where he and "de ladies" are seated after supper (115). Chloe's impetuous betrayal of Jeff is thus simultaneously a rejection of Aunt Peggy and the resources of her cabin for the supposed powers of the white slaver's porch.

Chloe's subsequent regret at this course, I would suggest, expresses Chesnutt's as well; in her figurative "I wish I hadn't done that" one can read his own lament, "I wish I hadn't *had* to do that." Further clues to Chesnutt's awareness of the painful retreats he has to stage in this story lie in the closing frame's overdetermined rewriting of "The Dumb Witness." Here again Mabel appears as Martha Todd—the northerner visiting a relative who has moved to the South—but this time she intends to marry Malcolm Murchison, not renounce him. Unlike Martha in "The Dumb Witness," who "learned some things about" Murchison that made it "impossible" for her to marry him (165), in "Hot-Foot Hannibal" Mabel is ready to excuse "things said that no woman of any spirit could stand" (108). Fair enough; though Mabel and young Murchison had had "something more than a mere lovers' quarrel" (108), she had not (like Martha) been told tales of rape, incest, and miscegenation. But John's final description in "Hot-Foot Hannibal" of the newly happy couple bears ominous traces of this repressed past that register for the knowing reader—or the regretful writer—what Chesnutt has been forced to unwrite. "They were walking arm in arm," John observes, "and their faces were aglow with the light of love" (119). "Arm in arm" with Murchison (recalling "*vis-à-vis*") describes just what Viney, both figuratively and literally, resists in the opening frame of "The Dumb Witness." (As Murchison begs Viney to tell him where the papers are, he offers to "take her hand, which lay on the arm of the chair"—but Viney "drew her hand away" [161].) Even more tellingly, "faces . . . aglow with the light of love" conspicuously recasts Viney's powerfully angry eyes—the earlier tale's central image of black resistance, which "glow . . . like the ashes of a dying fire" (160) whenever Murchison threatens Viney—as the radiant countenance of sanctioned union. If the silent changing of "young Murchison's" name from Roger to Malcolm (metaphorically marrying Mabel to the worst of the clan) could be said to mark Chesnutt's private protest against the literary "family" into which he has been co-opted, "They were walking arm in arm, and their faces were aglow with the light of love" might bitingly parody Chesnutt's public display of cheerful complicity with the preferred fictions of his white readers.[60]

Preferring to Leave

"Hot-Foot Hannibal" does not end on this parodic note, however. Chesnutt instead appends a narrative postscript that subtly reemphasizes the importance for African Americans in the late nineteenth century of validating memory by claiming ground. In the last paragraph of the story a befuddled John wonders why Julius, who apparently has not only "a most excellent understanding" with Murchison but also an offer of employment, declines to enter Murchison's service after his marriage to Mabel. Why would Julius decide to stay where he was? Why not take the presumably better offer? "For some reason or other," John concludes, Julius "preferred to remain with us" (120), meaning himself and Annie. But given the preoccupations of the earlier conjure tales, particularly the stories of the second phase that "Hot-Foot Hannibal" seems so regretfully to revise, it is more likely that what Julius prefers—like Cindy and Skundus, Lonesome Ben, and Viney before him—is to remain in *his* home, with his family, on the land he has known all his life. It is the power of place and memory—good and bad—that Julius reaffirms by preferring to remain where he is instead of following the prevailing winds of economic opportunity. That is not what Julius's dealings with John have been all about anyway. Indeed, rather than claim that Julius "disappears as a coherent pragmatic character" at the end of "Hot-Foot Hannibal," one might instead say that he reemerges as one.[61]

Of course this is not where Chesnutt preferred to remain. As interested in the politics of his own literary "place construction" as the politics within his stories, Chesnutt was ready once again to leave Julius behind for more contemporary ground. More than two decades would pass before he wrote another conjure tale. But the evidence of Chesnutt's imaginative investment in the social experience of American architecture, much muted in the third phase of the conjure stories, would reappear in the major work that soon followed, his color line novels *The House behind the Cedars* (1900) and *The Marrow of Tradition* (1901). *The House behind the Cedars*, in particular, bears heavy traces of Chesnutt's deepening interest in architectural form, social relations, and narrative construction. Initially drafted in 1889 as the short story "Rena," the tale would go through multiple revisions, expansions, and reorganizations during the 1890s—the precise years Chesnutt was exploring the complex crossings of race, memory, and the built environment we have been reviewing—before finally being accepted for publication by Houghton Mifflin in March 1900 under its new, architecturally resonant title.[62] No longer primarily a character study but instead a layered investigation into the lived structures of racism, *The House behind the Cedars* pays conspicuous attention to architectural space as both setting and symbol. The detailed description in the opening chapter of John Walden's walk through Patesville past exactly the same market-house that preoccupies the narrator at the beginning of the revised version of "The Goophered Grapevine," for example, carefully marks the debt in Chesnutt's first published novel to the socio-spatial interests of the conjure tales. In the novel, moreover, the market-house comes in for even closer scrutiny. Comparing the structure of the Reconstruction present with John Walden's memories of the antebellum past, the narrator muses, "Perhaps the surface of the red brick, long unpainted, had scaled off a little more here and there. There might have been a slight accretion of the moss and lichen on the shingled roof. But the tall tower, with its four-faced clock, rose as majestically and uncompromisingly as though the land had never been subjugated."[63]

As William Andrews aptly notes, the narrator's description makes clear that Patesville's simultaneously decaying and indomitable monuments "weigh heavily, not nostalgically, on the South's moral slate."[64] These monuments also weigh heavily on the narrative itself. Whereas in *The Conjure Woman*, as I have suggested, the market-house and its four-faced clock tower brood over the final collection despite appearing only in the opening story, in *The House behind the Cedars* this structure appears repeatedly (like clockwork, one might almost say), chiming again and again what Daniel Worden has characterized as the novel's architectural allegorization of racial hierarchy.[65] Counterpointed against these public edifices stands the text's eponymous "house behind the cedars," an ostensibly private space whose visual vulnerability—passersby can look onto the front and rear piazzas as well as into the house itself through gaps in the cedar hedge—further allegorizes both the precariousness of black homeownership and the instability of racial categorization by skin color. Although screened and shaded as picturesquely as any Downingesque cottage, complete with its own "honeysuckle vine" and "Virginia creeper" (11), the "gray, unpainted" (10) house shields no one, inside or out, from the deadly legacies of racial segregation.[66]

Whereas *The House behind the Cedars* nearly overflows with architectural signification, repeatedly invoking the preoccupations of the conjure tales (whose temporal frames the novel also shares), *The Marrow of Tradition*, set at the end of the century, consolidates its socio-spatial interests into a smaller range of representative sites.[67] The later novel nonetheless powerfully suggests that what is fundamentally at stake in its fictionalized account of the 1898 coup by the white residents of Wilmington, North Carolina, is nothing less than the right of African Americans to occupy—to own, to inhabit, and to shape—public and private space. The "trope of violated inheritance" that Eric Sundquist discerns at the core of the novel, in other words, is spatial as well as genealogical.[68] Framed as a story of architectural dispossession, the ancestral home of the impoverished slaveowning Carteret family having been sold after the war to the industrious father of the novel's contemporary black protagonist, Dr. William Miller (whose own constrained access to "white" spaces the text similarly foregrounds), *The Marrow of Tradition* builds to a scene of destruction that revisits Chesnutt's very first architectural narrative, "Uncle Peter's House." In the earlier story, the Klan burns Peter's house as a protest against black advancement. At the end of Chesnutt's novel, Wellington's modern white avengers analogously, and far more dramatically, incinerate Dr. Miller's hospital—the town's most prominent black structure—in an act that illuminates the true face of racist violence. "The flames soon completed their work," Chesnutt's narrator reflects,

> and this handsome structure, the fruit of old Adam Miller's industry, the monument of his son's philanthropy, a promise of good things for the future of the city, lay smouldering in ruins, a melancholy witness to the fact that our boasted civilization is but a thin veneer, which cracks and scales off at the first impact of primal passion. (310)

It was undoubtedly passages like this that led William Dean Howells, who only a year earlier had hailed the artistry of *The Conjure Woman* in a glowing review, to reject the "bitter, bitter" tone of Chesnutt's latest work. Indeed, the novel suffered from poor sales, ultimately moving only a handful more copies than *The House behind the Cedars*, a disappointing showing that precipitated Chesnutt's sudden literary decline. Incisive commentary on race and the built environment—perhaps particularly when carried uncomfortably close to contemporary readers' own historical moment—did no more to bring a reluctant white audience to Chesnutt's novels than it did to his middle phase of conjure tales. If many of Julius's stories commemorated a past white readers wanted to forget, the color line fictions of *The House behind the Cedars* and *The Marrow of Tradition*, we might say, inversely re-created a present those same readers wanted to ignore. And largely did.[69]

Despite his white audience's lukewarm embrace of his work, in Chesnutt's hands the landscapes of slavery and segregation could function as instructive sites of both remembrance and resistance at the precise moment that American collective memory, energized by resurgent national myths of racial superiority, aggressively sought to muffle that landscape in pastoral nostalgia. (Even Howells had to admit that, for all its bitterness, *The Marrow of Tradition* was also both powerful and just.) Countering historical amnesia with concrete memories, and doing so, as it were, from the very porch that symbolized the hoped-for return to a time of less complicated social relations, Chesnutt's conjure stories in particular challenge the dominant culture's revisionism by articulating revisions of their own. The piazzas in these tales thus operate, in the end, as powerful African American *lieux de mémoire*, sites of memory willfully recalled in order to "block the work of forgetting," in the words of Pierre Nora.[70] And yet they do so, as we have seen, not simply to establish a countertradition but to try to reframe white understandings of race and the built environment. That the task of this reframing was both difficult and crucial is made even more clear, as we will see in the next chapter, by the role that racialized space was already beginning to play in U.S. imperial adventurism in the Americas and beyond.

3

Imperial Bungalow

*Structures of Empire in Richard Harding
Davis and Olga Beatriz Torres*

What the map cuts up, the story cuts across.
— Michel de Certeau, *The Practice of Everyday Life* (1984)

At 4:30 in the morning on 28 June 1914, thirteen-year-old Olga Beatriz Torres boarded the first of four trains that would take her from her home outside Mexico City to the militarized Gulf port of Veracruz, nearly 300 miles away. Amid patrolling U.S. Marines, who had seized the port on President Woodrow Wilson's orders only two and a half months earlier, Torres and her family—refugees from the escalating chaos of the Mexican Revolution—waited for a ship to take them north to Texas, where they would seek a new home in exile. Several days later, a crude cargo vessel refitted for passenger use finally arrived. After four queasy days at sea—and another twenty-four exasperating hours under medical quarantine in the Galveston harbor—Torres finally stepped onto American soil. It was 5:00 in the afternoon on a blisteringly hot eighth of July, and what greeted Torres, as she recorded in a letter to an aunt who had remained behind in Mexico, greatly disillusioned her:

> Imagine a wooden shack with interior divisions which make it into a home and store at the same time. The doors were covered with screens to keep the flies and mosquitos out. Outside, it had a little dirty wooden bench used by passengers waiting for the train, and that shack, the "property" of a Mexican married to a German woman, was the only building in sight.
> I could not restrain myself and asked, "Is this the United States?"[1]

Torres's interjection encodes multiple disenchantments. Expecting cleanliness, she found dirt; expecting grandeur, she found insignificance; expecting Americans, she found none. Not a little of Torres's disillusion stems from her specific class position, for in Mexico she had been accustomed to the privileges of comparative wealth. But Torres's query also reflects certain geopolitical expectations: after all, shouldn't the region's supposedly most powerful nation have a correspondingly impressive—and distinctively "American"—port of entry? Something more significant, surely, than a mere "wooden shack"?

This chapter explores the expectations and disappointments at stake in Torres's question by placing her fascinating yet relatively obscure narrative—*Memorias de mi viaje* (*Recollections of My Trip*), a book-length compilation of the letters Torres wrote to her aunt during her journey—in conversation with two much more widely known texts of transit, revolution, and the buildingscape of empire: Richard Harding Davis's travelogue *Three Gringos in Venezuela and Central America* (1896) and his follow-up imperial romance, *Soldiers of Fortune* (1897). In many respects, of course, Davis and Torres could not be more disparate figures. At the time of his trip with two friends through Belize, Guatemala, Honduras, Nicaragua, Panama, and Venezuela, the thirty-year-old Davis was already a popular author and former managing editor of *Harper's Weekly*. By 1900 he would be not only a famous war correspondent but also—particularly in the wake of the publication of the immensely popular *Soldiers of Fortune*—a household name. By contrast, when Olga Torres accompanied her family on their journey out of Mexico into the U.S., she was an unknown teenage immigrant. And although Torres's letters were eventually published in *El Paso del Norte*, the Spanish-language daily of El Paso's Mexican exile community (where Torres and her family finally settled) before being reissued in book form in 1918, the story of her family's flight from political persecution would languish for nearly eighty years until an enterprising scholar resurrected it from the archives. Indeed, part of the work of this chapter will be to highlight the revealing ways in which these narratives diverge: in their contrasting notions of what it means to be displaced or dislocated; in their chiastic longings for safety and return; and, not least, in their conflicting perspectives on the uses of U.S. military power.

At the same time, there are surprising and important points of convergence between these texts that can help us think in productive ways about race, architecture, and empire at the turn of the twentieth century, particularly within the material context of what Kirsten Silva Gruesz has identified as "not simply an *object* of U.S. expansionism but the original *engine* of it": the Gulf of Mexico.[2] I will argue in part that Davis's and Torres's writings can in fact be productively understood as Gulf narratives, texts that explore what Gruesz terms the "complex entanglements" (470) of the greater Gulf region or "system." I will also suggest that, taken together, the texts of Davis and Torres provide a surprisingly revealing examination of the architecture of empire, reflected not only through official structures of state (with which all three narratives are particularly concerned) but also through what we might call the correlative forms of imperial domesticity, especially the turn-of-the-century bungalow, which despite its democratic iconography is freighted by a complexly imperial heritage.[3]

Gulf Crossings

The vectors of motion and emotion driving Davis's and Torres's texts—particularly the travel narratives *Three Gringos* and *Memorias*—cross almost exactly. Where the chapters in *Three Gringos* drop leisurely south, the letters that make up *Memorias* struggle anxiously east, then finally north. For Davis, the geographic dislocation of his journey is not only welcome, it is a professional opportunity: he has been urged to go to Central America to write about an outlawed Louisiana lottery surviving in exile on the eastern coast of Honduras. Torres's dislocation, on the other hand, is forced upon her. Although early in her trip she wishes she could simply turn around and go home to Mexico City, "thoughts of father's political persecution, of the horrifying destruction of the charming city by Zapata's hordes, of the unjust vengeance in the hands of government partisans, of the assassination by unknown assassins of people who were thought to be against the government and, finally, hearing of the horror the war was spreading throughout the land," she reports, "made me realize that returning to the City of Palaces would be total stupidity" (31).[4] Unlike Torres, Davis at times seems to court danger out of sheer boredom, as when in Panama he and his traveling partners are suspected—rightly—of giving aid to an antigovernment revolutionist. Of course Davis can use his connections to seek asylum on an American warship when Panamanian soldiers breathe a little too hotly down his neck. "I was impressed," he confides, "with the comforting sense that comes to a traveller from the States when he knows that one of our White Squadron is rolling at anchor in the harbor." This is in fact not far from the vision Davis has for the political future of the region. At the midpoint of his narrative, appalled by the volatility of governance in Central America, Davis notoriously asserts: "What [the Central American citizen] needs is to have a protectorate established over him, either by the United States or by another power."[5]

Although Torres does not condemn the U.S. military exclusively for the invasion of Veracruz—she has even more contempt for "the citizens who with their excesses submit their nation to such trials and tribulations" (34)[6]—as a war refugee she is understandably more skeptical than Davis about the use of force in the pursuit of political ends.

These differences are important because they help historicize and particularize the positions and experiences of Davis and Torres. Just as Davis's nonchalant risk-taking brings Torres's constrained options into sharper relief, so too elsewhere does Torres's dependence on her family makes us more aware of Davis's bachelor swagger. And yet by focusing exclusively on such differences, we risk overlooking patterns and points of contact that are otherwise less easy to discern. Only by reading Davis's and Torres's narratives side by side, for example, literally mapping their separate journeys within a single frame, can we recognize the extent to which the larger Gulf region—rather than more traditionally conceived national borders—helps shape the concerns and scope of both texts. As Gruesz has argued, our ability to discern larger regions or systems of contact and exchange in the Americas has in part been hampered by the dominance of the "reified map of the land border, *la línea*," as a privileged site in U.S.-Mexican border studies. Even Juanita Luna-Lawhn, who resurrected *Memorias de mi viaje* for contemporary scholars and oversaw its reprinting in 1994, characterizes Torres's text somewhat imprecisely as an account of "movement across political borders" rather than as one of movement within a far less linear system of continent, port, and sea.[7] For although *Memorias* begins in Mexico City and concludes in El Paso, Torres's journey does not travel due north from the one city to the other. Instead, *Memorias* first travels east by train to Veracruz, then north by ship to Texas City, then inland by streetcar to Houston, then southeast to the Galveston coast—and then back, once more, to Houston—before finally, and only near the very end of the narrative, heading northwest to El Paso. Given this route—with multiple entries and exits rather than a single, momentous line crossing, and with so much time actually spent in and on the Gulf itself—it seems more appropriate to consider Torres's text as mapping what Gruesz (drawing on the work of cultural geographer D. W. Meinig) would call a Gulf "circuit" (or perhaps half circuit) than as chronicling a simple border passage. Thus while *Memorias* can still contribute productively to studies of "transculturalization" along the U.S.-Mexican border, as in Luna-Lawhn's pioneering reading, it can also help construct what Gruesz calls the "as-yet-unwritten comparative ethnography of the Gulf's gateway settlements."[8] Indeed, Torres's disenchantment with what greets her when she disembarks at her first U.S. port—"Is this the United States?"—has everything to do with her understanding of what a "real" port city, such as, in her experience, Veracruz, is supposed to look like.

The classification of *Memorias de mi viaje* as a Gulf narrative draws on more than geography. As she moves through the Gulf, Torres repeatedly registers the region's commercial and social interconnectedness. In Galveston she notes the presence of "merchant ships of all types and from all over the world, as could be inferred by the variety of flags and their sailors. Close to the large ships, motorboats slithered in and out like small fish of countless colors; some, coarsely wrought, are meant to carry cargo; others, meant to be passenger boats, are beautifully finished, with a row of seats on each side and mounted above the deck" (64).[9] Commenting on the profusion of train lines in Houston, Torres describes for her aunt the circuits that connect many of the Gulf's major cities: "[Houston] is situated in continuous contact with Galveston, Texas City, and New Orleans; four steam locomotives leave daily for New Orleans. Two steam locomotives and hourly electric trains depart for Galveston daily. Eight electric trains and two steam locomotives depart for Texas City daily" (67).[10] Even Torres's annotated list of the destinations of the other passengers on the ship that takes her from Veracruz to Texas—two nuns headed to San Antonio, a cavalry captain on his way to Sonora, a Mexican woman looking for her husband in Galveston, an English woman meeting yet another ship to take her to England—maps a region traversed by multiple crossings rather than one neatly bifurcated into "Mexico" and "U.S." Torres's sense of the Gulf's vibrant, varied richness finds its way even into her description of the "enormous beauty" of the sea itself:

> [I felt] admiration because the landscape is grandiose and beautiful—the sunlight as it broke over the waves produced an arabesque of different colors so varied so those who speak of the 'blue sea,' of the 'green sea' are mistaken. The sunlight projects so many colors on the moving surface of the sea that it is neither green nor blue; it is an infinite variety of colors. It is an admirable polychrome. (38)[11]

And what of Davis? Because critics have primarily been interested in mining *Three Gringos* for the ways it anticipates the political themes of *Soldiers of Fortune* (set in South America but understood to refract Davis's interest in the Cuban independence struggle) or Davis's later reportage from Cuba itself—which registers in such accounts more as a Caribbean site than as part of the Gulf—we have never thought of *Three Gringos* as a Gulf narrative, even though Davis embarks from New Orleans, sails south through the Gulf to the Yucatán coast, and then docks in Belize to begin the land portion of his journey. To be fair, it is possible Davis never quite thought of the narrative this way himself. He does not explicitly describe New Orleans or the Gulf as a conduit to Latin America, nor does he foreground the geographic, economic, or cultural connections between this U.S. port and the greater Mexican/Central American region he is about to explore—Gruesz's implicit criteria for a self-aware Gulf-system narrative.[12] If anything, Davis characterizes the Gulf region below New Orleans as a wholly separate, almost alien place. Leaving the city on a steamer bound "for Central American ports" (1), Davis and his companions slowly "[push] down the last ninety miles of the Mississippi River" (2) toward the Gulf. This portion of the journey, including the racialized landscape of Jim Crow, is familiar to Davis from past images: "The great river steamers, with paddle-wheels astern and high double smoke-stacks, that were associated in our minds with pictures of the war and those in our school geographies, passed us . . . on their way to St. Louis, and on each bank we recognized, also from pictures, magnolia-trees and the ugly cotton-gins and the rows of negroes' quarters like the men's barracks in a fort" (2–3). In the very next paragraph, however, this familiar landscape darkens into a far stranger space:

> At six o'clock, when we had reached the Gulf, the sun sank a blood-red disk into great desolate bayous of long grass and dreary stretches of vacant water. Dead trees with hanging gray moss and mistletoe on their bare branches reared themselves out of the swamps like gallows-trees or giant sign-posts pointing the road to nowhere; and the herons, perched by dozens on their limbs or moving heavily across the sky with harsh, melancholy cries, were the only signs of life. On each side of the muddy Mississippi the waste swampland stretched as far as the eye could reach, and every blade of the long grass and of the stunted willows and every post of the dikes stood out black against the red sky as vividly as though it were lit by a great conflagration, and the stagnant pools and stretches of water showed one moment like flashing lakes of fire, and the next, as the light left them, turned into mirrors of ink. It was a scene of the most awful and beautiful desolation, and the silence, save for the steady breathing of the steamer's engine, was the silence of the Nile at night. (3)

This is a far cry, to be sure, from the "admirable polychrome" of Torres's Gulf. In this extraordinary passage, Davis represents New Orleans as a gateway not to a space of invigorating Latin American contact and exchange but instead to a hellish yet almost erotically mesmerizing terrain of fire and decay, a figurative "road to nowhere" animated by tropes of contagion and waste, on the one hand, and exoticism and sensual pleasure, on the other, with an underlying frame of reference that is African ("the silence of the Nile at night") rather than Latin.[13] In Gruesz's terms, this description would link Davis with other nineteenth-century Anglo-American commentators who so often failed to apprehend the transnational connectedness of New Orleans with the greater Latin Gulf. When Davis's steamer eventually emerges from this inky night, and three days later finds a new shore, Davis continues to imagine he has been transported to another world: "Land, when it came, appeared in the shape of little islands that floated in mid-air above the horizon like the tops of trees, without trunks to support them, or low-lying clouds" (4). Even the first sign of human settlement—a "ruined temple" rumored to be the site of "wild Indian" massacres—affirms distance, not proximity, to the U.S. he has left behind. "It was interesting," Davis observes, "to find such a monument a few days out from New Orleans" (4–5).

And yet despite these opening gestures of estrangement, Davis's narrative betrays considerable interest in the Gulf as both a physical and a geopolitical region. He becomes obsessed, for example, with an issue Gruesz identifies as the central preoccupation of many nineteenth-century Gulf-system narratives: the acquisition of transit rights across Latin America. Throughout *Three Gringos*, Davis is passionate about securing U.S. access to the Pacific across Central America, although his preferred route is through Nicaragua, where the U.S. already has interests, rather than Panama, where the French are still in charge. (For a sense of the mid-1890s U.S. interest in the Nicaraguan route, see Fig. 19.) Whatever may transpire politically in the region does not matter, Davis suggests, "so long as it leaves the Nicaragua Canal in our hands" (146). Thus although Davis's narrative at its close swerves east to Venezuela, leaving the greater Gulf region behind, its emotional energy remains chiefly invested in the completion of an arterial route west through Central America. This trans-isthmian desire may even be said to infect the micronarrative patterns of *Three Gringos*, which is inordinately—even for a travel narrative—obsessed not merely with crisscrossing difficult terrain but also with getting around or cutting through various frustrating delays or government officials during the trip.

Although *Soldiers of Fortune* bears a less overt relationship to the Gulf, there are unmistakable traces of the wider region's influence on the staging and even the conception of the story. Some of these traces have their ori-

Figure 19. "Uncle Sam's Next Duty," Marshall Everett, ed., *Exciting Experiences in Our Wars with Spain and the Filipinos* (1899), n.p.

gins in *Three Gringos*. After all, as John Seelye notes, Davis went to Central America in the first place "in part to obtain . . . realistic detail of the sort that would loan verisimilitude to romantic fiction."[14] Thus in *Soldiers*, for example, Davis provides the Valencia Mining Company—the American-owned concern extracting ore from the coastal cliffs of a fictional republic on the northeastern coast of South America—with a paddle-wheeled steamer commandeered from "the levees in New Orleans" that recalls the ones Davis describes at the opening of *Three Gringos*. Other details, central to *Soldiers*, link it directly to the Gulf. For example, Davis imagines a backstory for the novel's main character, civil engineer Robert Clay, that locates his most formative experiences within the circuit of the Gulf. We come to learn, for example, that as a young man, "an orphan and without a home," Clay journeys from Colorado to the Gulf, eventually "sail[ing] away from New Orleans to the Cape." We also learn that Clay's most recent engineering feat took place in Mexico, where he was responsible for putting new road and rail lines through some of the most dangerous and inaccessible terrain in the country. To contemporary readers this would have signaled Clay's involvement in the extensive late nineteenth-century modernization of Mexico's transportation infrastructure by President Porfirio Díaz—a project criticized by many Mexicans for disproportionately benefiting the imperial designs of rail- and road-dependent industries dominated by foreign capital, such as mining and agriculture, that sought efficient new routes to the Pacific and especially the Gulf, for Mexico's raw materials. Since it was primarily U.S. capital that controlled these markets, this seemingly innocuous biographical detail makes Clay's behavior as an active imperial agent in South America merely a follow-up to his earlier involvement in the Gulf.[15] Nor is Clay the only character who has prepared for imperial ventures in South America by first honing his skills in the Gulf region. MacWilliams, for example, the Valencia Mining Company's chief railroad engineer, has "spent [his life] in Mexico and Central America," where he "learned what he knew of engineering at the transit's mouth" (45). It is a cast of quintessentially Gulf characters, in other words, that Davis places at the center of *Soldiers*'s imperial drama.

In what follows I will retrace the scope and function of architectural representation in each of the three main texts under consideration here—*Three Gringos*, *Soldiers*, and *Memorias de mi viaje*—before returning at the chapter's end to reconsider the ways the spatial concerns of these texts can be productively linked and contrasted. That they belong in the same conversation seems even more clear if we keep in mind this small but evocative detail: the very rail lines on which Torres and her family flee Mexico City to escape the turmoil of the Mexican Revolution turn out to be part of the same national network built by Díaz in the late nineteenth century with the help of the real-life models for Robert Clay—rail lines whose role in the domination of Mexico by foreign capital the revolution itself was partly launched to challenge.

Palm Trees and Mud Huts

Given the importance of spatial concerns within *Three Gringos*, it comes as no surprise to find that the narrative provides an extensive inventory of architectural structures, from humble huts and sheds to the grander spaces of hotels and palaces. In this text, moreover, architectural details do more than simply describe the built environment. Instead, they typically serve as a telling index of a given country's level of "civilization" as well as reliable indicators of the stability of the local political landscape. Davis is charmed, for example, by the architecture he finds in the capital of British Honduras, his first stop in Central America. "Belize is a pretty village of six thousand people," he reports, "living in low, broad-roofed bungalows, lying white and cool-looking in the border of waving cocoanut-trees and tall, graceful palms" (5). The noteworthiness of this particular scene is heightened by Davis's reflection on its atypicality. "It was not necessary to tell us," he notes, "that Belize would be the last civilized city we should see until we reached the capital of Spanish Honduras. A British colony is always civilized; it is always the same, no matter in what latitude it may be, and it is always distinctly British" (5–6). Official structures are just as appealing as the domestic housing. The seat of colonial power, the Government House—where Davis and his two companions are treated to breakfast and lunch—"is a very large building, fronting the bay, with one of the finest views from and most refreshing breezes on its veranda that a man could hope to find on a warm day" (11).[16] Not only is Belize "one of the prettiest ports" Davis would visit, but its "cleanliness and order . . . were in so great contrast to the ports we visited later as to make them most remarkable" (16).

Once Davis leaves Belize, however, the three gringos are "met at every step with the despotic little rules and safeguards"—not to mention, in Davis's view, the shoddy buildings—"which mark unstable governments" (19). Livingston, the chief Gulf seaport of Guatemala, "was like a village on the coast of Africa in comparison with Belize": presenting nothing like the political or structural sophistication (or indeed the "cleanliness and order") of either the British colonial capital or indeed of the "Pacific side" of Guatemala itself, where "her civilization lies" (19). Reflecting further on this contrast, Davis delivers an extended commentary on the ways the architecture of empire can disfigure rather than beautify colonial space:

> There are two opposite features of landscape in the tropics which are always found together—the royal palm, which is one of the most beautiful of things, and the corrugated zinc-roof custom house, which is one

of the ugliest. Nature never appears so extravagant or so luxurious as she does in these hot latitudes; but just as soon as she has fashioned a harbor after her own liking, and set it off at her best so that it is a haven of delight to those who approach it from the sea, civilized man comes along and hammers square walls of zinc together and spoils the beauty of the place forever. The natives, who do not care for customs dues, help nature out with thatch-roofed huts and walls of adobe or yellow cane, or add curved red tiles to the more pretentious houses, and so fill out the picture. But the "gringo," or the man from the interior, is in a hurry, and wants something that will withstand earthquakes and cyclones, and so wherever you go you can tell that he has been there before you by his architecture of zinc. (19–21)

Although Davis here presents himself as a defender of the "delightful" structures of "extravagant" nature against the unsightly incursions of the white man's "architecture of zinc," it would be a mistake to take this passage, as Seelye does, as the sign of a pervasive critique of colonialism in *Three Gringos*. For Seelye, this disdain for colonial ugliness affirms Davis's belief that "the impulse that is the heart of imperialism may be counted on to create a Conradian shambles, not the outlines of an emerging civilization."[17] And yet as Davis makes clear in Belize, he admires colonial enterprises that enhance rather than mar the picturesqueness of the native landscape. Nor can he even sustain for long the enthusiasm he expresses in this passage for the "natives" who "help nature out" by building with nature's materials rather than man's manufactures. Turning from the customhouse, the "picture" Davis sees "filled out" is not a haven of delight but instead a monotonous local landscape made up of "no houses but those which have been created out of the mud and the trees of the place itself," populated by mostly "coal-black" natives (21). No walls of yellow cane or roofs with curved red tiles accessorize the native architecture here. "There are no streets to the village nor doors to the houses; they are all exactly alike," Davis reports, "and the bare mud floor of one is as unindividual, except for the number of naked children crawling upon it, as is any of the others" (21). Davis's suggestive linking of the "naked" black children with the "bare" mud floors ensures not only that the houses appear unindividuated from each other but also that the inhabitants appear unindividuated from the houses. That Guatemala is not technically a colonial space—although, as we have seen, Davis considers all of Central America ripe for intervention—does not diminish the fact that *Three Gringos* registers Davis's appreciation for the physical results of certain kinds of "civilized" intervention and disdain for the results of other kinds.[18] If anything, this sequence suggests, Livingston's particular disarray might be improved by the right kind of imperial reconstruction.

As Davis moves farther south, his distaste for disarray only grows. The three gringos' next stop is Honduras. After a brief respite in the unexpected comfort of the large and airy Puerto Cortez mansion housing the exiled Louisiana State Lottery, followed by the better part of a week in a surprisingly clean hotel in the drowsy inland city of San Pedro Sula, Davis and his companions embark on an arduous two-week cross-country expedition by mule to the mountain capital of Tegucigalpa. There is little in the way of formal shelter along this rural route. "Even in the larger towns and so-called cities," Davis notes, "we slept in private houses, and on the solitary occasion when we were directed to a hotel we found a bare room with a pile of canvas cots heaped in one corner, to which we were told to help ourselves" (79). Davis finds the inhabitants of these private houses—who are "apparently quite hardened to having their homes invaded by strangers, and their larders levied upon at any hour of the day or night" (79)—sufficiently generous. But the houses themselves, "as near an approach to the condition of primitive man as one can find on this continent" (92), he finds unbearably uncomfortable. "The walls of a Honduranian hut are made of mud packed round a skeleton of interwoven rods," Davis reports; "the floor is of the naked earth, and the roof is thatched with the branches of palms" (91). On cold nights the damp floor chills their bones, even when they sleep in hammocks rather than on the ground. And when the buildings in which they are to sleep are already full, with either people or (as on one miserable night) livestock, sleeping outside is not an option because of the bugs. Indeed, the ubiquity of biting insects "transcends mere discomfort," Davis complains. "It is an absolute curse to the country, and to every one in it" (111).

Davis's frustrations with the conditions in Honduras, both physical and political, boil over shortly after they reach Tegucigalpa (where, not incidentally, expecting clean lodgings after such an arduous trip, they discover only yet another dirty hotel). Exasperated in particular by the revolutionary culture of Central America—"the value of stability in government is something they cannot be made to understand. It is not in their power to see it, and the desire for change and revolution is born in the blood" (143)—Davis casts about for the right metaphor to express his profound sense of the unsuitability of Central America for self-government. "The Central-American citizen is no more fit for a republican form of government," he sputters, "than he is for an arctic expedition." But this does not quite fit the bill. Trying a second comparison, Davis alludes to a statue in Costa Rica in which "the Republic in the form of a young woman" stands "with her foot on the neck of General Walker, the American filibuster" (146). Irritated by the anti-Americanness of this gesture, Davis imagines its symbolism inverted: "It would have been a very good thing for Costa Rica if Walker, or any other man of force, had put his foot on the neck of every republic in Central America and turned it to some account" (147).[19] While this image has received much critical attention, it does not quite do the trick for Davis either. Instead, the many-layered simile on which he finally does land is architectural at the core:

> There is no more interesting question of the present day than that of what is to be done with the world's land which is lying unimproved; whether it shall go to the great power that is willing to turn it to account, or remain with its original owner, who fails to understand its value. The Central-Americans are like a gang of semi-barbarians in a beautifully furnished house, of which they can understand neither its possibilities of comfort nor its use. They are the dogs in the manger among nations. . . . Nature has done so much that there is little left for man to do, but it will have to be some other man than a native-born Central-American who is to do it. (147–48)

Nearly as unstable as the republican governments he condemns, Davis's comparison—which imagines Central Americans as the "original owner" of an "unimproved" lot, then abruptly recasts them as ignorant squatters in a metaphorical house, before exiling them from the house of humanity itself ("They are the dogs in the manger among nations")—seems to bubble up viscerally from his torturous experience with Honduran native lodgings.[20] The domestic thrust of the simile's central comparison—"The Central-Americans are like a gang of semi-barbarians in a beautifully furnished house"—reworks a trope Amy Kaplan has identified as a common midcentury justification for U.S. national expansion: as John L. O'Sullivan's *Democratic Review* put it, "When a nation keeps a 'disorderly house,' it is the duty of neighbors to intervene."[21] Davis's exasperated outburst also seems at once to invoke and yet ignore his earlier reflections on the architectural degradations of that spoiler of nature, "civilized man" (20). After all, the natural environment that according to Davis the Central Americans have squandered through their ignorance and sloth—"great pasture-lands, wonderful forests of rare woods and fruits, treasures of silver and gold and iron, and soil rich enough to supply the world with coffee" (147–48)—sounds very much like the naturally "extravagant" surplus whose beauty, according to Davis, the native enhances and the gringo, with his architecture of zinc, despoils. And yet here Davis insists that while there "is little left for man to do," it will "have to be some other man" than a Central American "who is to do it" (148). A few more zinc roofs, one suspects Davis would say, is a small price to pay to turn a region "to account." Or better yet—imperialism done right—why not a score more of those clean and orderly bungalows from Belize?

Indeed, nowhere else in his travels through Central America will Davis find the equal of that "remarkable" Belizean buildingscape. Managua, Nicaragua's capital, cannot measure up: it is "a most dismal city, built on a plain of sun-dried earth, with houses of sun-dried earth, plazas and parks and streets of sun-dried earth, and a mantle of dust over all" (178). Nor can Panama, which "is like any other Spanish-American city of the second class" (201). Colon, "a large town of wooden houses, with a floating population of Jamaica negroes and a few Chinese" (219) on the isthmus's Caribbean shore, fails equally to impress. Only the gringos' final stop, with its clean, trim, pretty, and restful plazas, Venezuela's capital, Caracas, which Davis praises as "the Paris of South America" (221)—and on which he will model some of the features of Valencia, the capital of the fictional republic in *Soldiers of Fortune*— offers a built environment worthy of the "civilized" traveler.

A Fairy Palace on the Coast

If Davis's imagining of the physical appearance of Valencia in *Soldiers* bears the imprint of his architectural impressions of Caracas—whose principal plaza, for example, lends both its physical features and its romantic aura to Valencia's own[22]—this is nonetheless not simply more evidence for the importance of Venezuela to Davis's novel. Although Gretchen Murphy has argued persuasively that scholars have too quickly dismissed the centrality of Davis's Venezuelan sojourn, particularly Davis's commentary in *Three Gringos* on the relevance of the Monroe Doctrine to the controversial border dispute engulfing Venezuela during his visit, what is now in danger of being lost is the significance of the Central American context of *Three Gringos*, particularly for our readings of *Soldiers*. Not only had Davis undertaken his Central American journey in part to gather detail for the novel, but for a period of time after his return Davis worked on both texts simultaneously. And yet we have still not sufficiently understood the relationship between the buildingscape Davis encounters in Central America and the one he elaborates in *Soldiers*.[23]

Most of the architectural inventory of *Three Gringos* finds its way, in some form, into *Soldiers*. In many instances the structures seem transplanted directly from the travel narrative's notebooks into the novel's own pages. Zinc sheds and palm huts, for example, make up the crude lodgings of the imported U.S. laborers (300 "wild Irishmen and negroes" [130]) and the native Olanchan soldiers at work on the fictional mines, producing a visual contrast similar to the one Davis fretted over in *Three Gringos* by the harbor at Livingston. At one point in the novel Davis has Clay arrange an architectural tour of Olancho's capital city for Mr. Langham, Clay's stateside employer, and his two young daughters, recently arrived from the U.S. Led by Clay himself, this tour in effect condenses the range of structures Davis encountered in Central and South America into a single, almost evolutionary display. First to appear is a set of "mud cabins thatched with palm-leaves," recalling, right down to the "naked, little brown-bodied children" (101) crawling on the mud-brown floors, the primitive huts and "naked children" (21) Davis finds in the hills above Livingston's customhouse. The tour quickly moves on, as well as up, in building height and social class:

> From the mud cabins they came to more substantial one-story houses of adobe, with the walls painted in two distinct colors, blue, pink, or yellow, with red-tiled roofs, and the names with which they had been christened in bold black letters above the entrances. Then the carriage rattled over paved streets, and they drove between houses of two stories painted more decorously in pink and light blue, with wide-open windows, guarded by heavy bars of finely wrought iron and ornamented with scrollwork in stucco. (101–2)

Once in the heart of the city, they progress from houses to shops and cafés, "all wide open to the pavement and protected from the sun by brilliantly striped awnings" (102). The tour finally terminates at "the Government palace, which stood in an open square in the heart of the city" (105).

A building not on this tour, yet central to the narrative, is the one structure the Langhams have already claimed as their own: the "low-roofed bungalow" (97) overlooking the harbor, built expressly for the visitors by Clay, the railroad engineer MacWilliams, and Mr. Langham's young son Teddy, who has been sent to Olancho to learn the family business. This magnificent house re-creates—indeed, exponentially magnifies—the cool, clean, comfortable bungalows Davis longs for in *Three Gringos* from the moment he leaves Belize. Davis devotes a full paragraph to the account of the house's construction and the landscaping of the surrounding site:

So they cleared away the underbrush, and put a double force of men to work on what was to be the most beautiful and comfortable bungalow on the edge of the harbor. It had blue and green and white tiles on the floors, and walls of bamboo, and a red roof of curved tiles to let in the air, and dragons' heads for water-spouts, and verandas as broad as the house itself. There was an open court in the middle hung with balconies looking down upon a splashing fountain, and to decorate this *pátio*, they levied upon people for miles around for tropical plants and colored mats and awnings. They cut down the trees that hid the view of the long harbor leading from the sea into Valencia, and planted a rampart of other trees to hide the iron-ore pier, and they sodded the raw spots where the men had been building, until the place was completely transformed as though a fairy had waved her wand above it. (40–41)

There is no more important structure in *Soldiers* than this one. Dubbed "the Palms" (42) by Teddy Langham, this palatial home not only figuratively re-creates Davis's soothing memories of imperial Belize—merging that city's "cool-looking" bungalows with its harbor-view Government House—but also serves as the locus for the novel's most consequential energies and desires. Its design seems at once fantastically implausible (dragons' head spouts? a splashing fountain?) and aggressively amalgamative, combining vernacular elements borrowed, it would seem, from around the globe. Part Central American hut (by way of the curved red tiles, first mentioned in *Three Gringos*), part southwestern hacienda (via the open court *pátio*), part Asian temple (those dragon spouts), even part New England cottage (the Langhams are said to enjoy rocking quietly on its porches), this "fairy palace" (42) is imperial not just in its omnivorous stylistic appropriations but also in its commanding physical location (looming as it does over the plain zinc village of the black and brown mine workers) and even in its tributary fur-nishings, "levied" peremptorily from the local population "for miles around."

The popularization of the bungalow in early twentieth-century American culture as a quintessentially democratic architectural form, favored for its inex-pensive, unpretentious, easily constructed designs, has helped mask the ways in which this most humble of house types is thickly shadowed by an imperial past. Published just before the bungalow had fully exploded on the national scene, *Soldiers* helps recover the more complex story of global invention, appropriation, and expansion that lay behind this deceptively simple form. The word "bungalow" itself, which originated among seventeenth-century Brit-ish colonial officers in India to describe the primitive dwellings built for them from native designs, is derived from the Bengali term *bangla*, meaning a low house surrounded by galleries or porches. Over time, the English word came to denote a range of housing forms in the multiple outposts of the British Empire. Local vernacular adaptations slightly modified the bungalow's external appearance, but the basic spatial arrangements remained consistent: a single-story dwelling with a prominent horizontal roofline, a fully or partially surrounding veranda, and a central, open living room to maximize the circulation of air.[24] Ironically, despite the bungalow's debt to native forms, it quickly came to signify a place of colonialist escape rather than embrace. As architectural historian Paul Duchscherer suggests, for the British the bungalow "became associated with the concept of a retreat from the foreign ways of the native societies that populated their colonial outposts. . . . Idealized visions of pleasantly sited enclaves, such as those in the Himalayan foothills that provided seasonal relief from the scorching heat of the Indian plains, fed into a kind of escapist fantasy about bungalows that raised them beyond the level of mere cottages."[25]

Domestic iterations of this colonial form began to appear first in England, then in the U.S., in the 1870s. In addition to its associations via England with the "East," the American bungalow had more local strands of imperial ancestry as well. Historians have identified at least three regional house types that likely helped shape the inflection of the bungalow idea in the Western Hemisphere. These antecedents include seventeenth-century Spanish colonial adobe residences, with partially enclosed patios, in the U.S. Southwest; eighteenth-century French colonial dwellings with galleries and double-pitched roofs along the Mississippi River and in the Upper Midwest; and single-story, axially arranged houses with recessed porches in the Caribbean. (Davis himself may have been familiar with such forms even before his 1895 visit to Central America, having spent time in the 1880s in Cuba at La Cruz, the harborside mansion of Bethlehem Iron Company president William W. Thurston, a house that may in part have inspired the grandiosity of the harbor bungalow in *Soldiers*.)[26] By the 1880s, the increasing familiarity and appeal of the bungalow form meant that detailed construction plans drawing on these multiple influences— imperial as well as transnational—began appearing in American pattern books.[27] By the 1890s, the decade just before truly affordable versions of the bungalow would hit the market, grand American homes in the bungalow style—such as the monumental house built in 1893 by W. W. Kent for J. R. Pitcher at Grindstone Neck, Maine, pictured in Figure 20—modeled almost exactly the palatial sweep and hilltop siting Davis would conjure up in *Soldiers* for the Palms.

Figure 20. Perspective and plan of bungalow house for J. R. Pitcher at Grindstone Neck, Maine, W. W. Kent, architect, *Architecture and Building* 18.12 (25 March 1893), n.p. Courtesy Marquand Library of Art and Archaeology, Princeton University Library.

Despite its resolutely imperial connotations, Davis's central structure is urged on the reader as a democratizing space. This is the particular refrain, for example, of Clay's chief assistant, MacWilliams, who is amazed how easily he and Clay assimilate into the Langhams' social world, as though money and class do not matter on the bungalow's verandas. "Oh, I tell you, Clay," MacWilliams exults after the first night the Langhams have spent at the Palms, "we're mixing right in with the four hundred, we are! I'm substitute and understudy when anybody gets ill. We're right in our own class at last!" (94). There are limits to the leveling admired here, of course, as the Palms, staffed by dark-skinned servants, is understood within the novel's racial hierarchy to be "white" space. And yet it is on these same verandas that Clay will successfully woo Langham's tomboyish younger daughter, Hope, who is depicted, in contrast to her stately and emotionally contained sister, as unaffectedly "open" (149), unpretentious, and democratic in her enthusiasms—much like the bungalow form itself. Davis further emphasizes the democratizing energies of the Palms by contrasting it with the aristocratic trappings of the capital, whose colonial grid reinforces hierarchical gradations of wealth and poverty and whose own magisterial palace houses not the seat of power but political and physical impotence. And yet the Palms is unmistakably—and simultaneously—a space for the staging of imperial desire. After the revolutionist Mendoza finally orchestrates his long-planned military coup, for example, it is at the Palms that Clay and the other colonialists plot the reconquest of Olancho. This grand bungalow even activates imperial fantasies in Olanchans themselves. At a breakfast Clay holds as a "test" (65) of the bungalow's readiness prior to the Langhams' arrival, his guests—Olancho's most prominent planters, bankers, generals, and cabinet officers—interrupt a round of polite toasts to shout, "To President Alvarez, Dictator of Olancho!" (68), prematurely spilling Alvarez's secret plan to dissolve the presidency and turning the sedate breakfast into an "uproarious scene of wild excitement" (69). There are other imperial desires the Palms deliberately conceals. When Clay plants a screen of trees "to hide the iron-ore pier," cutting down others to create a view instead of the "long harbor leading from the sea into Valencia" (41), he conceals not merely the pier's unsightliness but its operational mission of the relentless extraction of Olancho's ore.

There are still further desires that the Palms helps fuse together. Mingled with the discourse of benevolent imperialism and particularly that of the imperial house, for example, is a profound, inward longing for a purified national "home." Clay's assistant MacWilliams—"a man who had visited almost every spot in the three Americas, except his home, in ten years" (88)—is the most prominent source for this longing. Inordinately fond of balladry, MacWilliams ends every gathering with a plaintive rendition of Felix McGlennon's popular tune "He Never Cares to Wander from His Own Fireside; Or, There's No Place Like Home, Sweet Home" (1893), which the novel depicts as the ironic lament of an American who travels the world but is never at rest. The chorus intones:

> He never cares to wander from his own fireside,
> He never cares to wander or roam.
> With his babies on his knee,
> He's as happy as can be,
> For there's no place like Home, Sweet Home. (88)

If on one level MacWilliams's nightly renditions of this chorus register as idiosyncratically personal, in a novel so preoccupied with the meanings of architecture and place the insistent invocation of a desired yet out-of-reach "Home, Sweet Home" simultaneously voices the more broadly felt nostalgia for American colonial forms that had begun to emerge at the end of the nineteenth century. As we saw in chapter 2, this nostalgia found its most emphatic expression in the architecture of the Colonial Revival, which sought a return to the supposedly purer structures of American national culture—quite literally to the colonial "home, sweet home"—as an antidote to a polyglot modernity. Although the bungalow was not technically a revivalist form, the clean lines of its simpler iterations complemented rather than challenged the revivalist agenda.[28] Not surprisingly, MacWilliams, who casually uses terms like "nigger" (94) and "half-breed" (123), also serves as the novel's mouthpiece for racial and class hierarchy, as when he jokingly refers to the Langhams (in contrast not only to South Americans but also to working-class whites like himself) as "white people" (124).

In her illuminating discussion of MacWilliams's attachment to this particular song, Murphy highlights the way in which the engineer retains his national identity even though he is physically absent from home. His enjoyment of the song, she suggests, "comes from his ability to share the veneration of domestic tradition without impractically residing in it." Murphy links this ability to the way Clay, too, can remain "quintessentially American" despite his own homelessness. (As Clay tells Hope, "I travel because I have no home. . . . I'm different from the chap that came home because all the other places were shut. I go to other places because there is no home open" [169].) Citing the scene near the end of the novel in which a U.S. Marine salutes Clay as his superior officer, even though Clay has never worn the uniform of a U.S. soldier, Murphy argues that, "in this cathartic moment, Clay's nationality is secured." And yet Murphy's subsequent conclusion that through this process "home is thus dislocated" in the novel—even "dematerialize[d]"—overlooks the ways in which the bungalow, as a physical and symbolic site, refuses to disappear in this text. Thus when Murphy notes that the Palms demonstrates "the power that a reconstructed home retains even in the jungles of South America," she is only half right. For if "Americanness and a connection to home and tradition cease to be placebound in *Soldiers of Fortune*"—that is, if they are no longer bound to the physical space of the U.S.—they nonetheless remain firmly *structure*-bound in the novel, in the form of the bungalow.[29]

By the end of the text, after defeating Mendoza, restoring the puppet republic, preserving the mining company's financial interests, and sweeping Hope off her feet (even as she, in turn, literally sweeps him off his), Clay no longer travels because he has no home but because he is suddenly at home everywhere. This is the final ironic imperial twist of *Soldiers*. Clay's success in Olancho (including his success in wooing Hope) convinces him that he no longer need serve as anyone's foreign "Resident-Director" but can instead roam the world as expert-American-at-large. Indeed, although the novel ends with Clay and Hope on board a steamer heading to New York City to get married and settle down, the last images are not of their anticipated home but of their being *at home* anywhere in the world. Rather than return Clay and Hope to some clapboard Colonial, in other words, Davis turns the steamer into a traveling bungalow, with the same terraced and open structure as the Palms itself, as the newlyweds-to-be lean against the ship's railings exactly as they had done on their Olanchan verandas. The bungalow rematerializes, as it were, under their feet. "Do you see that long line of lamps off our port bow?" Clay asks Hope as they pull into international waters. "Those are the electric lights along the ocean drive at Long Branch. . . . Over there is the coast of Africa. . . . If it wasn't for Gibraltar being in the way, I could show you the harbor lights of Bizerta, and the terraces of Algiers" (345). They plan trips to Mexico and Peru, "or wherever they want me," Clay says (346). Their motto could be "Have bungalow, will travel." Clay and Hope's newfound mobility thus signals not simply the freeing of U.S. power "from the confines of national boundaries," as Murphy suggests, but also, and more concretely, the versatility and portability—indeed *exportability*—of what would soon become the quintessential American house form.[30] For if *Soldiers* helps make visible the largely forgotten imperial origins of the bungalow, through this final image the novel simultaneously foreshadows the rapid spread of the American bungalow form not merely in the U.S. but also abroad, an emphatically material effect of the new reach of U.S. power in the late nineteenth and early twentieth centuries.

One Should Buy Postcards

By that hot July day in 1914 when Olga Beatriz Torres stepped off the ship that had taken her family from Veracruz to Texas only to find a mere "wooden shack" where she expected a more impressive port of entry, the material effects of U.S. power imaged forth in the last scene of *Soldiers* should have been in evidence almost everywhere. As historian Gwendolyn Wright observes, "By the late nineteenth century, most of the world saw America as the epitome of modernity, with architectural advances assuming a key role in this mental construction: towering skyscrapers, rationalized factories, vibrant settings for popular culture, verdant parkways and mass-produced, moderate-cost dwellings." The bungalow in particular—not J. R. Pitcher's monumental 1893 seaside home but the far more affordable versions that circulated with increasing frequency in the early 1900s—flourished like no U.S. house form before it, becoming not only the "characteristic and dominant style" during the domestic "explosion" of U.S. home building at the turn of the century but also a popular and profitable export commodity for prominent mail-order housing firms like the Aladdin Company of Bay City, Michigan.[31] The success of the mail-order bungalow, as Scott Erbe explains, had much to do with the canny exploitation by Aladdin and its competitors of the relatively simple form's capacity for standardization. Not only did manufacturers use precut lumber and such mass-produced components as millwork, windows, and lock sets—reducing their own costs as well as the final ticket price for the consumer—they created an artificially expansive inventory of styles by making minor variations in what was essentially a limited arrangement of "interchangeable, similarly sized spaces." Shrewd marketing that highlighted the mail-order bungalow's unique combination of low price, high quality, and aesthetic desirability played no small role in the national embrace of the form as well.[32]

The modernity expressed by these bungalows and the companies that produced them was full of contradictions. On the one hand, they reflected the most up-to-date American manufacturing and distribution processes, consolidating, as Erbe notes, "several decades of development in the industrialization of housing into a single, buyer-friendly package."[33] Extolling the efficiency of the company's production methods, Aladdin's house-plan catalog for 1912 boasted, "We reduce waste in everything down to less than two percent." On the other hand, these sleek, easy-to-assemble bungalows—such as the 1915 Aladdin model featured in Figure 21—were supposed to deliver just the right touch of snug comfort. "A cosy and charming home," the ad copy promises. "This particular Aladdin Bungalow has delighted many owners." Nor was this simply the age-old marketer's trick of turning "small" into "good." Other Aladdin advertisements applied the vocabulary of precious delight to much larger homes as well. Purred one 1919 ad: "That charming bungalow Home—bordered in flowers—bathed in sun-light—the one you have dreamed of can now be yours. It may be a snug and cosy cottage complete with five rooms on one floor, or a more pretentious bungalow of charming proportions."[34] In applying the latest technological and industrial expertise to the production of houses that in many ways represented an aesthetically if not ideologically "snug" retreat from the urban itself, the mail-order companies perhaps unwittingly helped affirm the mass-produced bungalow's status as, in Michael Eldridge's apt formulation, an "ironic talisman of modernity . . . representing that aspect of the modern which is historically, vestigially—perhaps schizophrenically—*anti*-modern."[35]

Figure 21. "$595 for This Complete Aladdin Bungalow," advertisement, North American Construction Company, *Independent* 84 (24 May 1915): n.p.

A related cluster of contradictions issues from the fact that mail-order bungalows were designed by experts to be assembled by amateurs. Before being released to consumers, each of the Aladdin Company's house plans was given "the acid test of perfection" by its self-dubbed "Famous Board of Seven," a group of "high-priced" "master" designers, builders, and factory technicians whose job was not just to design the perfect house but also to ensure that even the least skilled purchaser would have no difficulty putting it together (or hiring other unskilled laborers to do so). On the one hand, this agglomeration of expertise would not have been possible without the broadly successful professionalization of architecture and design in the latter half of the nineteenth century, a period that saw the founding of the first American architectural society (the American Institute of Architects), the first university architecture programs (at MIT, Cornell, and the University of Illinois), and the first professional architecture and design journals. Each of these institutions helped create and maintain modern standards of professional training, practice, and conduct embodied in Aladdin's "Famous Board of Seven." On the other hand, the mail-order house-plan firms made a point of contrasting their expertise with what they saw as the inferior methods of professional architects. Architects, the sales catalogs explain, are wasteful. "The architect, in designing a house, seldom considers the subject of cutting material to waste," the 1917 Aladdin catalog informs the reader. "He lays out the dimensions of the house, places windows, doors, etc., without any thought of how the material will cut." The unlucky consumer ends up paying for all the extra lumber the contractor will trim away to cut pieces with the dimensions specified in the architect's plans. Given that most professional architects touted the superiority of their services to potential customers by stressing how much more *personal* attention a home buyer would receive compared with ordering from a catalog, Aladdin ingeniously inverts that relationship by depicting the architect—not the catalog—as distant and out of touch. All that architects (and their evil henchmen, the contractors) appear good for in the mail-order catalogs is adding the "hundred and one little extra fittings and things that you never thought of when the estimates were made" and that cost a small fortune.[36]

The repeated appeal in the mail-order catalogs to the budget-conscious workingman brings yet another contradiction into relief: the same system that made it possible for thousands of working- and middle-class American families to buy the "cosy" single-family dwellings they had always "dreamed of" was equally well suited to the mass production of industrial housing. Look again at the advertisement in Figure 21. As the inset box headed "Tenant Houses" notes, "The Aladdin mills are especially equipped for large orders. Large corporations, mine operators and railroad companies have recognized the low cost advantages of the Aladdin System." Thus at the same moment Aladdin was helping workingmen and workingwomen attain the independence associated with owning their dream homes, it was also helping to supply low-cost, corporate-controlled housing for, in many cases, the unskilled laborers who were increasingly coming to define factory and industrial work in the U.S. at the turn of the century. That is an irony of the modern mail-order house business likely lost on the happy homeowners whose testimonials fill the pages of the Aladdin catalogs.[37]

A final irony concerns the involvement of companies like Aladdin in precisely the global expansion of U.S. architectural influence prefigured by Davis at the end of *Soldiers of Fortune*. In the early twentieth century, mail-order firms began shipping precut houses not just across the continent but also across the seas, in correlation with (and often along the routes of) the growth and reach of U.S. imperial power. Not that this process—or its connection to empire—was entirely new. According to Jeffrey W. Cody, one of the foundations for the post-1898 boom in the exportation of American architecture was the success certain firms in Boston and New York had as early as the 1860s marketing versions of slave cabins to West Indian plantations. As Cody notes, "Many of the designs for slave dwellings were for one-storey, rectilinear structures whose uncomplicated joinery made them easy to erect, probably by those very slaves who lived in them." By the mid-1870s, exporting simple houses or house plans to the West Indies was apparently routine enough that one firm advertised its patented "ready-made houses" as "particularly adapted for Camp Grounds, Seaside and Summer Resorts, Pioneer Settlements, the West Indies, etc."—a fascinating chain of locations that marks out a spectrum from (predominantly) white leisure on the one end to (predominantly) black labor on the other.[38]

As one of the most significant early twentieth-century house exporters, Aladdin sent its houses, including bungalows, in all directions. "Let Us Ship You This Complete Home," proposes a 1913 advertisement that looks as though it could serve as an illustration for Davis's novel (Fig. 22): "Distance need not deter you from owning this handsome Aladdin dwelling—for we have sent them all over the world to buyers who realize the immense savings we offer by our methods of manufacture." The concomitantly immense bungalow pictured sitting aft in the ship, as if it were to be delivered fully assembled instead of efficiently packed away in its containers, gives surprisingly concrete shape to the image Davis offers of Clay and Hope at the end of *Soldiers* leaning against their ship's railings as though on a floating bungalow, imagining themselves at home anywhere in the world. In an Aladdin house, perhaps they could be. A testimonial produced by the Curtis Publishing Company's *Saturday Evening Post*, *Ladies' Home Journal*, and *Country Gentleman* that appeared in the 1916 Aladdin catalog vouches

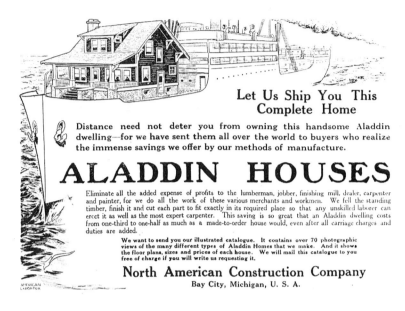

Figure 22. "Let Us Ship You This Complete Home," advertisement, North American Construction Company, *American Exporter* 73.6 (1913): 137.

for the company's international omnipresence, claiming, "Today Aladdin's houses stand in every part of the world, from Saskatchewan to the Tahiti Islands, in hot and cold climates."[39] The regions most dramatically affected by the exportation of American architecture and design in the years immediately following 1898, perhaps not surprisingly, were Central and South America. As Cody reports, not only did the work of urban planners, architects, and military engineers from the U.S. significantly alter the morphology of many cities in the Southern Hemisphere, the American variant of the bungalow "was being actively promoted and constructed" in many of the zones newly controlled, through either formal or informal imperial relationships, by the U.S.[40]

Thus when Olga Beatriz Torres arrived in Texas on that hot July day—exiled from one home, seeking another—she did so during a crucial period in the twinned histories of American architecture at home and abroad. If the bungalow style, which rose so quickly to prominence in the U.S. in the early twentieth century in large part by means of mail-order firms like Aladdin, was on the one hand helping rapidly to redefine both the American suburb *and* the American city (by what it embraced in the one and by implication left behind in the other), it was simultaneously reshaping the buildingscapes of the Greater Gulf region as well. Although we have no way of knowing, it would in fact not have been impossible for the "wooden shack" that so disappointed Torres to turn out to be one of Aladdin's (or a competitor's) most basic designs. Perfect for temporary (or pioneering) communities, the company's simplest structure—the "Aladdin Two-Room Dwelling House, Style A," which opened every Aladdin catalog from 1909 through 1913—featured exactly two eight-by-ten-foot rooms, side by side, mirroring the humble building Torres saw, with its "interior divisions which make it into a home and store at the same time." And although Luna-Lawhn appropriately translates Torres's word for that structure (*jacalón*) as "shack," in order best to convey Torres's disgust at its dirt and ugliness, the use of the term itself—which can also, less judgmentally, simply mean cabin or cottage—does not necessarily signal (as it might in English) that what she saw was a crudely or haphazardly built structure, as though someone had nailed together a random collection of boards. In fact, as we will see shortly, in other letters to her aunt Torres uses the same noun to describe urban train stations, whose architecture disappoints her but which are clearly not "shacks" in any literal sense. (In these instances, Luna-Lawhn will translate Torres's term, also appropriately, as "shed.")

Indeed, had Torres ventured only a little farther from the Texas City docks before making her judgment, she would have seen that rather than represent something run-down and inconsequential, the wooden shack could be read as a sign of bigger and better things to come, and to come quickly. "You see, child, this very recent town, these lands so ugly for you, will be within a short period of time a big city," explains the owner of the store to Torres. "Three years ago when I built this building, there were only one hundred persons; now there are eight thousand people" (47–48).[41] While waiting for the train that would take them to Houston, Torres takes a brief tour of the port city by car and is surprised to discover that it is already far more developed than she had imagined. "Asphalt streets, sprinkled with rows of houses on both sides of the street, clothing stores, bars, hotels of three and four stories, movie houses filled with people, drugstores, restaurants, cafés, and musicians could be seen," marvels Torres. "It was truly an emerging town" (48).

Texas City's rapid growth owes everything to its founders' belief that it has the potential to become a major Gulf port. "Four years ago there was nothing in this place," Torres learns from the store owner; "but a company constructed some docks and warehouses here and made it known that this place was a place with a great future, that it was a better location than New Orleans or Galveston to ship out merchandise destined for Panama from the United

States" (47).⁴² With the completion of the Panama Canal having occurred only a few months before Torres arrived in the U.S., Texas City's dream of funneling the future commercial traffic of the Gulf through its docks and warehouses—however realistic or unrealistic—was nothing to laugh at. At this moment, however, Texas City is not only a nascent commercial hub but also a military transit station. Torres notes that "thousands of soldiers who are waiting to be shipped to Mexico" (48)—to enforce the U.S. occupation of Veracruz, the Gulf port city from which she has just arrived—mill about the town. Not only is it not yet clear which U.S. cities will become dominant Gulf ports; it is not yet clear which country, the U.S. or Mexico, will control, and thus shape the future of, the Gulf itself.⁴³

Torres's text drops the reader into the middle of this volatile and uncertain moment, making *Memorias de mi viaje* a fascinating counterpoint to, and in some ways counterpart of, both the political commentary of *Three Gringos* and the imagined economies (imperial, libidinal) of *Soldiers*. Written in the shadow of U.S. imperialism rather than as a harbinger of it, traveling into the U.S. rather than out of it, Torres's text explores Davis's terrain, as it were, from the other side, not just physically but also ideologically and—because she writes after the imperial adventurism launched in 1898 rather than before it—temporally. At the same time, there are important points of contact within the personal and political orientations of these writers that should not be overlooked. As a member of a well-to-do family, for example, Torres occupies a class position more comparable to Davis's than one might at first assume. Although certain stages of Torres's journey are arduous, and at times she suffers the indignities of her refugee status (as when she is forcibly vaccinated on the train to Veracruz or when U.S. health inspectors in Texas City insist on fumigating her ship before permitting the passengers to disembark), Torres is shielded by her family's means from some of the discomforts of travel. And although Torres's actions are in part constrained by regional exertions of U.S. power, it would be too simplistic to say (as one might be tempted) that where Davis writes as an imperialist, Torres writes as an anti-imperialist. If anything, as Luna-Lawhn has suggested, Torres perhaps writes instead from the perspective of transnational acculturation, as *Memorias* records the young immigrant's gradual movement "away from a familiar culture and language and toward a foreign language and culture" (14). Indeed, Torres's ability to live in both cultures at the same time gives her more of a mobile, even transnational perspective than simply an anti-imperial one. At the same time, the fact that Davis and Torres quite literally almost crossed paths—Davis the celebrity journalist had been rushed to Veracruz in April 1914 by the *New York Tribune* a few days after his fiftieth birthday to report from the invasion zone; was then arrested on his way to Mexico City for an exclusive interview with Victoriano Huerta, the Mexican president; and only finally left the country, from Veracruz, in June, just before Torres and her family fled for the coast—suggests the extent to which the experiences and reflections of *Memorias* may be said provocatively to overlap with the passions and interests of the far better known author. (Whether Torres was familiar with any of Davis's work is an open question.)[44] One of these shared interests turns out to be the practice and politics of architecture, imperial and otherwise.

Like Davis, Torres is an acute observer of the built environment. Not only does she refer to specific structures in almost every letter (at one point devoting an entire letter to the "Other Buildings" of Houston); she frequently stops to provide architectural commentary, beginning in Mexico City. "Train stations all identical," she complains to her aunt in her very first letter. "Large, poorly constructed wooden sheds, others of stone, but always of the same architectural design—angular and unattractive" (28). Torres is also well aware of the symbolic power buildings can have. Just before they reach Veracruz, for example, she and her family are treated to "frightening accounts" (31)[45] of the American invasion of the city by some lemonade vendors. The most dramatic of these accounts focuses on the shelling by U.S. forces, months earlier, of the Veracruz Naval Academy, an important public building along the waterfront. "They spoke of battleships shooting grenades at buildings, especially at the marine school which was eventually destroyed," Torres writes; "they recounted the incident with such frenzy thus producing a sensation of horror and hate against the assailants" (31).[46] Although Torres is indeed frightened by this story—"I was tempted to ask that we return to Mexico" (31)—she does not share the same intensity of hate that the building's loss generates in others. Later, in Veracruz, she visits the academy to see the destruction for herself and to take her own measure of the building's symbolism. "As I contemplated the windows broken by the battleship cannon balls," she tells her aunt, "the windows seemed to me to make a horrible gesture of anger: less against the invaders and more for the citizens who with their excesses submit their nation to such trials and tribulations" (34).[47] This is mature commentary from a child of thirteen, who though strongly influenced by her father's opinions on most political matters diverges here from his own bitter antipathy to the American forces. "It is sad that tyranny has obliged me to seek sanctuary among these men," he had told Torres "emotionally" when they first encounter U.S. soldiers (31).[48] But Torres has to see, and to judge, for herself.

By this I do not mean to suggest Torres is an apologist for U.S. power. Far from it. Her angry reaction to the forced vaccinations and the fumigation of their ship makes clear Torres's resentment, for example, of imperial anxieties about the vulnerability of port cities to contagion and contamination.[49] What I do wish to highlight is the earnestness with which Torres reads and interprets her surroundings, particularly the built environment. She even has her own method for doing so. As she explains to her aunt:

> I will tell you what is the most practical way of getting to know American cities, and, in general, those of other places. Even in Mexican cities, it has produced good results. As soon as one arrives at a place, one should buy postcards of the city that one is visiting because with these postcards one can quickly get an idea of the most important or the most picturesque buildings of the city. At once, one takes a carriage or an automobile (only automobiles are available here), and one tells the coachman or the chauffeur, as the case may be, that one wishes to see what is reproduced on the postcards. (61)[50]

There are potential limitations to this method, to be sure. It risks yielding to others (city boosters, say) the judgment of what counts as "most important" or "most picturesque" if one is limited to the buildings that commonly appear on postcards. It also risks superficiality, if the actual tours are as breezy as they sound in this passage. And yet Torres proves herself no casual tourist but instead a nascent architectural critic with clear aesthetic and ideological criteria of her own. This does not prevent her from making poor judgments, as we will see. But it does make the project of *Memorias* in part the shaping not only of a new cultural epistemology (as Torres gradually becomes familiar with, and adapts to, a new environment in a new country), but also of what we might call an architectural epistemology—by which I mean not simply what Torres knows *about* architecture but also what she learns, and what ideas she comes to express, *through* architecture.[51] And much as we saw with Davis, this knowledge, in at least one crucial instance, will founder on the intensely structural conundrum of racial difference.

Torres's postcard epistemologies also shape her own writing. As she adopts the method just described—purchase postcards; arrange tour to see what is pictured on the postcards; write letter about what she sees to her aunt—her own letters will reproduce, in a sense, the perspectival view of the postcards themselves. What they show, she visits; what she sees, she writes about. Even the way in which (as we shall see shortly) Torres incorporates English words into her letters—most often by transcribing English terms for the sites she visits—may be said to reproduce the topography of the postcard's architectural landscape, as those words effectively stand out like the buildings on the cards themselves. And although a letter is not quite the same as a postcard, a series of letters that chronicle a period of travel as it is taking place, like Torres's dispatches to her aunt, share with the postcard a tendency toward impressionistic reportage over retrospective narrative reflection, even though Torres certainly has a good sense of how to tell a story—how to keep her aunt interested, presumably, in what dispatch might come next. In this respect Torres's method is not unlike Davis's in *Three Gringos*, whose chapters not only first appeared individually in *Harper's* before being published in a single volume, but which also found their earliest expression in letters Davis wrote home to his family during his trip.[52]

Alegres Casitas

Though drawn to "important" structures, Torres is rarely impressed by them. During her first days in Houston, for example, her family's next stop after Texas City, Torres is alternately threatened and bored by the major commercial and public buildings of the region's largest city. Standing outside the imposing, seventeen-story Rice Hotel, looking up and down the street, Torres remarks: "All around, on all four sides, other buildings were under construction, not as tall as the **Rice Hotel**, but still of eight, ten, and twelve floors; consequently, my first impression was that I was in an enormous tomb, whose four walls were lost in space" (52).[53] Torres's first tour of the city does little to raise her spirits. Though the marble interior of the First National Bank makes it appear "truly elegant," it is the exception rather than the rule. "I will tell you this," Torres complains to her aunt: "almost all the buildings are made of monotonous architecture. They are gigantic square masses sprinkled with rectangular windows that make me think of gigantic pigeon houses, without art or beauty of any kind" (53).[54] Torres finds religious architecture in the U.S., for the most part, no more appealing. Although she admires the "stone construction" and "beautiful four story tower" of the Houston Presbyterian Church, the other houses of worship she sees fall far short of this standard. "Here Catholic churches are few, because most churches are Protestant," she explains. "The few that do exist are ugly; they look like rooms that are missing art pieces, even the paintings of the saints are not very good; at least, this is true in the few churches I have seen around here" (70).[55]

There is more than a little cultural chauvinism in these judgments. Torres not infrequently compares what she finds in the U.S. to that with which she is familiar in Mexico, architecturally and otherwise, usually to find the American version lacking. Having grown up in a suburb of Mexico City, however, Torres might be forgiven a certain measure of partisanship when it comes to architecture. Although in 1910 Houston was a city on the rise, with a population around 78,000, Mexico City had nearly ten times that many people, as well as a far more extensive and significant architectural infrastructure—as might be expected for a city founded in the 1300s rather than the 1800s. At the turn of the twentieth century, moreover, Mexican president Porfirio Díaz (when he was not paying the Robert Clays of the world to expand the national rail system) had spent heavily on new architectural and boulevard projects for the capital city. Diaz's aesthetic preferences tended toward "neoromantic and neo-Gothic designs," making Mexico City in 1910, at least for families of privilege such as Torres's, a "landscape of opulence."[56] These details may help explain not only Torres's general chauvinism but also her specific preference, for example, for the Venetian Gothicism of the Mexico City post office over the Beaux-Arts neoclassicism of its Houston counterpart. "The Post Office building," she explains to her aunt, "is a structure that occupies, with the garden that surrounds it, one block, but it is not as nice, beautiful nor as elegant as our General Post Office in Mexico" (53).[57] Indeed, when Torres complains about the monotony of American architecture, it is the increasing dominance of the Beaux-Arts style in U.S. cities, particularly for monumental government buildings and public squares, to which she objects.[58] Torres is far more attracted to a structure like Houston's City Hall (Fig. 23), whose Richardsonian Romanesque idiosyncrasies, such as its "two four-story towers" and its "circular balconies of stone," make it, for her, one of "the beautiful buildings" in the city (70).[59]

Although Torres does not actually use such classificatory terms as "Beaux-Arts" or "Richardsonian Romanesque," she does use specific architectural terminology (and gives their English equivalents where possible). In less technical language she also registers a strong preference for variety over monotony, bright colors over drab, and (in terms she does use frequently) "beauty" over "ugliness." These judgments extend not merely to public or parochial buildings but also to houses and their settings. The typical housing stock of Houston does not impress Torres at all. "Americans are not concerned with architectural beauty," she laments. "This explains why with a few variations, all homes are the same hovels covered with uniform wooden tiles (**shingles**), square windows, and, in the front, they have some *porticos*, or

Figure 23. "City Hall and Market House, Houston, Tex.," postcard (ca. 1915).

verandas that here are called **Porchs**, and with the exception of the color, they are all the same. They all possess the same architectural design" (70–71). As Luna-Lawhn notes, Torres's increasingly frequent incorporation of English words into her letters serves as a gauge of her transculturalization; yet it is striking how many of these words are architectural in nature—as though she is learning to speak English primarily through the built environment, making "reading" architecture for Torres more than mere metaphor.[60]

Torres is far more impressed by Houston's picturesque upper-class residential neighborhoods than by its more ordinary houses. Waving away the economic constraints that might shape architectural and aesthetic decisions— indeed, that might give a homeowner only the very smallest say in the exterior design of his or her house (although perhaps Torres's targets here are the builders, not the inhabitants)—Torres gushes over the homes of the well-to-do. "Between the asphalt streets and the sidewalks are English grass meadows," Torres informs her aunt, "an endless grove that provides shade to pedestrians and gives the whole street a sense of beauty." This is one instance in which the U.S., not Mexico, comes out ahead. "The houses are surrounded by plants and grass," continues Torres. "You can visualize it better if you know that here it is not customary to have one house touch the other, side by side like in Mexico, so that each one is an isolated building and the garden in the front yard extends into the space between the buildings" (53).[61] The detached single-family dwelling, that staple of American individualism, strikes Torres as a marvelous innovation—at least as she finds it in this neighborhood.

Equally wonderful is the somewhat more modest yet comparatively novel house form she first sees in Galveston: the bungalow. Far humbler than the fantasy version imagined by Davis in *Soldiers* via the Palms, and bearing fewer overt trappings of empire than the clean and orderly specimens Davis had admired in Belize, Galveston's bungalows exude for Torres a kind of natural warmth and joy. "On one side of the highway," Torres observes, "extends the city with its happy, little houses which around here are called 'bungalows' and are decorated with plants and flowers. On the opposite side of the highway is the Gulf of Mexico whose final waves, converted into foam about fifty meters away from the highway, die out" (62).[62] Though these seaside homes are not ornate, neither are they the emotionless "pigeon houses" Torres finds so objectionable in U.S. public architecture. The Galveston bungalows are not just attractive, they are "happy" little houses—"alegres casitas" (119)—and their palpable joy introduces one of the most delightful moments Torres describes in the entire narrative:

> The scene is exquisite. Imagine, Tía, swimmers holding on and being supported by cables against the thrust of the waves; others grabbed by those holding on as the waves push them to shore and are thrown down on the sand; still others are stretched out on the beach.
> Here and there, groups of children suddenly disappear in the waves and then reappear dripping water when the waves break. And all around, there is endless cheer, laughter, and happiness. (63)[63]

Attuned to the visual pleasure and comfortable setting of this house form, which Torres appears to recognize as a regional type, rather than a unique invention of the U.S.—"which *around here* are called 'bungalows'" (62; my emphasis), she explains to her aunt—Torres will later make a point of noting other neighborhoods where bungalows appear. One such neighborhood is Houston Heights, an upscale streetcar suburb about four miles north of downtown Houston. Notes Torres, "The most modern homes of Houston are built here; some stand out because of the novelty of the common '**bungalow**' style of architecture." The bungalows of the Heights are further enhanced by the neighborhood's comfortable microclimate: "This place, . . . in addition to the garden which is beautiful, has the added attraction of the cool breeze that is always present since it is situated in the highest elevation of the city and a fairly high esplanade; the breeze kept the bothersome heat of the city away" (71).[64]

No advertising brochure or bungalow magazine from the period could have expressed Torres's enthusiasm for this form more vividly. Torres admires in the bungalow the same elements of freshness, simplicity, and natural comfort so vigorously heralded and marketed to potential homeowners both in the U.S. and outside of it as key aspects of what Gustav Stickley in 1907 called the bungalow's "spirit of individuality and freedom."[65] It is in fact quite likely that many of the actual bungalows Torres sees, while drawing for inspiration on the blend of regional building practices that helped give rise to the form itself, were built from specific designs found in such widely circulating U.S. mail-order house-plan magazines and catalogs as Stickley's *Craftsman* and Henry L. Wilson's *Bungalow Book*, which Martha Culbertson has identified as two important sources for bungalow construction in South Texas, including the Houston suburbs, in the early twentieth century.[66] Indeed, part of what Torres may find so appealing about the bungalow is not simply its individuality but its mobility. For, like Torres herself, the bungalow is a form that both travels and resides, in the process adapting itself to different environments. Torres's appreciation of the transnational dimension of the bungalow may thus help mark her own increasing comfort with the mobility that has been forced upon her and her family. If so, then the "exquisite" scene at the bungalow-dotted Galveston waterfront, with its joyous evocation of the back-and-forth movement of the waves and particularly the way the swimmers temporarily disappear, then reappear, like survivors of both a literal and a metaphorical flux, becomes for *Memorias* more than just an interlude of pleasant relaxation. Instead, it stands as a critical moment of spatial and architectural self-identification.

Yet as we saw with Davis in *Soldiers of Fortune*, even the transnational bungalow seems almost always shadowed by imperial designs. To Torres's dismay, the beautiful seascape of Galveston turns out to be pockmarked with traces of the intense U.S. military presence in the Gulf during the standoff with Mexico. At the end of the highway, beyond the happy, laughing children in the water, Torres somberly discovers "a military camp with its typical yellow tents; farther on, hidden between artificial hills that covered the green pasture, were some enormous cannons ready to defend the city." Later, on her way back to the city, she sees masses of debris alongside the road, "piles of sticks and the remains of tents in complete disarray, as if the sea had destroyed a big ranch house, and piled here and there the remainder of the house"—only to be told that the debris came from "an encampment of soldiers who were sent to Veracruz" (63).[67] She lets this information fall without comment, then abruptly ends the letter—one of the few in *Memo-*

rias to close this way—as though to reflect silently on this sober reminder of the U.S. military in the field, at once protecting but perhaps also destroying (at least metaphorically) those "happy, little houses."[68] We need only recall the comfort Davis takes in Panama in the knowledge that "one of our White Squadron [was] rolling at anchor in the harbor" (216) to register how differently Torres responds to the specter of a militarized coast in the Gulf.

Dirty Houses

One irony of Torres's postcard method for touring (and narrating) cities is that the longer she stays in a given place, the more likely it becomes she will run out of things to see. Or conversely—as turns out to be the case for Torres in Houston—the more likely she will see sites that do not typically appear on postcards. "The last days we spent in Houston," Torres writes, "we spent them getting to know the inner city, which in reality is a large and beautiful city" (67). It is in this letter that Torres sketches for her aunt Houston's place in the thriving regional circuit of Gulf cities, the way it stands in "continuous contact" with New Orleans, Galveston, and Texas City through their intricate network of train routes. She also puts her finger on the source of Houston's rise to regional prominence: "If to this is added the fact that Houston is the hub of cotton transactions, the secret for its development and wealth will be revealed" (67).[69] The network of associations called up by this fact leads Torres next to mention Houston's cotton fields and their African American workers, and then—at far greater length—to tell her aunt about the neighborhood where much of Houston's black population lives:

> With respect to Negroes—one morning we went through the center of the ghetto where colored people, as they are referred to here, live, and I was horrified. One can hardly imagine worse filth; dirty houses, broken wire fences, amidst dirty yards together with pigs and horses, little black children of all ages are seen lying on animal excrement like gigantic flies coming out of the garbage. (67)[70]

The contrast to the tree-lined streets of Houston's upper-class neighborhoods could not be more pronounced. Instead of plants and grass, the "dirty houses"—"casas sucias" (124)—in this section of town are surrounded by filth and excrement. After this initial description one could imagine Torres's horror turning to indignation. How could the city provide such subpar—indeed, subhuman—conditions for any part of its population? In describing black cotton workers in the previous paragraph, Torres had indeed seemed sympathetic to their exploitation, calling them the "men and women who for centuries have been used to harvest the fiber" (67).[71] But by "used" ("se ocupan") Torres appears to mean something closer to "utilized" than to "exploited"; for instead of holding the city culpable, in the next sentence she faults the neighborhood's residents for their contribution to the filth. "In several doors or in several windows or on the sidewalks, big ugly dirty Negro women stand smoking pipes which emit more smoke than a locomotive engine" (67).[72] Torres's metaphorical excess at the end of this sentence is of a piece with the descriptive surplus of the first half, in which the women are not merely "big ugly dirty" (Luna-Lawhn's translation of *cochinos*, which means "filthy" and is related to the word for "pig" or "sow"), but are everywhere at once—"in several doors or in several windows or on the sidewalks"—as though exceeding their architectural boundaries. For Torres not only is there no beauty here, there is no sense of marked-out, or even human, space.[73]

Later in this same letter Torres makes clear she understands the role of segregation in the creation of separate black environments. She notes that white customs forbidding public contact with blacks have "obligated them to have their own theaters, bars, hotels, casinos, and even neighborhoods which I have described above" (68).[74] At other times Torres appears genuinely to empathize with the plight of African Americans. She informs her aunt, for example, that although American blacks are "a hard working and untiring people," increased competition from Mexican immigrants has begun to displace black workers from various jobs. Torres further notes that these Mexican immigrants, including her own family—and very much unlike blacks—"have access to all public places; that is to say, they have the same rights as whites" (68).[75] She even concludes the letter by writing, "Unfortunate Negroes, they carry their blackness even in their luck" (69). And yet Torres seems ultimately to blame the horrifying conditions of African Americans not on the architecture of segregation but on the architecture of the self. In the middle of the letter, in a visceral explosion all too reminiscent of Davis's frustrated claim in *Three Gringos* that Central Americans "are like a gang of semi-barbarians in a beautifully furnished house," Torres similarly insists: "These people are so ugly and dirty that Americans are right to segregate them from all white public places" (68).[76] This condemnation is simultaneously racial and architectural. "Ugly," after all, is Torres's most consistently derogatory description of the buildings she cannot stand. Very much like Davis, in other words, Torres in the end confronts and condemns—"condemns" in both the human and the architectural sense: to disapprove and to *declare unfit*—the American "others" whom she cannot imagine inhabiting (her) civilized space.

The deep consonance of Torres's condemnation of African Americans and the spaces they inhabit with Davis's angry dismissal of Central Americans as "semi-barbarians in a beautifully furnished house" suggests that the transnational (or transcultural) perspective may not always be structurally distinct from the imperial one, particularly when race enters the picture. If, as Luna-Lawhn argues, one measure of the success of Torres's transculturalization is her ability at the end of her memoir—literally in the last letter—to translate for her aunt the "interlingual" (23) Spanish-English dialect of the Chicana maid who works for Torres's family in El Paso, then this distressing scene in Houston is surely another, if in a more negative sense than Luna-Lawhn describes. Indeed, Torres does more than simply translate U.S. racism for her aunt (who, as Luna-Lawhn points out, is likely already familiar with upper-class Mexican prejudice against indigenous Indians). Instead, Torres uses her own experiential "knowledge" ("These people are so ugly and dirty") to endorse discriminatory U.S. practices ("Americans are right to segregate them from all white public places"). And just as Davis expels Central Americans from the house of civilization by figuring them as "dogs in the manger among nations," Torres—despite her moments of sympathy for blacks—casts them as "flies" and "pigs" before effectively casting them out of the category "American" itself.

Bird's-Eye-View

The closing chapters of *Memorias* shift ground from Houston and the Texas Gulf Coast to the inland border city of El Paso. Directly across the Rio Grande from Mexico, and home to a prominent community of generally well-to-do Mexican exiles who called themselves El México de Afuera ("those living outside Mexico"), El Paso offers Torres's family a congenial place to settle until they can return to Mexico City. In her reading of these chapters, Luna-Lawhn emphasizes the ways they demonstrate the success of Torres's linguistic transculturalization. Noting that Torres spends a good deal of one of her last letters literally decoding for her aunt the *mexicano* dialect of her family's new Chicana housekeeper, Luna-Lawhn argues that Torres has become not just "a translator of the language of the border people" but also, "in essence, a translator of border culture." Although Luna-Lawhn is right to suggest that Torres's fascination and facility with her housekeeper's interlingual dialect indicates the difficulty of maintaining anything like a "pure" Mexican culture in the U.S., despite the insistence by members of El México de Afuera that this is precisely what they would do, there is evidence that Torres's understanding of "border culture" is far more limited than this example might indicate. For while it is true that Torres becomes a translator of language, she appears to understand little else about the life of her housekeeper. Part of this lack of understanding may have to do with Torres's age, but the greater part seems to stem from her class position and, in a related sense, from the spatial position of her family's new home. In this respect, Torres's response to her housekeeper seems quite similar to, rather than different from, her response to Houston's black "ghetto."

Torres's letters suggest that her family settles in the neighborhood of Sunset Heights, the part of the city in which many wealthy Mexican exiles lived, and which, according to Torres, featured "undoubtedly, some of the most beautiful homes of the city." (Although she does not specify the house types, this was, not surprisingly, a neighborhood known for its bungalows.)[77] As its name hints, Sunset Heights is an elevated suburb, reached "through a street that was sloping" (80) in the hills above the river. Torres even calls the chapter in which she describes her first visit to this part of town "A Bird's Eye View" (78),[78] in part because one can look out over the houses to the river below and even across into Mexico itself. But it is also, metaphorically speaking, a "bird's-eye-view" that Torres creates of Carlota, her Chicana housekeeper—a distant observation rather than a close one—especially if we consider more than the mere words Carlota speaks. For if we attend to the content of the lengthy explanation Carlota gives for arriving late to work rather than just the vocabulary, as in Torres's letter to her aunt, then we can recognize precisely what Torres fails to see—or at least what she has not yet learned to recognize.

This is the explanation Carlota gives:

"Yesterday, I was coming from the *Esmelda*, and I asked in the *carro* for a *trance* to go to the *dipo* where I had been told there was a *marqueta*, and I needed to buy some *mechas* and see if there was an inexpensive heater, for which I had enough wood in the *yardita*, but when I was about to arrive, the *traque* broke and I had to wait, so I went to the home of the López family of Chihuahua. The *babis* had torn opened [*sic*] a package of *espauda*, the kind that is used in *bisquetes*. The lady asked me to lend her a *daime* to buy another one, and since I didn't have any other except that one, I had to walk and I became sick. That's why I am late." (83)[79]

In her letter to her aunt, Torres asks, "Did you understand? You didn't, did you?" (83) and then provides definitions for each of the italicized words. At the end of the letter—which also marks the end of *Memorias*—Torres writes: "Now with these explanations, you should be able to translate the incomprehensible Spanish of Carlota" (84).[80] But what Torres's aunt might need more help to understand is the way this passage highlights the spatial segregation of El Paso. From Carlota's explanation, it seems likely that she lives far from Sunset Heights, presumably (given her class status) in one of the city's poorer Mexican barrios, such as East El Paso, located near the railroad yards, or perhaps South El Paso (Chihuahuita), just over the river from Cuidad Juárez and the densest of the barrios. She could also live in the barrio near the American Smelting and Refining Company, since she begins by saying that she was "coming from the *Esmelda*," or, as Torres translates this, the "neighborhood where the **Smelter** is located" (83),[81] although from the context it seems as though she describes leaving that neighborhood not to come to work at the Torres house (since this is the day before) but instead to go home, perhaps after a day's work at the smelter itself. The rest of Carlota's explanation—which includes multiple streetcar transfers, temporary refuge in someone else's home when she is stranded by a broken train, the donation of her last ten cents, and finally a long walk home during which she becomes sick, making her late for work at the Torres's the following day—touches concretely on the segregated physical and social landscape of El Paso, not to mention the gendered specificity (and spatiality) of the work of a domestic laborer. (It is typically working-class women, after all, who must travel from their homes to their employers' homes for their jobs.)

All these details Torres overlooks, both literally and figuratively. She overlooks them literally in the same sense that the panoramic photograph in Figure 24 does. Taken from Sunset Heights about the time Torres arrived there, this photograph looks out over El Paso and across the river, toward Cuidad Juárez and greater Mexico. Barely visible in the middle distance, left of center, just before the river, is the Chihuahuita barrio of El Paso, Carlota's likely neighborhood. Someone who takes in this view, without also visiting Chihuahuita, will miss all the details Carlota's explanation makes vivid. This is, after all, very much the nature of the bird's-eye view genre, which portrays cities "as if seen from an imaginary viewpoint high in the air," showing "every building, street, and open space of the urban community as well as the immediate surroundings."[82] One typically cannot make out those smaller details, however, unless one gets up close to the image. But Torres seems to prefer the more distant view. She also overlooks these details metaphori-

Figure 24. Panoramic view of El Paso from Sunset Heights looking toward Juarez, ca. 1910–20. Courtesy of the El Paso Public Library, Otis A. Aultman Photo Collection, Photograph A5058.

cally, in the sense that she simply does not notice Carlota's difficulties; they mean nothing to her, at least in this letter, other than a source of transcultural humor. This is not to say that Torres's perspective from Sunset Heights does not carry a measure of spatial and political awareness. She does register, in quiet parenthesis, the loss this landscape represents for the Mexican viewer: "The land has been taken away from the river (and, in passing, from us Mexicans) so the city has extended its building onto the mountains and the nearby hills" (80).[83] But in the end, like the panoramic photographer, she is more interested in the buildings in the hills than she is in the structures of the lives in the barrios that she literally and figuratively overlooks. Out of postcards, as it were—as had been the case in the Houston ghetto—Torres is left to shape her own narrative frames.

In this respect, if Torres's explosion in Houston mirrors Davis's outburst in *Three Gringos*, then the "bird's-eye-view" at the end of *Memorias* comes to look something not unlike the scene at the end of *Soldiers of Fortune*, in which Clay and Hope peer out over the guardrail of their ship/mobile bungalow, imagining they can see all the way to New York and Africa. If Torres's view does not quite have the proprietary—or should we say imperial—sweep of the one Davis imagines in *Soldiers*, it nonetheless situates Torres as a figure apart from, rather than acculturated within, the neighborhoods she surveys. And yet El Paso's poorer turn-of-the-century barrios condemned their residents to the same slum conditions Torres had blamed on blacks in Houston: "overcrowded homes with little or no sanitation, high infant mortality rates, many cases of tuberculosis and other diseases, and the highest crime rate in the city."[84] One wonders if a visit would have "horrified" Torres or politicized her. One's answer may depend on whether, in the end, Torres strikes us as Davis's antagonist or his uncanny double.

Stop at the Next Shack

For all the imperial posturing of *Soldiers of Fortune*, there is one episode near the end of the novel that takes a surprisingly empathetic view of a racialized architectural scene. In the middle of the night on the day Olancho's president is slain and the republic temporarily overtaken by military insurrection, after hours of exhausting effort delivering the president's wife to safety and escaping an ambush that nearly claims their lives, Clay, MacWilliams, Teddy Langham, and Hope travel by carriage on a slow ride along deserted roads back to the Palms. Overcome by hunger, Langham and MacWilliams ask Clay to drive faster so that they can find something to eat. Or, more precisely, so that they can get someone to feed them. "'Do you know we haven't had anything to eat since yesterday at breakfast?' asked Langham. 'MacWilliams and I are fainting. We move that we stop at the next shack we come to, and waken the people up and make them give us some supper'" (298).

When they finally reach a mud hut, MacWilliams takes charge, "beating and kicking at the door" and initiating a "long debate in Spanish" (300) with the native occupants, who finally consent to make the Americans some food. As Hope and Clay look on from the carriage, a surprisingly peaceful scene unfolds:

> A few minutes later a man and woman came out of the hut, shivering and yawning, and made a fire in the sun-baked oven at the side of the house. Hope and Clay . . . watched the flames springing up from the oily fagots, and the boys [Langham and MacWilliams] moving about with flaring torches of pine, pulling down bundles of fodder for the horses from the roof of the kitchen, while two sleepy girls disappeared toward a mountain stream, one carrying a jar on her shoulder, and the other lighting the way

with a torch. Hope sat with her chin on her hand, watching the black fig-ures passing between them and the fire, and standing above it with its light on their faces, shading their eyes from the heat with one hand, and stirring something in a smoking caldron with the other. Hope felt an overflow-ing sense of gratitude to these simple strangers for the trouble they were taking. She felt how good everyone was, and how wonderfully kind and generous was the world that she lived in. (300–301)

This midnight idyll is about the last thing one would expect from the author of *Three Gringos*. In that travelogue, as we have seen, mud huts are an afflic-tion, not a comfort, and their native inhabitants, while sufficiently willing to share, are never described as the "kind and generous" people they appear to be here—doubly surprising perhaps given the way MacWilliams bullies them into providing supper. The filter that Hope provides is surely important; hav-ing barely an hour earlier realized that she is in love with Clay—who returns her affection—her own view could not be rosier. The disgruntled MacWil-liams is by no means impressed with their hosts, for example, but his view is not the one that counts. After they have been fed, Hope insists that Clay and Langham give her all their money, which she in turns pours into the hands of the "uncomprehending" women. Sighs Hope as they depart: "The world is full of such kind and gentle souls" (305).

As surprising as this moment is, however, we should not be too quick to propose it as a sign of cross-racial empathy engendered by the humble buildingscape (and gentle peasants) of rural Olancho. For the scene remains entirely susceptible to an imperial reading quite consonant with the broader socio-spatial reckonings of both *Soldiers* and *Three Gringos*—and, for that matter, parts of *Memorias*. While the appreciation Hope expresses may seem in tension with the racial hierarchies Davis elsewhere bolsters, in the end it remains entirely safe, a romantic racialism that elevates the "souls" of the natives while preserving both the racial and the spatial distinctions that the novel's imperialism demands. The hospitality of the natives does nothing to interrupt the imperial plot of *Soldiers*; if anything, it helps to sustain it. In the context of the novel, then, the midnight idyll serves more as a representation of the kind of service a subordinate population might provide their superiors than as a challenge to the text's larger structural relationships.[85]

And it is in this sense, once again, that we find common ground—how-ever unexpectedly—between the Gulf writings of Davis and the travel mem-oir of Torres. Although, as we have seen, Torres is critical of the U.S. impe-rialism that makes her a subordinated subject even in her own country (as when she is forcibly vaccinated on the train from Mexico City to Veracruz) and that shadows the beautiful seascape of Galveston, with its "happy little" bungalows, her responses to the racially segregated neighborhoods of Houston and El Paso—visceral recoil, in the first case; unseeing indifference in the second—may be said to mirror the hierarchical blueprints of race, place, and power Davis so forcefully composes in *Three Gringos* and *Soldiers*. In the end, this unlikely pair thus also helps give us a fuller picture of the complex imbrications of race and architecture in the wider Gulf region at the turn of the last century. In the following chapter, yet another unlikely pair will help us trace the material and representational crossings of a very different form of architectural racialization that nonetheless emerges from its own imperial context.

4

Keyless Rooms

Frank Lloyd Wright and Charlie Chan

> Bring the outside of the world into the house, and let the inside
> of the house go outside.
> —Frank Lloyd Wright, "Building the New House" (1943)

Late in the first of Earl Derr Biggers's six Charlie Chan novels, *The House without a Key* (1925), the narrative visits, for the first time, the Chinese Hawaiian detective's home. Chan, we learn, lives in a modest bungalow "that clung precariously to the side of Punchbowl Hill." From his front gate a visitor—in this instance John Quincy Winterslip, a proper young Bostonian who is helping Chan solve the murder of his cousin Dan Winterslip, and who has hastened after hours to present the detective with a fresh clue—can see the "great gorgeous garden" of downtown Honolulu illuminated below. Turning to enter the house, however, John Quincy encounters increasingly dark spaces. Just beyond the gate lies a walkway in "the shadow of the palm trees." Inside the house are more shadows still, accentuated for John Quincy by the dark habiliments and friendly but distant demeanor of his host. "A Chinese woman—a servant, she seemed—ushered him into Chan's dimly-lit living-room. The detective . . . rose with dignity when he saw his visitor. In this, his hour of ease, he wore a long loose robe of dark purple silk, which fitted closely at the neck and had wide sleeves. Beneath it showed wide trousers of the same material, and on his feet were shoes of silk, with thick felt soles." The narrator reflects: "He was all Oriental now, suave and ingratiating but remote, and for the first time John Quincy was really conscious of the great gulf across which he and Chan shook hands."[1] John Quincy's sense of this "gulf" abates as they discuss the case, only to return a short while later when Chan leaves the room. After observing a New Year's scroll on one wall and a picture painted on silk on another, John Quincy slowly takes inventory of the rest of Chan's "Oriental" objects:

Beneath the picture stood a square table, flanked by straight, low-backed armchairs. On other elaborately carved teakwood stands distributed about the room were blue and white vases, porcelain wine jars, dwarfed trees. Pale golden lanterns hung from the ceiling; a soft-toned rug lay on the floor. John Quincy felt again the gulf between himself and Charlie Chan. (245–46)

If this gulf does not quite connote fear, the combination of Chan's dimly lit house and what we might call John Quincy's material essentialism nonetheless gestures toward the foreboding "Oriental" spaces of much late nineteenth- and early twentieth-century "yellow peril" writing. In these stories of Asian threat, which William Wu has identified as "the overwhelmingly dominant theme in American fiction about Chinese Americans" from the 1850s through the 1940s,[2] menacing structures and claustrophobic interiors—often filled with stereotypically Asian décor—are as essential to the genre as sinister villains. And yet as Biggers himself maintained, he created Chan as an alternative to this insidious pattern of representation. If "sinister and wicked Chinese were old stuff in mystery stories," as Biggers told a *New York Times* interviewer in 1931,[3] so too by that time were darkly ominous "Oriental" rooms. By the mid-1920s many readers of *The House without a Key* were perhaps more likely to see in Chan's living room images of cosmopolitan desire than of alien terror. As Kristin Hoganson has shown, by the early twentieth century not only had "foreignness" in household decoration come to seem, for many, "desirable as an end in itself," but Orientalist goods quickly became the most popular imports gracing the newly furnished sitting rooms of scores of middle- and upper-class white households, helping to create a kind of "consumers' imperium." These households had their tastes simultaneously served and shaped by import companies that sold most (if not all) of the items Biggers places in Chan's house. Indeed, when Sandra Hawley, in her analysis of the depiction of Chan's cultural identity in the novel, offhandedly suggests that Biggers presents the detective in an "almost gift-shop Chinese setting," she is even more right than this casual metaphor might suggest.[4]

Closely related to the turn-of-the-century fascination with "Oriental" decorative goods was a contemporaneous effort by American architects to incorporate principles of Asian building design into the theory and construction of American dwellings. Although "Oriental" building motifs may be found in the very earliest American pattern books, architectural historians mark the installation of Japanese buildings first at the 1876 Philadelphia Centennial Exposition and then at the 1893 Chicago World's Fair as catalytic events in the growing influence of Asian architectural design in the U.S. Among American architects, Frank Lloyd Wright—whose exposure to and interest in Asian forms shaped his design aesthetic throughout his career—was only the most prominent figure to make the horizontal lines, open floor plan, and integration of built forms with their natural settings common to Japanese domestic architecture dominant elements of his own groundbreaking house plans.

Although the middle-class embrace of "Oriental" goods (which often tilted toward sumptuous profusion) and the dissemination of Japanese architectural principles (which typically emphasized more spare interiors) were not always organized around the same goals, it remains striking how persistently the imagery of "Oriental" space in turn-of-the-century popular American literature rejects the very possibility that Americans might find themselves "at home" either with, or within, Asian design. Which makes Biggers's Charlie Chan novels all the more unusual for the ways they revise, even as they invoke, as in the scene in Chan's living room, stereotypical representations of Asian material otherness. In what follows I will examine the strategies of architectural racialization in popular American Orientalist narrative—which, as Robert G. Lee has shown, often collapses differences among Asian nations and ethnicities into a single, "ahistorical category of Oriental Otherness"[5]—in order to show how a novel like *The House without a Key* attempts to destabilize that racialization. I will argue not only that Biggers's text deliberately (and quite literally) confronts the typical spaces of "Oriental" popular fiction but also that it enlists a new set of structures and metaphors surprisingly consonant with the Asian-influenced aesthetics nurtured by designers like Wright and the importers of Asian-themed furnishings. By forwarding these claims I do not mean to wave away the deeply problematic characterization of Charlie Chan himself, whom Asian American critics have assailed as the forerunner of the demeaning model minority Asian stereotype—the nonthreatening, obliging ally of white authority[6]—although my focus will be less on Chan than on the spaces and objects with which Biggers surrounds him. Indeed, I will ultimately suggest that even as *The House without a Key* attempts to refurbish popular notions of "Oriental" spatial and decorative identity, it cannot entirely escape the strictures (and structures) of Orientalist representation.[7]

"In the Oriental Style"

Before examining the architectural and decorative idioms of popular American Orientalist narrative, it will be helpful briefly to trace the rise and reach of Asian material culture in the U.S. before 1900. Objects from Asia first began to appear in North America at least as early as the mid-1500s, when Spanish traders started bringing Chinese export porcelain to Mexico.[8] By the mid-1700s—largely as an elaboration of British fascination with the Far East—well-to-do American colonists had not only developed a taste for Asian decorative objects but in some cases had already begun to incorporate "Oriental" architectural motifs into their homes. American builders' handbooks of the late eighteenth century highlight Chinese designs for such features as lattice roof and stairway banisters, examples of which can be found in the colonial and early republican built environment from Connecticut to Charleston.[9] Interest in Asian decorative and architectural arts then accelerated after 1785, with the return to New York of the *Empress of China*, the first U.S. ship to make port at Canton. The consequent breaking of the East India Company monopoly and the opening of direct trade with China introduced more and more Americans to Chinese porcelains, silks, lacquerwares, carvings, and wallpapers, to name only a few of the decorative objects that were making their way—through a process John Kuo Wei Tchen has helpfully termed "patrician orientalism"—into select upper-class U.S. households by 1800.[10]

More and more examples of Chinese architecture, or architecture modeled on an "Oriental" style, also began to appear in the U.S. during this period. In 1792, for example, a former supercargo of the Dutch East India Company and newly made American citizen built a Chinese-accented house north of Philadelphia in part to display articles he had collected during his years trading in Macao. Dubbed China Retreat, and topped by a small pagoda "hung with little bells," the former trader's house impressed visitors with its power to evoke the exotic "East." Noted one guest: "The furniture, ornaments, everything at Mr. van Braam's reminds us of China. It is even impossible to avoid fancying ourselves in China while surrounded at once by living Chinese [van Braam's Chinese servants], and by representations of their manners, their usages, their monuments, and their arts."[11] The phrase "fancying ourselves" is worth pausing over, for it suggests that Americans were prone to imagining that the architectural and decorative elements (not to mention the people and the customs) they encountered in the U.S. were authentic representations of Asian culture rather than Orientalist interpretations of Asian-influenced idioms. (Such fancies, in fact, would increase through the century.) More public "Oriental" structures would soon appear as well. In 1827, for example, British émigré John Haviland designed a towering pagoda for the Philadelphia Pagoda and Labyrinth Garden, a pleasure resort located between the Eastern State Penitentiary (which Haviland also designed) and the Fairmount Waterworks.[12]

China was not the only inspiration for architectural designs from the "East." Egyptian forms were increasingly popular for monumental architecture (especially obelisks), as well as for courthouses, prisons, churches, and cemeteries. Within domestic architecture in particular, "Oriental" could signal almost anything from Egyptian, to Persian, to East Indian, to Far Eastern. In Alexander Jackson Davis's seminal *Rural Residences* (1837), for example, his "Villa in the Oriental Style" draws its inspiration from India. As Davis explains in the text accompanying the elevation and floor plan, "This design is termed Oriental (East Indian) from its veranda shades, the window lintels, and eaves' ornaments." In Andrew Jackson Downing's *Treatise on the Theory and Practice of Landscape Gardening* (1841), on the other hand, the "oriental air" of former China trader Nathan Dunn's large Mount Holly, New Jersey, cottage derives from its Chinese rather than East Indian features. Still others built in what might be called "Moorish" forms. P. T. Barnum's enormous villa Iranistan, which he erected overlooking Long Island Sound in the late 1840s after visiting the Indo-Saracenic Royal Pavilion while on tour in Brighton, England, resembled nothing so much as a "mythical Arabian palace." (Downing criticized its pretension, objecting that it "looks like the minareted and domed residence of a Persian *Shah*.")[13]

In 1852, amid growing objections that "Oriental" forms were inappropriate for American domestic architecture—Downing had insisted as early as 1841 that only "the Grecian and Gothic styles" could be "thoroughly adapted to our domestic purposes"[14]—Samuel Sloan would nonetheless include two different designs for "An Oriental Villa" inspired by "Spanish-Arabian" architecture in his pattern book *The Model Architect*. Only a few years later, Sloan would actually construct a version of one of these villas, topped by a massive onion-shaped dome, in Natchez, Mississippi, for the wealthy cotton baron Haller Nutt. When he published the octagonal design in his 1861 volume *Sloan's Homestead Architecture*, Sloan declared the style "particularly suitable for the home of the retired southern planter" and not at all out of place in an American setting (Fig. 25). "The choice of style in this example was less a matter of caprice than the natural growth of the ground-plan selected," Sloan maintained, although he admitted that elements of the design were based on a medley of popular ideas of the "East" (not to mention of the American South) rather than actual physical models. "Fancy dictated that the dome should be bulbiform," Sloan explained, "a remembrancer of Eastern magnificence which few will judge misplaced as it looms up against the mellowed azure of a Southern sky. In addition to this, the Moorish arch employed in the balconies and the foliated drapery

Figure 25. Samuel Sloan, "Design I: Oriental Villa," *Sloan's Homestead Architecture* (1861), 56. Courtesy Marquand Library of Art and Archaeology, Princeton University Library.

of the verandas will fully sustain us in the application of the term 'Oriental,' despite the Italian details of cornice and window."[15]

If George B. Tatum is correct in asserting that these midcentury designs, "because of their relatively high cost and because they would not have been considered sufficiently picturesque by later standards," could not have "exerted much influence on contemporary American architecture,"[16] the fantasies they expressed about Asian exoticism nonetheless helped lay the ground for much of the popular writing we will explore in the next section. Not long after this moment, however, a different set of ideas about and examples of Asian architecture would help transform American house building in the last decades of the nineteenth century. A watershed moment in this transformation was the popularity of the Japanese pavilion at the 1876 Philadelphia Centennial Exposition. Staged in Fairmount Park—not far from the site of Haviland's long since demolished 1827 Pagoda and Labyrinth Garden—the Centennial offered stateside Americans their closest look yet at Asian architecture. The Japanese delegation constructed two buildings at the exposition, a small bazaar and a larger two-story house, entirely from materials shipped from Japan. Fascinated crowds watched native Japanese craftsmen assemble the buildings like "an ingenious puzzle."[17] A souvenir book of lithographs from the exposition describes the unusual appeal of the two-story dwelling:

> This house, during its erection, created more curiosity and attracted infi-
> nitely more visitors than any other building on the grounds. It was erected
> by native Japanese workmen, with materials brought from home, and built
> in their own manner with curious tools and yet more curious manual pro-
> cesses. In fact, the whole work seemed to be executed upon exactly reverse
> methods of carpentering to those in use in this country. . . . It was put
> together without the use of iron. The different parts were mortised, bev-
> eled, dovetailed and joined, and where it was necessary to use any other
> fastenings wooden pins were employed. The woods are of fine grain, care-
> fully planed and finished, and the house, which is the best-built struc-
> ture on the Centennial grounds, was as nicely put together as a piece of
> cabinet-work.[18]

To judge from the diaries of contemporary fairgoers, the novel method of joinery struck many visitors as particularly compelling. "The Japanese build-ing is mentionable because it was brought from Japan and created without a nail, screw, or bolt," noted one appreciative onlooker. Jotted another: "The buildings put up by foreign nations are remarkable, as showing their differ-ent styles of architecture. The Japanese building was put up without the use of nails."[19]

It was less the absence of nails than the presence of design elements intriguingly consonant with recent developments in American architecture, however, that helped turn the Japanese pavilion from oddity to influence. As Marcus Whiffen and Frederick Koeper have argued, the emergence in the mid-nineteenth century of the "skeletal" stick style, popularized in domestic architecture by Downing and the pattern book genre, predisposed Ameri-cans to accept the "constructivist esthetic of Japanese building."[20] Americans appeared equally ready to appreciate Japanese innovations in the disposition of interior space, especially the open plan, in which adjacent rooms, instead of being cordoned off by walls, are conjoined or linked by large openings—as was the case with the Japanese pavilion. Simultaneously making its formal debut in the U.S. at the Centennial was British architect Richard Norman Shaw's Queen Anne style, whose unusual combination of central hall, stairway, and fireplace further modeled the openness that was not only already beginning to appear in American floor plans but would soon provide the core elements of what would be known as the shingle style. Thus while Americans would not literally adopt Japanese architectural forms until the late nineteenth century, the "spirit of Japanese architecture permeated and reinforced the direction of American architecture during the post-Centennial era."[21] This attraction to Japanese forms helps account for the ongoing American interest not only in the open plan but also, for example, in the deliberate exposure of framing, the accentuation of horizontal lines, the integration of structures with their landscape settings, and even the use of Asian-influenced window and wall treatments.[22]

The erection in 1893 of another distinctive Japanese building at the World's Columbian Exposition in Chicago brought even more attention to Asian architectural forms. Constructed on the fair's Wooded Island, in its central lagoon, and remaining on that site for more than fifty years (even as nearly all the rest of the fair's ephemeral structures had long been burned or bulldozed away), like its 1876 predecessor the Ho-o-den was also assembled by Japanese craftsmen out of imported materials. It featured a cruciform-plan central hall whose rooms were divided not by walls but instead by screens, several of which were removed during the fair to provide a better view for visitors, who were only permitted to look in from the surrounding veranda. As Kevin Nute suggests, from this vantage point it required only a short step "to imagine all the internal divisions removed, leaving essentially one large space serving several different functions."[23] One visitor to the Ho-o-den whom historians have long believed imagined precisely that scenario, later drawing on that inspiration in the design of his innovative Prairie Houses, was Frank Lloyd Wright.

The precise influence of Japanese architecture on Wright's designs is difficult to identify. While Wright openly acknowledged debts in his aesthetic to Japanese art, in particular to the compositional style of Japanese woodblock prints, he frequently, even vehemently, denied that Japanese architecture had guided his work in any formal way—even though the structural massing and roof forms in many of his late nineteenth- and early twentieth-century designs often appear to mine a structure like the Ho-o-den for inspiration.[24] (Compare, for example, the photograph of the Ward W. Willits House [1902] with that of the Ho-o-den in Fig. 26.) It is inside his houses, however, that we find the best evidence for Japan's influence on Wright. As Nute has carefully delineated, Wright's innovative contributions to the open plan in turn-of-the-century American house design can be most clearly illuminated by comparison to the spatial flexibility of a structure like the Japanese Ho-o-den. Whether Wright actually imitated Japanese forms or more loosely analogized them, his decision in the early Prairie House plan to reshape the American home into a "generic form consisting of a large communal space centred on a free-standing chimney and flanked by related dining and study areas" follows logically from the Japanese distribution of interior space he likely first encountered on the Wooded Island. Figure 27, for example, shows how closely allied the central design elements of the new Prairie House form were to the central hall of the Ho-o-den. Whatever inspiration Wright received from the shingle style, with which he had already become familiar in the 1880s, his first mature phase of house building in the early 1900s bears the unmistakable trace of his interest in, and admiration for, Asian architectural idioms. Even Wright's own language at times betrays this affinity, as when he speaks of aiming "to eliminate the room as a box and the house as another by making all walls enclosing screens—the ceiling and floors and enclosing screens to flow into each other as one large enclosure of space."[25]

If the "Japan craze" inaugurated at the Philadelphia Centennial and accentuated by the Chicago World's Fair ultimately helped shape Wright's respatialization of the American interior, it also gave rise to a related—and far more immediately visible—decorative aesthetic based on Japanesque design. American elites with opportunity to travel to Asia had begun to embrace this particular aesthetic even before 1876, decorating their homes with Japanese prints and other objects beginning in the 1860s, much like their wealthy Aesthetic Movement counterparts in London and Paris, where the "cult of Japan" had already struck. (The Japanese "screens and ornaments" in Henry Wadsworth Longfellow's living room, for example—praised in Charles Wyllis Elliott's *Book of American Interiors* (1876) for giving "life and piquancy to the room"—had been bought for him by his son Charley, who lived in Japan for two years in the early 1870s.)[26] One did not even have to travel to take part. Items of Japanese design could be purchased from high-end interior design and import companies like New York's Herter Brothers, which under the leadership of Christian Herter (who in the late 1860s had spent time in Paris, where he absorbed the Japan cult firsthand) became the most fashion-

Figure 26. Top: Frank Lloyd Wright, Ward W. Willits House, Highland Park, Illinois (1902), street facade, Stuart Cohen and Susan Benjamin, *North Shore Chicago* (2004), 74. Bottom: Ho-o-den Palace, central hall and side verandas, front view, James W. Shepp and Daniel B. Shepp, *Shepp's World's Fair Photographed* (1893), 243. Both images courtesy Marquand Library of Art and Archaeology, Princeton University Library.

8 The plan of the central hall of the Ho-o-den as it appeared in the official catalogue in 1893
9 The main functions of the central hall of the Ho-o-den
10 Generic plan configuration of the early Prairie House

Figure 27. Comparison of the spatial plans of the Ho-o-den and Frank Lloyd Wright's early Prairie House form, Kevin Nute, "Frank Lloyd Wright and Japanese Architecture" (1994), 172. By permission of Oxford University Press.

able decorating company in the U.S.[27] In the wake of the Centennial the allure of Asian decorative art spread quickly from elite collectors to the American middle class, who turned not to Herter Brothers but to specialty retailers like A. A. Vantine and Company, which later in the nineteenth century would simply call itself "The Oriental Store." For the first time since Asian material culture had begun appearing in select American homes in the mid-1700s, "Oriental" décor had become a mainstream fascination. Even Mark Twain was a Vantine's customer.[28]

Regardless of one's class position, decorating in the "Japanese taste" during the Victorian era typically meant crowding a room with as many items as possible. As Jane Converse Brown noted in her pioneering study of popular U.S. Japonisme, "Fans, porcelains, prints, hanging scrolls, pillows, and rugs, all together or in any combination completed the interior. The early room . . . was well filled." In his own analysis of the "Japan idea," William N. Hosley concurs: "A room filled with carefully chosen and placed bric-a-brac is unmistakably Japanesque and must be recognized as *the* look sought after at the height of the Japan craze. Cluttered corners, mantelpieces groaning with the weight of decorative accessories, and cabinets—little museums—filled with odd bits of china and glass, that is what the Japanesque interior was all about."[29] More recent scholars have shown that, far from being exclusively Japanesque, this cluttered aesthetic characterized "Oriental" decorative motifs more broadly, as consumers often mixed and matched objects from multiple Eastern sources, typically with more concern for decorative value than cultural authenticity. (In its early years Vantine's advertised itself as an importer of goods from India, China, Japan, and Turkey, and by the turn of the century it carried items from many different "Eastern" countries, all with the promise of providing "the largest stock of Oriental goods in the world.") As Mari Yoshihara has observed, "It was common during this period . . . to see a Persian rug, a Chinese scroll, and a Japanese umbrella displayed in a single setting."[30] For consumers who could only afford to decorate part of a room, the popular "cosey corner," sometimes of Japanese or Chinese design but more often Middle Eastern in inspiration, modeled a relatively inexpensive way to participate in the production of domestic "Oriental" profusion.[31]

Though similarly inspired by "Asian" forms, this decorative aesthetic is thus starkly different from—indeed almost antithetical to—Wright's effort to push back the walls of the domestic interior in order to create the more free-flowing and comparatively empty spaces characteristic of the open plan. Marilynn Johnson Bordes highlights precisely this contrast in a brief essay on Christian Herter and the "cult" of Japan. After describing the influence of

British Aestheticism (and in particular E. W. Godwin) on Herter's Japanese-style art furniture, Bordes concludes by juxtaposing images of two strikingly different rooms: the lush, overstuffed Japanese parlor designed by Herter (who was both architect and decorator on the project) for one of railroad magnate William H. Vanderbilt's Fifth Avenue homes in early 1880s New York City; and the spare, spacious "Northome" parlor designed by Wright for the Francis W. Little House in Wayzata, Minnesota, in 1912–13. The difference in the two rooms—both of which are clearly influenced by Japanese motifs—is a function not merely of chronology but also of ideology and interpretation. Where Herter used Japanese materials primarily as an "exercise in elaboration," Bordes argues, Wright, who had traveled to Japan in 1905 and then again in 1912 while working on Northome, transformed his encounter with Asia into a "supreme study in elimination."[32]

These interiors are worth looking at again (see Fig. 28 and Fig. 29). For Bordes, this difference suggests that Wright succeeded where Herter failed: in embracing Japanese art's powerful "sense of the void." But it seems more accurate to say that the Northome and Vanderbilt parlors epitomize two contrasting ways in which turn-of-the-century Americans not only imagined but also sought to inhabit "Oriental" space. By which I mean not simply a contrast between elaboration and elimination—between stuffed and empty—but also between inhabiting that space through, on the one hand, the display of objects and, on the other hand, through the redesigning of floor plans. If these modes, as Bill Brown suggests, were increasingly in tension—Wright was only one of many who assailed the prevalence of "bric-a-brac" and domestic decorative excess, offering his houses as partial remedies to ornamental disorder—they nonetheless existed side by side through the early years of the century. And indeed, even as profuse "Oriental" interiors gave way to more austerely modern ones, the embrace of the "East" they offered continued to be mediated through objects, however many fewer. Even in Wright's spare Northome interior one can see a low, white hexagonal coffee table evocative of the "Turkish" style in the right rear next to the piano.[33]

Chan's bungalow on Punchbowl Hill, in fact, evokes each of these contexts. By the early 1900s, American bungalow designers were drawing explicitly on the same Japanesque principles of horizontalization and respatialization central to Wright's aesthetic; Japanese-inspired bungalows, in particular, were prevalent in Hawaii.[34] As popularly understood, Biggers could have chosen no clearer architectural sign of the influence of the "East." Inside the house, moreover, Chan's objects illustrate both the spareness of the emerging modernist aesthetic and the residual excess of "elaborate" Orientalism. While on one wall

Figure 28. Christian Herter, Japanese parlor, William H. Vanderbilt House, New York (ca. 1882), Marilynn Johnson Bordes, "Christian Herter and the Cult of Japan" (1975), 26. Courtesy Marquand Library of Art and Archaeology, Princeton University Library.

Biggers places "a single picture, painted on silk," charming for its "simplicity," around the rest of the room he distributes "elaborately carved teakwood stands" topped with vases, wine jars, and dwarf trees. Add in the "pale golden lanterns" hanging from the ceiling and the "soft-toned rug" that presses up from below, and John Quincy turns out to be surrounded on all sides in the very room that, in a typical early twentieth-century Hawaiian bungalow,

Figure 29. Frank Lloyd Wright, parlor, "Northome," Francis W. Little House, Wayzata, Minnesota (1912–13), Marilynn Johnson Bordes, "Christian Herter and the Cult of Japan" (1975), 27. Courtesy Marquand Library of Art and Archaeology, Princeton University Library.

would be the most spacious and open. In a house that one might say both embraces the "void" and fills it, it is no small irony that John Quincy feels the "gulf" between himself and Chan in (for him) a strangely crowded room.

We will return to Chan's living room again shortly. Before we do, however, it is critical to register just how vigorously, and in what particular ways, popular American literature inscribed its own gulf between its readers and the "Oriental" structures, spaces, and persons that inhabit so many stories in the late nineteenth and early twentieth centuries—the stories Biggers and his readers knew so well and whose floor plans (and interior décor) *The House without a Key* would at once so deliberately invoke and revise.

A World of Narrow Streets

Asian American scholars have mapped with care the role that turn-of-the-century American literature played in creating and stoking anti-Asian stereotypes. What these studies help make vividly clear, yet without ever stating the case, is that architectural and decorative tropes assume a larger role in turn-of-the-century popular American literary representations of Asian scenes and characters than they do in the depictions of any other racial or ethnic group. Images of Chinatown both dominate and organize these tropes, which, as John

Tchen has shown, emerged powerfully just as, if not before, literal Chinatowns began to appear in major American cities. In New York, for example, as the midcentury "sunlight and shadow" genre of urban exposé writing "sought to redefine the cultural geography of the entire city," New York's Chinese, their living spaces, and the "Chinese quarter" itself came to represent most starkly "the opposite of the ideal Victorian individual, Victorian household, and Victorian city." The Chinese were regarded as low, vulgar, dirty, and diseased, just like the filthy neighborhoods and "rickety dens" in which they lived, presumably by choice. One visited "such a quarter" only at one's physical and moral peril. "This spatial remapping of New York City was not simply geographical," Tchen argues, "but essentially cultural and socioeconomic."[35]

The passage of the 1882 Chinese Exclusion Act, which severely restricted immigration from China and validated anti-Chinese racism, contributed significantly to the segregative relocation of countless American Chinese to urban Chinatowns. By the turn of the century these spaces had emerged as the "primary setting and subject" for fiction featuring Chinese Americans.[36] As Elaine Kim notes, "Anglo-American writers like Frank Norris, Gertrude Atherton, and a host of lesser writers used Chinatown for local color and exotic effect, filling their tales with tong wars, opium dens, and sinister hatchetmen lurking in dark alleyways where mysterious trapdoors and underground passages led to torture chambers and slave quarters."[37] Even in tales that treat Chinatown picturesquely rather than as a site of terror, Chinatown's simultaneous allure and threat are almost always embodied in and magnified by its overpowering, even constricting, buildingscape. Norris's description in his urban romance *Blix* (1898) of a white couple in San Francisco who are so engrossed in conversation that they accidentally find themselves in Chinatown highlights some of the specific ways architectural and decorative imagery had come to define the Anglo-American experience of "Oriental" space:

> "By the way—by Jove! Travis, where are we?"
>   They looked swiftly around them, and the bustling, breezy water-front faded from their recollection. They were in a world of narrow streets, of galleries and overhanging balconies. Craziest structures, riddled and honeycombed with staircases and passages, shut out the sky, though here and there rose a building of extraordinary richness and most elaborate ornamentation. Color was everywhere. A thousand little notes of green and yellow, of vermilion and sky blue, assaulted the eye. Here it was a doorway, here a vivid glint of cloth or hanging, here a huge scarlet sign lettered with gold, and here a kaleidoscopic effect in the garments of a passer-by.

Directly opposite, and two stories above their heads, a sort of huge "loggia," one blaze of gilding and crude vermilions, opened in the gray cement of a crumbling façade, like a sudden burst of flame. Gigantic pot-bellied lanterns of red and gold swung from its ceiling, while along its railing stood a row of pots—brass, ruddy bronze, and blue porcelain—from which were growing red, saffron, purple, pink, and golden tulips without number. . . .

"Chinatown!" exclaimed Travis.[38]

Travis's exclamation marks a wide-eyed recognition that Norris's readers would presumably have shared. In fact, by withholding the answer to the initial question—"where are we?"—until after the swirling description of the crooked streets, looming balconies, and blazing colors (the latter heightened by the magnification of "vermilion," colloquially known as China red, into "vermilions"), Norris encourages readers to decode the setting along with his characters. And because Norris plays the tropes out to their fullest, of course readers would recognize where they are. For where else but in Chinatown—or, more to the point, in Chinatown fiction—did streets become so narrow so quickly, did the "craziest structures . . . shut out the sky," did such rich, almost violent colors and objects "assault" the senses?

Indeed, the violence implicit even in what Wu terms Norris's "sympathetic lyricism"[39] marks the principal feature of the architectural topoi of the vast majority of popular Chinatown tales, in which the "trapdoors and underground passages" described by Kim proliferate. In these tales by white writers of abduction, murder, and revenge—some of which narrate Chinese-on-Chinese violence, while others imagine white characters, particularly women, in thrall to "Celestial" kidnappers—Chinatown's streetscape offers unsuspecting visitors not lunch (as it does the white couple in *Blix*) but entrapment and violation. The "riddled and honeycombed" structures of *Blix* thus have their unseemly doubles in networks of hidden tunnels, secret openings, and subterranean vaults.[40] One popular turn-of-the-century weekly magazine series that returns to Chinatown settings (in both New York and San Francisco) over and over, *Secret Service*, featuring the New York detectives Old and Young King Brady, employs such structures in virtually every one of its Chinatown stories. In *Hop Lee, the Chinese Slave Dealer; or, Old and Young King Brady and the Opium Fiends. A Story of San Francisco* (1899), for example, Chinese assassins, or "Highbinders," construct a "death trap" in a deserted house, luring each victim to a room fitted with unseen apertures through which venomous snakes, trained to kill, may be surreptitiously introduced. Although the Bradys solve the mystery of the house, in the penultimate chapter Old King Brady, while searching the building for the assassins, is only narrowly saved from this "most horrible" death by the intervention of his younger partner. In a later story, *The Bradys' Trip to Chinatown; or, Trailing an Opium Fiend* (1904), the partners spend much of the last half of the tale either trapped in, escaping from, or searching for other kidnapped characters in an underground vault—a space that eventually leads, via a system of collateral tunnels, to the discovery and rescue of the opium-ravaged wife of the distraught white millionaire whose hiring of the Bradys had initiated the tale in the first place.[41]

In popular Chinatown fictions "Oriental" décor often works hand in hand with architectural tropes to signify difference and danger—or even deliver it. In the stories of Hugh Wiley, for example, whom Wu identifies as one of the writers who most fully exploited Chinatown's "lurid reputation," Asian decorative art can turn into instruments of torture or death.[42] In "Jade," the title tale of Wiley's 1921 short-story collection, the Chinese owner of a beautifully appointed jewelry store exacts murderous revenge on the white woman who inadvertently thwarts his attempt to smuggle a Chinese bride into the country. The rooms of the store, "created from memories of the Palace of the Prince" in which the shopkeeper was born, evoke "Oriental" refinement and luxury. In one room, "the walls . . . were hung with pale grey silk. Rugs from the looms of Tientsin covered the floor. In one corner of the room a bronze jar as high as a man's shoulder stood beside an ebony table on which rested a shrine of ivory and pearl and the dwarfed pine tree of delightful curves." Inviting the woman to his store under the pretense of giving her a present of three precious opals—"My Gawd, I never knew no Chink had a joint as grand as this," she declares upon entering the shop—the merchant contrives to overcome her with charcoal fumes. While she is unconscious, he pours the molten gold he had been pretending to use to set the opals down the woman's throat, choking and killing her. He then stuffs her into the tall bronze jar in the corner of the room, sealing it so her corpse cannot be discovered. In a final gruesome irony, the shopkeeper gives the store—with all its furnishings, including the bronze jar—to the white woman's husband, an Irish cabbie who for years had accepted money for steering customers to this very shop, while the merchant returns to China with his bride-to-be. Now in control of the shop, the cabbie "believes himself to be a widower" but has no idea what has happened to his wife.[43]

A spectacularly lethal combination of architectural and decorative terror haunts the Fu-Manchu novels of English writer Sax Rohmer, which were enormously popular (and published separately) in the U.S. Long singled out by critics for their powerful consolidation of some of the worst anti-Asian stereotypes, epitomized by the oft-quoted description of the evil genius himself near the beginning of the first novel in the series ("Imagine a person, tall, lean and feline, high-shouldered, with a brow like Shakespeare and a face like Satan"), the Fu-Manchu texts take equal care to locate "Oriental" menace not just in persons but in structures and particularly objects. One harrowing dream sequence recounted in *The Insidious Dr. Fu-Manchu* by the novel's narrator after he has been knocked unconscious and imprisoned in a dank cellar in London's Chinatown suggestively elaborates this terror:

> Tapestries covered the four walls. There was no door visible. These tapestries were magnificently figured with golden dragons; and as the serpentine bodies gleamed and shimmered in the increasing radiance, each dragon, I thought, intertwined its glittering coils more closely with those of another. The carpet was of such richness that I stood knee-deep in its pile. And this, too, was fashioned all over with golden dragons; and they seemed to glide about amid the shadows of the design—stealthily.
>
> At the farther end of the hall—for hall it was—a huge table with dragons' legs stood solitary amid the luxuriance of the carpet. It bore scintillating globes, and tubes that held living organisms, and books of a size and in such bindings as I never had imagined, with instruments of a type unknown to Western science—a heterogeneous litter quite indescribable, which overflowed on to the floor, forming an amazing oasis in a dragon-haunted desert of carpet. A lamp hung above this table, suspended by golden chains from the ceiling—which was so lofty that, following the chains upward, my gaze lost itself in the purple shadows above.

The luxurious pile of the carpet, the heavily ornamented table with its "heterogeneous litter" of the evil scientist's wholly alien "globes, and tubes, . . . and books," seem almost like one of Christian Herter's overstuffed rooms come terrifyingly to life. (There is also an unmistakable erotics of terror in the descriptive excess, fitting since the dreamer will later imagine his aching forehead is being caressed by a woman's hand.) Fu-Manchu's hideous face soon materializes behind the huge table, snapping the narrator momentarily out of his reverie: "The walls no longer lived, but were merely draped in exquisite Chinese dragon tapestry. The rich carpet beneath my feet ceased to be as a jungle and became a normal carpet—extraordinarily rich, but merely a carpet." But his relief is only short-lived. In a "cloud of gray horror" the narrator suddenly slips back into delirium, imagining himself being choked by the curling, sinuous tips of a pair of exotic red slippers on his own feet. [44]

If the repeated denigration and demonization of Asian character in Orientalist narratives functioned in part to affirm Anglo-American readers' sense of their own whiteness, then the obsessive depiction of malignant decorative objects and menacing architectural structures undoubtedly helped, for many, to shore up an analogously racialized architectural and decorative identity. More than simply providing an "exotic setting for otherwise hackneyed plots," these fictions aggressively define, typically through negative example, what truly "American" interiors and exteriors should look like.[45] In so doing, popular Chinatown fictions could be said to take part in the heated debate over architecture and national identity that was central, as we have seen in previous chapters, to the Colonial Revival. For these revivalists, decorative "purity" was an important as architectural purity. As Kristin Hoganson notes, opponents of "cosmopolitan domesticity"—the embrace by primarily middle- and upper-class white women of decorative imports, especially from Asia—denounced "foreign" interiors as inappropriately heterogeneous, unhygienic, and emblematic of "old world" luxury and corruption.[46] Houses that entrap, carpets that engulf—not to mention slippers that kill—would represent a nightmarish elaboration of the anticosmopolitans' worst fears. When Americans passed laws revoking citizenship from American women who married unnaturalizable aliens—as they did in the early twentieth century, specifically targeting Asians—were they not acting on analogous fears, hoping to prevent more literal instances of unacceptable heterogeneity? Indeed, for David Palumbo-Liu, the "intensification in the segregation and partitioning of Asia from America" in the 1920s "is entirely in keeping with a general and increased anxiety over what modernity had brought to America."[47]

Confronting Chinatown

Even amid this intensified partitioning, which Palumbo-Liu does not see fading until the 1930s, there were challenges raised, implicitly and explicitly, to the insistence on "Oriental Otherness" advanced by fictions like *The Insidious Dr. Fu-Manchu*. If on the one hand the imagined buildingscape of Chinatown sometimes indeed leapt out of the books and into real public space—as when Sid Grauman constructed a phenomenally popular "Underground Chinatown" exhibit, featuring a "chamber of horrors" of opium smokers and drug fiends, on the Joy Zone at San Francisco's Panama-Pacific International Exposition in 1915[48]—on the other hand more and more Americans were encountering hybridized Asian American forms in relatively benign settings. Indeed, in the very pages of the magazines from which Hoganson suggests turn-of-the-cen-

The East is East and the West is West, and it's a far cry from the Colonial to the Oriental, yet this breakfast room, at Locust Valley, shows a successful mingling of the two, an achievement in restraint. Its lines are Colonial, the decorations Chinese and Japanese. The walls and woodwork are tinted a faint green, and the rug is bluish green with maroon figures. On the consol is kept a little green Japanese bird

Figure 30. Frontispiece, *House and Garden* 26.6 (December 1914), 346. Courtesy, The Winterthur Library: Printed Book and Periodical Collection.

tury cosmopolitan homemakers were most likely to get new ideas for decorating and furnishing, one finds not just samplings of "Oriental" products (Vantine's was a frequent advertiser) but even praiseworthy blends of East and West. The full-page photograph frontispiece of the December 1914 issue of *House and Garden* shown in Figure 30, for example, depicts an interior of decidedly mixed origins. With an obligatory nod to Kipling, the caption effuses:

The East is East and the West is West, and it's a far cry from the Colonial to the Oriental, yet this breakfast-room, at Locust Valley, shows a successful mingling of the two, an achievement in restraint. Its lines are Colonial, the decorations Chinese and Japanese. The walls and woodwork are tinted a faint green, and the rug is bluish green with maroon figures. On the consol is kept a little green Japanese bird.[49]

There are traces here of imperial condescension, to be sure—that diminutive, "kept" Japanese bird, for example. This photograph and its editorial caption nonetheless express the evident interest by magazines like *House and Garden* in encouraging their readers to accept tastefully composed, "mixed-race" architectural and decorative forms. That this image could appear practically alongside advertisements for none other than Rohmer's *Insidious Dr. Fu-Manchu*—which ran in both the July and August 1914 issues of the very same magazine[50]—further suggests that American consumers might often have been called to navigate a world in which the denigration and acceptance of Asians and their material products could take place in virtually the same spaces. (Or at least be issued by the same publishers: after all, the U.S. imprint house for the first edition of *The Insidious Dr. Fu-Manchu*, McBride, Nast and Company, was also the parent company behind *House and Garden*, which used the pages of its magazine to plug its fiction.)[51] Perhaps this juxtaposition even suggests that Americans could read Rohmer's novels or visit "Underground Chinatown" and yet still be interested in decorating their houses in the latest "Oriental" style—particularly if the latter process were understood to be safe and sanitary, an "achievement in restraint," in the words of the *House and Garden* frontispiece, say, rather than a yielding to seduction.

For many readers, the Charlie Chan novels must have seemed the epitome of "restraint" in an era so strongly marked by the almost hysterically anti-Asian menace of a figure like Rohmer's Fu-Manchu. After all, Chan was a law-abiding detective, not an arch-criminal. He was polite, even self-effacing. "An amiable Chinese acting on the side of law and order had never been used up to that time," Chan's creator Biggers noted in 1931. Indeed, Biggers claims that Chan played a larger role in *The House without a Key* than he had first anticipated. Starting "as a minor and unimportant character," Biggers explains, Chan "modestly pushed his way forward, and toward the end he had the lion's share of the spotlight." Biggers even suggests that he wrote the next Chan novel only at the demand of readers. "Scarcely had the story stopped running in the 'Post' [the *Saturday Evening Post*, where all six Chan novels were originally serialized before appearing in novel form], when I began to hear from people all over the country who wanted another Charlie Chan story. The idea had never occurred to me to write a series."[52] This new type of Asian character must have been deeply appealing to many readers. And yet as countless critics have suggested, Chan's law-abiding self-effacement, though the complete opposite of Fu-Manchu's self-aggrandizing villainy, served to shape equally denigrating—and in some ways even more insidious—stereotypes about "Oriental" character. For Gish Jen, reflecting on depictions of Asians in twentieth-century American popular culture, "the benign images . . . are typically no more tied to reality than their malign counterparts; vilification is merely replaced by glorification. . . . More message than human being, [Charlie Chan] recalls the ever-smiling black mammy that proliferated during Reconstruction: Don't worry, he seems to say, no one's going to go making any trouble."[53]

At first glance, Biggers would appear to have aimed for a similar restraint in choosing the settings for *The House without a Key*. In fact, in telling the story of how Chan solves the murder of John Quincy's wealthy cousin Dan Winterslip, Biggers almost seems intent on avoiding Chinatown and its negative associations altogether. Though the novel spends an early chapter in San Francisco, for example, where John Quincy stops on his way to the islands, and though his cousin Roger treats him to "an exhilarating afternoon of motoring over the town" (31), no mention is made of their driving by, let alone stopping in, Chinatown. Later that night, when John Quincy and Roger are ambushed in an old house and John Quincy suffers a cut on his face, the attack happens not in Chinatown but above it, in Russian Hill. Chinatown does appear briefly at the very end of the chapter but only obliquely—indeed, at first only metonymically—when John Quincy's young cousin Barbara suggests they take "this Boston boy" out for some "chop suey."[54] Exhausted, John Quincy protests internally. "Good lord, John Quincy thought. Was there anything in the world he wanted less? Barbara took him among the Chinese" (31). But Biggers does not provide any details of the trip or suggest that a visit to Chinatown is anything other than an evening out for "foreign" food. Indeed, in John Quincy's account, Chinatown is apparently merely one among many stops they were to make that night. "He didn't give a hang about the Chinese. Nor the Mexicans, whose restaurants interested the girl next. At the moment, he was unsympathetic toward Italy. And even toward France. But he struggled on the international round, affronting his digestion with queer dishes, and dancing thousands of miles with the slim Barbara in his arms. After scrambled eggs at a place called Pete's Fashion, she consented to call it an evening" (31). John Quincy's provincial squeamishness leads him to sneer at all the "queer dishes" of this global buffet, allowing Biggers to invoke Chinatown yet not assign any special stigma to it. In fact, in this episode, Biggers never even uses the term "Chinatown."

Although Charles J. Rzepka does not discuss this early scene, the decidedly unsensational depiction of one of the most notorious Chinatowns in popular fiction would seem further evidence of what Rzepka sees as the text's challenge to the "generic topography of . . . Chinatown regionalism." That is, instead of mimicking the "sensationalistic images of Chinese secrecy, cunning, and depravity, fed by nostalgia for a Chinatown that existed nowhere but in white imaginations," *The House without a Key*, according to Rzepka, shifts the scene to the "radically counterintuitive" space of Hawaii. "By choosing Honolulu as his inaugural mise-en-scène," Rzepka argues, "Biggers decisively rejected Chinatown regionalism as a generic context for the debut of his Chinese American detective, replacing the 'architectural uncanny' of its dark alleys, tunnels, and opium dens with sunshine, fresh air, and broad, sandy beaches." The value of this reading, the first to assess the significance of the physical setting of *The House without a Key*, lies in Rzepka's analogy between Biggers's choice of locale and a range of other "generic inversions of white stereotypical expectations" in the Charlie Chan series.[55] Foremost among these inversions is the change Biggers rings on the genre of detective fiction itself by making a Chinese American his lead character.

Because Rzepka's interest is primarily in exploring this link between region, race, and genre, he pays little specific attention to architectural or spatial representations in the text beyond noting that the typical markers of popular Chinatown fictions go missing. And yet these markers do in fact eventually surface. A few days after John Quincy's visit to Chan's bungalow on Punchbowl Hill, he receives a phone call from someone pretending to be Chan, hoping to lure him into a trap. The voice on the phone directs him to "the drug and grocery emporium of Liu Yin" on River Street, in Chinatown (254). Unable to borrow a car, John Quincy takes a trolley until its slow progress becomes too frustrating and he gets off to walk the rest of the way. His walk takes him through the streets of Chinatown, "past noodle cafés and pawn shops." As he hurries to River Street, he sees "a couple of tourists" drifting aimlessly and a few military men enjoying themselves at a commercial shooting gallery. The atmosphere in the neighborhood "was one of somnolent calm" (255). Much like John Quincy's "chop suey" evening in San Francisco, Honolulu's Chinatown—though Biggers once again does not use the term—seems anything but dark, dangerous, or threatening.

The "dark" version makes its appearance, however, after John Quincy reaches his destination, realizes he has been tricked, and tries to escape. Greeted at the door by an "old Chinaman," John Quincy's would-be kidnapper turns out to be not Chinese but white, a "huge red-haired man with the smell of the sea about him" (255). John Quincy outsmarts this bigger opponent by dousing the lights and laying him out with a football tackle. Seizing the opportunity to flee, it is at this moment John Quincy finally encounters something like the Chinatown of popular representation:

> He passed hurriedly through a cluttered back yard and climbing a fence, found himself in the neighborhood known as the River District. There in crazy alleys that have no names, no sidewalks, no beginning and no end, five races live together in the dark. Some houses were above the walk level, some below, all were out of alignment. John Quincy felt he had wandered into a futurist drawing. As he paused he heard the whine and clatter of Chinese music, the clicking of a typewriter, the rasp of a cheap phonograph playing American jazz, the distant scream of an auto horn, a child wailing Japanese lamentations. Footsteps in the yard beyond the fence roused him, and he fled. (258)

The "crazy alleys" of this passage take us right back to the "craziest structures" of Norris's *Blix* and share a common shorthand for the supposed architectural dementia of Chinatown. (Indeed, the word "crazy" itself originated as a structural metaphor, denoting an object or building that is full of cracks and thus liable to collapse into pieces.) Although the passage identifies this part of town as the "River District"—a descriptor not found in any of the contemporary guidebooks to Honolulu[56]—this seems part of Biggers's larger effort to avoid using the term "Chinatown" itself rather than an attempt to pinpoint a separate location. What is so striking about this eruption of sensationalist Chinatown imagery is the associative leap the narrative makes from spatial to racial confusion, registered initially in an equally disorienting present tense: "There in crazy alleys that have no names, no sidewalks, no beginning and no end, five races live together in the dark." The anxiety produced by this physical space, in other words, appears to derive from the "dark" (and ongoing) secret of racial mixture rather than the terror of Asian menace. Surrounded by a modernist cacophony ("whine," "clatter," "click," "rasp") perhaps more suited to a Dos Passos novel than to popular Chinatown fiction, John Quincy pauses to register the strangeness of this "futurist drawing" into which he feels he has wandered. On the one hand this pause might be understood as the moment at which the text simply gives in to the common Chinatown stereotypes it has tried so hard to avoid. On the other hand there is fascination here as well as fear, suggested by the way John Quincy picks out each of the sounds and identifies them one by one: the Chinese music, the typewriter, the American jazz, the auto horn, the child's lamentations. (Though one might well ask, by what mechanism does he distinguish some of these sounds? Does he really know what "Chinese music" sounds like, or "Japanese lamentations"?) By noting that John Quincy has to be "roused" from this moment of intense listening by the sound of approaching footsteps, the narrative seems to confirm that he is as mesmerized as he is appalled.

John Quincy's tangled attraction to this "dark" Chinatown moment, I would argue, has much to do with the novel's insistent yet repeatedly repressed conjunction of race, place, and sexuality. John Quincy has been sent to Hawaii on a family mission to coax his elderly, unmarried Aunt Minerva away from the sensuous gardens of Honolulu and back to "her calm, well-ordered life behind purple window-panes on Beacon Street" (20). It is not so much that Minerva is in danger of some sexual escapade, as that she is simply not behaving like a Winterslip. The family secret, however, is that there are two "strains" of Winterslip, the Boston Puritan and the wandering "gypsy." At the beginning of the novel, John Quincy represents the Puritan strain, with a vengeance. "He's a dear boy," Minerva observes, "but oh, so proper. . . . The gypsy strain missed him completely" (7). But the plot of the novel dictates that John Quincy will discover his repressed "gypsy" self away from home. The first sign of this discovery is his uncanny connection to San Francisco. Although he has "never [been] west of New York," as his ferry pulls into San Francisco harbor he gets "the oddest feeling" he has been there before (23). The eventual outcome of John Quincy's embrace of the Far West as his true home—and of the implicitly racialized "wandering gypsy" as his true identity—will be his romantic involvement with (and proposal of marriage to) a mixed-race girl of the islands, whom he not only meets on the very same ferry but to whom he tries to explain the uncanniness of this connection. That this girl, Carlota Egan, is not Asian but instead part Portuguese suggests the limits to the novel's endorsement of race-mixing, while also keeping the famously asexual Chan, even by association, away from the story's miscegenational subplot.[57]

At the precise moment John Quincy is trying to escape the red-haired sailor in the River District, however, he has not yet fully realized that he desires Carlota rather than his proper Boston fiancée (who is so appalled by the West and all it represents that she will later abandon a trip to meet him in San Francisco after making it as far as Wyoming) or his vivacious cousin Barbara. Thus the intensity of John Quincy's "Chinatown" experience makes fresh sense if we recognize the psychosexual anxiety it appears simultaneously to trigger, or at least subconsciously reflect. For even after he is roused by approaching footsteps and flees, John Quincy cannot seem to find his way out of a Chinatown that is quickly becoming a racialized space of terrifyingly intimate claustrophobia:

> He must get out of this mystic maze of mean alleys, and at once. Odd painted faces loomed in the dusk; pasty-white faces with just a suggestion of queer costumes beneath. A babel of tongues, queer eyes that glittered, once a lean hand on his arm. A group of moon-faced Chinese children under a lamp who scattered at his approach. And when he paused again, out of breath, the patter of many feet, bare feet, sandaled feet, the clatter of wooden clogs, the squeak of cheap shoes made in his own Massachusetts. Then suddenly the thump of large feet such as might belong to a husky sailor. He moved on. (258)

After the initial alliterative determination of "*m*ust get out of this *m*ystic *m*aze of *m*ean alleys," John Quincy's sentences collapse into fragments as his anxiety increases, particularly as the "pasty-white" faces and "queer" costumes (recalling the "queer dishes" he had eaten in San Francisco's Chinatown) press closer, even touch him. As though in a nightmare from which he cannot awake, a moment later John Quincy finds himself back where he started, in front of Liu Yin's shop. He is abducted again and driven to the docks, where he is saved from being "Shanghaied" (260) only by the last-minute intervention of a dockside reporter, prowling for news.

This episode complicates Rzepka's suggestion that Biggers's Honolulu glorifies racial harmony by offering "a utopian prototype of assimilation-ist multiculturalism."[58] Although earlier in the novel John Quincy is indeed impressed during one memorable trolley ride by the city's vibrant mix of "all colors and all creeds," which he sees reflected even in its architectural commingling—"[he] saw great houses set in blooming groves, a Japanese theater flaunting weird posters not far from a Ford service station, then a huge building he recognized as the palace of the monarch" (120)—his terrifying escape from Chinatown registers on a physical as well as symbolic level anxieties about Hawaii's spatial and multiracial admixture that the novel must work hard to push away. In other words, this is not simply a scene Biggers presents in order that he may then reject it in a gesture of anti-Orientalist triumphalism. Rather, it seems a necessary and necessarily vexed encounter with the potentially threatening yet also potentially appealing racial disorientation of Chinatown, a grappling with precisely the setting the novel has tried unsuccessfully to repress. Biggers thus does not merely "replace" the "architectural uncanny" of Chinatown with sunshine and beaches, as Rzepka suggests. Instead, *The House without a Key* actively struggles with its generic prototype in a not entirely successful attempt to leave it behind—or perhaps, we could even say, in an entirely successful attempt *not* to leave it behind.[59]

A similar if more subtle dynamic is at work in John Quincy's encounter with Chan's living room on Punchbowl Hill—the scene that opens the chapter that ends with John Quincy's Chinatown escape. Decorative echoes from stories like "Jade" and *The Insidious Dr. Fu-Manchu* seem everywhere in Chan's house, from the "pale golden lanterns hung from the ceiling" (nearly matching Fu-Manchu's hanging lamp, "suspended by golden chains from the ceiling"), to the "dwarfed trees" on Chan's teakwood tables (so like the "dwarfed pine tree" on the "ebony table" in "Jade"), to the "shoes of silk" (recalling the hallucinatory slippers in *Fu-Manchu*) on Chan's feet. Like the "crazy alleys" of Chinatown, these details mark the novel's conscious evocation of the lurid tradition with which Biggers's readers were so familiar. And yet as we have seen, these objects remain decidedly inert. Chan's slippers never lunge for John Quincy's throat; his "soft-toned rug" never threatens to swallow up his guest—nor would readers suspect for a moment they might. Unlike the episode in Chinatown, in which John Quincy feels truly in danger, in this scene he must grapple primarily with his own lingering discomfort with racial difference.

What is surprising about this scene is that John Quincy should feel as uncomfortable among Chan's possessions as he does. Although these cues might well come from popular fiction itself, by the 1920s in the world outside the novel Asian décor had become so thoroughly domesticated that one could have outfitted most of Chan's living room from a Montgomery Ward catalog. "The exotic holds no terrors for the American woman," declared a 1922 article in the advertising journal *Printer's Ink* on the "main street" success of the respected Asian import store Vantine's. Even this famous concern, one of the oldest in the country, had by the 1920s largely modulated its sales pitch from the mystery and craftsmanship of the "East"—"a permanent exposition of things unique and rare," as one early catalog put it—to something much closer to slightly exoticized ordinariness. By 1914, for example, Vantine's was pitching consumers an array of "Oriental Articles for Occidental Men" (Fig. 31), featuring "foreign" versions of such around-the-house items as ashtrays (Japanese),

No. 4400

No. 4400. Men's Pajamas of hand-loom Oriental silk or Chinese pongee, very soft and durable; well made throughout. In ordering please state color and size (chest measure.)

Silk, price prepaid, $12
Pongee, price prepaid, 10

173

No. 173. Vantine's Natural Color Pongee or Black Habutai Silk Office or House Coat. Excellently made and finished throughout. Sizes up to and including 42-inch chest measure.
Price prepaid, $7.00
Size 44 and larger Price prep'd, 7.50

171

No. 171. Vantine's Four-in-hand Scarf with patented neckband, designed to permit easy adjustment with folding collar. In any color desired. Price prepaid, $1

34965

No. 34965. Japanese Lacquered Ash Receiver. Heavy nickel top with revolving disk that automatically drops ashes into a removable tin receptacle; size 3¾x3¾.
Price prepaid, $1

5511

No. 5511. Vantine's Sirdar Egyptian Cigarettes, straw, cork, gold or plain tip.
Price per box of ten, 25c.; box of fifty, $1.15; box of one hundred, $2.25. Ladies' size, plain, box of ten, price, 20c.

35421

No. 35421. Japanese Cigarette Box. Press the spring and the stork dives down into the box and automatically picks up a cigarette; size 5½ x4½x2¾ inches. Price prepaid, $2.75

2229

No. 2229. Antimony Metal Cedar-lined Cigar Box, heavy embossed dragon and bamboo design; size 5½x 5½x2 inches. Price prepaid, $2.75

176

No. 176. Men's Turkish Leather Slippers, leather lined, soft and pliable. Colors, red, brown, and black; sizes 6½ to 11. Price prepaid, $1.25

3043

No. 3043. Japanese Embossed Leather Tobacco Pouch, assorted landscape designs. Colors, black and brown; size 4½x3½.
Price prepaid, $1.50

·A·A·VANTINE·&·CO·Inc·

Figure 31. "Oriental Articles for Occidental Men," A. A. Vantine and Company, *Vantine's: The Oriental Store*, catalog (1914), 44. Courtesy, The Winterthur Library: Printed Book and Periodical Collection.

cigarettes (Egyptian), cigarette boxes (Japanese), pajamas ("Oriental"), and slippers (Turkish). By 1917 you could turn to "The House of the Orient" for a one-pound box of pagoda-shaped chocolate crackers. By the 1920s Edmund Wilson—yes, that Edmund Wilson—lamented that even shopping at Vantine's in person "has lost a good deal of its fascination."[60]

John Quincy's anxiety, however, would seem to have less to do with the specific artifacts in the room than with Chan's presence among them, as though their conjunction confirms his host not as a middle-class consumer but as a racial alien. John Quincy's sense of the "great gulf" between himself and Chan mimics the reaction some visitors to Chinatown apparently felt when seeing Asian persons in their "native" setting. As one diarist wrote in 1915 after visiting San Francisco's Chinatown on his way to the Panama-Pacific Exposition: "The Oriental is stamped on every thing and one sees an alien race 'at home.'"[61] This sentiment precisely captures John Quincy's state of mind in Chan's living room and is one reason he feels relief when Chan reappears not in his purple robe and silk slippers but in "the conventional garb of Los Angeles or Detroit" (246). Although Biggers does not dramatize John Quincy's "escape" from his confining assumptions as he does his flight from Chinatown, the rest of the novel works to diminish the remoteness this "Boston boy" feels from Chan. Indeed, it is only after this chapter that John Quincy finally begins to shed his "New England inhibitions" (56) once and for all, subtly separating himself from the transplanted easterners who "had kept in their exile the old ideals of culture and caste" (281). As he separates from New England, he draws closer to both the people and the structures of Honolulu, developing a preference not merely for Carlota (whom the "blue-bloods" [108] shun for her mixed-race caste status until they discover she is related to a British admiral) over Agatha, but also for "bungalow[s] buried under purple alamander" (180) over the "particularly unlovely type of New England architecture" (181) favored by the island's leading Brahmin exile. Near the end of the novel, John Quincy will finally shake hands with Chan once again, this time sensing no "great gulf" between them but instead the pleasure of association. And in the novel's final dismantling of John Quincy's own Brahmin reserve—for that, rather than Chan's alienness, is what the text tries to suggest has been at stake all along—he will impetuously convince Carlota that he is not, as she had come to believe, "too dignified—and remote" (284) to fall in love with. For that matter, to the readers who demanded Biggers produce a sequel, one might say, neither was Chan.[62]

Through the Bamboo Curtain

If the brief scenes in Chan's living room and the claustrophobic alleys of Honolulu's River District mark the ways *The House without a Key* evokes the stereotypical settings of popular Chinatown fictions in order to try—if not entirely successfully—to distance itself from them, then a second, more pervasive set of architectural structures and metaphors works to foreground a very different spatial idiom in Biggers's text, one more consonant with the Asian-inspired open plan of Frank Lloyd Wright. These range from literal buildings like Dan Winterslip's "great, rambling house" (5) with its spacious living room and broad veranda; to the outdoor gardens like the one in the Hawaiian quarter under whose "fragrant" (64) date palms Minerva attends a luau; to Chan's recurring comparison of his progress in solving the murder to the act of breaking down a wall. The predominant spaces of the novel, in other words, both physical and figurative, emphasize fluidity of access and the expansion, rather than the contraction, of built forms.

Dan Winterslip's house, for example, where a good deal of the story's action takes place, is large, spacious, and open to the elements. His living room, which can be accessed directly through a door at the side of the house, is, after Wright's fashion, wide and uncluttered, and moreover "walled on but three sides," with the fourth consisting of "a vast expanse of wire screening" (6). Even from the dining room, Minerva can hear the ocean "murmur[ing] restlessly" (8) beyond the screens. Just off one end of the living room is a deep lanai, accessible through one of the many bamboo curtains that act as interior doors in Winterslip's house and that themselves economically express the interpenetration of inside and outside, of the natural and the built environments so characteristic of both the house's and, more generally, the novel's spaces. The lanai, of "generous size, screened on three sides and stretching far down on to the white beach" (10), functions in part as an extension of the living room, much like the broad verandas Wright often incorporated into his Prairie Houses. The illustration of the lanai by artist William Liepse that appeared in the serialized version of the novel in the *Saturday Evening Post* strongly emphasizes this openness (Fig. 32).[63]

Indeed, although Wright himself did not design specifically for the tropics, the spatial arrangements of vernacular Hawaiian architecture—which, as we have seen, were already strongly influenced by Japanese designs, and with which Wright may have become familiar when laying over in the islands on his trips to Japan—have much in common with his Prairie House phase. In their horizontal lines, open floor plans, and seamless integration of structure and setting, Wright may well have recognized principles similar to his own. As Kevin Nute notes, one of Wright's main objectives in the Prairie House designs was "the merging of interior and exterior." As Wright himself would later observe about his work during this phase: "My sense of 'wall' was no longer the side of a box. It was enclosure of space affording protection against storm or heat only when needed. But it was also to bring the outside

Figure 32. William Liepse, "Barbara Appeared on the Lanai, Dressed for a Drive. Her Eyes Were Somewhat Happier, a Bit of Color Had Come Back to Her Cheeks," illustration for Earl Derr Biggers, *The House without a Key*, *Saturday Evening Post* (21 February 1925), 25.

world into the house, and let the inside of the house go outside. In this sense I was working away at the wall as a wall and bringing it towards the function of a screen, a means of opening up space." Thus when Biggers makes Winterslip's house, with its spacious living room/lanai, the principal setting of his novel—the titular "house without a key"—he introduces a spatial aesthetic analogous to Wright's that serves as an explicit countersetting to the traditional buildingscape of Chinatown fiction.[64]

The novel's many gardens function similarly and are often represented either as extensions of the houses they enhance or as hybrid spaces of their own, as at the private backyard luau Minerva attends, where "pale golden Chinese lanterns, inscribed with scarlet letters" (64), hang from the trees above her head. The garden at Dan Winterslip's house is visible from the living room and the lanai, and characters repeatedly pass through it on their way into and out of the house, almost as though it were a part of the structure itself. At the aged Reef and Palm Hotel, owned by Carlota's father, John Quincy appreciates the way an adjacent garden helps both prop up and beautify the tottering facade: "Flowering vines clambered over [the hotel] in a friendly endeavor to hide its imperfections from the world" (101). As we have seen, even Honolulu itself is figured as a "great gorgeous garden" when viewed from Punchbowl Hill.

Chan's repeated figuration of the work of detection as the dismantling of a wall further carries the novel's interest in architectural openness into its metaphorical register. Chan first introduces the trope about halfway through the book, after two promising clues lead nowhere. "The page ripped from guest book, the brooch lying silent on floor. Both are now followed into presence of immovable stone wall," Chan tells John Quincy. "We sway about, looking for other path" (151–52). Each time another clue fails them, Chan repeats the figure. "'Filled with nothing,' murmured Chan," referring to an empty ohia wood box each hoped might hold the secret to the murder. "Another dream go smash against stone wall" (186). The excessive use of this metaphor, often rendered in Chan's stilted English, can at times seem designed to mock his penchant for mystical "Oriental" aphorisms. "'Stone wall surround us,' [Chan] said dreamily, 'But we circle about, seeking loophole. Moment of discovery will come'" (248). And yet near the end of the novel Biggers pointedly has Chan lay claim to this figure as a more accurate description of his professional labors than a metaphor the chief of police casually tosses out. As they close in on a potentially important suspect, the chief says to Chan, "Charlie, you old rascal, you've got the scent at last." But Chan refuses this metaphor. "With your gracious permission," he says, "I would alter the picture. Stone walls are crumbling now like dust. Through many loopholes light stream in like rosy streaks of dawn" (275). More architect or structural engineer than bloodhound, Chan indeed deserves credit for figuring out how to tear down these "walls"—which are coming down largely through his efforts, despite the passive voice of "are crumbling"—and break the case, as it were, wide open.

In *The House without a Key* even the staging of murder works to reconfigure the spatial expectations of popular Chinatown fiction. Where a novel like *The Insidious Dr. Fu-Manchu* depends on the architectural puzzle of the "locked room" mystery—the apparent impossibility of someone either entering a closed space to commit murder or vanishing from it without opening a door or window—Dan Winterslip is killed on his lanai, ostensibly one of the most "open" spaces in the text. Rohmer's novel in particular fetishizes the locked room conundrum, in which terror lies in the breaching of an unbreachable space, symbolizing an assault on one's deepest personal and spatial integrity. (As the leader of a secret society whose supposed goal is to take over the West, Fu-Manchu threatens to breach the integrity of national/political space as well.) In *The House without a Key*, on the other hand, terror arises from the impossibility of locking the door in the first place. "In all Dan's great house," Minerva later reflects, "she could not recall ever having seen a key. In these friendly trusting islands, locked doors were obsolete" (73). The lanai, where Winterslip keeps a cot and prefers to sleep, is the most vulnerable space of all. From the outside, one can enter through a simple screen door; from the inside, one can merely push aside the bamboo curtain. Already frightened for his life, having recently learned that the son of a man he long ago robbed of a great fortune is on his way to Honolulu, perhaps to settle old scores, Winterslip can do nothing but wonder through what opening his avenger will arrive. "He sat in the dark to think. His face was turned toward the curtain of bamboo between him and the living-room. On that curtain a shadow appeared, was motionless a second, then vanished. He caught his breath—again the shadow. 'Who's there?' he called" (17).

This is a fascinating moment. Here the spatial terror in *The House without a Key* is heightened by the vulnerability of openness itself, accentuated by structures and floor plans that offer access, not entombment.[65] This is not the vulnerability of total exposure; it is not like standing in an open field, or in a room without walls. Rather, it is the vulnerability of only partially screened protection, the terror of not quite knowing what to expect around the next corner—or on the other side of that bamboo curtain. This is a terror analogized in the novel's romance subplot as well. The anxiety that makes John Quincy hesitate to act on his desire for the mixed-race Carlota—and thus to commit to building a new life in the cities of the West—is also very much a fear of what lies ahead.[66]

If uncertainly about what lies ahead marks one way in which the novel's fluidity of access (to persons as well as places) carries certain risks, for at least one scholar it also defines, in architectural terms, what we might call the spatial narrative of a Frank Lloyd Wright interior. As H. Allen Brooks first suggested in his influential essay on Wright's "destruction of the box," we fundamentally misunderstand Wright's adherence to the "open plan" and "flowing space" if we think it means simply an increase in "the degree of openness between the rooms." Instead, Brooks argues, as his Prairie House plans matured, Wright increasingly (and ingeniously) sought to "interlock" rooms by making them share overlapping space, such that the view from one room into the next is in fact not wide open but instead "diagonal and pinched at the point of intersection." Thus while Wright did enlarge the openings between the rooms of the boxed-in domestic interior to create "a sense of greater openness," the effect of this pinched overlapping is to introduce "a sense of mystery into the spatial sequence," into the way one literally moves through a Wright interior. As Brooks explains:

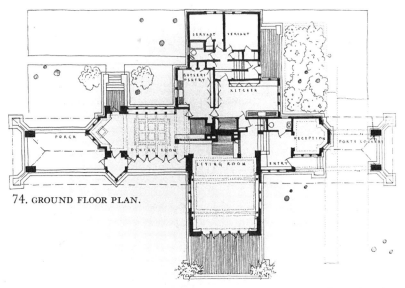

74. GROUND FLOOR PLAN.

Figure 33. Frank Lloyd Wright, Ward W. Willits House, Highland Park, Illinois (1902), ground-floor plan, Henry-Russell Hitchcock, *In the Nature of Materials* (1942), ill. 74. Courtesy Marquand Library of Art and Archaeology, Princeton University Library.

Mystery is an essential element in Wrightian space; he never resolves all visual questions at once; rather he holds in reserve something to be examined later. To assist in this process of limiting and controlling the view and guarding the privacy of the adjoining spaces, Wright screens openings by various means—for example, vertical wooden slats combined with low bookshelves (Willits house), walls that do not reach the ceiling (Roberts and Hanna houses), fireplaces or chimneys that open into the neighboring space (Martin and Robie houses).[67]

It is the careful management of opened space, in other words, not the simple fact of spaciousness, that characterizes Wright's interiors. The floor plan of the Willits House (Fig. 33), whose facade we saw in Figure 26, for example, shows how Wright pinches the living room and the dining room at their interlocking point to limit and control the view from one room into the other, while still giving each room access to a different face of the same central fireplace, in the process maintaining almost quite literally an "open hearth" around which the principal first-floor rooms circulate. (Only the servants' rooms, behind the kitchen, are kept off this main circuit.) The photograph in Figure 34, which looks from dining room past the interlocking point toward the living room hearth, gives an intimate sense of what it might mean, in a Wright Prairie House, to wonder "what lies ahead." You can almost see into the living room, but not quite. The other screening mechanisms Brooks highlights can be seen here as well, including the low bookshelf on the left that partially screens the dining room fireplace from the living room view, and the vertical wooden slats at the rear center that half screen, half allow a view of the entry and reception areas. Were we able to move through the house, room to room, we would have an even clearer sense of the "mystery" to which Brooks refers.[68]

Thus if it seems something of a stretch to think of Charlie Chan as an architect, it might not be so odd to imagine Frank Lloyd Wright as a detective—or a mystery novelist. For in a more figurative sense, may we not say that Brooks here describes, quite eloquently, the mechanisms of the detective genre itself? And is this not, in particular, also a metaphor for Biggers's management of *The House without a Key*? Never resolving all questions at once, holding in reserve "something to be examined later," introducing

Figure 34. Frank Lloyd Wright, Ward W. Willits House, Highland Park, Illinois (1902), looking toward entrance foyer from dining room, Bruce Brooks Pfeiffer, *Frank Lloyd Wright: Selected Houses*, vol. 1 (1991), 116. Courtesy Marquand Library of Art and Archaeology, Princeton University Library.

devices to screen the novel's most consequential openings, even moving two detectives forward along overlapping trajectories (Chan the professional and John Quincy the amateur) rather than one sleuth with a single perspective. Indeed, it is only when Chan and John Quincy both come, finally, to the same view—that Barbara's fiancé Jennison must be the murderer—that the mystery of *The House without a Key* can at last be solved.

But there is even more to Dan Winterslip's lanai scene in the novel than this. We have left poor Dan alone, awaiting his murderer. "He caught his breath—again the shadow. 'Who's there?' he called." Suddenly a "huge brown arm" is thrust through the bamboo—Winterslip flinches—but it is only his Hawaiian housekeeper bringing him some fruit.

In this moment Winterslip's spatial vulnerability is figured in explicitly racial terms: sitting in the dark, he cowers from the "shadow" that appears on the curtain and then flinches as the "huge brown arm" of his housekeeper breaches his private space. That the arm is followed by Kamaikui's "friendly brown face" only momentarily relieves Winterslip's anxiety. "What was the matter with him, anyhow? He who had fought through unspeakable terrors in the early days—nervous—on edge" (17). These "unspeakable terrors," the novel will slowly reveal, are those that had shadowed Winterslip as a young man plying his trade as a "blackbirder" (59)—an illegal trafficker in black contract labor for the South Pacific plantation economy. This particular breach of the "bamboo curtain" (which would not become a widely used metaphor for the supposed divide between Asia and the West until the 1940s) thus not only anticipates the later eruption of the novel's repressed "dark" Chinatown motif, in which Asian bodies threaten white characters by their sudden, almost claustrophobic proximity; it also marks a return of the repressed crime of enslavement, whose profits built the very house in which the breach takes place.

Thus in *The House without a Key*, despite Biggers's sincerest efforts, not even the structures most clearly intended to counter the architectural and decorative idioms of popular Chinatown fictions—and that resonate most strongly with the Asian-inspired practice of someone like Frank Lloyd Wright—can fully escape the constraints of Orientalist, or indeed, more broadly, racialist representation. We might have suspected as much even earlier in the novel, as John Quincy's dilatory Aunt Minerva, looking out at the tropical night from this very same lanai, warms to the view:

> For this, after all, was the time she loved Waikiki best. So brief, this tropic dusk, so quick the coming of the soft alluring night. The carpet of the waters, apple-green by day, crimson and gold at sunset, was a deep purple now. On

top of that extinct volcano called Diamond Head a yellow eye was winking, as though to hint there might still be fire beneath. Three miles down, the harbor lights began to twinkle, and out toward the reef the lanterns of Japanese sampans glowed intermittently. Beyond, in the roadstead, loomed the battered hulk of an old brig slowly moving toward the channel entrance. Always, out there, a ship or two, in from the East with a cargo of spice or tea or ivory, or eastward bound with a load of tractor salesmen. Ships of all sorts, the spic and span liner and the rakish tramp, ships from Melbourne and Seattle, New York and Yokohama, Tahiti and Rio, any port on the seven seas. For this was Honolulu, the Crossroads of the Pacific—the glamorous crossroads where, they said, in time all paths crossed again. Miss Minerva sighed. (12)

Seated on the screened and covered lanai, Minerva in her reverie nonetheless collapses the distinction between inside (the enclosed space of the lanai) and outside (Honolulu and its harbor), figuring the waters as an expanse of "carpet" spread out around her. Once again architectural space dilates rather than contracts. No "dark" Chinatown here—nothing threatens; even the volcano only winks. Instead everything allures, especially the ships in the water, which Minerva imagines "crossing" at sea almost erotically, led by the mingling of the "spic and span liner" with the "rakish tramp." But of course this is where the racialist tropes finally surface. Opposites merge; East meets West ("Melbourne and Seattle, New York and Yokohama"); and suddenly the Orientalist fantasy of contact with the exotic other—safely managed in the U.S.-controlled Honolulu harbor—takes center stage. Minerva sighed, indeed.

The Empty Chair

In closing this chapter it would be well for us to remember that, as Mari Yoshihara and Kristin Hoganson have demonstrated, fantasies of contact with exotic others, particularly through decorative and architectural Orientalism, do not necessarily produce structures of dominance and submission. More neutral and in some cases even more liberatory impulses were often at work, for example, among the middle- and upper-class American women at the turn of the century who chose to "embrace" the "East."[69] And yet in The House without a Key it is striking how few "Orientals"—within a story that places the longing for tropical otherness at the heart of its plot—play even minor roles. Despite the novel's setting, beyond Chan there are precious few Chinese, Japanese, or Hawaiian characters that speak, let alone advance the story. For all the imagined couplings of East with West, in other words, there

Figure 35. "Chairs from China," advertisement, Vantine's: The Oriental Store, *House and Garden* 25.4 (April 1914), n.p. (inside front cover). Courtesy, The Winterthur Library: Printed Book and Periodical Collection.

seem to be many more characters from the latter region than the former, even as the "presence" of the "East" is felt so strongly throughout.

This dependence on and desire for a material Asian presence despite the conspicuous absence of actual Asian referents embodies the contradiction at the heart not just of Biggers's novel but also, ironically, of the architectural and decorative embrace of "Oriental" forms in U.S. culture, which flourished during precisely the years in which Americans sought the tightest possible restrictions on immigration from Asia. Nowhere is this contradiction more forcefully modeled than in an advertisement placed by Vantine's in the April 1914 issue of *House and Garden*. This full-page, full-color ad for Vantine's "Canton Chairs" appeared in the most costly and visible position in the issue, the reverse of that month's cover (Fig. 35). The top half of the ad shows a light-colored, comfortable-looking rattan chair on a screened-in porch. Titled "Chairs from China," the ad extols the virtues of these popular designs, "woven by hand in Canton." "There is not a visible nail in the entire construction," the ad asserts, invoking the analogous architectural quirk that so intrigued visitors to the Japanese pavilion almost four decades earlier at the 1876 Philadelphia Centennial. In addition to being "strong and durable and the most comfortable furniture made," these chairs have special appeal for the aesthetically inclined: "Because of their artistic lines they are the favored studio chairs of the nation's most famous artists." Biggers chooses almost exactly this kind of chair—or perhaps a slightly more expensive and exclusive version—in furnishing Dan Winterslip's house. "Winterslip strolled back to his living-room. He sat down in a rattan chair that had been made especially for him in Hong-Kong, and glanced complacently about at the many evidences of his prosperity" (6).

The irony of Vantine's ad, of course, lies in its subtitle: "Our Annual Importation." Did the copywriters recognize when they chose these words that they were unintentionally affirming the hard distinction in the early twentieth century between "Oriental" goods and Asian persons as desirable import objects? (Did Biggers, for that matter, recognize when he placed chairs like these around Winterslip's house that he was employing a symbol not simply of his character's wealth but of the broader Orientalist economy in which he participated?) The boldface type in the ad—along with the specificity of the word "annual"—seems to announce both an arrival and a quota, as though to communicate, without intentional irony, the significance of the product's availability through the vocabulary of immigration itself, while at the same time making clear the distinction between the chairs' "unique Oriental craftsmanship" and the actual craftspersons who made them. Leaving the chair empty turns out to be an effective touch, too—all the better to see the product, but also easier to dissociate it from the hands that made it. (When Dan Winterslip is murdered, his chair will finally go empty, too.)

Which brings us back, once more, to Frank Lloyd Wright. On the one hand, Wright has always seemed immune from the charges of Orientalism that have been levied against creative work in so many fields during this period. If anything, Wright has been felt to have imbibed Asian architectural and decorative ideas so thoroughly and so naturally (in large part through his love affair with Japanese wood-block prints) that he did not need to acknowledge—indeed would be hard-pressed to acknowledge—any specific influence. Coupled with the generally high regard with which he was held in Japan for his work on the new Imperial Hotel in Tokyo (1916–22)—especially after his structure was one of the few buildings to survive the Great Kanto Earthquake of 1923—it is little wonder that we tend not to think of Wright in the same company as other Anglo-American popularizers of Asian idioms or materials. And yet to the extent that he so resolutely denied any influence from Asian architecture on his spatial reconception of the American domestic interior—"Do not accuse me of trying to 'adapt Japanese forms,'" Wright excoriated English Arts and Crafts architect C. R. Ashbee in 1911; "THAT IS A FALSE ACCUSATION AND AGAINST MY RELIGION"—Wright, too, if only analogously, would seem to embody the same contradiction we have seen at work so potently in both the broader Orientalist movement and the imagined world of Charlie Chan: that one might draw deeply on Asian forms while holding Asians themselves at bay.[70]

Coda
Black Cabin, White House

Architecture is politics by other means.
>—Russell L. Mahan, "Political Architecture: The
>Building of the President's House" (2004)

In 1891, architect George F. Barber of Knoxville, Tennessee, published his third booklet of house designs, *Cottage Souvenir No. 2, A Repository of Artistic Cottage Architecture and Miscellaneous Designs.* His first two
booklets, produced in 1887 and 1888 while he was still practicing in DeKalb,
Illinois, had been modestly successful, but *Cottage Souvenir No. 2* made Barber, so to speak, a household name. Advertised nationally in high-circulation
periodicals such as *The Cosmopolitan* (Fig. 36), Barber's booklet attracted
customers interested in his "very attractive" and "artistic dwellings" from
all parts of the country, and soon, from abroad. Over the next twenty years,
thousands of homes modeled on Barber's designs, often known colloquially as "Barber Houses," were erected in the U.S., Canada, and as far away as
China, South Africa, and the Philippines, making him one of the most popular mail-order house plan designers of the nineteenth century. Operating just
before the heyday of precut mail-order companies like Aladdin—Barber sold
plans, not build-it-yourself kits—by 1900 his firm employed close to thirty
draftsmen and twenty secretaries to copy his nearly 800 designs and handle
the firm's voluminous correspondence. Barber's houses, too, differed from
Aladdin's. Instead of bungalows, he specialized in the more quirky vertical-
ity of the Romanesque and Queen Anne styles. (The house pictured in the
advertisement in Figure 36, Design 36, is fairly typical of the types of homes
that appear in *Cottage Souvenir No. 2.*) Many of Barber's houses still stand
today.[1]

Inside *Cottage Souvenir No. 2* Barber featured designs for fifty-nine different homes as well as plans for a few nondomestic structures (barns, store-
fronts, a church, a chapel). To prospective buyers he touted his broad experi-

Figure 36. Advertisement, George F. Barber's *Cottage Souvenir No. 2* (1891), *Cosmopolitan* 12.6 (April 1892), "Advertising Department," 16.

ence designing for different regions and classes. "I have had several years of personal practice in the West, and especially in the North, . . . and have lately had two years experience traveling over the South, from the Ohio River to the Gulf of Mexico, planning, arranging and designing residences for every class of people, thus gaining a very clear knowledge of the various requirements of house planning for any section of the country."[2] Judging from his widespread success, such credentials convinced. In our own period, many of Barber's designs have been reprinted and analyzed in histories of American architecture and domesticity, offering as they do tremendous insight into late nineteenth-century ideas about, and attitudes toward, design theory, building practice, craftsmanship, gender relations, and a whole host of other social, cultural, economic, and aesthetic issues surrounding the American home.

What has received significantly less attention, however—indeed, almost total silence—are two prominent images from the book that provide equally valuable insight into late nineteenth-century ideas about, and attitudes toward, race: the pair of engravings Barber asks his readers to study before turning to the house plans themselves, "Uncle Tom's Cabin" and "Old Cabin Home" (Fig. 37). Jointly captioned "Contrasted Architecture," these images of impoverished African Americans standing in front of crude one- or two-room cabins in the rural South appear just after Barber's twin prefaces ("Remarks on the Principles of Design, Harmony of Form and Proportion in Architecture" and "Hints to Home Builders") and immediately before the first actual house design. Barber explains the purpose of the images in a brief note on the facing page:

The two scenes on the opposite page were engraved direct from photographs taken from real life in the Great Smoky Mountains of North Carolina in the vicinity of Asheville. The engravings are given for their oddity
and picturesqueness. The contrast between these two homes and those on
the following pages gives us an idea of the advancement of modern architecture in this country. (12)[3]

Within the pattern book genre, these images are nothing short of remarkable. As we have seen, although American house-plan books were often
founded on a range of racial assumptions, the "direct" depiction of persons
of color, let alone reference to the housing styles or standards of nonwhite
people, particularly African Americans, is extremely rare. In Barber's book
these engravings appear to function as a kind of inverted or ironic frontispiece: they illustrate the type of architecture absolutely *un*characteristic of
the houses featured in the volume, the very homes—and by association, the
very persons—one is guaranteed *not* to find in the book itself.

Barber may have seen the images more benignly. His explanatory note
does not refer to the people in the photographs, only the structures; nor
does he mention race at all. In declaring that the "two homes" pictured in
the engravings provide "an idea of the advancement of modern architecture
in this country," Barber may have simply been trying to illustrate what had
become a common trope in late-century pattern books: that American architecture had evolved from the "log cabin" to the "modern house." According
to Linda E. Smeins, only a few years before Barber published *Cottage Souvenir No. 2*, for example, Robert Shoppell included in his own pattern book,
Modern Houses, an illustration purporting to show precisely that trajectory.[4]
Perhaps Barber just wanted to be up to date. And yet the iconography of the
houses in Barber's engravings does not quite seem to say "log cabin." Instead,
it seems quite clearly to say "slave cabin." Calling one of the images "Uncle
Tom's Cabin" suggests that at some level Barber understood this all too well.

The titles of the images, in fact, reveal more than the images themselves
about the ways Barber expected his audience to respond to them. Rather
than call to mind a specific part of North Carolina "in the vicinity of Asheville," as Barber's note would have it, "Uncle Tom's Cabin" and "Old Cabin
Home"—the title of the second image—gesture, in the cultural shorthand of
late nineteenth-century America, toward generalized white idealizations of
black home life under slavery, nostalgic inventions that found their broad-
est expression on the minstrel stage. (Barber seems to acknowledge as much
by designating the images "scenes.") "The Old Cabin Home" was in fact the

"UNCLE TOM'S CABIN."

"OLD CABIN HOME."

Figure 37. "Contrasted Architecture," George F. Barber, *Cottage Souvenir No. 2* (1891), rpt. as *Victorian Cottage Architecture: An American Catalog of Designs, 1891* (Mineola, NY: Dover, 2004), 13.

title of an antebellum minstrel song, first published in 1858 and still popular at the end of the century. And of course by 1891, "Uncle Tom's Cabin" no longer primarily connoted Stowe's outrage against slavery but the popular "Tom shows" that toured the country.[5] When Barber notes that he has provided the engravings for their "picturesqueness," he is invoking the charms of the "good old days" of slavery apotheosized in the plantation school genre, not the harmonious irregularity of the ideal cottage home championed by Andrew Jackson Downing—the characteristic idiom, in fact, of most of Barber's own home designs. Indeed, he invokes these cabin charms not once but twice.

Thus even though Barber does not refer directly to the African American figures in these engravings, he does not have to: the doubled invocation of the plantation genre, which sutures person to place, subject to site, ensures that his readers will understand the connection. What Barber's readers are being asked simultaneously to recognize and reject, in other words, is not merely "cabin" architecture but, however inaccurately and stereotypically, "black" architecture. In which case, we might say that the evolutionary history of American home building Barber invokes—"the advancement of modern architecture in this country"—runs not simply from "old cabin" to "modern house" but more particularly from "old *black* cabin" to "modern *white* house."

And yet perhaps "reject" is not quite the right word. Evolution implies a chain of connection, not outright rejection. In an evolutionary model, the "black" architecture of the cabins would represent both a superseded phase and a point of origin, at once antithetical to yet also necessary for the emergence of "modern architecture." Toni Morrison's analysis of the necessary dependence of white American writers on an often hidden "Africanist" presence in their narratives, though not addressed to architecture, might nonetheless offer a further gloss on the functions of these two images in Barber's catalog. "Through significant and underscored omissions, startling contradictions, heavily nuanced conflicts, through the way writers peopled their work with the signs and the bodies of this presence," Morrison argues, "one can see that a real or fabricated Africanist presence was crucial to their sense of Americaness."[6] May we not make an analogous claim for Barber's catalog? After all, it is through these engravings—which offer a striking combination of both a "real" (i.e., photographic) *and* a "fabricated" (i.e., plantation-schooled) Africanist presence—that *Cottage Souvenir No. 2* works to shore up the identity of Barber's prospective house-plan buyers, their sense of being not just "advanced" and "modern" but also "American" ("the advancement of modern architecture *in this country*") and thus implicitly "white." Perhaps nowhere else have the often unspoken racial assumptions of the American pattern book genre been so clearly articulated.

The apparent unremarkableness of these images for past scholarly examinations of Barber's catalog is symptomatic of one of the central concerns of this book: that we have not yet trained ourselves to notice powerful connections between race and American architecture even when, figuratively speaking, they are looking us right in the face. In tracing the multiple ways race has shaped the literary and cultural meanings of American architecture from the beginning of the pattern book era to the early twentieth-century designs of Frank Lloyd Wright, *Sites Unseen* has attempted to remedy this blind spot in the interdisciplinary study of literature and the built environment—to clarify, for the first time, the central importance of race in the study of architecture at precisely the moment architecture became centrally important to American culture.

I close this book in the early twentieth century at a moment of transition, and also continuity. By the 1920s, American architecture had firmly consolidated itself as a profession and begun to receive international recognition. New forms, and new phases, would soon take center stage, as pluralist experimentation in the arts of building—accelerated by dynamic postwar economic growth and a concomitant intensification of land values in and around American cities—would give rise to the classic era of the modern skyscraper, to ambitious (if not always fulfilled) plans for the redesign of urban space, and to "modern" ideas about the organization and appearance of suburban neighborhoods.[7] American literary production would find itself at a similar crossroads, marked by the advent (in general) of a more experimental modernism and the transformative emergence (in particular) of the Harlem Renaissance. At the same time, the central questions that animate this book do not in any sense disappear with the closing of this formative period. If, as I have argued, the built environment is always shaped in some way by race, whether such shaping is explicitly acknowledged or understood, then one might productively investigate the ongoing contact between race, writing, and architecture in the decades that follow the close of this study. Or, for that matter, in the decades before this study—not, in either case, to reproduce the specific findings here but instead to historicize and particularize this intricate interrelationship as thoroughly as possible. I hope this book will provoke just such future work.

This is a propitious moment in which to conduct this analysis. Attention to race in the study of architecture and the built environment, though not yet as advanced as that taking place in some other interdisciplinary fields, has grown encouragingly since I first began to examine Chesnutt's porches. As collateral disciplines such as cultural geography, material culture, and landscape architecture bring race more to the center of their own inquiries, moreover, the analytical tools on which literary scholars and cultural historians may draw will continue to become more sophisticated and various. And contemporary events—particularly the ascension of the first African American to the presidency, and the resulting (and highly public) move by a black family into the nation's most symbolic house—have brought fresh attention to questions of race, space, and national identity. Indeed, the election of Barack Obama in November 2008 produced a brief surge of popular interest in the relationship between race and the built environment, as U.S. news organizations rushed to report the apparently surprising historical irony—well known to scholars but not the general public—that the White House, like many official structures in the nation's capital, was built in part by African American slaves.[8]

If the history of the impact of race on the American architectural landscape—a history, as we have seen, that has often been hidden in plain sight—still has the power to surprise, it is only because the work of forgetting, as Chesnutt surely learned while trying to publish his conjure tales in the late 1800s, has been so efficient and so thorough. This is as true for the White House as it was for the colonnaded plantation porches on which Chesnutt centered his revisionary stories or, for that matter, for the midcentury architectural pattern books that tried to pretend slavery did not exist. In fact, the president's house—a structure whose past and present intersect powerfully with many of the histories (and stories) that make up this book—is an apt site with which to bring this investigation to a close and to point ahead in new directions. As we saw with Barber's *Cottage Souvenir No. 2*, what is at stake in such investigations is nothing less than a set of vital questions: Who belongs in what spaces? How are our experiences, understandings—and narratives—of those spaces shaped, in the end, by race? What better place, indeed, to examine these questions than the *nation's* "white house."

Initially envisioned by George Washington as a "President's Palace," the structure already known unofficially in the early 1800s as the White House because of the snowy whitewash on its stone exterior not only was built by slaves but also was staffed predominantly by black servants, both slave and free. The original house, which in all likelihood drew part of its inspiration from the statehouse in Charleston, South Carolina, bore multiple traces, if one knew where to look, of its complexly multicultural heritage—from the single-story plantation-style porch that was supposed to run the full length of the building's south facade (and that, had it been built, would have elevated the racially amalgamated porch we examined in chapter 2 from a southern to a national symbol), to the West Indian mahogany finish wood that eventually did grace the interior. This last feature was a luxury imported from, of all places, Santo Domingo, a source in the early nineteenth century not only for "richly figured, dark and durable" wood but also for deep-felt white anxieties about slave insurrection.[9]

Whether these design elements would have been recognized as racial in nature at the time, early in its history the White House as a symbolic site was vigorously defended as white space. At least one commentator decrying the raucous mob that attended the open house at the Executive Mansion following the inauguration of Andrew Jackson in 1829, for example, was more shocked by the apparent racial desecration of the president's home than by the leveling disruptions of class. In a private letter written shortly after the president's welcoming "levee," Congressman James Hamilton of South Carolina fulminated about the "regular Saturnalia" he personally witnessed:

> The Mob broke in, in thousands—Spirits black yellow & grey, poured in in one uninterrupted stream of mud & filth, among the throng many subjects for the penitentiary and not the fewest among them [were] Mr Mercer's tyros for Liberia.—It would have done Mr Wilberforce's heart good to have seen a stout black wench eating in this free Country a jelley with a gold spoon at the President's House.[10]

As cultural historian Jeff Smith notes, for Hamilton—who found the entire scene distasteful—the "key index of disorder" in this scene of spatial violation is race, figured first as murky color ("spirits black yellow & grey"), then as noxious sewage ("one uninterrupted stream of mud & filth"), before provocatively congealing—almost in anticipation of the very "jelley" she eats—into the "stout black wench" who defiles the president's house not simply by her presence but by her presumption of belonging.[11]

It is Jackson's presidency, ironically, that largely gave us the White House we know today. Whereas the comparatively bare structure of the early 1800s would look odd to contemporary viewers, accustomed as we are in particular to the dramatic pillared embellishments of the north and south porticoes, these elements were not fully completed until Jackson took office. As White House historian William Seale observes, the uniform white color scheme, maintained as the house expanded, kept these striking additions from seeming tacked on once the north portico was finished in 1830: "White paint melded existing house and new portico into a single composition. With the completion of the north portico the White House—or better said, the *image* of the White House—was permanently established."[12] Within a generation the structure had become iconic, representing not merely national power but white privilege. When African American author William Wells Brown, for example, wanted to dramatize in his novel *Clotel; or, The President's Daughter: A Narrative of Slave Life in the United States* (1853) the "appalling tragedy" of his title character's decision to kill herself rather than return to slavery, he has her leap into the Potomac "within plain sight of the president's house," depicting the structure as a shamed witness to the racial crimes its tacit approval helps perpetuate. Hannah Crafts shapes a similar scene in *The Bondwoman's Narrative*, commenting on the "extraordinary contrast" between the "splendid show made by the President's House and the Capitol" and the appalling spectacle of a "negro designed for sale" being "dragged, though shrieking and praying, and struggling, manacles placed on his limbs, . . . to the market."[13] By 1869, as we have seen, Smith's Pictorial Parlor Oracle (the board game that suggestively linked human physiognomy with architectural space) would implicitly identify the "face" of the White House as Anglo-Saxon. Even at the public reception celebrating Lincoln's second inauguration—as Elizabeth Keckley, Mary Todd Lincoln's black dressmaker, reports in her memoir *Behind the Scenes; Or, Thirty Years a Slave and Four Years in the White House* (1868)—people of color, including Frederick Douglass, were prevented by armed policemen from entering the president's home. In stark contrast to the chaos of what Congressman Hamilton had decried in 1829 as Jackson's racial "Saturnalia," only a private intervention with Lincoln himself—by none other than another U.S. congressman—gained special admission for Douglass that night.[14]

What social custom accomplished inside the White House, the Colonial Revival, one might say, helped bring to pass on the outside. Or, more precisely, helped bring to stasis. As we have seen, the late-century neocolonial turn in American architecture—fueled by a potent mix of preservationist zeal and racial nostalgia—admired (and sought to protect) structures with the clean lines and boxy shapes of the early republic. The White House, like Washington's own Georgian neoclassical Mount Vernon estate (the object, beginning in the 1850s, of the first sustained historic preservation effort in the U.S.),[15] was a natural candidate for such attention. And thus despite the desire of nearly every president between Ulysses S. Grant and Theodore Roosevelt to see the aging structure—which they regarded as too outdated to meet its uniquely complex bureaucratic and domestic needs—either razed, redesigned, or relocated (a sentiment Mark Twain captured in his novel *The Gilded Age* [1873] when he mocked the outside of the building as ugly and the inside for its "dreariness, flimsiness, [and] bad taste"), there was, according to Seale, "strong, quiet opposition on all fronts to the destruction of the historic house."[16] Roosevelt would oversee the most thorough renovation of the White House since the British burned much of it to the ground during the War of 1812 only by making sure McKim, Mead, and White—the architectural firm most closely identified with the Colonial Revival—preserved the "external image" of the building and the general layout of the interior. Although Roosevelt would outrage many whites in 1901 by inviting the African American educator Booker T. Washington to dine at the White House (a gesture felt to endorse race mixing of all types), it was also Roosevelt's idea to change the official name of the structure itself from the Executive Mansion to the White House, giving the century-old nickname a legal status to match its cultural one.[17]

And yet even as the White House's exterior (and new title) bespoke the orderly white facade of the Colonial Revival, its interior would continue to be shaped by more heterogeneous racial markers. Though Charles McKim pulled up the old pine and mahogany flooring in the main building, for example (replacing it with bleached northern oak), just a few years later Nathan C. Wyeth, the architect chosen by Roosevelt's successor, William Howard Taft, to redesign what is now known as the West Wing, installed in the first Oval Office a checkerboard parquet floor featuring—perhaps in tribute to Taft's years as governor-general of the U.S.'s most recent colonial acquisition—dark mahajua wood from the Philippines.[18] Indeed, Taft and his wife, Helen Herron Taft, brought to the White House a special enthusiasm for Asian furniture and décor, installing in the mansion precisely the kind of profusely decorated "Oriental" room that, as we have seen, was so broadly fashionable in the late nineteenth and early twentieth centuries. Even *Good Housekeeping*, the popular domestic advice monthly, took notice, marveling in a nine-page insider's tour of the Taft White House in 1911 that Mrs. Taft's Asian-themed library, located "just over the blue rooms of the state apartments," was "one of the most interesting rooms in the White House." Instead of featuring "conventional drawing-room furniture," the magazine informed its readers, the octagonal library offered

an Oriental interior with all the cunningly carved teakwood chairs and tables and cabinets, wonderful Eastern fabrics for curtains and brilliant splashes of gold dragons on rich backgrounds, a screen of soft wistaria bloom, and wall panels of the tender grays of Japanese art; a tea-table covered with an exquisite piece of embroidery and Oriental pottery. Nowhere has Mrs. Taft's gift as a decorator found fuller and truer expression. These precious bits were collected by her all over the world.[19]

If in Helen Taft's library the White House's interior aesthetic embraced Orientalist cosmopolitanism, in other rooms the lines separating one race from another were drawn much more firmly, in keeping with the increasingly strict segregationist practices of Jim Crow. Of the twenty-five full-time servants working for the Tafts, for example, the majority of African American staff were restricted to basement and state floor positions, while white staff predominated in the upstairs family quarters. Mealtimes were even more strictly segregated. For years in the White House, servants' meals had been stratified by rank: regardless of race, staff at the same job level ate together. The Tafts' new housekeeper, Englishwoman Elizabeth Jaffray, put an end to such mixing, deciding almost immediately after the Tafts moved in that servants' meals would be segregated by race, regardless of rank. For the rest of Jaffray's time in the White House—seventeen years through four administrations—blacks and whites ate separately in the home of the president.[20]

The White House of the late nineteenth and early twentieth centuries thus reproduced American socio-spatial mores even as it modeled them anew and on a grander scale. *Good Housekeeping*, which made no mention of the White House's racial segregation (perhaps because of its all-too-American turn-of-the-century ordinariness), encouraged readers to look to the president's house for example and inspiration. In particular, it averred that Mrs. Taft's "executive and intellectual activity" as head of the president's household could provide "a good national pattern for American housewives, coming as it does from the White House in which dwell [*sic*] the personality of the government and around which have centered the imagination, emotions and affections of the Republic."[21] Though here the magazine invokes the special affective relationship that had helped make the White House so important for preservationists, it could just as easily have been referring to the concomitant frequency with which the president's home, as site and symbol, had begun to appear in American fiction (and, soon, film). And while we have already seen how a midcentury writer like William Wells Brown used the structure to personify white indifference to slavery in his novel *Clotel*, at the turn of the century an American narrative would attempt to imagine something far more radical: a black man in charge of the president's house.

Note that I did not say the White House. Although many of the speculative political narratives and utopian fictions that flourished during the Progressive Era reimagine the qualifications for (and functions of) the U.S. presidency, none venture to depict a black chief executive at 1600 Pennsylvania Avenue. Sutton Griggs's *Imperium in Imperio* (1899), however, offers a tantalizing alternative: an African American president of a parallel black government—with its own Executive Mansion—operating covertly within the U.S. The imagined site of this parallel government, moreover, located far from the stately buildings of Washington, D.C., suggests Griggs's keen awareness of the ways American landscapes of power are marked both overtly and covertly by race. Constructed outside Waco, Texas, the Capitol of the Imperium masquerades as the campus of a black college. No disguise could be more fitting. Turn-of-the-century black colleges were one of the few physical environments African Americans could control without automatically drawing interference or suspicion. Typically relegated to whatever land was considered the least valuable within a given community, historically black colleges and universities (HBCUs) were thus also usually regarded by whites as intrinsically inferior—degraded institutions erected, as Kenrick Ian Grandison has argued, on "degraded ground"—which ironically made these potentially threatening spaces more, rather than less, agreeable to powerful whites.[22] Griggs accentuates the benign isolation of his fictitious Thomas Jefferson College by placing it a full five miles out of town, much farther from the center of Waco than even the actual HBCU located there in the late nineteenth century had been.[23]

Grandison's groundbreaking work on HBCU campuses as "multicultural" spaces allows us also to see how Griggs has cannily inverted other expected features of the Thomas Jefferson College landscape to give it a provocative mixture of "black" and "white" spatial characteristics. Although most HBCU campuses, according to Grandison, are "laid out 'backwards,'" putting their "'best' façades inward not outward"—not as a result of poor or haphazard design but rather as a protective shield from white hostility—Griggs's imaginary HBCU places its landmark structure in the most visually dominant position, after the fashion of a typical "majority" (white) campus.[24] The narrator's description of the approach to the college by the novel's two main protagonists makes this strikingly clear:

> After going about five miles, they came in sight of a high stone wall enclosure. In the middle of the enclosed place, upon a slight elevation, stood a building four stories high and about two hundred feet long and one hun-

dred and eighty feet wide. In the center of the front side arose a round tower, half of it bulging out. This extended from the ground to a point about twenty feet above the roof of the building. The entrance to the building was through a wide door in this tower.

A similarly wide gravel driveway curves past the tower to bring visitors directly to the front of the building, on the steps of which are carved "in large letters" the name of the school.[25] No spatial camouflage here—instead it is the "high stone wall enclosure" that provides protection and fairly announces there is something of significance inside. Indeed, this central building is immense: at 200 feet by 180 feet its dimensions closely approximate those of the White House, while its prominent tower recalls both the semicircular White House porticoes and the rising dome of the U.S. Capitol Building. Griggs, in other words, presents Thomas Jefferson College—the hidden-in-plain-sight headquarters of the black Imperium—as not just the most visually and architecturally striking HBCU ever planned or built but the most carefully fortified as well.

All of which makes Griggs's design for the Imperium's actual White House—the large building houses only its Congress—even more significant. Located innocuously "off a few paces" to the side of the central structure, the Executive Mansion is none other than a small white Downingesque cottage, a "remarkably pretty" structure with "green vines clinging to trellis work all around it" that could have stepped right out of a midcentury pattern book. Or, indeed, out of the imagination of Hannah Crafts, whose novel *The Bondwoman's Narrative*, as we have seen, is structured by a powerful arc of desire for precisely such a space, which serves in her text as a marker of black independence through homeownership. Griggs's small white cottage—synecdochically asserting black independence through nation-ownership—combines a Downingesque exterior with an interior décor suited to the White House itself, including "rare and antique furniture" displayed in rooms "so tastefully arranged as to astonish and please" even the Imperium's wealthy, mixed-race president-elect. (By contrast, the interior of the Imperium's enormous Capitol Building is furnished with simple desks.) It is within this "president's mansion," moreover, that the novel will not only reveal the secret history of the Imperium but also stage the final confrontation between its competing political philosophies of passive resistance and militant confrontation.[26] That in the end neither philosophy carries the day—the novel ends with the betrayal and presumed destruction of the Imperium—suggests that the desire for an adequate structure in which to house the hopes, rights, and freedoms of Americans of color, both literally and metaphorically, remains, for Griggs, unfulfilled.

Not for a quarter century would another American narrative explore the possibility that a black man could take control of the White House; nor would the end result be any less grim. This narrative, moreover, would come from the pen of not a U.S. writer but a South American one, suggesting the broad hemispheric interest in U.S. structures of power. In his novel *O Choque das Raças; ou, O Presidente Negro* (1926), written in Portuguese and subtitled *Romance Americano do Anno de 2228*, Brazilian author José Bento Monteiro Lobato imagines a distant future in which the American electorate chooses an African American as the eighty-eighth president, only to have him end up dead—and all American blacks eugenically sterilized—before he can take office. As the defeated Anglo-Saxon incumbent in *O Presidente Negro* warns the doomed black candidate near the end of the novel, "Não subirás os degraus da Casa Branca, Jim. . . . Não penetrarás na Casa Branca" ("You will not go up the steps of the White House, Jim....You will not penetrate the White House"). Lobato's black president, in other words, would have no more success integrating the White House (or replacing it with a substitute) than Griggs's would.[27]

The only safe way to explore the paradox of a nonwhite White House before the contemporary era, it turns out, would be deliberate parody. In 1933, at roughly the end of the formative period we have been examining in *Sites Unseen*, Vitaphone released the musical farce *Rufus Jones for President*, introducing a seven-year-old Sammy Davis Jr. as Jones and starring blues and jazz vocalist Ethel Waters as Jones's mother. The film imagines Jones elected president in an elaborate dream sequence that only heightens the supposed absurdity of a black chief executive. Interspersing dialect comedy with interludes of song, the film depicts Jones as a tap-dancing prodigy whose oath of office (which he takes with his hand on a telephone book, not a Bible) includes such cavalier promises as "from now on pork chops will be free" and "the tax on razors will be refused!"[28] Moving swiftly from this mock inauguration to the initial meeting of the U.S. Senate (in which African Americans have also apparently won all the seats), the film then showcases Waters's performance of the songs "Am I Blue" and "Underneath a Harlem Moon." Waters's rendition of the latter song, popular with white audiences but full of demeaning stereotypes of African Americans ("They just live on dancing, / They're never blue or forlorn. / 'Tain't no sin to laugh and grin, / That's why darkies were born") marks a slyly subversive high point of the film. As music critic Yuval Taylor has argued, by rewriting the lyrics to suggest empowerment rather than objectification—changing "They" pronouns to "We," skipping some of the more objectionable sections entirely, and adding new verses of her own, for example—Waters refashions demeaning racism into defiant triumph.[29] At the center of Waters's revised version, moreover, is a powerful socio-spatial pronouncement: "We don't live in cabins like our old folks used to do; / Our cabin is a penthouse now on St. Nicholas Avenue / Underneath *our* Harlem Moon." By the premise of the film, the "old folks" cabin—an architectural trope dating well back into our period, and capitalized in particular, as we have seen, by George F. Barber in the immensely successful *Cottage Souvenir No. 2*—has been transformed not just into a penthouse but the White House, even though no scenes are actually staged inside the new president's home. And while young Jones ultimately reawakens, no longer president, on the porch of his mother's simple cabin (where Waters gently reminds him, "Stay on your own side of the fence, / And no harm will come to you"), the film's conservative frame cannot quite repress the exuberant spatial ambition of its dream-sequence interior.

By the time Barack Obama declared his own intention to run for the presidency in 2007, the idea of an African American president—both serious and satiric—had become a staple of American fiction, television, and film, from Irving Wallace's *The Man* (1964) and Philip K. Dick's *The Crack in Space* (1966) to more recent incarnations brought to life by such actors as Morgan Freeman, Dennis Haysbert, and Chris Rock.[30] That it is no longer incongruous in our era to imagine a black man in the White House, however, does not mean that the anxieties surrounding this scenario, so evident in the late nineteenth and early twentieth centuries, have subsided. Quite the contrary: in the months leading up to the 2008 presidential election, then to Obama's inauguration (and beyond), manifestations of this anxiety have continued to erupt in the broader culture, almost always expressed in racialized terms of architectural or decorative violation. These eruptions have included satirical news accounts or editorial cartoons of Obama painting (or planning to paint) the White House black; images of the White House topped with Islamic domes or Russian towers (signaling its transformation into either a Muslim or a socialist stronghold); as well as an anti-Obama campaign button, circulated at the June 2008 Texas Republican state convention, bluntly asking: "If Obama is President . . . will we still call it the White House?"[31] Even the notorious Barry Blitt cover illustration for the *New Yorker* depicting Barack and Michelle Obama in terrorist garb inside the Oval Office (and intended, Blitt claimed, to poke fun at "the politics of fear," as the cartoon was titled) drew a good deal of its power from the apparent incongruity of radical Muslims making themselves "at home" within perhaps the single most recognizable room in American politics. The architectural and decorative details Blitt highlights—including the room's oval shape, the American eagle rug beneath the Obamas' feet, and the portrait of Osama bin Laden where Washington's image should be—intensify the sense not only of unlawful and surreptitious occupation but also of radical (political) redecoration. That the image could work so powerfully yet so controversially (it was condemned by liberals and conservatives alike) suggests the depth of the anxiety into which it tapped.[32]

The actual move of the Obama family into the White House in January 2009 has made new narratives possible and given long-forgotten stories about race and place fresh relevance. For the first time since being elected to the U.S. Senate in 2005, for example, President Obama now lives full-time in the same house as his wife and daughters—inadvertently refiguring the White House as an agent for strengthening black family life rather than (as in William Wells Brown's *Clotel*) destroying it. Indeed, after a fashion, this arrangement simply refreshes the conclusion of Crafts's *Bondwoman's Narrative*, in which Crafts strategically links black homeownership not merely to personal and economic freedom but also to the restoration of the black family. The decision of Michelle Obama's mother to join the family in the White House even symbolically reproduces the joyful inclusion of Crafts's own mother in her "neat little Cottage" at the end of the narrative.

Even more strikingly, perhaps, the Obamas' move resonates provocatively with the architectural message Frederick Douglass sought to deliver when he moved in 1877 from Rochester to the nation's capital. As Sarah Luria notes (and as we saw in chapter 1), on his move to Washington Douglass bought a "large white house on a hilltop high above the Capitol Building and the Washington Monument," not just metaphorically overlooking the federal city but offering through his presence a "visible challenge to the increasing 'Ku Klux spirit' of the nation." Inverting a myriad of spatial and social relationships, Douglass positioned himself as at once master of the reclaimed plantation home of his enslaved childhood (which his new white house resembled) and the "overseer" of the nation, both highly ironic positions for an ex-slave to occupy. The most unusual inversion, however, was embodied in the slave cabin–like structure Douglass built behind the house, which he turned into a "gentleman's private study" for reading and writing, the very pursuits slavery had so vigorously striven to deny him.[33] As rightful occupants, indeed residents, of the White House itself, the Obama family does not merely complete Crafts's arc of desire, they reinvert Douglass's inversions. Instead of inhabiting the symbolic position of master to claim authority over presumptively white space, the Obamas' legitimacy permits them to act as a "normal" family, treating the house as their own through the routines of inhabitation rather than the gestures of mastery. Instead of refashioning a slave cabin into a gentleman's study to ironize cultural assumptions about African American literacy, the Obamas can share the newly discovered story of Michelle Obama's own great-great-grandfather, raised in bondage in a slave cabin on a plantation in South Carolina.[34]

At the same time, it remains no small irony that the president who integrated the nation's whitest house presides over a country that in many respects has become more segregated since the passing of the Fair Housing Act in 1968 than it was before, or that one of the most complex tasks this president has inherited is the management of a global financial crisis experienced most profoundly in the U.S. at the intersection of race and housing—indeed, a crisis in large part triggered by the bursting of a domestic housing bubble overinflated by predatory loans concentrated in minority communities.[35] The impact of this collapse has been felt not only in those communities, where hundreds of thousands of primarily African American and Latino homeowners have lost their houses, but also in many middle-class white communities, where home values have plummeted so precipitously that many residents are either locked into houses they cannot afford to sell or hamstrung by debt from purchasing a new home. One wonders what new stories, set in what kinds of structures, will emerge from this particular moment.

Which returns us to the place we began, with questions that will continue to resonate in the American social and cultural imagination. How does race shape the meanings our physical environments convey? How do the stories we tell—or inherit—shape the social experience of the built environment? Who belongs in which spaces, and at which times? No longer merely fiction or farce, a black president in the White House has already irrevocably changed, and will continue to change, the ways we think and talk not only about race and architecture but also about the stories and circumstances that shape, interrogate, and perhaps even renew the built environment of our national (indeed, transnational) imagination—and in turn, we might hope, of the nation itself.

Notes

NOTES TO INTRODUCTION

1. Though illuminating in their own terms, the majority of book-length studies situated at the interdisciplinary crossroads of architecture and literature, even those that treat the American context specifically, have paid virtually no attention to race as a category of analysis. These works include Frank, *Literary Architecture*; Knapp, *Archetype, Architecture, and the Writer*; Fryer, *Felicitous Space*; Ruzicka, *Faulkner's Fictive Architecture*; Antoniades, *Epic Space*; Sweeting, *Reading Houses and Building Books*; Olsen, *Transcending Space*; and, most recently, Bernstein, *Housing Problems*. One notable exception is Lois Leveen's unpublished dissertation, "The Race Home," which examines the ways American houses articulate and enforce constructions of identity, particularly race and gender.

The few published book-length studies of literature and architecture (or related intersections, such as literature and material culture, or literature and geography) that include at least partial discussions of race and the built environment (and from whose examples I have benefited) include Chandler, *Dwelling in the Text*, half of whose last chapter analyzes Toni Morrison's *Beloved*; Hines, *William Faulkner and the Tangible Past*, which in part considers how race and class help structure Faulkner's architectural imagination; Villa, *Barrio-Logos*, which analyzes the production and regulation of Chicano social space and the built environment in Los Angeles; Brady, *Extinct Lands, Temporal Geographies*, which examines the spatial transformation of the American Southwest in the late nineteenth and twentieth centuries; Heneghan, *Whitewashing America*, which includes architecture among the "white things" that helped define race through objects in antebellum America (xiii); Luria, *Capital Speculations*, which includes a chapter on Frederick Douglass's role in the creation of a "new social landscape" in Reconstruction-era Washington, D.C. (75); Klimasmith, *At Home in the City*, which includes a chapter on Nella Larsen's *Quicksand*; Shamir, *Inexpressible Privacy*, which includes a chapter that examines the relationship between slavery and privacy in Stowe and Douglass; McKittrick, *Demonic Grounds*, which includes a chapter on Harriet Jacobs's garret in *Incidents in the Life of a Slave Girl*; and Faherty, *Remodeling the Nation*, which briefly discusses the role of slavery in the design of Jefferson's Monticello and also assesses the impact of Native American architectural relics in the formation of early American national identity.

A small number of important individual essays on race, architecture, and American representation may supplement this list, including Smith, "'Loopholes of Retreat'"; Curtis, "Race, Realism"; Gelder, "Reforming the Body"; Kawash, "Haunted Houses, Sinking Ships"; and Machlan, "Diseased Properties and Broken Homes."

2. Although vernacular architectural historians, material culture scholars, and cultural geographers, whose discoveries have been crucial to my work, have paid more attention than literary critics to the intersections of race and architecture in the U.S., no single architectural study treats in detail the period that is the focus of this book, roughly 1850–1930. And despite important early calls for more attention to race within architectural theory and collateral fields by such figures as Cornel West (including "A Note on Race and Architecture") and such publications as the interdisciplinary journal *Appendx* (founded in 1993), the turn to race as an analytical category within architectural studies has nonetheless been slow to develop and selective in its areas of inquiry. While my work is thus also informed by the important contributions to this field made by such edited volumes as Noble's *To Build in a New Land*; Lokko's *White Papers, Black Marks*; Barton's *Sites of Memory*; Breisch and Hoagland's *Building Environments*; and Schein's *Landscape and Race in the United States*, this study breaks new ground through its extended focus on the U.S. cultural context at the turn from the nineteenth to the twentieth century.

3. Upton, "White and Black Landscapes," 59.

4. This study also draws crucially on the work of countless scholars who have helped make race a central category in the analysis of literary representation. The title of this introduction, "Race, Writing, Architecture," is meant to evoke one of the pioneering efforts in this regard, Henry Louis Gates Jr.'s *"Race," Writing, and Difference*. Much as Gates asks in his introduction to that volume, "What importance does 'race' have as a meaningful category in the study of literature and the shaping of critical theory?," *Sites Unseen* in effect begins by asking: What importance does race have in the study of literature and architecture?

One additional field that has only recently experimented with putting race at the center of its place-based inquiries is landscape architecture. Although Barton's important collection *Sites of Memory* (2001) features essays by prominent landscape architects, including, for example, Kenrick Ian Grandison (to whose groundbreaking work on the cultural-historical landscapes of historically black colleges and universities I will return in the coda), not until 2007—when Dianne Harris guest-edited a special issue of *Landscape Journal* under the rubric "Race, Space, and the Destabilization of Practice"—did the major journal in the field specifically address race. In their introduction to this volume the journal's editors note that while "the content of this issue may seem to stretch the mandate of *Landscape Journal* into new territory," the time has come to "crack open hidden or forgotten doors" both in the scholarly analysis and in the professional practice of landscape architecture, which, as they note, is "an overwhelmingly white profession." See Harris, "Race, Space," v.

5. I will examine the prevalence of "Oriental" designs in early American pattern books and builders' guides in detail in chapter 4.

6. Trafton, *Egypt Land*, 143.

7. As Adam Sweeting notes, pattern books began to replace the earlier builders' guides in the 1840s and 1850s. Where the guides had provided detailed instructions and technical specifications, the pattern books "were read primarily by patrons who were less interested in technical information and more concerned with a house's style and amenities." Pattern books thus soon became "a vehicle for architects to market their tastes and talents and helped to forge a new professional consciousness among architects." See Sweeting, *Reading Houses and Building Books*, 39. The pattern book era lasts through the

nineteenth century, until it is eventually supplemented (if not replaced) by the rise of popular home design periodicals and the mail-order catalog. For more on the history of the pattern book and its corollary forms—which in general have not been understood as having any racial dimension—see Reiff, *Houses from Books*, and Upton, "Pattern Books and Professionalism."

8. Fiske, *A Rapid Tour*, 7. Subsequent references are from this edition and will appear parenthetically in the text.

9. "Young Peter's Preface" even states: "Authors older and wiser than Young Peter are responsible for all the facts; and therefore I think my readers may rely upon everything in this book as being strictly true" (Fiske, *A Rapid Tour*, 5).

10. Fowler, *A Home for All*, 11, 12.

11. Downing, *The Architecture of Country Houses*, 159–60. For another example of Downing's discussion of racial instinct, see his *Rural Essays*, 131. In a related vein, Downing also believed strongly in regional fitness in architecture, arguing that certain national forms were better suited aesthetically for particular American topographies, such as Rural Gothic for the "broken country" of the North and Modern Italian for the "plain and valley surfaces of the Middle and Southern States." See Downing, *The Architecture of Country Houses*, 274.

12. Smith, *The Domestic Architect*, 24, iii, 118.

13. As David Schuyler observes in his introductory essay to a modern reprint edition of Henry W. Cleaveland et al.'s pattern book, *Village and Farm Cottages* (1856), "True, the sectional traumas that threatened the nation are absent, but so they were from most books devoted to the principles of design published during that decade." See Schuyler, "Villages and Farm Cottages," n.p.

14. Sloan, *The Model Architect*, 55.

15. Ibid., 81 (my emphasis).

16. Wheeler, *Rural Homes*, 136, 134.

17. Elliott, *Cottages and Cottage Life*, 4. Subsequent references are from this edition and will appear parenthetically in the text.

18. Upton, *Architecture in the United States*, 117.

19. Rev. of Elliott, *Cottages and Cottage Life*, *Merchants' Magazine and Commercial Review*, 460.

20. Downing, rev. of Elliott, *Cottages and Cottage Life*, *Horticulturist*, 179.

21. In *To Live in the New World*, 86–87, Judith K. Major notes that Downing had started working on *The Architecture of Country Houses* by December 1847.

22. Loudon, *An Encyclopaedia of Gardening*, 613. Elliott, himself a landscape gardener, of course would have known Loudon's work well and even drops in a mention of Loudon by name in *Cottages and Cottage Life* (38). In *Bees in America*, Tammy Horn reports an incident of bees swarming a parlor through an open window in 1882, but the practice of actually hiving bees in a window device that opened into a house was unknown in the U.S. in the 1840s. Horn has discovered instances of Indian and Nepalese kitchen beehives constructed with two doors, one to the inside and one to the outside, somewhat as in Elliott's diagram, but it is not clear to what extent this type of beekeeping influenced Western beekeepers in the nineteenth century. Horn herself suspects that Elliott would have had no way of knowing about these practices (e-mail communication, 19 March 2008). Noted bee scholar Gene Kritsky also observes that while it was common for people

to bring hives closer to their houses to avoid theft, it was not common to bring them inside the house (telephone conversation, April 2008).

23. Hedrick, *Harriet Beecher Stowe*, 172.

24. Ibid., 92. My principal source for identifying Elliott and Stowe's relationship by marriage is a privately distributed book written by Sarah Elliott Perkins's granddaughter in 1907, which discusses the family tree, including the connection to the Stowes, in some detail. See Edith Perkins Cunningham, *Owl's Nest*.

25. The very fact that John has to ask one of their neighbors whether he has "not been on the Ohio River," for example, suggests that although *Cottages and Cottage Life* was published in Cincinnati, it is not set in Cincinnati (which is on the Ohio River). The broker who swindles Uncle Tom and has an office "in town" appears to have close connections to New York. At one point Tom mocks a sparkling wine offered by John as being from the "cider cellars of New Jersey" (24).

26. Smith, "Loopholes of Retreat," 215. On *Incidents* as a revision of Downing, see Gelder, "Reforming the Body," 252–66.

27. Hersey, "Godey's Choice," 104.

28. While most historians of scrapbook houses agree that they take shape in dialogue with consumer culture, out of whose very scraps they are made, critics disagree on the nature and meaning of that dialogue. Some, such as Rodris Roth, have seen paper doll houses primarily as "tools" for the "consumer education" and gender training of their young users. At the other interpretive pole, for Linda Roscoe Hartigan scrapbook collage is always a "radical medium" resisting its consumerist frame. In her extensive study of the genre, Beverly Gordon finds a middle ground, seeing scrapbook houses providing opportunities for cross-generational bonding, lessons in aesthetics and decoration (rather than consumption, strictly speaking), as well as a way to imagine women's space. See Roth, "Scrapbook Houses"; Hartigan, "The House That Collage Built"; Gordon, "Scrapbook Houses for Paper Dolls"; and Gordon, *The Saturated World*, especially ch. 2, "The Paper Doll House."

29. In Clara Andrews Williams's popular *House That Glue Built* (1905), for example, the scrapbook house comes with a black cook named Dinah who is meant to be glued into the kitchen.

30. Gordon, "Scrapbook Houses for Paper Dolls," 125.

31. Collage album, ca. 1880–1900, Joseph Downs Collection, Winterthur Library.

32. Garvey, "Scrapbook, Wishbook, Prayerbook," 111.

33. Gordon, *The Saturated World*, 54. See also Gordon, "Scrapbook Houses for Paper Dolls," 125.

34. Brown, *A Sense of Things*, 18.

35. Not only did the commercial versions typically mark precisely where everything should go—every precut object had a number and a corresponding location in its appropriate room—many of the books present themselves as narratives about their own construction and decoration. Williams's *House That Glue Built*, for example, tells the story of four children who have decided to build a paper house for the "Glue" family, who will arrive at the end of the story to live there. "Into the Hall of the House that Glue Built the little housekeepers come," the story explains. "Much work awaits the tiny hands under whose magic touch the rooms will soon appear homelike." Most of the narration is concerned with directing the children, for whom the book buyer stands as proxy, in the

proper placement of the home's possessions. "One thing we must not forget," the book at one point reminds, is "to place the furniture exactly as the diagram shows." When it comes to servants, moreover, these commercial books seem invested in reinforcing racial stereotypes, not merely through their visual representations but also through their imagined narratives. When the Glue family finally arrives at the end of *The House That Glue Built*—Mr. Glue, Mrs. Glue, their children Gertrude and Frank, their nurse, Elise (who appears to be French), and their African American cook, Dinah—Dinah responds in dialect to the newly decorated kitchen with stereotypical rapture. "'Aint dis yere kitchen lubly,' said Dinah, the good old coloured cook, 'dese chilluns am de smartest I eber done see.'"

36. In her detailed history of the professionalization of American architecture, Mary N. Woods identifies the antebellum period as the era in which architecture first became a profession, and the late nineteenth century as the era in which that profession then expanded and consolidated itself into most of the forms by which we know it today, including the creation of "university programs, professional societies, certification of practitioners, and codes of ethics traditionally associated with professionalization." See Woods, *From Craft to Profession*, 4. As Woods notes, the American Institute of Architects was formed in 1857; the first university courses were offered at MIT in 1868; the first program at a historically black college or university was implemented at Tuskegee in 1881; the first licensing law for architects was passed in 1897; the first detailed code of professional ethics for architects was approved in 1909.

37. Upton, *Architecture in the United States*, 11; Barton, Foreword, *Sites of Memory*, xv.

38. Fuss, *The Sense of an Interior*, 4.

39. Upton, *Architecture in the United States*, 12.

40. By playing often leading roles in the historic preservation and hereditary society movements that flourished at the turn of the century, moreover, American women also helped shape the implicit racialism of the Colonial Revival, whose interest in architectural "purity" will be a touchstone in the final three chapters of this study.

41. Levander and Levine, Introduction, *Hemispheric American Studies*, 399.

42. Manson, *Frank Lloyd Wright to 1910*, 37–38.

43. Indeed, while I have aimed only to provide powerful examples, not an exhaustive history, I am aware of potential texts and topics that would fit well in this study that are nonetheless not included here. One such text, fascinating for its potential connections to some of the history traced in this introduction, is Helen Hunt Jackson's popular romance *Ramona: A Story* (1884), set in the American Southwest—for as it turns out, Jackson's father was none other than N. W. Fiske, the author of *A Rapid Tour around the World*.

44. On the racial "crisis" in the architectural profession, see Mitchell, *The Crisis of the African-American Architect*; and Kaplan, *Structural Inequality*.

NOTES TO CHAPTER 1

1. Crafts, *The Bondwoman's Narrative*, 211, 212, 213, 214, 215. Subsequent references are from this edition and will appear parenthetically in the text.

2. On yet another level, this scene touches insightfully on the psychology of place attachment among African American slaves, whose legal status as property rather than persons made the question of belonging to a physical place or landscape particularly

acute. For more on place attachment theory, see Altman and Low, eds., *Place Attach-ment*; on place attachment and American slavery, see Morgan, *Slave Counterpoint*, 519–30.

3. hooks, Eizenberg, and Koning, "House, 20 June 1994," 23.

4. Throughout this chapter I will refer to the author as Crafts and will assume, follow-ing Henry Louis Gates Jr., "that she was female, mulatto, a slave of John Hill Wheeler's, an autodidact, and a keen observer of the dynamics of slave life." See Gates, Introduction, lxxii.

5. The seemingly unusual floor plan of the fictional De Vincent mansion, in which the original drawing room later becomes part of Lindendale's "southern turret," reflects a typical construction pattern for "ancient mansions" in colonial Virginia: a gradual expan-sion of a modest structure over time. In Virginia (and also elsewhere in the South), the original so-called mansion—which despite the appellation may have had as few as four rooms, since larger structures were exceedingly uncommon—may or may not have been incorporated into the final house design. Thomas Jefferson's first house at Monticello, for example, an eighteen-by-eighteen-foot box erected in 1770, eventually became his "South Pavilion" once the estate was complete. See Sobel, *The World They Made Together*, 100. Readers who may object that the "turret" design of Lindendale makes it inappropriately European for Crafts's American setting may be surprised to know that it was precisely during the 1850s that literal towers were becoming fashionable (on paper, if not always in practice) in the American South. Consider, for example, Hawkwood, a Louisa County, Virginia, plantation designed for Richard Overton Morris by Alexander Jackson Davis in 1851 (completed in 1852–54) as an Italianate villa. See Brownell, *The Making of Virginia Architecture*, 278–79. For a broader discussion of the interest in Italianate domestic architecture in the antebellum period, including the South, see Lancaster, "Italianism in American Architecture before 1860," 127–48.

6. Of course the cottage's proximity to Lindendale and the overseer's apparent jurisdic-tion within it suggest that it is owned by Hannah's master, already compromising its ability to offer Hannah a home outside of slavery.

7. See Crowley, "'In Happier Mansions, Warm, and Dry,'" 170; and Lounsbury, ed., *An Illustrated Glossary of Early Southern Architecture and Landscape*, 97.

8. Downing, *Cottage Residences*, i, iii, ii. Subsequent references are from this edition and will appear parenthetically in the text. Downing did include a brief section on rural architecture at the end of *A Treatise on the Theory and Practice of Landscape Gardening*.

9. See Wheeler, *Library Catalogue*. For more on Downing's cultural standing, see Tatum, "The Downing Decade"; Sweeting, *Reading Houses and Building Books*. In *Avery's Choice: One Hundred Years of an Architectural Library, 1890–1990*, Adolf Placzek and Angela Giral describe Downing's next book, *The Architecture of Country Houses* (1850), as "arguably the most important work on domestic architecture of the antebellum decades" (159). On Downing's popularity in the South, see Bishir, "A Spirit of Improvement," 138–42, 149–50.

10. Downing, *The Architecture of Country Houses*, 1. Subsequent references are from this edition and will appear parenthetically in the text.

11. On the steamboat fire and Downing as an "apostle" of middle-class taste, see Schuyler, *Apostle of Taste*. Nathaniel Hawthorne's sister Louisa was also killed in the *Henry Clay* fire.

12. Despite the imposing length of *Rural Essays*, one reviewer declared that "there is not a chapter or page which we would spare. . . . It must take its place as a domestic classic." See the *New Englander and Yale Review* 11 (August 1853): 474–75. During the 1850s alone, Downing's four main books were reprinted at least twenty times. His *Treatise* (already in its fourth edition) was reprinted in 1850, 1852, 1853 (new edition), 1854, 1855, 1856, 1857, and 1859 (new edition); *Cottage Residences* was reprinted in 1852 (new edition), 1853, and 1856; *The Architecture of Country Houses* (first edition 1850) was reprinted in 1851, 1852, 1853, 1854, 1855, and 1856; and *Rural Essays* (first edition 1853) was reprinted in 1854, 1856, and 1857. See Hitchcock, *American Architectural Books*, 31–34.

13. Even the party of hunters that discovers Hannah and her mistress avow the cabin is too frightening a place to sleep in. "Faith, I wouldn't stay here a night for all ~~your master's~~ that was once your master's fortune" (69), declares one.

14. The one direct reference I have come across to slavery in Downing's writings is in itself deliberately oblique. In his November 1850 essay for the *Horticulturist*, "The Favorite Poison of America" (republished in the posthumous collection *Rural Essays*), Downing facetiously lists several possible (but incorrect) candidates for the "national poison" he wishes to expose. Moreover, Downing delivers this list in the voice of an imagined interlocutor to his essay: "'A national poison? Do you mean slavery, socialism, abolition, Mormonism?' Nothing of the sort. 'Then, perhaps, tobacco, patent medicines, or coffee?' Worse than these." Downing's national poison is instead "a foe more insidious than these": "the vitiated air of *close stoves*." It is interesting to see Downing list both slavery *and* abolition as possible national poisons, even in giving voice to an imaginary speaker. See *Rural Essays*, 278–79.

15. Alterations to subsequent editions of Downing's texts sometimes changed the numbering of his illustrations. Design XXVI was renumbered XXVII in the 1851 edition of *The Architecture of Country Houses*, while Design XXXII (itself adapted from Design VIII in *Cottage Residences*) was renumbered XXX in 1851. See Davies, "Davis and Downing," 119–20. For clarity, like Davies I will use Downing's original 1850 numbering.

16. For more on the dispersal of slave accommodations, see Vlach, *Back of the Big House*.

17. Sweeting, *Reading Houses and Building Books*, 43. This is not to say, of course, that slaves did not routinely circumvent such segregatory and circulatory regulations in the South. See, for example, Vlach, *Back of the Big House*, 235–36.

18. Identifying the figure on the veranda as a southern planter might seem unremarkable given the southern context provided in this section of *The Architecture of Country Houses*. And yet this specific "variation" sketch originally appeared in the first issue of Downing's *Horticulturist* in 1846, where it was captioned "Design for a Simple Country House" and given no southern inflection. According to Jane B. Davies, this sketch—recaptioned "Exterior of Southern Country House" in *The Architecture of Country Houses*—was drawn by Alexander Jackson Davis, who contributed many of the designs in Downing's text. Davies confirms, however, that Downing himself designed and delineated the engraving for Design XXVI. See Davies, "Davis and Downing," 121.

19. Upton, "Pattern Books and Professionalism," 124–27. Even when in *The Architecture of Country Houses* Downing urges that "the humblest laborer" should have an equal opportunity to own a "future country-house," he still manages to intimate that the "lord of the soil" is the "true American." "The just pride of a true American," Downing writes,

"is not in a great hereditary home, but in greater hereditary institutions. It is more to him that all his children will be born under wise, and just, and equal laws, than that one of them should come into the world with a great family estate. It is better, in his eyes, that it should be possible for the humblest laborer to look forward to the possession of a future country-house and home like his own, than to feel that a wide and impassable gulf of misery separates him, the lord of the soil, from a large class of his fellow beings born beneath him" (*The Architecture of Country Houses*, 270).

20. Downing, "Warwick Castle," 481.

21. See, for example, Parsons, *Inside View of Slavery*. The travel narratives of Frederick Law Olmsted—a protégé of Downing's as a landscape architect—frequently included illustrations of precisely the type of slave housing and work arrangements that the pattern books tended to ignore. See, for example, the illustrations in his *Journey in the Seaboard Slave States*, especially 16, 71, 344, 385, 423, 629. Given Olmsted's interest in both design and slavery, his travel texts might be said to mediate between the architect's (Downing's) efforts to evade discussions of race and the novelist's (Crafts's) efforts to reexamine pattern book ideology from a slave's perspective. My thanks to Bernard Herman for suggesting this possibility.

22. Jacobs depicts the perversion of cottage space by slavery not only through the confining garret but in the "lonely cottage" that Mr. Flint begins building for her "four miles away from the town." In many ways, Jacobs's narrative pivots on this structure: Jacobs evades Flint's cottage trap only by making her "plunge into the abyss" by initiating her sexual relationship with the white Mr. Sands. See Jacobs, *Incidents in the Life of a Slave Girl*, 82–87. Some of the best work on race and the built environment is focused on Jacobs's text, including Smith, "Loopholes of Retreat," 212–26; Gelder, "Reforming the Body," 252–66; and the second chapter of McKittrick's *Demonic Grounds*, "The Last Place They Thought Of: Black Women's Geographies," 37–63. Frederick Douglass, too, paid increasing attention to domestic space in the revisions he made in expanding his 1845 *Narrative* into *My Bondage and My Freedom* in 1855. One of the most striking additions to Douglass's second autobiography is the lengthy reminiscence of his grandparents' "little hut" at the beginning of *My Bondage and My Freedom*, the log cabin in which Douglass lived so "snugly" during his early childhood and from which "good old home" he dreaded being removed to work on his master's distant plantation. Crafts's account of Hannah's days in Aunt Hetty's cabin bears some similarity to Douglass's tribute to this sheltering yet deeply vulnerable space. See Douglass, *Autobiographies*, 141–44.

23. Stowe, *Uncle Tom's Cabin*, 1.

24. Much as Stowe locates the main action of *Uncle Tom's Cabin* on three plantations—Shelby, St. Clare, and Legree—Crafts places Hannah at Lindendale, then Forget-me-not, and finally the Wheeler's plantation. There is also a certain correspondence within the trajectories: like Stowe, Crafts makes the second plantation (at least initially) the most desirable, and it is at the third that her main character is for the first time brought in contact with "vile, foul, filthy" slave huts (205).

25. Page, *Uncle Robin in His Cabin in Virginia*, 23.

26. For more on representations of architectural space by Stowe and her rebutters, including Eastman, see Handlin, *The American Home*, 76–78. As Handlin notes, sectional commentators "often cited the houses of North and South to compare the two societies.

The ideas about houses mentioned in this debate had been formulated in the discussion of other issues. But when used to measure the progress of North and South, they assumed some of their most powerful meanings" (76). The man believed to be Crafts's final owner, John Hill Wheeler, had several anti-*Uncle Tom's Cabin* texts in his library in the 1850s, including Page's *Uncle Robin in His Cabin in Virginia*, according to an auction catalog prepared after his death.

27. Robbins, "Blackening *Bleak House*," 73–74. Robbins notes that in serializing *Bleak House* in his *Paper* Douglass praised Dickens for his "true to life" depictions of the "dense ignorance, squallid [*sic*] misery, and pressing wants of 'the London poor'" (73).

28. Dickens, *Bleak House*, 61. Subsequent references are from this edition and will appear parenthetically in the text.

29. Robbins, "Blackening *Bleak House*," 74.

30. Some of the "British" details Crafts excises from the borrowed passages actually have a racial aspect, as they link Bleak House to British imperial ventures. For example, Crafts elides Dickens's mention of a "Native-Hindoo chair" and also a series of paintings showing "the whole process of preparing tea in China, as depicted by Chinese artists." See Dickens, *Bleak House*, 61–62.

31. Rohrbach, "'A Silent, Unobtrusive Way,'" 8. For a reading of this scene as evidence that Crafts "testifies knowledgeably about the interplay of power that defines not only the relationship between master and slave, between mistress and slave, but also between the mistress and the master," see Byrd, "The Outsider Within," 348–50.

32. Robbins, "Blackening *Bleak House*," 80–83.

33. By having Hannah note in the final paragraph that, in becoming free, Charlotte's husband, William, "has learned the carpenter's trade" (239), Crafts further underscores the importance of black command over built space in her text. As hooks has argued, "Black folks equated freedom with the passage into a life where they would have the right to exercise control over space on their own behalf. They would imagine, design, and create spaces that would respond to the needs of their lives, their communities, their families" ("House, 20 June 1994," 23). In Jacobs's novel, Linda Brent's father and first love are both carpenters. See *Incidents in the Life of a Slave Girl*, 11, 58.

34. Luria, "Racial Equality Begins at Home," 27. Hannah, moreover, uses her respectable cottage home as "a school for colored children" (Crafts, *The Bondwoman's Narrative*, 237), further radicalizing the Downing and Dickens models.

35. See Luria, "Racial Equality Begins at Home," 34–35, 32.

36. Many of the essays in Gates and Robbins's *In Search of Hannah Crafts: Critical Essays on The Bondwoman's Narrative* address the ways Crafts's text locates itself within and against various midcentury genres, including the slave narrative, the sentimental novel, and African American gothic.

37. Hannah's "Oh" also fittingly recalls the intensity of feeling Hannah experiences during expulsion from Aunt Hetty's cottage ("My horror, and grief, and astonishment were indescribable. I felt Oh how much more than I tell" [12]). In fact, if Hannah's mother replaces Mrs. Henry, she also fully maternalizes Aunt Hetty, Hannah's original aged and "venerable" (229) mother figure. Pointedly, Crafts has Hannah reunite briefly with Aunt Hetty—who once again resides in "a neat little cottage, tidy and comfortable" (229)—just before she rediscovers her biological mother.

1. Charles W. Chesnutt to Albion W. Tourgée, 26 September 1889, McElrath and Leitz, eds., *"To Be an Author,"* 44–45.

2. Brodhead, *Cultures of Letters*, 208. "Rena Walden" would finally see publication in 1900 as *The House behind the Cedars*, Chesnutt's first novel.

3. Chesnutt announced his plan to "strike for an entering wedge in the literary world" in a journal entry of 26 March 1881 (Brodhead, ed., *The Journals of Charles W. Chesnutt*, 155). Page's term "cunjure" appears in a letter to Chesnutt, 30 March 1898 (Chesnutt, McElrath and Leitz, eds., *To Be an Author,"* 106n). The phrase "preferred fictions of racial life" is Brodhead's, from *Cultures of Letters*, 210.

4. Upton, "White and Black Landscapes," 59.

5. The three phases of Chesnutt's conjure tale production divide as follows (initial publication dates, where applicable, follow each story in parentheses; the seven tales that Page selected for *The Conjure Woman* volume in 1899 are further designated by an asterisk): (1) first phase (1887–89): "The Goophered Grapevine"* (1887), "Po' Sandy"* (1888), "The Conjurer's Revenge"* (1889), "Dave's Neckliss" (1889); (2) second phase (1893–97): "A Deep Sleeper" (1893), "Lonesome Ben" (1900), "The Dumb Witness"; (3) third phase (March–May 1898): "A Victim of Heredity" (1900), "The Gray Wolf's Ha'nt"* (1899), "Mars Jeems's Nightmare"* (1899), "Sis' Becky's Pickaninny"* (1899), "Tobe's Tribulations" (1900), "Hot-Foot Hannibal"* (1899). For more detailed publication information, see Chesnutt, *The Conjure Woman and Other Conjure Tales*, 23–26.

6. Isaac, *The Transformation of Virginia*, 19.

7. Quoted in Kammen, *Mystic Chords of Memory*, 122.

8. Clearly I am also invoking Herman Melville's collection *The Piazza Tales* (1856) in my naming both of this chapter and of Chesnutt's stories, though a full account of the relation of Chesnutt's imaginative investment in the piazza to Melville's is beyond the scope of this chapter. In brief, I read Melville's *Tales* (and particularly his lead story, "The Piazza") as at once an affirmation of what I call the "legibility" of architecture and an indictment of the ideological assumptions of midcentury pattern book design theory, such as that expressed in the works of Andrew Jackson Downing and Calvert Vaux. What Chesnutt does (insistently, provocatively) is make the matters of race and memory even more central to these inquiries.

9. Stepto, "'The Simple but Intensely Human Inner Life of Slavery,'" 31, 46. Brodhead also briefly discusses the piazza in his introduction to *The Conjure Woman and Other Conjure Tales* (see p. 11). For broader analyses of southern architecture in literary texts, see, for example, Gaines, *The Southern Plantation*; Guttmann, "Images of Value and the Sense of the Past"; Cardwell, "The Plantation House"; Ruzicka, *Faulkner's Fictive Architecture*; and Hines, *William Faulkner and the Tangible Past*. For a more focused study of the role of the porch in African American storytelling, see Harris, *The Power of the Porch*.

A word on terminology: following Stepto, in this chapter I use the terms "piazza" and "porch" as synonyms for the same basic structure, a covered shelter "supported by columns or pillars and attached to the outside of a building" (Lounsbury, ed., *An Illustrated Glossary of Early Southern Architecture and Landscape*, 269). According to Lounsbury's *Glossary*, while "porch" was the earliest word for such structures, beginning in the 1730s the term "piazza" began to designate those coverings that stretched "the full length of the facade," a style that soon became "the most common form of entrance shelter" in the South. In the antebellum period, under the influence of the Classical Revival, the term "portico" gained popularity (as did "veranda"), while "porch" was finally revived in the late nineteenth century "to indiscriminately describe most varieties of sheltered entrance structures" (285). Chesnutt uses "piazza" and occasionally "porch" in his Uncle Julius tales.

10. Hayden, *The Power of Place*, xii.

11. Kammen, *Mystic Chords of Memory*, 121.

12. As noted in the introduction, nearly all the current work at the interdisciplinary crossroads of architecture and literature, though illuminating, focuses primarily on white writers, grand spaces, and/or genteel traditions. Only Fryer's *Felicitous Space* and Hines's *William Faulkner and the Tangible Past* are particularly attentive, for example, to vernacular American structures, though neither discusses nonwhite writers.

13. Chesnutt, "Uncle Peter's House," 168, 169, 170, 172, 174, 175. Subsequent references are from this edition and will appear parenthetically in the text.

14. Isaac, *The Transformation of Virginia*, 38.

15. Ibid., 36; Vlach, *Back of the Big House*, 43. Bishir's comprehensive study of architecture in North Carolina suggests that detached kitchens had moved inside southern homes by the late nineteenth century, corresponding, presumably, to social, not climatic, change. See her *North Carolina Architecture*, 291, 304.

16. On the possible English roots of these changes in plantation design, see Carson, "Segregation in Vernacular Buildings," 24–29, where he suggests that the reorganization of interior domestic space in sixteenth- and seventeenth-century England (to separate servants from masters) may have influenced later colonial developments. For further discussion of the impact of architectural design on the regulation of slave life, see Wright, "The 'Big House' and the Slave Quarters," in *Building the Dream*, 41–57. Wright also explains how the slaves' use of African American craft traditions and construction techniques in assembling their quarters, while not necessarily forging "a secret weapon of active resistance to white domination," did help "mediate between two very different ways of viewing black culture in the South" (48).

17. We might also say that Chesnutt's story foregrounds the historical presence and skill of black carpenters, house builders, and other artisans (slave and free) who played "central role[s]" in the creation of architecture throughout the South (Bishir, "Black Builders in Antebellum North Carolina," 424). As Bishir reports, although black craftsmen were widely recognized for their talent and ingenuity, black construction sites (like Peter's) were also at times sabotaged by angry white mechanics. For more on the history of black craftsmen during this period, see DuBois, "The Ante-bellum Negro Artisan," 175–82; Vlach, *By the Work of Their Hands*, esp. 86–89.

18. I would suggest that it is predominantly this deadpan irony and neither a "superior and self-consciously 'literary' point of view" nor excessive sentimentality, as William L. Andrews has suggested, that not only guides the narrative but makes its political allegiances hard to read (*The Literary Career of Charles W. Chesnutt*, 18–19). And rather than adopt this irony in an effort to maintain a "strict detachment from his subject," as Andrews has argued (though Andrews views "Uncle Peter's House" more favorably in this regard than he does Chesnutt's other early sketches), Chesnutt in my view is trying on irony here, if not always successfully, as a possible vehicle for his social criticism.

19. Chesnutt, *Charles Waddell Chesnutt*, 48.

20. Chesnutt, "The Goophered Grapevine," 254. Shelley's poem, which early on describes "Two vast and trunkless legs of stone / Stand[ing] in the desert," closes with these lines: "Nothing beside remains. Round the decay / Of that Colossal Wreck, boundless and bare / The lone and level sands stretch far away."

21. Stepto, "The Simple but Intensely Human Inner Life of Slavery," 46; Sundquist, *To Wake the Nations*, 376.

22. Chesnutt, *The Conjure Woman and Other Conjure Tales*, 70. Unless otherwise noted, all subsequent citations from the conjure tales will come from this edition and will appear parenthetically in the text.

23. Mugerauer, "Toward an Architectural Vocabulary," 111. See also Perry, "The Front Porch as Stage and Symbol in the Deep South," 14.

24. Beckham, "The American Front Porch," 75.

25. Chesnutt, "The Conjurer's Revenge," 623. In the original version of this story Annie is described as a "strict Presbyterian" who "employed her time reading religious books and playing sacred music on the parlor organ." She is "quite a zealous missionary," John says, "but confined her ministrations chiefly to the colored element of the population." Julius is a particular target: "Sometimes old Julius McAdoo, our colored man-of-all-work, would come up to the house and sit on the piazza and listen to the music; and Annie would come out and exchange religious experiences with him, and supply him with religious literature, although she was aware that he did not know his letters." On this Sunday afternoon Annie gives Julius a hymn book, announcing, "If you know of any of your friends who would like to have one, I have several others which were sent to me for distribution." Julius mocks her zeal by making much of paging through the book while holding it conspicuously upside down. He also asks for one without red edges (even though it is supposedly his favorite color), because "folks"—in this case, Annie—"is alluz sayin' cullud people lubs red so" (623–24).

Many critics have commented on the importance of the connection between Julius and Annie; see, for example, Selinger, "Aunts, Uncles, Audience." Selinger's intriguing reading of Julius as a "metaphorical conjure woman" would also make Julius's connection with Annie resemble the woman-to-woman bonding that Beckham argues takes place in the "liminal space" of the porch.

26. Chesnutt varied his spelling of "Mars" from story to story, writing "Mars," "Marse," or "Mars'." My spellings will change as Chesnutt's do, depending on the story.

27. See, for example, the house designs in such popular nineteenth-century books as Downing's *Cottage Residences* (1842) and his *Architecture of Country Houses* (1850); Vaux's *Villas and Cottages* (1857); Woodward and Thompson's *Victorian Housebuilder's Guide* (1869); and *Bicknell's Victorian Buildings*, 5th ed. (1878); or in recent collections like Berg's *Country Patterns, 1841–1883*. Even when house plans do put dining rooms in the fronts of houses, there are often no windows looking out onto the front piazzas.

28. Stepto, "The Simple but Intensely Human Inner Life of Slavery," 51. Recent critics to treat one or more of these tales include Sundquist on "The Dumb Witness" and "Lonesome Ben" (*To Wake the Nations*, 389–92, 404–6), and Wideman on "A Deep Sleeper" ("Charles Chesnutt and the WPA Narratives"). My reading of "A Deep Sleeper" is particularly indebted to Wideman's essay. Stepto has called these three tales "slight," though "fascinating in terms of Chesnutt's struggle to vary his form" ("The Simple but Intensely Human Inner Life of Slavery," 30).

29. Wideman, "Charles Chesnutt and the WPA Narratives," 67.

30. Vlach, *Back of the Big House*, 235, 230, 235, 235–36.

31. Brodhead, *Cultures of Letters*, 202.

32. Ironically, in the end Ben figuratively receives the beating that he had tried to avoid: "He laid dere 'til he died, an' de sun beat down on 'im, an' beat down on 'im, an' beat down on 'im, fer th'ee er fo' days" (156).

33. Sundquist, *To Wake the Nations*, esp. 405–6.

34. Gowans, *Styles and Types of North American Architecture*, 101, 94. Vlach's discussion of plantation architecture points up an ironic permutation of this zeal for porches: to embellish the appearance of his own house an antebellum planter might also build his big house quarters (for nearby house slaves) not only with better materials than those used for field quarters but in scaled-down imitation of his own mansion—including miniature porches, that is, themselves squared to look back at the big house. See *Back of the Big House*, 23.

35. Bishir, *North Carolina Architecture*, 195.

36. Bishir, "A Proper Good Nice and Workmanlike Manner," 51, 58.

37. Bishir, *North Carolina Architecture*, 199.

38. Another "dumb witness" is Murchison, who does not seem able to imagine the piazza as a possible hiding place. In catechizing Viney he skips right over it: "Is it in the house? . . . In the yard? . . . In the barn? . . . In the fields?" (167). As "between" space, the piazza disappears from view in this catalog of the plantation grounds even as Chesnutt underscores its importance by hiding the papers there.

39. Edwards, "The Complex Origins," 48; Little-Stokes, "The North Carolina Porch," 105. As Little-Stokes explains, the "mature Southern porch" is "Classical" in its "decorative detail" but "dependent upon the West Indian model in overall form" (105). For more on the Caribbean origins of the North Carolina/Southern porch, see also Johnston and Waterman, *The Early Architecture of North Carolina*, 41–42. Edwards presents by far the most thorough history of the full-length piazza, outlining a five-stage process of "American Architectural Creolization": (1) ca. 1518–1630: proto-Creole culture; (2) ca. 1630–80: Antillian Creole cultural florescence; (3) ca. 1680–1730: the creolization of coastal North America; (4) ca. 1730–1830: diffusion of the veranda within North America; (5) ca. 1830–1920: modeling on the vernacular.

40. The Caribbean influence on the vernacular architecture of eighteenth-century and early nineteenth-century southeastern North America was also strongly felt in the Creole cottages of the Gulf Coast, particularly Louisiana, albeit primarily as a result of French rather than English settlement. See Edwards, "The Origins of Creole Architecture." A note on the dating of the Old Plantation House in Figure 15: although it was originally dated 1742 (and so listed in the 1990 edition of Bishir's *North Carolina Architecture*), dendrochronology in the early 1990s indicates that the timbers were actually cut in 1786. See Bishir, *North Carolina Architecture*, portable edition, 27.

41. Vlach, *The Afro-American Tradition in Decorative Arts*, 138, 136.

42. First published in 1896, Fletcher and Fletcher's tome (cowritten by Banister Fletcher and his son, Banister F. Fletcher, who was responsible for revisions after his father's death in 1899) was "unrivaled as a textbook for architectural history" until the 1940s (Gowan, *Styles and Types of North American Architecture*, x). The original 1905 version of the tree is drawn with less ornamentation and does not include the all-white

Greco-Roman figures at the bottom, but otherwise presents the same array of nations and regions as depicted in Figure 18 excepting the very top branch, which had not yet sprouted its American shoot. The tree reproduced here (from the sixth edition) first appeared in 1921—ironically at almost precisely the moment that Chesnutt returned to the conjure (and piazza) genre to blast "the trope of the family tree" (Sundquist, *To Wake the Nations*, 378) in his story "The Marked Tree" (1924). The 1905 frontispiece does appear with a cautionary caption—"The Tree must be taken as suggestive only, for minor influences cannot be indicated in a diagram of this kind"—but the reader will not find African forms in the main text either. The first discussion of African architecture in Fletcher and Fletcher's *History* would not appear until 1987, in the nineteenth edition.

43. Luke Bresky, untitled seminar presentation (Department of English, UCLA, 10 March 1992), 1.

44. Marling, *George Washington Slept Here*, 155, 158, 90. On architecture and the Colonial Revival, see also Kammen, *Mystic Chords of Memory*, esp. 146–53; May, "Progressivism and the Colonial Revival"; and Schlereth, "American Homes and American Scholars." Beginning in the early 1890s, "an unabashed and pervasive craze for colonial furniture, silver, various other artifacts, and entire homes . . . became an absorbing passion of American society, the upper crust as well as segments of the middle class, for more than a decade," Kammen reports (148). On the shifting meanings of "colonial" beginning in the 1870s, see also Scully, *The Shingle Style and the Stick Style*, 38–39.

45. In "purer" I am quoting Mary H. Northend, a prominent turn-of-the-century neocolonialist who used such phrases as the "purest colonial type" in identifying American buildings. See, for example, her *Colonial Homes and Their Furnishings*, 7. The phrase "antidotes to the poison[s]" is Marling's (*George Washington Slept Here*, 76). The list of neocolonial keywords is drawn from both Northend's *Colonial Homes and Their Furnishings* (e.g., 6, 17, 57) and May's "Progressivism and the Colonial Revival," 110. The phrase "instinctive need for order" is Marling's (89), and "visual cues" is May's (117).

46. While it is difficult to say how aware Chesnutt himself may have been of the polycultural origins of the piazza, critics have affirmed his "emblematic" role in "the drama of African retentions and black cultural survival" taking place in the late nineteenth century (Sundquist, *To Wake the Nations*, 312). I would suggest that architecture offers yet one more field in which Chesnutt plays his part in this drama. We do know that in the 1890s he was reading Lafcadio Hearn's *Two Years in the French West Indies* (1890), a lengthy travel narrative that often lingers over architectural detail. See Chesnutt, *Charles Waddell Chesnutt*, 63; Hearn, *Two Years in the French West Indies*, e.g., 23, 36, 73. It also appears that Chesnutt had an interest in contemporary public architecture, including structures with racial and political significance; in an 1897 letter to his daughter Ethel upon returning from Boston (where he met with Page to discuss his literary prospects), Chesnutt writes, "I saw the [Robert Gould] Shaw Memorial and the new Public Library building, which are 'out of sight'" (Chesnutt, *Charles Waddell Chesnutt*, 81).

47. My reading of Viney's "house-keeping" is indebted to Bresky's.

48. Chesnutt to Walter Hines Page, 20 May 1898, McElrath and Leitz, eds., *"To Be an Author,"* 105.

49. See Brodhead's *Cultures of Letters* for a description of the ways that the "social markers" Chesnutt adds to this paragraph give John "an unusual precision of historical identification" (197). My reading of the significant *place* markers that Chesnutt

also adds is partly influenced by Brodhead's subsequent discussion of the "sense of space" in the conjure tales (199–200), although Brodhead does not discuss Patesville specifically.

50. For more on the political, economic, and architectural history of the Fayetteville Market House (particularly its dominance of the city's "trade, its government, and the pace of daily life"), see Bishir, *North Carolina Architecture*, 172. Other discussions of Chesnutt's treatment of Fayetteville in his fiction include Andrews, "Chesnutt's Patesville"; and Render, "Tarheelia in Chesnutt." Chesnutt calls further attention to the historical actuality of Patesville in his revisions to "The Goophered Grapevine" when he has John announce that he "shall call [it] Patesville, because, for one reason, that is not its name" (32). On the significance of Fayetteville to Chesnutt, see also his letter to Page of 4 April 1898, in which Chesnutt describes it as "the town where I spent my own boyhood and early manhood, and where my own forbears have lived and died and laid their bones" (McElrath and Leitz, eds., *"To Be an Author,"* 107). For another account of Chesnutt's revisions to "The Goophered Grapevine," see Burnette, "Charles W. Chesnutt's *The Conjure Woman* Revisited."

51. Page, *In Ole Virginia*, 1; Semple, "Old Kentucky Home," 32–33.

52. Vlach, *Back of the Big House*, 5.

53. Upton, "White and Black Landscapes," 64, 66. Semple's story offers a remarkably detailed processional narrative, moving stage by stage from town to plantation, through numerous gates and stiles, up steps, down steps, onto the porch, into the house, around the house, behind the house, and so on. And even though as a family relative the speaker is a house "insider," not merely a guest, and appears to move around the grounds by her own routes, in the end her experience of the plantation matches the planter's desired "articulation": "Slavery had its shadowed side in Kentucky as elsewhere," she observes, "but what we saw of it here was bright and sunny" ("Old Kentucky Home," 37).

54. Semple, "Old Kentucky Home," 33; Chesnutt, *The Conjure Woman and Other Conjure Tales*, 33. Upton's analysis is useful here: "Since the meaning of spaces depends as much on how we got to them as it does on our being in them—on the shifting states of awareness as we pass one barrier after another—it is evident that in circumventing the formal barriers of the processional entrance, . . . the slaves' route undercut the social statement made by the formal approach" ("White and Black Landscapes," 68). Here Chesnutt's replacement of the dozen tumbling slaves with the "straight" and solitary black girl (pointedly a "human being" [33], not a caricature) undercuts the social statement about black character typically made by stories like Semple's.

55. In drawing this contrast I do not mean to slight the importance of Aunt Peggy as a powerful female narrative counterpart (and sometimes rival) to Uncle Julius. For a reading of the gender relations inscribed in the conjure tales (and their writing), see Selinger, "Aunts, Uncles, Audience."

56. Where Julius is seated in "Tobe's Tribulations" is not clear; in every other story from this phase, however, when John asks Julius "to sit down," he means the top step.

57. The one significant new space that Chesnutt does elaborate in the six tales from 1898 is Aunt Peggy's cabin, which becomes almost as obligatory a site for Julius's stories as John and Annie's piazza had already become for Chesnutt's frames. Though an insignificant character in the first two phases of tales (appearing only in "The Goophered Grapevine"), Peggy appears in every tale of the third set, even naming the final collection,

as characters visit her cabin to enlist (or, more accurately, to purchase) her aid. Chesnutt does not anatomize the cabin or its contents as fully as he does John and Annie's piazza, but what he does do is affirm—through insistent reiteration—Peggy's address. In every tale he identifies her as the conjure woman who lives "down by de Wim'l'ton Road." The exact language may differ, but the point is the same: Peggy has a location outside of slavery. Her cabin thus complicates any simplistic division of the antebellum South into "white" space and "black" space. Though Peggy is not part of any plantation, she consistently influences plantation space, much as the presence of free blacks (and even non-slave-owning whites) shaped the conceptual if not the physical landscape of southern slavery. The endlessly repeated signature of Peggy's (business) address thus allegorizes a crucial space of free black female enterprise, if not racial independence, that Chesnutt was also trying to explore in his non-Julius work and that conventional southern fictions summarily excluded.

58. Quoted in Andrews, *The Literary Career of Charles W. Chesnutt*, 35.

59. Selinger, "Aunts, Uncles, Audience," 684.

60. Evidence that Chesnutt may privately have scorned the reconciliatory North-marries-South endings of popular fictions like his own "Hot-Foot Hannibal" surfaces in a 1901 letter to Booker T. Washington in which Chesnutt reports being unable to finish Winston Churchill's novel *The Crisis* (1901), which features such a denouement. "It is in the popular vein," Chesnutt writes, "which is sufficient to account in large measure for its popularity" (McElrath and Leitz, eds., *"To Be an Author,"* 167–68).

61. Selinger, "Aunts, Uncles, Audience," 685. In my use of the term "pragmatic" here I am recalling Vlach's description of territorial appropriation as a way for slaves to establish "defensible social boundaries" in both "pragmatic and symbolic terms" (*Back of the Big House*, 235).

62. On the multiple versions of the story that would eventually become *The House behind the Cedars*, see Sedlack, "The Evolution of Charles Chesnutt's *The House Behind the Cedars."* According to Joseph R. McElrath, Jr., the final title change appears to have been the suggestion of Chesnutt's editor, Walter Hines Page. See McElrath, "Collaborative Authorship," 163.

63. Chesnutt, *The House behind the Cedars*, 3. Subsequent references are from this edition and will appear parenthetically in the text.

64. Andrews, *The Literary Career of Charles W. Chesnutt*, 158.

65. See Worden, "Birth in the Briar Patch," 7.

66. While a full reading of the architectural resonances of the novel are beyond the scope of this chapter, I disagree with Worden's conclusion that the house behind the cedars "remains illegible" in the novel ("Birth in the Briar Patch," 14). I would argue instead that it is far too legible (whether the "reading" produced by each character is mistaken or not), to too many people, to preserve any sense of safety for its occupants. For additional readings of the architectural significance of *The House behind the Cedars*, see Leveen, "The Race Home" (Diss. UCLA, 1999), 259–99; and Moddelmog, *Reconstituting Authority*, 129–59. Moddelmog also helpfully compares Chesnutt's treatment of race, place, and property in *House* with similar tropes found in "The Sway-Backed House," which appeared in *Outlook* in November 1900. The publication of this latter story shows Chesnutt's architectural imagination continuing to move out of the conjure tales into his color line fiction.

67. These representative sites include Olivia Carteret's estate ("saved" by Polly Ochiltree from grasping black hands); the historic Clarendon Club, housed in a "dignified old colonial mansion"); the house of William and Jane Miller; and the "little group of public institutions"—hospital, schoolhouse, and church—that will become the locus of black resistance at the end of the novel. See Chesnutt, *The Marrow of Tradition*, 138, 155, 299. Subsequent references are from this edition and will appear parenthetically in the text.

68. Sundquist, *To Wake the Nations*, 432.

69. Howells, "A Psychological Counter-current in Fiction," 882. According to McElrath and Leitz, by the end of 1904 *The Marrow of Tradition* had sold only 3,387 copies, *The House behind the Cedars* only 3,244 copies. See *"To Be an Author,"* 214n6. Chesnutt would publish only one more novel, *The Colonel's Dream*, in 1905. Ironically, it was in this final novel that he would bring the piazza back to narrative prominence, in part by weaving a new version of "The Dumb Witness" (which was still unpublished) into the text—although he revised the earlier story in such a way as to soften much of its critique. For more on Chesnutt's "dilution" of the original story's import through revision, see Sundquist, *To Wake the Nations*, 90n.

70. Nora, "Between Memory and History," 295–96.

NOTES TO CHAPTER 3

1. Torres, *Memorias*, 47. In the original Spanish Torres wrote: "Figúrate un jacalón de madera que con divisiones interiores era a la vez habitación y tienda: las puertas estaban cubiertas de tela de alambre, para evitar la entrada de moscas y zancudos. Afuera, una banca de madera algo sucia, era utilizada para esperar el tren. Y aquel 'establecimiento' propiedad, entre paréntesis, de un mexicano casado con una alemana, era todo que de edificios había allí.

"No pude contenerme más y pregunté: ¿pero esto es Estados Unidos?" (104).

Subsequent references are to this edition and will appear parenthetically in the text. For each citation I will provide the original Spanish version in the endnotes.

2. Gruesz, "The Gulf of Mexico System," 472–73.

3. My reading of the imperial dimensions of domestic architectural space in this chapter draws in part on the groundbreaking work of Amy Kaplan, particularly her essays "Manifest Domesticity" (1988) and "Romancing the Empire" (1990), both of which also appear in revised form in her later volume *The Anarchy of Empire in the Making of U.S. Culture* (2002). My analysis brings an architectural specificity to Kaplan's broader readings of ideology and empire. I am particularly indebted to her explication of the domestic "logic" of American national expansion. See "Manifest Domesticity," 584. At the same time, by bringing Torres into the conversation I explore new ways of thinking about architecture, identity, mobility, and narrative in a transnational context.

4. "Pero el recuerdo de las persecuciones que pretexto de política había sufrido mi papá, los estragos espantosos que las hordas zapatistas hacían en las goteras de la gallarda Cuidad, las venganzas injustificadas de los partidarios del Gobierno, los asesinatos cometidos por misteriosos matadores de personas a quienes se creía desafectas al Gobierno, y en fin, los horrores, que oía contar que iba extendiendo por todas partes la guerra, me hicieron pensar que la vuelta a la Cuidad de los Palacios, sería el más grande de los disparates" (88).

5. Davis, *Three Gringos*, 216, 146. Subsequent references are from this edition and will appear parenthetically in the text.

6. "Más que . . . para los nacionales que con sus intemperancias someten a la Patria a semejantes pruebas!" (91).

7. Gruesz, "The Gulf of Mexico System," 470; Luna-Lawhn, Introduction, 10.

8. Gruesz, "The Gulf of Mexico System," 474. Gruesz uses "circuit" in D. W. Meinig's sense: "Meinig notes that once access to the Gulf was secured through the Louisiana Purchase, 'a whole circuit of coasts—Florida, Cuba, Yucatán, Mexico, Texas—suddenly took on new meaning for Americans, and before long such places were being declared to be of compelling national interest'" (474). See Meinig, *The Shaping of America*, 23. "Transculturalization" is Luna-Lawhn's term for Torres's process of moving from one language and culture toward/into another (Introduction, 12).

9. "Barcos mercantes, de todas clases y de todas las naciones del mundo, según se ve por la variedad infinita de sus banderas y de sus marinos. Junot a los grandes barcos se deslizan como pequeños peces de colores innumerables botes de gasolina, unos destinados a carga, toscamente labrados, y otros para pasajeros, primorosamente acabados, con los asientos en hilera, a ambos lados y más altos que la cubierta" (121).

10. "Houston está situada en contacto continuo con Galveston, Texas City, y con Nueva Orleans, para donde salen cuatro trenes de vapor diarios. Para Galveston hay eléctricos cada hora, y dos de vapor al día y para Texas City, ocho trenes eléctricos y dos de vapor al día" (124).

11. "Enorme grandeza"; "Admiración porque el paisaje es grandioso y bello, la luz al quebrarse sobre las olas produce arabescos de colores tan variados, que los que hablan del 'mar azul' del 'mar verde' están en un error. La luz le dá a la superficie movediza del mar tantos colores, que ni es verde ni es azul, es una infinita variedad de colores, es una policromía admirable" (95).

12. In "The Gulf of Mexico System," Gruesz suggests that a self-aware Gulf-system narrative would resemble Domingo Faustino Sarmiento's "apprehension of the city [New Orleans] as a liminal zone between the Anglo and Latin worlds—the North and the South, the future and the past, mingling in the Gulf like fresh water and saline. Throughout the nineteenth century, Hispanophone commentators tended to be more trenchantly aware of the profound historical and economic links between the U.S. Gulf Coast and sites that lay outside the nation: Mexico, Cuba, Texas, Yucatán, Belize, Honduras" (469).

13. Unless we think of the hanging moss as "Spanish" (Spanish moss).

14. Seelye, *War Games*, 167. Seelye, however, goes on to maintain that while the travel narrative may have "nourished" (164) the novel, the two texts otherwise have little in common: "One is hard pressed to find any but the most superficial connections between the two narratives" (167). As will become clear, I believe the Central American context of *Three Gringos* is very important to the political and architectural landscapes of *Soldiers*.

15. Davis, *Soldiers of Fortune*, 31, 96. Subsequent references are from this edition and will be cited parenthetically in the text. On the controversy surrounding Díaz's modernization of the rail and road network and in particular the role of U.S. capital in the Mexican economy in the late nineteenth and early twentieth centuries, see Gonzalez and Fernandez, *A Century of Chicano History*, esp. 36–39. Davis makes it clear in *Soldiers* that the role of Clay's work in Mexico before the novel begins is understood in precisely these terms. Describing the work of the engineers who were building Mexico's new rails and

roads, one character explains to another: "And they knew all the time that whatever they decided to do out there in the wilderness meant thousands of dollars to the stockholders somewhere up in God's country [i.e., the U.S.], who would some day hold them to account for them" (12–13).

16. Belize's Government House was built between 1812 and 1814, during the British slave trade, possibly after a design by Christopher Wren. It combines Caribbean and European architectural forms. See Pariser, *Explore Belize*, 119.

17. Seelye, *War Games*, 169.

18. Guatemala achieved independence from Spain in 1821. See Bethell, *The Cambridge History of Latin America*, 471.

19. The General Walker in this statue is American filibuster William Walker (1824–60), who in 1855 took advantage of a civil war in Nicaragua to seize control of the country, make himself commander in chief of the army, and declare himself president in 1856. Defeated and turned out in May 1857, he tried to return later that year only to be arrested and forcibly expelled. Walker made one last unsuccessful attempt to filibuster in Central America in 1860 and was eventually executed by firing squad in Honduras. See Greenberg, *Manifest Manhood*, 31–33. For the most thorough treatment of Davis's attraction to Walker, one of the later author's "freebooting heroes" (1), see Harrison, *Agent of Empire*.

20. Davis is also exasperated by the bullet holes in all the chief buildings in the capital—a sign of the endless revolutionary turmoil and the neglect (indeed degradation) of the built environment.

21. Quoted in Kaplan, *The Anarchy of Empire*, 27. The "disorderly house" metaphor originally appeared in *Democratic Review* 20 (February 1847): 101. See Kaplan, *The Anarchy of Empire*, 219n7.

22. In *Three Gringos*, Davis recalls sitting in the Plaza de Bolívar, "looking up at the big statue [of the South American liberator Simón Bolívar] on its black marble pedestal, under the shade of green palms and in the moonlight, with a band of fifty pieces playing Spanish music, and hundreds of officers in gold uniforms, and pretty women with no covering to their heads . . . circling past in an endless chain of color and laughter and movement" while across the plaza "rose the towers and broad façade of the cathedral, white and ghostly in the moonlight" (282). In *Soldiers*, Davis imagines a very similar plaza scene: "At one end of the plaza the President's band was playing native waltzes that came throbbing through the trees and beating softly above the rustling skirts and clinking spurs of the señoritas and officers, sweeping by in two opposite circles around the edges of the tessellated pavements. Above the palms around the square arose the dim, white façade of the cathedral, with the bronze statue of Anduella, the liberator of Olancho" (111).

23. See Murphy, *Hemispheric Imaginings*, ch. 4, "Gringos Abroad: Rationalizing Empire with Richard Harding Davis." According to Seelye, Davis "had already started writing what would become *Soldiers of Fortune* before leaving" the U.S. on his trip through Central America, "and he would finish it while seeing the account of his Central American trip through the press" (*War Games*, 164). Like most critics, however, Seelye downplays the significance of the Central American trip to *Soldiers*; instead, he offers Cuba as the most important context for understanding the novel. See *War Games*, 192–213.

24. On the bungalow's origins and adaptations, see Lancaster, "The American Bungalow"; King, *The Bungalow*; and Faragher, "Bungalow and Ranch House."

25. Duchscherer and Keister, *Bungalow*, 2.

26. On Davis's earlier Cuban visit, see Lubow, *The Reporter Who Would Be King*, 28. One of Lubow's sources for this inference is William Harley Porter's 1902 *Bookman* essay, "Mr. Davis and the Real Olancho." Even if the size and scope of the imagined bungalow in *Soldiers* were based in part on this Cuban visit, Davis's Central American experiences, particularly his encounter with "imperial" bungalows in Belize, provide a much more immediate context for the Palms.

27. In *The American Bungalow*, Lancaster notes that bungalow patterns may be found in New York architect Arnold W. Brunner's *Cottages; Or, Hints on Economical Building* (1884). See Lancaster, *The American Bungalow*, 79–80.

28. On the consonance of simple bungalow forms with the "minimalist aesthetic" of the Colonial Revival, see Clark, *The American Family Home*, 163, 189. For a fascinating example of an early twentieth-century house design that explicitly merged neocolonial and bungalow forms, see the Aladdin Company's "Kentucky" model. As the 1912 Aladdin catalog explains, "While it reminds one of the stately colonnades of old colonial mansions, it still retains the delightful atmosphere of modern American bungalows" (*Aladdin Houses: "Built in a Day*," Catalog No. 23, 34–35).

29. Murphy, *Hemispheric Imaginings*, 142–44.

30. Ibid., 141.

31. Wright, *USA*, 8; Faragher, "Bungalow and Ranch House," 154. On the Aladdin Company's bungalow exports, see Cody, *Exporting American Architecture*, 5.

32. Erbe, "Manufacturing and Marketing the American Bungalow," 46–47. In addition to Aladdin, which started selling its "Readi-Cut" homes in 1906, other early twentieth-century national mail-order firms specializing in bungalows included Lewis Homes, also based in Bay City, Michigan; Gordon-Van Tine, in Davenport, Iowa; and the Sears Roebuck Company.

33. Erbe, "Manufacturing and Marketing the American Bungalow," 47.

34. "Aladdin Homes: Make This Your Home Building Year," 89.

35. Eldridge, "There Goes the Transnational Neighborhood," 633. Another sign of the tension between modern and antimodern embodied in the mail-order bungalow can be seen in the stock "Arabian Nights" imagery in many Aladdin Company advertisements, which often feature an image of a genie holding a lamp, out of which the house emerges.

36. *Aladdin Homes: "Built in a Day*," Catalog No. 29, 4, 6; *Aladdin Houses: "Built in a Day*," Catalog No. 23, 9.

37. The 1916 Aladdin sales catalog elaborates the company's increasingly influential role in the construction of industrial housing. In a section titled "Industrial Housing Problems," the catalog copy notes that "a special study of housing problems as related to industrial institutions has been made by the Aladdin organization. This study has been based on actual experience in building six new cities with Aladdin houses, and in furnishing groups of houses for many manufacturing concerns, mines in many localities and government projects." This section further notes that the firm has built not only houses but also "dormitories, bunk houses, community dining halls, guard houses, bath houses, school houses, churches, offices and gymnasiums." See *Aladdin Homes: Built in a Day*, Catalog No. 28, 14. For more on the contradictions between the American dream of homeownership and the standardization of modern assembly-line production, see Banta, *Taylored Lives*, 215–29.

38. Cody, *Exporting American Architecture*, 4–5; "Ready-Made Houses," 10, cited in Darnall, "Innovations in American Prefabricated Housing," 53.

39. *Aladdin Homes: Built in a Day*, Catalog No. 28, 8. The house depicted in the 1913 export advertisement is the Mardsen, a "pretty bungalow of six rooms" commended to the reader of Aladdin's 1913 domestic brochure as "without question the most complete, convenient, and attractive design that we are showing"—a fitting home for Clay and Hope. See *Aladdin Houses: "Built in a Day,"* Catalog No. 24, 64. For another reading of the Aladdin Company's global involvement, see Hoganson, *Consumers' Imperium*, 211ff.

40. Cody, *Exporting American Architecture*, 87–88.

41. "'Verá usted más adentro, niña, la cuidad naciente: estos terrenos tan feos para usted serán una inmensa cuidad dentro de poco . . . hace tres años me instalé aquí y sólo había cien gentes; ahora ya hay ocho mil'" (105).

42. "Hace cuatro años no había nada en aquel lugar . . . ; pero una compañía estableció allí sus muelles y bodegas y entonces se vino en cuenta que aquel lugar iba a ser de gran porvenir, porque era nada menos que el destinado para que, con mayores ventajas que por Nueva Orleans O Galveston, se enviaran todas las mercancías que de Estados Unidos van destinadas a Panamá" (104).

43. "Diez mil soldados que están esperando de un momento a otro embarcarse para México" (105). Texas City would in fact become one of the busiest U.S. ports on the Gulf, outstripping Galveston although not New Orleans. Surpassing both Texas City and New Orleans, however, would be yet another U.S. Gulf port—just up the Galveston bay—that opened in November 1914, the Port of Houston, which as of 2009 remains the second-busiest port on the Gulf (and in the U.S.; the busiest U.S. port on the Gulf is the Port of South Louisiana). See "U.S. Port Ranking by Cargo Tonnage 2009," publication of the American Association of Port Authorities (http://www.aapa-ports.org, accessed 4 December 2010). The U.S. occupied Veracruz in part in retaliation for "the arrest of several American sailors and their commanding officer" at Tampico, another major Gulf port. See Quirk, *An Affair of Honor*, 1. The completion of the Panama Canal, which in part spurred the fight among Texas cities to be the next great Gulf port, was also important in showcasing American design and engineering expertise, and thus ultimately helped spur the increased exportation of American building and construction technology, including architecture, around the world. See Cody, *Exporting American Architecture*, 3.

44. Both *Three Gringos* and *Soldiers* were reprinted multiple times between their initial publications and Torres's departure for the U.S. and were thus widely available. *Three Gringos*, for example, was reprinted in 1903 and 1913, while *Soldiers* appeared even more frequently, with as many as thirteen new or reprinted editions issued between 1897 and 1914. In *Memorias* Torres appears to refer to at least one book that she would likely have read in English, Samuel Griswold Goodrich's *History of All Nations, from the Earliest Periods to the Present Time; or, Universal History* (1851). Torres compares a building she sees in Houston that resembles "the temple of Diana of Ephesus, that I saw in my *Manual of Universal History*" ("el templo de Diana de Éfeso que ví en mi Manual de Historia Universal" [79, 136]). Goodrich's *Universal History* includes an illustration of this same temple on page 274.

45. "Las estaciones todas iguales: jacalones de madera unos, otros de piedra; pero siempre en la misma forma: angulares y nada bellos" (85); "Asombrosos relatos" (88).

46. "Contaban cómo los grandes acorazados lanzaban granadas tremendas sobre los edificios, principalmente sobre la Escuela de marina, quedando destruída ésta y en fin, todo lo relataban de manera atropellada produciendo una sensación de horror y de odio hacia los alsaltantes" (88). On the Naval Academy and the other prominent buildings targeted by U.S. troops, see Langley, *The Banana Wars*, 101–2.

47. "Me ví tentada a pedirle que nos regresamos a México" (88); "Al contemplar las ventanas destrozadas por los cañonazos de los acorazados me pareció que hacían un gesto horrible de cólera, más que para los invasores, para los nacionales que con sus intemperancias someten a la Patria a semejantes pruebas!" (91).

48. "'Es triste verse obligado por la tiranía a buscar bajo el amparo de estos hombres paz y seguridad'" (88). Ironically, the soldiers they see are "dressed in khaki and wearing wide-rim felt hats traveling in the front cow guard" of a locomotive—as though in imitation of a famous scene from *Three Gringos* in which Davis and his two traveling companions ride on the front of a train in Honduras in exactly the same fashion. I should note here that it is possible Torres revised her original letters, which were first published in the Spanish-language newspaper *El Paso del Norte*, before they were republished in book form in 1918. Luna-Lawhn notes that she was not able to locate the original issues of *El Paso del Norte*, even "to document the exact date or dates that Torres's work appeared in the newspaper, because a complete microfilm copy of *El Paso del Norte* is unavailable in the United States" (Introduction, 8–9). Which means that what I am taking for the surprisingly mature comments of a thirteen-year-old may actually be the more reflective thoughts of a seventeen-year-old.

49. See Gruesz for a discussion of the ways that port cities and gateway settlements in the Gulf typically "function in the representational economy as morally ambiguous places that leave the continental interior of the national body vulnerable to contamination" ("The Gulf of Mexico System," 474).

50. "Te diré cuál es el sistema más práctico para conocer las ciudades americanas, y en general las de todas partes, pues hasta en las mexicanas nos ha dado resultado: inmediatamente que se llega hay que comprar una colección de tarjetas postales de la población que se visita, con lo cual se logra tener rápida idea de cuáles son los edificios principales o los lugares más pintorescos. En seguida toma uno un coche o un automóvil (aquí sólo hay automóviles), y se le indica al cochero o chauffeur en su caso, que desea uno conocer lo que las tarjetas postales reproducen" (118).

51. Luna-Lawhn's very helpful introduction to *Memorias* does pay some attention to Torres's architectural descriptions and judgments, offering them as (in part) an index of Torres's increasing cultural adaptation (or transculturalization) to the U.S. My goal in this chapter is to push this analysis even further, especially in relation to the broader hemispheric picture that becomes visible when we put Torres's text in conversation with the writings of someone like Davis.

52. For a selection of Davis's letters written from Central and South America during the *Three Gringos* trip, see Davis, ed., *Adventures and Letters of Richard Harding Davis*, 140–72. Discussion of Torres's actual letter writing also raises several additional questions about the mechanics of their publication. Not only do we not know whether the letters were revised before appearing serially in *El Paso del Norte* (or in the 1918 book version, for that matter), we also do not know whether Torres kept copies of the letters as she wrote them, or whether her aunt returned them to her after receiving them, or whether she may

even have written the letters but not mailed them. More information about the composition of the letters at any of these three phases would add greatly to our understanding of them as narrative documents.

53. "Junto a ese y enfrente, y a todos lados, se elevaban otros edificios, si no tan altos como el Rice; sí de ocho, diez y doce pisos; de manera que mi primera impresión fué la de encontrarme en una enorme tumba, cuyas paredes laterales se perdían en el espacio" (109). Following Luna-Lawhn's practice, when quoting from the English translation of Torres's text, I will use boldface type to highlight words that appeared in English in the original published version of *Memorias*.

54. "Verdaderamente elegante"; "Te diré: casi todos los edificios son de monótona arquitectura, son enormes moles cuadradas, salpicadas de ventanas rectangulares que me hacen pensar en palomares gigantesco, sin arte alguno o, sin belleza de ninguna clase" (110).

55. "Construcción de piedra"; "Hermosa torre de cuatro pisos"; "Aquí son pocas las iglesias católicas, pues ésta es protestante, y las pocas que hay son feas, parecen salones en los cuales escasean las obras de arte, pues hasta las pinturas, de los santos no son muy buenas, cuando menos en las iglesias católicas que hasta ahora he conocido por aquí" (127).

56. Herzog, *From Aztec to High Tech*, 32.

57. "El Correo es un edificio que ocupa, con el jardín que lo rodea, una cuadra, pero no es tan bello, ni tan elegante como nuestra Dirección General de Correos de México" (110). I have taken the phrase "Venetian Gothicism" from Fyfe, *Real Mexico*, 97. Fyfe is describing the architectural beauty of Mexico City in what is otherwise a somewhat breezy popular account of Mexico and its revolution.

58. On the rise of this style in Texas, including the Houston Post Office, see Henry, *Architecture in Texas*, 82. Torres would have found a sympathetic ear in this regard from at least one prominent American architect, Louis Sullivan, who famously asserted that the Chicago World's Fair of 1893—a grand showcase for the Beaux-Arts style—had set back American architectural practice for half a century. See Giedion, *Space, Time and Architecture*, 275.

59. "Dos torres de cuatro pisos"; "Balcones circulares de piedra"; "Es otro de los edificios hermosos" (127).

60. "Los americanos no se preocupan de la belleza arquitectónica; y así se explica que con ligeras variantes, todas las casas sean iguales, jacolones techados de una teja de madera (shingles) uniforme, ventanas cuadradas y al frente porticos o terrazas que aquí llaman Porchs, y con que excepción del color, afectan todas la misma forma" (127–28); Luna-Lawhn, Introduction, 17–19.

61. "Entre las calles, pavimentadas de asfalto y la banqueta, hay prados de pasto inglés y una interminable arboleda que presta sombra a los peatones y le da un aspecto de hermosura a toda la calle" (110).

62. "A un lado de esta calzada . . . se extiende la ciudad con sus alegres casitas del tipo que llaman aquí 'bungalow' cuajadas de plantas y flores; y al otro lado, el Golfo de México cuyas últimas olas vienen a morir, convertidas en espuma a unos cincuenta metros de la calzada" (119).

63. "El aspecto es primoroso: figúrate, Tía: unos bañistas, sosteniéndose de unos cables contra el empuje de las olas, otros alcanzados por estos en su fuga hacia la playa y der-

ribados sobre la arena, otros tendidos sobre ésta, y sepultadas de repente por la espuma de las últimas olas. Aquí y allá, grupos de muchachos que de repente desaparecen entre las olas, para volver a aparecer chorreando agua cuando aquellas se van. Y en todas partes gritos, risas y alegría sin fin!" (119–20).

64. "Las casas más modernas de Houston, algunas de las cuales sobresalen por su novedad dentro del tipo común de los 'bungalows'"; "Este lugar tiene, . . . además del jardín, que es hermosos, el atractivo del aire fresco que en él se recibe, puesto que, como está colocado a mayor altura que la cuidad y en una explanada bastante alta, el aire allí le quita a uno el fastidio del fuego de horno de la cuidad" (128).

65. Stickley, "The California Bungalow," which originally appeared in the *Craftsman* in October 1907; reprinted in Stickley, ed., *Craftsman Bungalows*, 12.

66. See Culbertson, *Texas Houses Built by the Book*, ch. 5, "Bungalows from Books: Mail-Order Bungalow Catalogues," 60–78.

67. "Un campamento de soldados americanos con sus típicas tiendas de campaña de color amarillo; y más adelante, ocultos entre cerritos artificiales que cubre un pasto verde, unos enormes cañones destinados a la defensa de la cuidad"; "Montones de palos y restos de tiendas en completo desorden, como si el mar hubiera destruido un gran ranchería, y apilado aquí y allá los restos de las chozas" (120).

68. Her feelings here are perhaps precisely the opposite of those we have already seen Davis express in Panama when he takes refuge on an American warship to stay out of trouble: "I was impressed with the comforting sense that comes to a traveller from the States when he knows that one of our White Squadron is rolling at anchor in the harbor" (216).

69. "Los últimos días que pasamos en Houston, los pasamos en conocer el fondo de la cuidad, que es en verdad una grande y bonita población" (124); "Contacto continuo"; "Si a esto se agrega que Houston es el centro de las transacciones algodoneras, se descubrirá el secreto de su desarrollo y riqueza" (124).

70. "A propósito de negros: una mañana pasamos por el centro de una barriada de gentes de color, como les llaman aquí; y me quedé aterrorizada; apenas se puede imaginar cochinada mayor; unas casas sucias, con el alambrado roto, entre patios asquerosos, en donde junto a los marranos y los caballos, se miran, tirados sobre el esti-rol, chiquil- los negros de todos tamaños, que paracen moscas gigantes salidas de aquel montón de materias en putrefacción" (124).

71. "Hombres y mujeres que por centenares, se ocupan en cosechar la fibra" (124).

72. "En unas puertas o en algunas ventanas, o sobre las aceras, negrasos cochinos, fumando sendas pipas de donde sale más humo que de una locomotora" (124).

73. Torres's sense of the black women's excess also extends to their clothes and their speech. "They go from here to there wearing extravagant dresses, with large, worn out straw hats," she tells her aunt. "The Negroes are wailing in incomprehensible English so that not even the chauffeur could easily understand their language" (67–68). ("Yendo de aquí para allá con extravagantes vestidos y con sombreros de paja enormes y rotos, los negros ahullan un inglés ininteligible, puesto que ni el chauffeur podía entenderles con facilidad" [124]). It is also worth noting that the adjective Torres uses to express the feeling she has when she sees this scene, which Luna-Lawhn translates as "horrified," is actually "aterrorizada," which means "terrified" or "terrorized," suggesting that her response is deeply marked by fear.

74. "Dado por resultado que se vean obligados a tener ellos sus teatros especiales, cantinas y fondas, casinos y hasta colonia especial, que es la que te describo más arriba" (125).

75. "Son gente trabajadora e incansable y en general"; "Tienen entrada libre a todas partes, es decir, tienen todos los derechos de los blancos americanos" (125).

76. "¡Infelices negros, llevan la negrura hasta en la suerte!" (126); "Son estos prójimos gente tan fea y tan sucia, que hacen bien los americanos de segregarlos de todo centro de blancos" (125).

77. See "Sunset Heights," City of El Paso, Texas, Development Services Web site: http://www.elpasotexas.gov/development_services/sunset.asp (accessed 14 November 2008).

78. "Indudablemente, las casas más bonitas de la población"; "Por una calle bastante pendiente" (137); "A Vuela Pájaro" (135).

79. "'Venía yo de la **Esmelda ayer**; y pedí en el **carro** un **trance** para ir al **Dipo**, en donde me habían dicho que había una **marqueta**, y yo necesitaba comprar unas **mechas**, y ver si había un calentón barato, para el cual ya tengo bastante leña en la **yardita**; pero cuando ya iba llegando, se descompuso el **traque** y tuve que esperar, dirigiéndome a la casa de **la familia** López, de Chihuahua. Allí los **babis** habían rotó un paquete de **espauda**, de ese que se usa en los **bísquetes**; y me pidió la señora prestado un **daime**, para comprar otro, y como yo no tenía más que ese, tuve que hacer el viaje a pie, y me puse mala, por eso no vine temprano'" (139). All the boldface words in this selection also appeared in boldface in the 1918 text. As Luna-Lawhn notes, in preparing the Spanish section of the reprint edition of Torres's book, she retyped everything "exactly as it appeared in the original," including boldface words. See Torres, *Memorias*, 85 n.1.

80. "¿Entendiste? ¿Verdad que no?" (139); "Ya con estas explicaciones podrás traducir el incomprensible castellano de Carlota" (140).

81. "Al barrio en donde está la fundición de metales que en inglés se llama **Smelter**" (139; boldface in original).

82. Reps, *Bird's Eye Views*, 7.

83. "El terreno . . . se le ha ido quitando al río (y de paso a nosotros los mexicanos) de manera que la cuidad ha ido ascendiendo las lomas y los cerros cercanos" (137).

84. Garcia, *Desert Immigrants*, 127.

85. The imperialism of this moment is related to, yet also different from, Renato Rosaldo's "imperialist nostalgia," in which the agents of colonialism "mourn the passing of what they themselves have transformed." The imperialism imagined in *Soldiers* does not so much transform or destroy native ways of life as it either ignores them (by extracting ore without paying much attention to native needs) or preserves them (by giving them a new, subordinate role to play in the imagining of the empire to come). See Rosaldo, *Culture and Truth*, 69.

NOTES TO CHAPTER 4

1. Biggers, *The House without a Key*, 244. Subsequent references are from this edition and will appear parenthetically in the text.

2. Wu, *The Yellow Peril*, 1.

3. "Creating Charlie Chan," 29.

4. Hoganson, *Consumers' Imperium*, 9, 16; Hawley, "The Importance of Being Charlie Chan," 138.

5. Lee, *Orientals*, 115. Here Lee is specifically discussing the treatment of Sax Rohmer's infamous character, Fu-Manchu, who though identified initially as Chinese is later described more generally as being from "Tartary" or "Tibet" or simply "the East." Lee sees this collapse of national/racial specificity occurring in many genres, including film.

6. See, for example, Kim, *Asian American Literature*, 18–19.

7. While in using the terms "Orientalist" and "Orientalism" I am indebted to the field-shaping work of Edward Said, especially *Orientalism* (1978), I am also guided by the more recent reformulations of Said's terminology for a specifically American context—in which China and Japan are the primary "objects" of "Oriental" fascination, rather than the countries of what is traditionally known as the Near East or Middle East—by such scholars as Mari Yoshihara, Kristin Hoganson, and June Hee Chung. At the same time, as I will discuss in the next section, U.S. Orientalism, particularly in its architectural and decorative guises, included Near Eastern and Middle Eastern structures and artifacts as well as those of Chinese and Japanese origin, derivation, or influence. See, for example, Yoshihara, *Embracing the East*; Hoganson, *Consumers' Imperium*; and Chung, "From Fu-Manchu."

8. Avril, *East Meets West*, 10.

9. Lancaster, "Oriental Forms," 191.

10. My summary of this early trade draws on Crossman, *The China Trade*; Jehle, *From Brant Point to the Boca Tigris*; Avril, *East Meets West*; Mudge, *Chinese Export Porcelain*; and Lancaster, "Oriental Forms." See also John Kuo Wei Tchen for his excellent discussion of "patrician orientalism" in late nineteenth- and early twentieth-century New York City in *New York before Chinatown*, esp. pt. 1, "A Culture of Distinction."

11. Lancaster, "Oriental Forms," 192. As Lancaster notes, a picture of van Braam's house was included in William Birch's views of *The City of Philadelphia* (1800). Other "Chinese features" included windows "that slide back into pockets in the walls like the screens in a Chinese house." The house was finally demolished in 1970. See also Goldstein, "Cantonese Artifacts," 43–55.

12. On the Philadelphia Pagoda and Labyrinth Garden, see Lancaster, "Oriental Forms," 191; Goldstein, "Cantonese Artifacts," 49; and Maynard, *Architecture in the United States*, 82–83. Lancaster says the pagoda was ten stories high; Maynard says it was seven stories high; Goldstein says it was 100 feet tall.

13. Lancaster, "Oriental Forms," 184; Davis, *Rural Residences*, n.p.; Downing, *Treatise*, 345; Holliday, *Leopold Eidlitz*, 91; Downing, "A Few Words," 217.

14. Downing, *Treatise*, 306.

15. Sloan, *The Model Architect*, 72 (see Designs XVIII and XLIX); Sloan, *Sloan's Homestead Architecture*, 57–58.

16. Tatum, review of Davis, *Rural Residences*, 357.

17. Harris, *Cultural Excursions*, 34.

18. Westcott, *Centennial Portfolio*, n.p.

19. Busher, "The Great Centennial Exhibition of 1876" (in 1876 Busher was eighteen), n.p.; Marsh, "Memoir of the Centennial Exhibition of 1876," n.p.

20. Whiffen and Koeper, *American Architecture*, 294.

21. Ibid., 295; Hosley, *The Japan Idea*, 103. Here Hosley also draws on the seminal views expressed by Vincent J. Scully Jr. in *The Shingle Style* (1955). Scully suggests that the "open interior space" of the Queen Anne style was "reinforced by the architectural influence represented by wooden buildings at the Centennial; that is, Japan" (21).

22. Whiffen and Koeper, *American Architecture*, 294; Hosley, *The Japan Idea*, 111. Also important in the growth of interest in Japanese forms was the publication of Edward S. Morse's *Japanese Houses and Their Surroundings* (1886), the first book published by an American author on Japanese architecture in the U.S. The first book on Japanese architecture to appear in the U.S. was British writer Christopher Dresser's *Japan: Its Architecture, Art, and Art Manufactures* (1882), published in both London and New York. Interestingly, Dresser apologizes in his introduction for producing yet another book on Japan—but notes that Japanese architecture represents a new topic.

23. Nute, "Frank Lloyd Wright and Japanese Architecture," 172.

24. Ibid., 169.

25. Quoted in Whiffen and Koeper, *American Architecture*, 295. On Wright's affinity for Japanese forms, see also Scully, *The Shingle Style* (1955), 159–60.

26. Elliott, *The Book of American Interiors*, 71. On Charley Longfellow's contributions to his father's living room, see Guth, *Longfellow's Tattoos*, 182–83. As Guth notes, as the manager of Boston's Household Art Company, which sold Japanese decorative objects, Elliott had a vested interest in encouraging readers to emulate the aesthetic taste of the subjects of his book, which besides Longfellow featured multiple members of the East Coast literary and cultural aristocracy, including William Cullen Bryant and Donald G. Mitchell (the essayist better known by his pseudonym "Ik Marvel"). That this happens to be the same Charles Wyllys Elliott who in Cincinnati in 1848 published the fascinating hybrid pattern book novel *Cottages and Cottage Life* examined briefly in the introduction is evidence not only of his knack for finding the forward edge of more than one house design innovation in the nineteenth century, but also of the midcentury cultural logic that might eventually lead a Downing-trained landscape architect to a career as a high-end dealer in decorative art. It is also evidence of the increasingly close relationship between architecture and interior decoration in the later nineteenth century. Indeed, as Marilynn Johnson Bordes notes, Christian Herter, besides being a decorator and designer, also occasionally offered his clients his services as an architect ("Christian Herter and the Cult of Japan," 20).

27. Bordes, "Christian Herter and the Cult of Japan," 23.

28. According to an invoice provided by the Mark Twain Papers and Project at Berkeley, in February 1881 Mrs. S. L. Clemens placed an order with the New York branch of Vantine's for 2 teapoys (tall oblong stands), 2 trays, 2 dolls, and 5 boxes of magic flowers. On the growth in mainstream fascination with "Oriental" décor, see Tchen, *New York before Chinatown*, esp. pt. 2, "Port Exchanges," which discusses the rise of "commercial orientalism" in New York during the first two-thirds of the nineteenth century; and pt. 3, "The 'Chinese Question,'" which analyzes the rise of the "political orientalism" that developed alongside residual forms of both patrician and commercial Orientalism from the end of the Civil War through 1882.

29. Brown, *The "Japanese Taste*," 280; Hosley, *The Japan Idea*, 111. Both Brown and Hosley are also indebted to Clay Lancaster's pioneering volume, *The Japanese Influence in America* (1963).

30. A. A. Vantine and Co., *Vantine's: The Oriental Store* (1915), inside cover; Yoshihara, *Embracing the East*, 25. Concurs Hoganson: "Late nineteenth-century domestic Orientalism generally entailed fanciful productions passed off as Moorish, Turkish, Chinese, Japanese, or a combination thereof" (*Consumers' Imperium*, 16). Yoshihara suggests that

there was nonetheless a "clear cultural hierarchy" among Asian objects selected for display in U.S. homes, with Japanese material culture—as a reflection of Japan's more favored political status in the late nineteenth century—at the top of the scale.

31. In *Consumers' Imperium*, Hoganson describes the typical contents of a turn-of-the-century "cosey corner": "an upholstered divan, a profusion of cushions, a rug, a Turkish coffee table, a few decorative objects (such as screens, fans, lanterns, and pottery), and lush draperies to frame the entire ensemble"—all in a single corner (16–17). In *Culture and Comfort*, Catherine C. Grier also emphasizes how important the "fabric-swaddled interior" and "overstuffed" Turkish furniture were to nineteenth-century "orientalized" taste. See 50, 112, 149, and esp. 163–99 passim. Both Grier and Hoganson note that the interest in Orientalist ornament and furnishings had as much to do with a desire to imitate European fashion as to access Asia—although such desires also often mirrored imperialist enthusiasms of the era, with their own programs of "access." See in particular Hoganson, *Consumers' Imperium*, 48–54.

32. Bordes, "Christian Herter and the Cult of Japan," 25.

33. Ibid., 27; Brown, "A Thing about Things," 223–24. As Brown notes, other prominent figures who criticized bric-a-brac included Edward Bok, and Edith Wharton and Ogden Codman Jr. Modernist writers such as Willa Cather complained analogously about the "overfurnished" novel, calling for a less superfluous narrative style. In *The "Japanese Taste,"* Jane Brown suggests that twentieth-century Japanese rooms became increasingly "austere," as the aesthetic of profusion gradually gave way to one of "minimalism" (283). Hexagonal Turkish coffee tables, sometimes inlaid with mother-of-pearl, were a stock item in Vantine's catalogs.

34. On the Japanese influence in American bungalow design at the turn of the century, particularly the work of Greene and Greene, see Lancaster, "The American Bungalow" (1958), esp. 245ff. Bordes also identifies the Greene brothers as turn-of-the-century architects who, unlike Herter, shared Wright's appreciation for Japanese art's powerful "sense of the void" ("Christian Herter and the Cult of Japan," 27). For a discussion of the more specific influence of Japanese idioms on Hawaiian vernacular architecture, particularly the bungalow, see Faulkner, "Island Gems," 33–39.

35. Tchen, *New York before Chinatown*, 277, 260–61, 277.

36. Wu, *The Yellow Peril*, 71. As Wu notes, the rise in violence in the 1870s and 1880s against Chinese in America, who were typically unprotected by the U.S. legal system and thus susceptible to white terror, "drove them out of the frontier and many of their smaller communities into the larger Chinatowns where numbers offered greater safety" (71–72). In "California Chinatowns," Christopher L. Yip describes the specific ways "political, social and economic discrimination" affected the "structure and location" (75) of American Chinatowns.

37. Kim, *Asian American Literature*, 10–11. Other commentaries on the treatment of the Chinese and Chinatown in this literature include, for example, Fenn, *Ah Sin and His Brethren in American Literature*; Foster, "China and the Chinese in American Literature"; Chu, *The Images of China and the Chinese*; Chung, "From Fu-Manchu"; Wu, *The Yellow Peril*; Hoppenstand, "Yellow Devil Doctors and Opium Dens"; Wong, "Chinatown"; Lee, *Orientals*; Lye, *America's Asia*; and Chung, "Asian Object Lessons."

38. Norris, *Blix*, 62–63. The description continues for nearly another full paragraph, marked here by the ellipsis, moving from the "craziest" structures and the riot of color

to the sounds and smells of Chinatown, creating a deeply synaesthetic experience of the spatial environment.

39. Wu, *The Yellow Peril*, 104.

40. In the typical association of underground spaces with terror in popular Chinatown fictions there are obvious correspondences to Jung's comparison of the unconscious to a cellar as well as Freud's distinction between the "homely" and the "unhomely" (or uncanny). See also Gaston Bachelard on the polarization between the cellar and the attic in understanding the phenomenology of the imagination in *The Poetics of Space*, 17ff.

41. *Hop Lee, the Chinese Slave Dealer*, 19, 27. So essential a device are the tunnels and dungeons in *The Bradys' Trip to Chinatown*, they become emblems not merely of Chinatown's unseen evils but also the stealthy detective (and narrative) work required to solve the crime.

42. Wu, *The Yellow Peril*, 137. Wiley's stories, especially "Jade," are often mentioned by critics, including Rzepka, but usually only to recapitulate Wu's brief summaries. My analysis is the first to look specifically at the role of "Oriental" decorative art in the title story.

43. Wiley, *Jade*, 22, 33, 13. Knopf's imprint on this lurid collection indicates the extent to which popular Chinatown fiction was not simply the province of the dimes and the pulps but was produced and endorsed by some of the most respected publishing houses.

44. Rohmer, *The Insidious Dr. Fu-Manchu*, 25, 161–62, 164. In England the title of this volume was *The Mysterious Dr. Fu-Manchu*. The eroticized portion of the dream follows immediately after the narrator imagines himself being choked by his slippers: "Came an interval, and then a dawning like consciousness; but it was a false consciousness, since it brought with it the idea that my head lay softly pillowed and that a woman's hand caressed my throbbing forehead. Confusedly, as though in the remote past, I recalled a kiss—and the recollection thrilled me strangely" (164). The novel suggests the narrator may actually be reliving these scenes through the fog of his semiconscious state rather than simply dreaming them, since later in the novel he will visit a room exactly like the one in his dream. He is also befriended by a woman enslaved by Fu-Manchu, who may have cared for him while he was unconscious.

45. Many critics have read Orientalist fiction as shoring up Anglo-American notions of whiteness (see, for example, Kim, *Asian American Literature*, 6, 20; Wong, "Chinatown," 4), though none has quite articulated an architectural version of this argument. Kim comes close: "After shuddering at the poisonous scorpions, snakes, and spiders, [Anglo-American readers] could then retire to the wholesome human normality of their own unequivocally 'American' neighborhoods" (*Asian American Literature*, 11); as does Wong: "Chinatown became a site of negation and definition. Conflicting images were used to portray a community that was forever foreign to American sensibilities and completely unacceptable. At the same time, these images perversely helped define what American communities 'ought' to be like: clean, without odor, safe, and Christian" ("Chinatown," 4). My reading both broadens and gives material specificity to these arguments by suggesting that these images also help define, for some readers, accepted notions of "American" architectural and decorative practice. The strongest analysis of Chinatown as a socio-architectural space is Teng's "Artifacts of a Lost City," which nonetheless suggests that in popular fiction Chinatown only provides an "exotic setting for otherwise hackneyed plots" (75). Teng's essay, which draws on Anthony Vidler's "architectural uncanny,"

examines the ways the architectural environment of the "old Chinatown" that existed in San Francisco before the devastating fire of 1906 appealed deeply as a "symbol for the darkest aspects of human nature that lie beneath the surface of civilized society" (56) to a broad range of bohemian whites, who embraced Chinatown's danger rather than recoiled from it and were disappointed when its seductive charms seemed to disappear once a new and "cleaner, better, brighter" Chinatown emerged after the 1906 earthquake and fire (72). Indeed, after 1906 Chinatown architecture was redesigned as a carefully planned fantasy, featuring applied chinoiserie designed to appeal to the modern tourist. For more on this reinvention of Chinatown, see also Yip, "California Chinatowns."

46. Hoganson, *Consumers' Imperium*, 38–42. As Hoganson notes, other scholars have outlined the ways that both Colonial Revivalism and Orientalism fed imperial fantasies, if of different kinds. See, for example, Brody, "Fantasy Realized," 1, 48.

47. Palumbo-Liu, *Asian/American*, 30.

48. Rydell, *All the World's a Fair*, 228. As Rydell notes, Exposition officials closed Grauman's popular exhibit in the face of protests from "the local Chinese business community," replacing it with one called "Underground Slumming," which depicted Chinatown as the source for illicit entertainment (228–30).

49. *House and Garden* 26.6 (December 1914), 346.

50. *House and Garden* 26.1 (July 1914), 8; *House and Garden* 26.2 (August 1914), 64. Advertisements for Rohmer's novel, sometimes by itself and at other times grouped with other McBride, Nast and Co. books, also appeared in the October and December 1913 issues (twice in the latter) as well as the January 1914 issue.

51. McBride, Nast published scores of home-oriented volumes during this period as well, including a whole series of books on the building—and furnishing—of bungalows. These "mixed-race" architectural images thus also competed with more insidious mass-market advertisements that exploited race in architectural and/or decorative contexts, such as Glidden's "Jap-a-lac" varnish and the Ohio Varnish Company's "Chi-Namel" brand, which feature diminutive Asian figures applying varnish or paint to the woodwork of American homes, either as exotic spectacles (as in the Jap-a-lac ads) or as industrious "coolies" (as in the Chi-Namel ads). For more on the exoticism of the Jap-a-lac ads in particular, see Lee, "Journalistic Representations," 253–58.

52. "Creating Charlie Chan," 29.

53. Jen, "Challenging the Asian Illusion," B1.

54. In *San Francisco's Chinatown*, Robert W. Bowen and Brenda Young Bowen note that by the 1920s "chop suey" had become a metonym for all Chinese food, and that in San Francisco "chop suey" signs were typically larger than the names of the restaurants themselves. The Bowens also note that in the early 1920s Chinatown's Grant Avenue (where Barbara likely takes John Quincy) "was already being heavily promoted as a major San Francisco tourist attraction because of its large number of exotic shops and Chinese restaurants" (83).

55. Rzepka, "Race, Region, Rule," 1469, 1474. In referring to the "architectural uncanny" of Chinatown fictions, Rzepka is citing Teng, "Artifacts of a Lost City," 55, who in turn is citing Vidler, *The Architectural Uncanny*. See also note 45 above.

56. For example, Schnack's *Aloha Guide* repeatedly refers to "Chinatown and the Oriental section" (87, 101) but never identifies a separate "River District." I should also note that, contrary to the suggestion left by Rzepka's essay, Honolulu's Chinatown not only was

rebuilt after the fire of 1900 but was very much a recognizable part of the city in the 1920s. Rzepka suggests that Chinatown's importance as a location was severely diminished; the guidebooks, however, do not suggest that at all.

57. Critics have long noted Biggers's insistence on making Chan appear sexless, even though, as the father of many children, he is clearly procreative. See, for example, Chan, *Chinese American Masculinities*, 63; Hagedorn, Introduction, xiii.

58. Rzepka, "Race, Region, Rule," 1469.

59. *The House without a Key* thus also delivers a much more complex version of the "South Seas tale" which Rzepka sees the novel invoking. Far from offering "a pastoral, prelapsarian haven from the restraints of Western class and race prejudice" ("Race, Region, Rule," 1469), Biggers's novel registers the tensions endemic to any multirace or multiclass society.

60. Henle, "Selling the Exotic to Main Street," 80; A. A. Vantine and Co., *Vantine's: The Oriental Store* (ca. 1910–15), 23; *Vantine's: The Oriental Store* (1914), 44; *Vantine's: The Oriental Store* (1917), 65; Wilson, "Vantine's in Five Floors," 86. Wilson complains that the store lost its fascination when it moved uptown to Fifth Avenue. "To wander about the old Vantine's gave a taste of the Arabian Nights. I do not remember using elevators; it was by staircases that one made one's way among galleries, tearooms and basements, and one never knew what one was going to find" (86). Wilson's lament recalls Teng's description in "Artifacts of a Lost City" of the bohemian nostalgia for San Francisco's "old Chinatown" in the early 1900s.

61. Hardy papers, vol. 2, Joseph Downs Collection, Winterthur Library, 42.

62. This dismantling of John Quincy's remoteness, of course, does not wave away the fact that for many contemporary readers, particularly Asian Americans, the only possible love for Charlie Chan, as Frank Chin and Jeffrey Paul Chan first observed in 1972, remains "racist love." See Chin and Chan's "Racist Love," 65–79.

63. Winterslip's lanai is the only architectural space Liepse elected to represent in detail in the seven issues of the *Post* in which *The House without a Key* appeared. In his illustrations Liepse focuses primarily on characters, not spaces, although strikingly he does not depict Chan. On the veranda as an important element of Wright's Prairie House design, see Twombly, *Frank Lloyd Wright*, 81–82.

64. Nute, *Frank Lloyd Wright and Japan*, 41; Wright, "Building the New House," 142–43. On Wright's stopping in Hawaii on his trips to Japan, see Langmead and Johnson, *Architectural Excursions*, 18. For more on Hawaiian vernacular architecture, see Faulkner, "Island Gems," 33–39.

65. This spatialization is thus precisely the opposite of Bachelard's formulation in *The Poetics of Space*—so evocative for popular Chinatown fiction—in which the basement or the cellar is the site of maximal terror.

66. By contrast, the fear that leads Harry Jennison (and not, as it turns out, the son of Winterslip's old rival) to murder Winterslip—Jennison is afraid Winterslip will expose him by telling his daughter Barbara the truth about Jennison's role in an opium smuggling ring—is analogous to the fear of total exposure.

67. Brooks, "Frank Lloyd Wright and the Destruction of the Box," 8–9.

68. Ironically, it can be difficult to locate images of Wright Prairie House interiors that adequately demonstrate the effects Brooks is describing. I suspect this is partly a result of the photographer's desire to capture images of individual rooms, not of the relationship between rooms.

69. By suggesting that decorative Orientalism in the U.S. context could at times emerge from motives other than imperialist domination, Yoshihara and Hoganson offer an important revision to Said's Foucauldian focus in *Orientalism* on "cultural domination" (28).

70. Nute, *Frank Lloyd Wright and Japan*, 153; Nute, "Frank Lloyd Wright and Japanese Architecture," 169. In saying that perhaps Wright, too, "hold[s] Asians themselves at bay," I do not mean to suggest that Wright did not have any personal Japanese friends, but rather that he was capable (metaphorically) of holding certain elements of Asian culture close and other elements at arm's length.

NOTES TO CODA

1. On Barber's publishing and designing career, including the extent of his firm's reach, see Tomlan's "Toward the Growth of an Artistic Taste," his invaluable introduction to a 1982 reprint edition of *Cottage Souvenir No. 2*, itself reprinted in 2004 by Dover. For further discussion of Barber's significance in late nineteenth-century American culture, see Woods, *From Craft to Profession*, 86–92; Reiff, *Houses from Books*, 114–20.

2. Barber, *Cottage Souvenir No. 2* (1891), rpt. as *Victorian Cottage Architecture* (2004), 6. Subsequent references are from this edition and will appear parenthetically in the text.

3. Two notable exceptions to the general silence about these images are Banta, *Taylored Lives*, 220–22; and Smeins, *Building an American Identity*, 31.

4. Smeins, *Building an American Identity*, 13–14.

5. "The Old Cabin Home," composed and arranged by T. Paine (Boston: Henry Tolman and Co., 1858), the Lester S. Levy Collection of Sheet Music, Special Collections, Johns Hopkins University, Box 128, Item 033 (http://levysheetmusic.mse.jhu.edu/otcgi/llscgi60). On the continuing popularity of this song in the late nineteenth century, see "Illustrating Slavery" (http://etext.lib.virginia.edu/railton/wilson/slavery/minslav7.html).

6. Morrison, *Playing in the Dark*, 6.

7. Two excellent accounts of these new forms and phases may be found in Upton, *Architecture in the United States*, esp. 197–223; and Wright, *USA*, esp. 79–112.

8. Both CNN and the CBS Evening News, for example, aired stories in early December 2008 emphasizing (in CBS's words) the "surpris[ing]" fact that slaves were used to build the White House. See Jim Axelrod, "The White House's History of Slave Labor" (http://www.cbsnews.com/stories/2008/12/10/eveningnews/main4661606.shtml); Susan Roesgen and Aaron Cooper, "Slaves Helped Build the White House, U.S. Capitol" (http://www.cnn.com/2008/US/12/02/slaves.white.house/index.html#cnnSTCText). For recent scholarly accounts of the role of slaves in the construction of the White House, see Allen, "History of Slave Laborers"; Holland, *Black Men Built the Capitol*.

9. William Seale's monumental two-volume study, *The President's House: A History*, offers the most detailed and thorough account of the White House as physical structure, workplace, and sociocultural site. On Washington's initial interest in a "President's Palace," see 1:3–22; on the nickname "White House," see 1:160–61; on the Charleston, South Carolina, statehouse as partial inspiration, see 1:13–14; on the full-length porch planned for the original south facade, see 1:32–33; on the importation of Santo Domingan mahogany finish wood, see 1:142.

10. Smith, *The Presidents We Imagine*, 48. As Smith observes in a footnote, the persons to whom Hamilton refers in this letter (British abolitionist William Wilberforce and colonizationist Charles Fenton Mercer) were prominent in the transatlantic antislavery movement. Hamilton's letter was penned to New York governor (and later president) Martin Van Buren. See 297n9.

11. Ibid., 49. We may also register the intensity of Hamilton's disgust in his almost stutteringly inadvertent repetition of the preposition "in" ("The Mob broke in, in thousands"; "Spirits . . . poured in in one uninterrupted stream"), which seems to mark, in its repeated use, the threat of invasion symbolized by the mix of races attending the levee.

12. Seale, *The President's House: A History*, 1:161. The south portico, incidentally, finally replaced the long-proposed full-length southern porch.

13. Brown, *Clotel*, 217; Crafts, *The Bondwoman's Narrative*, 196.

14. Keckley, *Behind the Scenes*, 158–60. Although Keckley does not mention armed policemen preventing people of color from attending the reception, Douglass himself does. See Douglass's chapter in Allen Thorndike Rice's edited collection, *Reminiscences of Abraham Lincoln*, 191–93.

15. For accounts of the preservation efforts at Mount Vernon, see Fitch, *Historic Preservation: Curatorial Management of the Built World*, 88–89; Barthel, *Historic Preservation: Collective Memory and Historical Identity*, 19–20; and Caspar, *Sarah Johnson's Mount Vernon*.

16. Twain and Warner, *The Gilded Age*, 173; Seale, *The President's House*, 1:517. On the desires of late nineteenth-century presidents to move, rebuild, or tear down the White House, see also Seale, "The White House." Seale notes that in 1867 the Army Corps of Engineers not only proposed a new site for the White House (within what is now called Rock Creek Park) but actually drew up designs for the new structure, which was to be "a suburban mansion with deep porches, set in the large and picturesque acreage, with miles of pleasure drives and walks" (12)—a design that would finally have given the White House the southern-style porch that had been part of architect James Hoban's original plan (but had been replaced with the south portico).

17. Seale, *The President's House*, 1:634; 1:624–25; 1:626.

18. Ibid., 1:643; 2:20. Taft served as governor-general of the Philippines from 1900 to 1904.

19. Busbey, "Mrs. Taft's Home-Making," 292.

20. Jaffray threatened to fire anyone who complained about this new arrangement. See Seale, *The President's House*, 2:4–6.

21. Busbey, "Mrs. Taft's Home-Making," 292–94.

22. Grandison, "Negotiated Space," 75–76.

23. Waco's original HBCU, Paul Quinn College, was located on the former Grandison Plantation, approximately 1.6 miles from downtown Waco, across the Brazos River in East Waco. (The school has since moved north to a location outside Dallas.) Griggs himself attended an HBCU (Bishop College), in Marshall, Texas.

24. Grandison, "Negotiated Space," 76–77. See also 79–83.

25. Griggs, *Imperium in Imperio*, 178–79.

26. Ibid., 179, 188, 249.

27. Lobato, *O Choque das Raças*, 161. As Daphne Patai observes, the grim ending Lobato imagines for presidential candidate Jim Roy and the rest of the African American race was not necessarily intended as a critique of U.S. race relations, as Lobato ultimately subscribed to a form of racist eugenics that favored strict racial segregation for his own country, Brazil. See her article "Race and Politics in Two Brazilian Utopias." Although Lobato had hoped his book would be published in the U.S. as well as in Brazil—indeed, he anticipated it might become a best seller and make him rich—no American publishing house would touch it. His novel, which has still not been issued in an English translation, was hastily republished in 2008 during the U.S. presidential election campaign in part because another subplot in the novel involves the competition between a white woman and a black man for the presidency, an imagined scenario that to some seemed uncannily to anticipate the contest between Hillary Clinton and Barack Obama for the Democratic nomination.

Anxiety during this period about a nonwhite president ascending to the White House was not limited to imaginary black candidates for office. In the eighth novel of English writer Sax Rohmer's Fu-Manchu series, Rohmer imagines the evil Asian villain scheming to take over the White House by helping elect an Anglo-Saxon puppet candidate whom he can control once he takes office. See Rohmer, *President Fu-Manchu*.

28. *Rufus Jones for President.* A copy of the original film is available at http://www.dailymotion.com/video/xqgez_rufus-jones-for-president_music.

29. Taylor, "Underneath the Harlem Moon."

30. For discussions of many of these fictional and filmic presidents, see Smith's compendious study *The Presidents We Imagine*.

31. For a selection of images and articles, see, for example: "Obama All Set for Black House," *Daily Squib*, 17 July 2008, http://www.dailysquib.co.uk/?c=117&a=1413; "Ma'ariv Prints Racist Obama Cartoon," *SabbahBlog*, http://sabbah.biz/mt/archives/2008/02/23/maariv-racist-obama-cartoon/; "White House Website Transformed within Minutes of Transition," *Greglouck's Daily Journal*, http://gregloucks.wordpress.com/2009/01/25/white-house-website-transformed-within-minutes-of-transition/; "The House Obama Built," *Conversations with Brit and Grit*, http://britandgrit.com/?p=2648; and "Texas GOP Disavows Knowledge of Racist Obama Button," *TPM Election Central*, 17 June 2008, http://tpmelectioncentral.talkingpointsmemo.com/2008/06/texas_gop_we_didnt_know_about.php

32. Blitt, "The Politics of Fear."

33. Luria, "Racial Equality Begins at Home," 27, 31, 32.

34. On Michelle Obama's slave ancestors, see Shailagh Murray, "A Family Tree Rooted in American Soil: Michelle Obama Learns about Her Slave Ancestors, Herself and Her Country," *Washington Post*, 2 October 2008, C01; and James Bone, "From Slave Cabin to White House, A Family Rooted in Black America," *London Times*, 6 November 2008, http://www.timesonline.co.uk/tol/news/world/us_and_americas/us_elections/article5092944.ece.

35. On the worsening of segregation within the U.S. since the 1960s, see Massey and Denton, *American Apartheid*. On the role of race in the predatory lending that helped trigger the U.S. housing market collapse, see Satter, *Family Properties*, 372–76.

Bibliography

Aladdin Homes: Built in a Day. Catalog No. 28. Bay City, MI: North American Construction Company, 1916. 118 pp.

Aladdin Homes: "Built in a Day." Catalog No. 29. Bay City, MI: Aladdin Company, 1917. 125 pp.

"Aladdin Homes: Make This Your Home Building Year." Advertisement. *Popular Science Monthly* 94.1 (January 1919): 89.

Aladdin Houses: "Built in a Day." Catalog No. 23. Bay City, MI: North American Construction Company, Spring 1912. 68 pp.

Aladdin Houses: "Built in a Day." Catalog No. 24. Bay City, MI: North American Construction Company, Spring 1913. 96 pp.

Allen, William C. "History of Slave Laborers in the Construction of the United States Capitol." Washington, DC: Office of the Architect of the Capitol. 1 July 2005. 1–27.

Altman, Irwin, and Setha M. Low, eds. *Place Attachment: Human Behavior and Environment.* New York: Plenum, 1992.

Andrews, William L. "Chesnutt's Patesville: The Presence and Influence of the Past in *The House Behind the Cedars.*" *CLA Journal* 15 (March 1972): 284–94.

———. *The Literary Career of Charles W. Chesnutt.* Baton Rouge: Louisiana State University Press, 1980.

Antoniades, Anthony C. *Epic Space: Toward the Roots of Western Architecture.* New York: Van Nostrand Reinhold, 1992.

Avril, Ellen. *East Meets West: Chinese Export Art and Design.* Cincinnati: Taft Museum, 1998.

Bachelard, Gaston. *The Poetics of Space.* Trans. Maria Jolas. Boston: Beacon Press, 1994.

Banta, Martha. *Taylored Lives: Narrative Productions in the Age of Taylor, Veblen, and Ford.* Chicago: University of Chicago Press, 1993.

Barber, George F. *Cottage Souvenir No. 2: A Repository of Artistic Cottage Architecture and Miscellaneous Designs.* 1891. Rpt. as *Victorian Cottage Architecture: An American Catalog of Designs, 1891.* Mineola, NY: Dover, 2004.

Barthel, Diane L. *Historic Preservation: Collective Memory and Historical Identity.* New Brunswick, NJ: Rutgers University Press, 1996.

Barton, Craig E. Foreword. *Sites of Memory: Perspectives on Architecture and Race.* Ed. Craig E. Barton. New York: Princeton Architectural Press, 2001. xiv–xvi.

———, ed. *Sites of Memory: Perspectives on Architecture and Race.* New York: Princeton Architectural Press, 2001.

Beckham, Sue Bridwell. "The American Front Porch: Women's Liminal Space." *Making the American Home: Middle-Class Women and Domestic Material Culture 1840–1940.* Ed. Marilyn Ferris Motz and Pat Browne. Bowling Green, OH: Bowling Green State University Popular Press, 1988. 69–89.

Berg, Donald J., ed. *Country Patterns, 1841–1883: A Sampler of American Country Home and Landscape Designs from Original 19th Century Sources.* Rev. 2nd ed. Pittstown, NJ: Main Street Press, 1986.

Bernstein, Susan. *Housing Problems: Writing and Architecture in Goethe, Walpole, Freud, and Heidegger.* Stanford: Stanford University Press, 2008.

Bethell, Leslie, ed. *The Cambridge History of Latin America.* Vol. 3, *From Independence to c. 1870.* Cambridge: Cambridge University Press, 1985.

Bicknell's Victorian Buildings: Floor Plans and Elevations for 45 Houses and Other Structures. 5th ed. 1878. Rpt. New York: Dover, 1979.

Biggers, Earl Derr. *The House without a Key.* New York: Grosset and Dunlap, 1925.

Bishir, Catherine W. "Black Builders in Antebellum North Carolina." *North Carolina Historical Review* 61 (October 1984): 423–61.

———. *North Carolina Architecture.* Chapel Hill: University of North Carolina Press, 1990.

———. *North Carolina Architecture.* Portable Edition. Chapel Hill: University of North Carolina Press, 2005.

———. "A Proper Good Nice and Workmanlike Manner: A Century of Traditional Building Practice, 1730–1830." *Architects and Builders in North Carolina: A History of the Practice of Building.* Ed. Catherine W. Bishir, Charlotte V. Brown, Carl R. Lounsbury, and Ernest H. Wood III. Chapel Hill: University of North Carolina Press, 1990. 48–129.

———. "A Spirit of Improvement: Changes in Building Practice, 1830–1860." *Architects and Builders in North Carolina: A History of the Practice of Building.* Ed. Catherine W. Bishir, Charlotte V. Brown, Carl R. Lounsbury, and Ernest H. Wood III. Chapel Hill: University of North Carolina Press, 1990. 130–92.

Blitt, Barry. "The Politics of Fear." Cover illustration. *New Yorker,* 21 July 2008.

Bordes, Marilynn Johnson. "Christian Herter and the Cult of Japan." *Records of the Art Museum of Princeton University* 34.2 (1975): 20–27.

Bowen Robert W., and Brenda Young Bowen. *San Francisco's Chinatown.* Charleston, SC: Arcadia, 2008.

Brady, Mary Pat. *Extinct Lands, Temporal Geographies: Chicana Literature and the Urgency of Space.* Durham, NC: Duke University Press, 2002.

The Bradys' Trip to Chinatown; or, Trailing an Opium Fiend. New York: Frank Tousey, 1904.

Breisch, Kenneth A., and Alison K. Hoagland, eds. *Building Environments: Perspectives in Vernacular Architecture X.* Knoxville: University of Tennessee Press, 2005.

Brodhead, Richard H. *Cultures of Letters: Scenes of Reading and Writing in Nineteenth-Century America.* Chicago: University of Chicago Press, 1993.

———, ed. *The Journals of Charles W. Chesnutt.* Durham, NC: Duke University Press, 1993.

Brody, David Eric. "Fantasy Realized: The Philippines, Orientalism, and Imperialism in Turn-of-the-Century American Visual Culture." Diss. Boston University, 1997.

Brooks, H. Allen. "Frank Lloyd Wright and the Destruction of the Box." *Journal of the Society of Architectural Historians* 38.1 (March 1979): 7–14.

Brown, Bill. *A Sense of Things: The Object Matter of American Literature.* Chicago: University of Chicago Press, 2003.

———. "A Thing about Things: The Art of Decoration in the Work of Henry James." *Henry James Review* 23.3 (2002): 222–32.

Brown, Jane Converse. *The "Japanese Taste": Its Role in the Mission of the American Home and in the Family's Presentation of Itself to the Public as Expressed in Published Sources—1876–1916.* Diss. University of Wisconsin, Madison, 1987. Ann Arbor: UMI, 1990.

Brown, William Wells. *Clotel; or, The President's Daughter: A Narrative of Slave Life in the United States.* London: Partridge and Oakey, 1853.

Brownell, Charles E. *The Making of Virginia Architecture.* Richmond: Virginia Museum of Fine Arts, 1992.

Brunner, Arnold W. *Cottages; Or, Hints on Economical Building.* New York: William T. Comstock, 1884.

Burnette, R. V. "Charles W. Chesnutt's *The Conjure Woman* Revisited." *CLA Journal* 30 (June 1987): 438–53.

Busbey, Katharine Graves. "Mrs. Taft's Home-Making." *Good Housekeeping Magazine* 53.3 (September 1911): 291–98.

Busher, William Sherwood. "The Great Centennial Exhibition of 1876" (December 1942). Document 1253. Joseph Downs Collection of Manuscripts and Printed Ephemera, Winterthur Library, Winterthur, DE.

Byrd, Rudolph P. "The Outsider Within: The Acquisition and Application of Forms of Oppositional Knowledge in Hannah Crafts's *The Bondwoman's Narrative.*" *In Search of Hannah Crafts: Critical Essays on The Bondwoman's Narrative.* Ed. Henry Louis Gates Jr. and Hollis Robbins. New York: Basic Books, 2004. 332–53.

Cardwell, Guy A. "The Plantation House: An Analogical Image." *Southern Literary Journal* 2.1 (Fall 1969): 3–21.

Carson, Cary. "Segregation in Vernacular Buildings." *Vernacular Architecture* 7 (1976): 24–29.

Caspar, Scott E. *Sarah Johnson's Mount Vernon: The Forgotten History of an American Shrine.* New York: Hill and Wang, 2008.

"Chairs from China." Advertisement. Vantine's: The Oriental Store. *House and Garden* 25.4 (April 1914), n.p.

Chan, Jachinson. *Chinese American Masculinities from Fu Manchu to Bruce Lee.* New York: Routledge, 2001.

Chandler, Marilyn R. *Dwelling in the Text: Houses in American Fiction.* Berkeley: University of California Press, 1991.

Chesnutt, Charles W. *The Colonel's Dream.* New York: Doubleday, Page, 1905.

———. *The Conjure Woman and Other Conjure Tales.* Ed. Richard H. Brodhead. Durham, NC: Duke University Press, 1993.

———. "The Conjurer's Revenge." *Overland Monthly* 13 (June 1889): 623–29.

———. "The Goophered Grapevine." *Atlantic Monthly* 60 (August 1887): 254–60.

———. *The House behind the Cedars.* 1900. Rpt. Athens: University of Georgia Press, 1988.

———. *The Marrow of Tradition.* 1901. Rpt. Ann Arbor: University of Michigan Press, 1969.

———. "The Sway-Backed House." *The Short Fiction of Charles W. Chesnutt.* Ed. Sylvia Lyons Render. Rev. ed. Washington, DC: Howard University Press, 1981. 223–31.

———. "Uncle Peter's House." *The Short Fiction of Charles W. Chesnutt.* Ed. Sylvia Lyons Render. Rev. ed. Washington, DC: Howard University Press, 1981. 168–76.

Chesnutt, Helen M. *Charles Waddell Chesnutt: Pioneer of the Color Line.* Chapel Hill: University of North Carolina Press, 1952.

Chin, Frank, and Jeffrey Paul Chan. "Racist Love." *Seeing through Shuck*. Ed. Richard Kostelanetz. New York: Ballantine, 1972. 65–79.

Chu, Limin. *The Images of China and the Chinese in the "Overland Monthly," 1868–1875, 1883–1935*. San Francisco: R. and E. Research Associates, 1974.

Chung, June Hee. "Asian Object Lessons: Orientalist Decoration in Realist Aesthetics from William Dean Howells to Sui Sin Far." *Studies in American Fiction* 36.1 (Spring 2008): 27–50.

Chung, Sue Fawn. "From Fu-Manchu, Evil Genius, to James Lee Wong, Popular Hero: A Study of the Chinese American in Popular Periodical Fiction from 1920–1940." *Journal of Popular Culture* 10.3 (March 1977): 534–47.

Clark, Clifford Edward, Jr. *The American Family Home, 1800–1960*. Chapel Hill: University of North Carolina Press, 1986.

Cleaveland, Henry W., et al. *Villages and Farm Cottages: A Victorian Stylebook of 1856*. Watkins Glen, NY: American Life Foundation, 1982. Rpt. of *Village and Farm Cottages*. New York, 1856.

Cody, Jeffrey W. *Exporting American Architecture, 1870–2000*. New York: Routledge, 2003.

Cohen, Stuart, and Susan Benjamin. *North Shore Chicago: Houses of the Lakefront Suburbs, 1890–1940*. New York: Acanthus Press, 2004.

Collage album. Ca. 1880–1900. Folio 252. Joseph Downs Collection of Manuscripts and Printed Ephemera, Winterthur Library, Winterthur, DE.

Crafts, Hannah. *The Bondwoman's Narrative*. Ed. Henry Louis Gates Jr. New York: Warner Books, 2002.

"Creating Charlie Chan." *New York Times*. 22 March 1931. Rpt. in David Manning White, *Popular Culture*. New York: Hudson Group, 1975. 28–29.

Crook, J. Mordaunt. *The Dilemma of Style*. Chicago: University of Chicago Press, 1987.

Crossman, Carl. *The China Trade: Export Paintings, Furniture, Silver, and Other Objects*. Princeton: Pyne Press, 1972.

Crowley, John E. "'In Happier Mansions, Warm, and Dry': The Invention of the Cottage as the Comfortable Anglo-American House." *Winterthur Portfolio* 32 (Summer/Autumn 1997): 169–88.

Culbertson, Martha. *Texas Houses Built by the Book: The Use of Published Designs, 1850–1925*. College Station: Texas A&M University Press, 1999

Cunningham, Edith Perkins. *Owl's Nest: A Tribute to Sarah Elliott Perkins*. Cambridge, MA: Riverside Press, 1907.

Curry, Milton S. F. "Emancipation Theory: Spatial Subtexts and Subjects." *Appendx* 1 (1993): 64–85.

Curtis, James C. "Race, Realism, and the Documentation of the Rural Home during America's Great Depression." *The American Home: Material Culture, Domestic Space, and Family Life*. Ed. Eleanor McD. Thompson. Winterthur, DE: Winterthur Museum, 1998. 273–99.

Darnall, Margaretta Jean. "Innovations in American Prefabricated Housing: 1860–1890." *Journal of the Society of Architectural Historians* 31.1 (March 1972): 51–55.

Davies, Jane B. "Davis and Downing: Collaborators in the Picturesque." *Prophet with Honor: The Career of Andrew Jackson Downing, 1815–1852*. Ed. George B. Tatum and Elisabeth B. MacDougall. Washington, DC: Dumbarton Oaks, 1989. 81–123.

Davis, Alexander Jackson. *Rural Residences: Consisting of Designs, Original and Selected, for Cottages, Farm-houses, Villas, and Village Churches, with Brief Explanations, Estimates, and a Specification of Materials, Construction, Etc.* New York: New York University, 1837.

Davis, Charles Belmont, ed. *Adventures and Letters of Richard Harding Davis.* New York: Charles Scribner's Sons, 1917.

Davis, Richard Harding. *Soldiers of Fortune.* 1897. Rpt. New York: Charles Scribner's Sons, 1910.

———. *Three Gringos in Venezuela and Central America.* New York: Harper and Brothers, 1896.

de Certeau, Michel. *The Practice of Everyday Life.* Berkeley: University of California Press, 1984.

Dickens, Charles. *Bleak House.* 1852–53. Rpt. New York: Bantam, 1992.

Dolan, Michael. *The American Porch: An Informal History of an Informal Place.* Guilford, CT: Globe Pequot Press, 2002.

Douglass, Frederick. *Autobiographies.* Ed. Henry Louis Gates Jr. New York: Library of America, 1994.

Downing, Andrew Jackson. *The Architecture of Country Houses.* New York: D. Appleton, 1850.

———. *Cottage Residences.* New York: Wiley and Putnam, 1842.

———. "The Favorite Poison of America." November 1850. Rpt. in Andrew Jackson Downing, *Rural Essays.* Ed. George William Curtis. New York: Putnam, 1853. 278–86.

———. "A Few Words on Our Progress in Building." June 1851. Rpt. in Andrew Jackson Downing, *Rural Essays.* Ed. George William Curtis. New York: Putnam, 1853. 214–23.

———. Rev. of C. W. Elliott, *Cottages and Cottage Life.* Cincinnati: H. W. Derby, 1848. *Horticulturist and Journal of Rural Art and Rural Taste* 3 (1848): 179–82.

———. *Rural Essays.* Ed. George William Curtis. New York: Putnam, 1853.

———. *A Treatise on the Theory and Practice of Landscape Gardening.* New York: Wiley and Putnam, 1841.

———. "Warwick Castle: Kenilworth: Stratford-on-Avon." June 1850. Rpt. in Andrew Jackson Downing, *Rural Essays.* Ed. George William Curtis. New York: Putnam, 1853. 475–84.

Dresser, Christopher. *Japan: Its Architecture, Art, and Art Manufactures.* London: Longmans, Green, 1882.

DuBois, W. E. B. "The Ante-bellum Negro Artisan." 1902. Rpt. in *The Other Slaves: Mechanics, Artisans, and Craftsmen.* Ed. James E. Newton and Ronald L. Lewis. Boston: G. K. Hall, 1978. 175–82.

Duchscherer, Paul, and Douglas Keister. *Bungalow: America's Arts and Crafts Home.* New York: Penguin Studio, 1995.

Eastman, Mary H. *Aunt Phillis's Cabin; or, Southern Life as It Is.* Philadelphia: Lippincott, Grambo and Co., 1852.

Edwards, Jay. "The Complex Origins of the American Domestic Piazza-Veranda-Gallery." *Material Culture* 21 (1989): 3–58.

———. "The Origins of Creole Architecture." *Winterthur Portfolio* 29.2/3 (Summer/Autumn 1994): 155–89.

Edwin Noah Hardy papers. Vol. 2. Joseph Downs Collection of Manuscripts and Printed Ephemera, Winterthur Library, Winterthur, DE.

Eldridge, Michael. "There Goes the Transnational Neighborhood: Calypso Buys a Bunga-low." *Callaloo* 25.2 (2002): 620–38.

Elliott, Charles Wyllys. *The Book of American Interiors, Prepared by Charles Wyllys Elliott from Existing Houses; With Preliminary Essays and Letterpress Descriptions; Illustrated in Heliotype*. Boston: James R. Osgood, 1876.

———. *Cottages and Cottage Life: Containing Plans for Country Houses, Adapted to the Means and Wants of the People of the United States; with Directions for Building and Improving; for the Laying Out and Embellishing of Grounds; with Some Sketches of Life in this Country*. Cincinnati: H. W. Derby, 1848.

Erbe, Scott. "Manufacturing and Marketing the American Bungalow: The Aladdin Com-pany, 1906–1920." *The American Home: Material Culture, Domestic Space, and Family Life*. Ed. Eleanor McD. Thompson. Winterthur, DE: Winterthur Museum, 1998. 45–69.

Everett, Marshall, ed. *Exciting Experiences in Our Wars with Spain and the Filipinos*. Chicago: Book Publishers Union, 1899.

Faherty, Duncan. *Remodeling the Nation: The Architecture of American Identity, 1776–1858*. Durham: University of New Hampshire Press, 2007.

Faragher, John Mack. "Bungalow and Ranch House: The Architectural Backwash of California." *Western Historical Quarterly* 32.2 (Summer 2001): 149–74.

Faulkner, Marlo. "Island Gems: Hawaii's Arts and Crafts Houses." *Style 1900: The Magazine of Turn-of-the-Century Design* 15.4 (Fall/Winter 2002): 33–39.

Fenn, William Purviance. *Ah Sin and His Brethren in American Literature*. Diss. University of Iowa, 1932. Peiping (Peking), China: College of Chinese Studies, 1933.

Fields, Darell W. "A Black Manifesto." *Appendx* 1 (1993): 18–45.

Fiske, N. W. *A Rapid Tour around the World; or Young Peter's Remarks to His Cousins upon the Different Nations*. Amherst, MA: J. S. & C. Adams, 1846.

Fitch, James Marston. *Historic Preservation: Curatorial Management of the Built World*. Charlottesville: University Press of Virginia, 1990.

"595 for This Complete Aladdin Bungalow." Advertisement. North American Construc-tion Company. *Independent* 84 (24 May 1915): n.p.

Fletcher, Banister, and Banister F. Fletcher. *A History of Architecture on the Comparative Method*. 5th ed. New York: Charles Scribner's Sons, 1905.

———. *A History of Architecture on the Comparative Method*. 6th ed. New York: Charles Scribner's Sons, 1921.

Foster, John Burt. "China and the Chinese in American Literature, 1850–1950." Diss. University of Illinois, 1952.

Fowler, Orson Squire. *A Home for All: or a New, Cheap, Convenient, and Superior Mode of Building*. New York: Fowler and Wells, 1848. Rpt. as *The Octagon House: A Home for All*. New York: Dover, 1973.

Frank, Ellen Eve. *Literary Architecture: Essays toward a Tradition*. Berkeley: University of California Press, 1979.

Fryer, Judith. *Felicitous Space: The Imaginative Structures of Edith Wharton and Willa Cather*. Chapel Hill: University of North Carolina Press, 1986.

Fuller, Kevin L. "Negative Affirmation." *Appendx* 1 (1993): 47–63.

Fuss, Diana. *The Sense of an Interior: Four Writers and the Rooms That Shaped Them*. New York: Routledge, 2004.

Fyfe, H. Hamilton. *Real Mexico: A Study on the Spot*. New York: McBride, Nast, 1914.

Gaines, Francis Pendleton. *The Southern Plantation*. 1924. Rpt. Gloucester, MA: Peter Smith, 1962.

Garcia, Mario T. *Desert Immigrants: The Mexicans of El Paso, 1880–1920*. New Haven: Yale University Press, 1981.

Garvey, Ellen Gruber. "Scrapbook, Wishbook, Prayerbook: Trade Card Scrapbooks and the Missionary Work of Advertising." *The Scrapbook in American Life*. Ed. Susan Tucker, Katherine Ott, and Patricia P. Buckler. Philadelphia: Temple University Press, 2006. 97–115.

Gates, Henry Louis, Jr. Introduction. *The Bondwoman's Narrative*. By Hannah Crafts. Ed. Henry Louis Gates Jr. New York: Warner Books, 2002. ix–lxxiv.

———. *"Race," Writing, and Difference*. Chicago: University of Chicago Press, 1986.

Gates, Henry Louis, Jr., and Hollis Robbins, eds. *In Search of Hannah Crafts: Critical Essays on The Bondwoman's Narrative*. New York: Basic Books, 2004.

Gelder, Ann. "Reforming the Body: 'Experience' and the Architecture of Imagination in Harriet Jacobs's *Incidents in the Life of a Slave Girl*." *Inventing Maternity: Politics, Science, and Literature, 1650–1865*. Ed. Susan C. Greenfield and Carol Barash. Lexington: University Press of Kentucky, 1999. 252–66.

Giedion, Siegfried. *Space, Time and Architecture: The Growth of a New Tradition*. 1941. Rpt. Cambridge: Harvard University Press, 1982.

Goldstein, Jonathan. "Cantonese Artifacts, Chinoiserie, and Early American Idealization of China." *America Views China: American Images of China Then and Now*. Ed. Jonathan Goldstein, Jerry Israel, and Hilary Conroy. Cranbury, NJ: Associated University Presses, 1991. 43–55.

Goldstein, Jonathan, Jerry Israel, and Hilary Conroy, eds. *America Views China: American Images of China Then and Now*. Cranbury, NJ: Associated University Presses, 1991.

Gonzalez, Gilbert G., and Raul A. Fernandez. *A Century of Chicano History: Empires, Nation, and Migration*. New York: Routledge, 2003.

Goodrich, Samuel Griswold. *A History of All Nations, from the Earliest Periods to the Present Time; or, Universal History*. Boston: Wilkins, Carter, 1851.

Gordon, Beverly. *The Saturated World: Aesthetic Meaning, Intimate Objects, Women's Lives, 1890–1940*. Knoxville: University of Tennessee Press, 2006.

———. "Scrapbook Houses for Paper Dolls: Creative Expression, Aesthetic Elaboration, and Bonding in the Female World." *The Scrapbook in American Life*. Ed. Susan Tucker, Katherine Ott, and Patricia P. Buckler. Philadelphia: Temple University Press, 2006. 116–34.

Gowans, Alan. *Styles and Types of North American Architecture: Social Function and Cultural Expression*. New York: Icon, 1991.

Grandison, Kenrick Ian. "Negotiated Space: The Black College Campus as a Cultural Record of Postbellum America." *Sites of Memory: Perspectives on Architecture and Race*. Ed. Craig E. Barton. Princeton: Princeton Architectural Press, 2001. 55–96.

Greenberg, Amy S. *Manifest Manhood and the Antebellum American Empire*. New York: Cambridge University Press, 2005.

Grier, Catherine C. *Culture and Comfort: People, Parlors, and Upholstery, 1850–1930*. Rochester, NY: Strong Museum, 1988.

Griggs, Sutton E. *Imperium in Imperio*. 1899. Rpt. New York: AMS Press, 1969.

Gruesz, Kirsten Silva. "The Gulf of Mexico System and the 'Latinness' of New Orleans." *American Literary History* 18.3 (2006): 468–95.

Guth, Christine. *Longfellow's Tattoos: Tourism, Collecting, and Japan*. Seattle: University of Washington Press, 2004.

Guttmann, Allen. "Images of Value and the Sense of the Past." *New England Quarterly* 35 (March 1962): 3–26.

Hagedorn, Jessica, ed. *Charlie Chan Is Dead: An Anthology of Contemporary Asian American Fiction*. New York: Penguin, 1993.

———. Introduction. *Charlie Chan Is Dead: An Anthology of Contemporary Asian American Fiction*. New York: Penguin, 1993. xxi–xxx.

Handlin, David P. *The American Home: Architecture and Society, 1815–1915*. Boston: Little, Brown, 1979.

Harris, Dianne. "Race, Space, and the Destabilization of Practice." *Landscape Journal* 26.1 (2007): 1–9.

Harris, Neil. *Cultural Excursions: Marketing Appetites and Cultural Tastes in Modern America*. Chicago: University of Chicago Press, 1990.

Harris, Trudier. *The Power of the Porch: The Storyteller's Craft in Zora Neale Hurston, Gloria Naylor, and Randall Kenan*. Athens: University of Georgia Press, 1996.

Harrison, Brady. *Agent of Empire: William Walker and the Imperial Self in American Literature*. Athens: University of Georgia Press, 2004.

Hartigan, Linda Roscoe. "The House That Collage Built." *American Art* 7.3 (Summer 1993): 88–91.

Hawley, Sandra. "The Importance of Being Charlie Chan." *America Views China: American Images of China Then and Now*. Ed. Jonathan Goldstein, Jerry Israel, and Hilary Conroy. Cranbury, NJ: Associated University Presses, 1991. 132–47.

Hayden, Dolores. *The Power of Place: Urban Landscapes as Public History*. Cambridge: MIT Press, 1995.

Hays, K. Michael, Catherine Ingraham, and Alicia Kennedy. "On the House." *Assemblage: A Critical Journal of Architecture and Design Culture* 24 (August 1994): 6–7.

Hearn, Lafcadio. *Two Years in the French West Indies*. 1890. Rpt. New York: Harper, 1903.

Hedrick, Joan. *Harriet Beecher Stowe: A Life*. New York: Oxford University Press, 1994.

Heneghan, Bridget T. *Whitewashing America: Material Culture and Race in the Antebellum Imagination*. Jackson: University Press of Mississippi, 2003.

Henle, James. "Selling the Exotic to Main Street: A. A. Vantine & Co. Succeed Where Carol Kennicott Failed." *Printer's Ink* 14 (September 1922): 77–80.

Henry, Jay C. *Architecture in Texas, 1895–1945*. Austin: University of Texas Press, 1993.

Hersey, George L. "Godey's Choice." *Journal of the Society of Architectural Historians* 18.3 (October 1959): 104–11.

Herzog, Lawrence A. *From Aztec to High Tech: Architecture and Landscape across the Mexico–United States Border*. Baltimore: Johns Hopkins University Press, 1999.

Hines, Thomas S. *William Faulkner and the Tangible Past: The Architecture of Yoknapatawpha*. Berkeley: University of California Press, 1996.

Hitchcock, Henry-Russell. *American Architectural Books*. New exp. ed. New York: Da Capo Press, 1976.

———. *In the Nature of Materials: The Buildings of Frank Lloyd Wright, 1887–1941*. New York: Duell, Sloan and Pearce, 1942.

Hoganson, Kristin L. *Consumers' Imperium: The Global Production of American Domesticity, 1865–1920*. Chapel Hill: University of North Carolina Press, 2007.

Holland, Jesse J. *Black Men Built the Capitol: Discovering African-American History in and around Washington, D.C.* Guilford, CT: Globe Pequot Press, 2007.

Holliday, Kathryn E. *Leopold Eidlitz: Architecture and Idealism in the Gilded Age.* New York: Norton, 2008.

hooks, bell, Julie Eizenberg, and Hank Koning. "House, 20 June 1994." *Assemblage: A Critical Journal of Architecture and Design Culture* 24 (August 1994): 22–29.

Hop Lee, the Chinese Slave Dealer; or, Old and Young King Brady and the Opium Fiends. A Story of San Francisco. New York: Frank Tousey, 1899.

Hoppenstand, Gary. "Yellow Devil Doctors and Opium Dens: A Survey of the Yellow Peril Stereotypes in Mass Media Entertainment." *The Popular Culture Reader.* 3rd ed. Ed. Christopher D. Geist and Jack Nachbar. Bowling Green, OH: Bowling Green University Popular Press, 1983.

Horn, Tammy. *Bees in America: How the Honey Bee Shaped a Nation.* Lexington: University Press of Kentucky, 2005.

Hosley, William N. *The Japan Idea: Art and Life in Victorian America.* Harford, CT: Wadsworth Atheneum, 1990.

Howells, William Dean. "A Psychological Counter-current in Fiction." *North American Review* 173 (December 1901): 872–88.

Isaac, Rhys. *The Transformation of Virginia, 1740–1790.* Chapel Hill: University of North Carolina Press, 1982.

Jackson, Helen Hunt. *Ramona: A Story.* 1884. Rpt. Boston: Little, Brown, 1900.

Jacobs, Harriet. *Incidents in the Life of a Slave Girl.* 1861. Rpt. New York: Oxford University Press, 1988.

Jehle, Michael A. *From Brant Point to the Boca Tigris: Nantucket and the China Trade.* Nantucket, MA: Nantucket Historical Association, 1994.

Jen, Gish. "Challenging the Asian Illusion." *New York Times,* 11 August 1991, B1, B12–13.

Johnston, Frances Benjamin, and Thomas Tileston Waterman. *The Early Architecture of North Carolina.* Chapel Hill: University of North Carolina Press, 1941.

Kammen, Michael. *Mystic Chords of Memory: The Transformation of Tradition in American Culture.* New York: Knopf, 1991.

Kaplan, Amy. *The Anarchy of Empire in the Making of U.S. Culture.* Cambridge: Harvard University Press, 2002.

———. "Manifest Domesticity." *American Literature* 70.3 (September 1998): 581–606.

———. "Romancing the Empire: The Embodiment of American Masculinity in the Popular Historical Novel of the 1890s." *American Literary History* 2.4 (Winter 1990): 659–90.

Kaplan, Victoria. *Structural Inequality: Black Architects in the United States.* New York: Rowman and Littlefield, 2006.

Kawash, Samira. "Haunted Houses, Sinking Ships: Race, Architecture, and Identity in *Beloved* and *Middle Passage.*" *CR: The New Centennial Review* 1.3 (Winter 2001): 67–86.

Keckley, Elizabeth. *Behind the Scenes; Or, Thirty Years a Slave and Four Years in the White House.* New York: G. W. Carleton, 1868.

Kim, Elaine H. *Asian American Literature: An Introduction to the Writings and Their Social Context.* Philadelphia: Temple University Press, 1982.

King, Anthony D. *The Bungalow: The Production of a Global Culture.* New York: Routledge, 1984.

Klimasmith, Elizabeth. *At Home in the City: Urban Domesticity in American Literature and Culture, 1850–1930*. Durham: University of New Hampshire Press, 2005.

Knapp, Bettina L. *Archetype, Architecture, and the Writer*. Bloomington: Indiana University Press, 1986.

Lancaster, Clay. "The American Bungalow." *Art Bulletin* 40.3 (September 1958): 239–53.

———. *The American Bungalow, 1880–1930*. 1985. Rpt. New York: Dover, 1995.

———. "Italianism in American Architecture before 1860." *American Quarterly* 4.2 (Summer 1952): 127–48.

———. *The Japanese Influence in America*. New York: Walton H. Rawls, 1963.

———. "Oriental Forms in American Architecture." *Art Bulletin* 29.3 (September 1947): 183–93.

Langley, Lester D. *The Banana Wars: United States Intervention in the Caribbean, 1898–1934*. Wilmington, DE: Scholarly Resources, 2002.

Langmead, Donald, and Donald Leslie Johnson. *Architectural Excursions: Frank Lloyd Wright, Holland and Europe*. Westport, CT: Greenwood Press, 2000.

Leach, Neil, ed. *Rethinking Architecture: A Reader in Critical Theory*. New York: Routledge, 1997.

Lee, Rachel C. "Journalistic Representations of Asian Americans and Literary Responses, 1910–1920." *An Interethnic Companion to Asian American Literature*. Ed. King-Kok Cheung. New York: Cambridge University Press, 1996. 249–73.

Lee, Robert G. *Orientals: Asians in Popular Culture*. Philadelphia: Temple University Press, 1999.

"Let Us Ship You This Complete Home." Advertisement. North American Construction Company. *American Exporter* 73.6 (1913): 137.

Levander, Caroline F., and Robert S. Levine. Introduction. *Hemispheric American Studies: Essays beyond the Nation*. New Brunswick, NJ: Rutgers University Press, 2008. 1–17.

Leveen, Lois. "The Race Home: Difference and Domestic Space in American Literature and Culture." Diss. UCLA, 1999.

Little-Stokes, Ruth. "The North Carolina Porch: A Climatic and Cultural Buffer." *Carolina Dwelling: Towards Preservation of Place: In Celebration of the North Carolina Vernacular Landscape*. Ed. Doug Swaim. Raleigh: North Carolina State University, 1978. 104–11.

Lobato, José Bento Monteiro. *O Choque das Raças; ou, O Presidente Negro: Romance Americano do Anno de 2228*. 1926. Rpt. Sao Paulo: Editora Brasiliense, 1979.

Lokko, Lesley Naa Norle, ed. *White Papers, Black Marks: Architecture, Race, Culture*. Minneapolis: University of Minnesota Press, 2000.

Loudon, J. C. *An Encyclopaedia of Gardening; Comprising the Theory and Practice of Horticulture, Floriculture, Arboriculture, and Landscape-Gardening*. New ed. London: Longman, Rees, Orme, Brown, Green, and Longman, 1835.

Lounsbury, Carl R., ed. *An Illustrated Glossary of Early Southern Architecture and Landscape*. New York: Oxford University Press, 1994.

Lubow, Arthur. *The Reporter Who Would Be King: A Biography of Richard Harding Davis*. New York: Scribner, 1992.

Luna-Lawhn, Juanita. Introduction. "Memorias de mi viaje (Recollections of My Trip): A Transcultural Voyage into El México de Afuera." *Memorias de mi viaje (Recollections of My Trip)*. By Olga Beatriz Torres. Albuquerque: University of New Mexico Press, 1994. 5–25.

Luria, Sarah. *Capital Speculations: Writing and Building Washington, D.C.* University Press of New England and the Center for American Places. Lebanon, NH: University of New England Press, 2005.

———. "Racial Equality Begins at Home: Frederick Douglass's Challenge to American Domesticity." *The American Home: Material Culture, Domestic Space, and Family Life.* Ed. Eleanor McD. Thompson. Winterthur, DE: Winterthur Museum, 1998. 25–43.

Lye, Colleen. *America's Asia: Racial Form and American Literature, 1893–1945.* Princeton: Princeton University Press, 2004.

Machlan, Elizabeth. "Diseased Properties and Broken Homes in Ann Petry's *The Street.*" *Representing Segregation: Towards an Aesthetics of Living Jim Crow, and Other Forms of Racial Division.* Ed. Brian Norman and Piper Kendrix Williams. Albany: SUNY Press, 2010. 149–63.

Mahan, Russell L. "Political Architecture: The Building of the President's House." *Life in the White House: A Social History of the First Family and the President's House.* Ed. Robert P. Watson. Albany: SUNY Press, 2004. 31–47.

Major, Judith K. *To Live in the New World: A. J. Downing and American Landscape Gardening.* Cambridge: MIT Press, 1997.

Manson, Grant Carpenter. *Frank Lloyd Wright to 1910: The First Golden Age.* New York: Reinhold, 1958.

Marling, Karal Ann. *George Washington Slept Here: Colonial Revivals and American Culture, 1876–1986.* Cambridge: Harvard University Press, 1988.

Marsh, E. S. "Memoir of the Centennial Exhibition of 1876." Document 113. Joseph Downs Collection of Manuscripts and Printed Ephemera, Winterthur Library, Winterthur, DE.

Massey, Douglas, and Nancy A. Denton. *American Apartheid: Segregation and the Making of the Underclass.* Cambridge: Harvard University Press, 1993.

May, Bridget A. "Progressivism and the Colonial Revival: The Modern Colonial House, 1900–1920." *Winterthur Portfolio* 26 (Summer/Autumn 1991): 107–22.

Maynard, William Barksdale. *Architecture in the United States, 1800–1850.* New Haven: Yale University Press, 2002.

McElrath, Joseph R., Jr. "Collaborative Authorship: The Charles W. Chesnutt–Walter Hines Page Relationship." *The Professions of Authorship: Essays in Honor of Matthew J. Bruccoli.* Ed. Richard Layman and Joel Myerson. Columbia: University of South Carolina Press, 1996. 150–68.

McElrath, Joseph R., Jr., and Robert C. Leitz, III, eds. *"To Be an Author": Letters of Charles W. Chesnutt, 1889–1905.* Princeton: Princeton University Press, 1997.

McKittrick, Katherine. *Demonic Grounds: Black Women and the Cartographies of Struggle.* Minneapolis: University of Minnesota Press, 2006.

Meinig, D. W. *The Shaping of America.* Vol. 2, *Continental America, 1800–1867.* New Haven: Yale University Press, 1993.

Melville, Herman. *The Piazza Tales.* New York: Dix and Edwards, 1856.

Mitchell, Melvin L. *The Crisis of the African-American Architect.* Rev. 2nd ed. New York: Writer's Advantage, 2003.

Moddelmog, William E. *Reconstituting Authority: American Fiction in the Province of the Law, 1880–1920.* Iowa City: University of Iowa Press, 2000.

Mooney, Barbara Burlison. "The Comfortable Tasty Framed Cottage: An African American Architectural Iconography." *Journal of the Society of Architectural Historians* 61.1 (March 2002): 48–67.

Morgan, Philip D. *Slave Counterpoint: Black Culture in the Eighteenth-Century Chesapeake and Lowcountry*. Chapel Hill: University of North Carolina Press, 1998.

Morrison, Toni. *Playing in the Dark: Whiteness and the Literary Imagination*. Cambridge: Harvard University Press, 1992.

Morse, Edward S. *Japanese Houses and Their Surroundings*. Boston: Ticknor, 1886.

Mudge, Jean McClure. *Chinese Export Porcelain for the American Trade, 1785–1835*. Newark: University of Delaware Press, 1962.

Mugerauer, Robert. "Toward an Architectural Vocabulary: The Porch as a Between." *Dwelling, Seeing, and Designing: Toward a Phenomenological Ecology*. Ed. David Seamon. Albany: SUNY Press, 1993. 103–28.

Murphy, Gretchen. *Hemispheric Imaginings: The Monroe Doctrine and Narratives of U.S. Empire*. Durham, NC: Duke University Press, 2005.

Noble, Allen G., ed. *To Build in a New Land: Ethnic Landscapes in North America*. Baltimore: Johns Hopkins University Press, 1992.

Nora, Pierre. "Between Memory and History: *Les Lieux de Mémoire*." Trans. Marc Roudebush. *History and Memory in African-American Culture*. Ed. Geneviève Fabre and Robert O'Meally. New York: Oxford University Press, 1994. 284–300.

Norris, Frank. *Blix*. New York: Grosset and Dunlap, 1899.

Northend, Mary H. *Colonial Homes and Their Furnishings*. Boston: Little, Brown, 1912.

Nute, Kevin. *Frank Lloyd Wright and Japan*. 1993. Rpt. New York: Routledge, 2000.

———. "Frank Lloyd Wright and Japanese Architecture: A Study in Inspiration." *Journal of Design History* 7.3 (1994): 169–85.

Olmsted, Frederick Law. *A Journey in the Seaboard Slave States*. New York: Dix and Edwards, 1856.

Olsen, Taimi. *Transcending Space: Architectural Places in Works by Henry David Thoreau, E. E. Cummings, and John Barth*. Lewisburg, PA: Bucknell University Press, 2000.

Page, J. W. *Uncle Robin in His Cabin in Virginia, and Tom without One in Boston*. 2nd ed. Richmond, VA: J. W. Randolph, 1853.

Page, Thomas Nelson. *In Ole Virginia*. New York: Charles Scribner's Sons, 1887.

Palumbo-Liu, David. *Asian/American: Historical Crossings of a Racial Frontier*. Palo Alto: Stanford University Press, 1999.

Pariser, Harry S. *Explore Belize*. Edison, NJ: Hunter, 1998.

Parsons, C. G. *Inside View of Slavery: or a Tour among the Planters*. Boston: John P. Jewett; Cleveland: Jewett, Proctor and Worthington, 1855.

Patai, Daphne. "Race and Politics in Two Brazilian Utopias." *Luso-Brazilian Review* 19.1 (Summer 1982): 67–81.

Perry, Richard L. "The Front Porch as Stage and Symbol in the Deep South." *Journal of American Culture* 8 (1985): 13–18.

Pfeiffer, Bruce Brooks. *Frank Lloyd Wright: Selected Houses*. Vol. 1. Ed. and photog. Yukio Futagawa. Tokyo: A.D.A. Edita, 1991.

Placzek, Adolf, and Angela Giral. *Avery's Choice: One Hundred Years of an Architectural Library, 1890–1990*. New York: G. K. Hall, 1997.

Porter, William Harley. "Mr. Davis and the Real Olancho." *Bookman* 15 (August 1902): 558–61.

Quirk, Robert E. *An Affair of Honor: Woodrow Wilson and the Occupation of Veracruz.* 1962. Rpt. New York: Norton, 1967.

"Ready-Made Houses." Advertisement. *Manufacturer and Builder* 8 (1876): 10.

Reiff, Daniel Drake. *Houses from Books: Treatises, Pattern Books, and Catalogs in American Architecture, 1738–1950: A History and Guide.* University Park: Pennsylvania State University Press, 2001.

Render, Sylvia Lyons. "Tarheelia in Chesnutt." *CLA Journal* 9 (September 1965): 39–50.

Reps, John W. *Bird's Eye Views: Historic Lithographs of North American Cities.* New York: Princeton Architectural Press, 1998.

Rev. of Alexander Jackson Downing, *Rural Essays. New Englander and Yale Review* 11 (August 1853): 474–75.

Rev. of C. W. Elliott, *Cottages and Cottage Life.* Cincinnati: H. W. Derby, 1848. *Merchants' Magazine and Commercial Review* 19.4 (October 1848): 460

Rice, Allen Thorndike, ed. *Reminiscences of Abraham Lincoln by Distinguished Men of His Time.* New York: North American Review, 1888.

Robbins, Hollis. "Blackening *Bleak House*: Hannah Crafts's *The Bondwoman's Narrative.*" In *Search of Hannah Crafts: Critical Essays on The Bondwoman's Narrative.* Ed. Henry Louis Gates Jr. and Hollis Robbins. New York: Basic Books, 2004. 71–86.

Rohmer, Sax. *The Insidious Dr. Fu-Manchu.* 1913. Rpt. New York: Robert M. McBride, 1920.
———. *President Fu-Manchu.* Garden City, NY: P. F. Collier, 1936.

Rohrbach, Augusta. "'A Silent, Unobtrusive Way': Hannah Crafts and the Literary Marketplace." *In Search of Hannah Crafts: Critical Essays on The Bondwoman's Narrative.* Ed. Henry Louis Gates Jr. and Hollis Robbins. New York: Basic Books, 2004. 3–15.

Rosaldo, Renato. *Culture and Truth: The Remaking of Social Analysis.* 1989. Rpt. Boston: Beacon Press, 1993.

Roth, Rodris. "Scrapbook Houses: A Late Nineteenth Century Children's View of the American Home." *The American Home: Material Culture, Domestic Space, and Family Life.* Ed. Eleanor McD. Thompson. Winterthur, DE: Winterthur Museum, 1998. 301–23.

Rufus Jones for President. Dir. Roy Mack. Vitaphone, 1933.

Ruzicka, William T. *Faulkner's Fictive Architecture: The Meaning of Place in the Yoknapatawpha Novels.* Ann Arbor: University of Michigan Press, 1987.

Rydell, Robert W. *All the World's a Fair.* Chicago: University of Chicago Press, 1984.

Rzepka, Charles J. "Race, Region, Rule: Genre and the Case of Charlie Chan." *PMLA* 122.5 (October 2007): 1463–81.

Said, Edward. *Orientalism.* New York: Pantheon, 1978.

Satter, Beryl. *Family Properties: Race, Real Estate, and the Exploitation of Black Urban America.* New York: Metropolitan Books, 2009.

Schein, Richard H., ed. *Landscape and Race in the United States.* New York: Routledge, 2006.

Schlereth, Thomas J. "American Homes and American Scholars." *American Home Life, 1880–1930: A Social History of Spaces and Services.* Ed. Jessica H. Foy and Thomas J. Schlereth. Knoxville: University of Tennessee Press, 1992. 1–22.

Schnack, Ferdinand J. H. *The Aloha Guide: The Standard Handbook of Honolulu and the Hawaiian Islands.* Honolulu: Honolulu Star Bulletin, 1915.

Schuyler, David. *Apostle of Taste: Andrew Jackson Downing, 1815–1852*. Baltimore: Johns Hopkins University Press, 1996.

———. "Villages and Farm Cottages: The Ideology of Domesticity." *Villages and Farm Cottages: A Victorian Stylebook of 1856*. By Henry W. Cleaveland et al. Watkins Glen, NY: American Life Foundation, 1982. Rpt. of *Village and Farm Cottages*. By Cleaveland et al. New York: 1856.

Scully, Vincent J., Jr. *The Shingle Style: Architectural Theory and Design from Richardson to the Origins of Wright*. New Haven: Yale University Press, 1955.

———. *The Shingle Style and the Stick Style: Architectural Theory and Design from Richardson to the Origins of Wright*. New Haven: Yale University Press, 1971.

Seale, William. *The President's House: A History*. 2nd ed. 2 vols. Baltimore: Johns Hopkins University Press, 2008.

———. "The White House: Plans Realized and Unrealized." *Our Changing White House*. Ed. Wendell Garrett. Boston: Northeastern University Press, 1995. 1–30.

Sedlack, Robert P. "The Evolution of Charles Chesnutt's *The House Behind the Cedars*." *CLA Journal* 19.2 (December 1975): 125–35.

Seelye, John. *War Games: Richard Harding Davis and the New Imperialism*. Amherst: University of Massachusetts Press, 2003.

Selinger, Eric. "Aunts, Uncles, Audience: Gender and Genre in Charles Chesnutt's *The Conjure Woman*." *Black American Literature Forum* 25 (Winter 1991): 665–88.

Semple, Patty B. "Old Kentucky Home." *Atlantic Monthly* 60 (July 1887): 32–33.

Shamir, Milette. *Inexpressible Privacy: The Interior Life of Antebellum American Literature*. Philadelphia: University of Pennsylvania Press, 2006.

Shepp, James W., and Daniel B. Shepp. *Shepp's World's Fair Photographed. Being a Collection of Original Copyrighted Photographs Authorized and Permitted by the Management of the World's Columbian Exposition*. Chicago: Globe Bible Publishing, 1893.

Sloan, Samuel. *The Model Architect: A Series of Original Designs for Cottages, Villas, Suburban Residences, Etc.* 2 vols. Philadelphia: E. S. Jones and Co., 1852.

———. *Sloan's Homestead Architecture, Containing Forty Designs for Villas, Cottages, and Farm Houses, with Essays on Style, Construction, Landscape Gardening, Furniture, etc., etc.* Philadelphia: J. B. Lippincott, 1861.

Smeins, Linda E. *Building an American Identity: Pattern Book Home and Communities, 1870–1900*. Walnut Creek, CA: AltaMira Press, 1999.

Smith, Jeff. *The Presidents We Imagine: Two Centuries of White House Fictions on the Page, on the Stage, Onscreen, and Online*. Madison: University of Wisconsin Press, 2009.

Smith, Oliver P. *The Domestic Architect: Comprising a Series of Original Designs for Rural and Ornamental Cottages*. Buffalo, NY: Derby, 1852.

Smith, Valerie. "'Loopholes of Retreat': Architecture and Ideology in Harriet Jacobs's *Incidents in the Life of a Slave Girl*." *Reading Black, Reading Feminist: A Critical Anthology*. Ed. Henry Louis Gates Jr. New York: Meridian, 1990. 212–26.

Sobel, Mechal. *The World They Made Together: Black and White Values in Eighteenth-Century Virginia*. Princeton: Princeton University Press, 1987.

Stepto, Robert B. "'The Simple but Intensely Human Inner Life of Slavery': Storytelling, Fiction and the Revision of History in Charles W. Chesnutt's 'Uncle Julius Stories.'" *History and Tradition in Afro-American Culture*. Ed. Gunter H. Lenz. Frankfurt: Campus, 1984. 29–55.

Stickley, Gustav. "The California Bungalow: A Style of Architecture Which Expresses the Individuality and Freedom Characteristic of Our Western Coast." *The Craftsman* (October 1907). Rpt. in *Craftsman Bungalows: 59 Homes from "The Craftsman."* Ed. Gustav Stickley. New York: Dover, 1988. 12–24.

Stowe, Harriet Beecher. *Uncle Tom's Cabin*. 1852. Rpt. New York: Bantam, 1981.

Sundquist, Eric J. *To Wake the Nations: Race in the Making of American Literature.* Cambridge, MA: Belknap Press, 1993.

Sweeting, Adam W. *Reading Houses and Building Books: Andrew Jackson Downing and the Architecture of Popular Antebellum Literature, 1835–1855.* Hanover, NH: University Press of New England, 1996.

Tatum, George B. "The Downing Decade." *Prophet with Honor: The Career of Andrew Jackson Downing, 1815–1852.* Ed. George B. Tatum and Elisabeth B. MacDougall. Washington, DC: Dumbarton Oaks, 1989.

———. Rev. of Alexander Jackson Davis, *Rural Residences, etc., Consisting of Designs, Original and Selected, for Cottages, Farm-Houses, Villas, and Village Churches: With Brief Explanations, Estimates, and a Specification of Materials, Construction, etc.* New York: New York University, 1837. Rpt. with new introduction by Jane Davies. New York: Da Capo Press, 1980. *Journal of the Society of Architectural Historians* 41.4 (December 1982): 357–58.

Tatum, George B., and Elisabeth B. MacDougall, eds. *Prophet with Honor: The Career of Andrew Jackson Downing, 1815–1852.* Washington, DC: Dumbarton Oaks, 1989.

Taylor, Yuval. "Underneath the Harlem Moon." *Faking It.* 11 August 2007. http://fakingit.typepad.com/faking_it/2007/08/underneath-the-.html.

Tchen, John Kuo Wei. *New York before Chinatown: Orientalism and the Shaping of American Culture, 1776–1882.* Baltimore: Johns Hopkins University Press, 1999.

Teng, Emma J. "Artifacts of a Lost City: Arnold Genthe's *Pictures of Old Chinatown* and Its Intertexts." *Re/collecting Early Asian America: Essays in Cultural History.* Ed. Josephine Lee, Imogene L. Lim, and Yuko Matsukawa. Philadelphia: Temple University Press, 2002. 54–77.

Thompson, Eleanor McD, ed. *The American Home: Material Culture, Domestic Space, and Family Life.* Winterthur, DE: Winterthur Museum, 1998.

Tomlan, Michael A. "Toward the Growth of an Artistic Taste." Introduction. *Cottage Souvenir No. 2.* By George F. Barber. 1982. Rpt. Mineola, NY: Dover, 2004. v–xxi.

Torres, Olga Beatriz. *Memorias de mi viaje (Recollections of My Trip).* Trans. Juanita Luna-Lawhn. 1918. Rpt. Albuquerque: University of New Mexico Press, 1994.

Trafton, Scott. *Egypt Land: Race and Nineteenth-Century American Egyptomania.* Durham, NC: Duke University Press, 2004.

Tucker, Susan, Katherine Ott, and Patricia P. Buckler, eds. *The Scrapbook in American Life.* Philadelphia: Temple University Press, 2006.

Twain, Mark [Samuel L. Clemens], and Charles Dudley Warner. *The Gilded Age: A Tale of Today.* 1873. Rpt. New York: Penguin, 2001.

Twombly, Robert C. *Frank Lloyd Wright: His Life and His Architecture.* New York: Wiley, 1979.

Upton, Dell. *Architecture in the United States.* New York: Oxford University Press, 1998.

———. "Pattern Books and Professionalism: Aspects of the Transformation of Domestic Architecture in America, 1800–1860. *Winterthur Portfolio* 19.2/3 (Summer/Autumn 1984): 107–50.

———. "White and Black Landscapes in Eighteenth-Century Virginia." *Places* 2.2 (1984): 59–72.

Upton, Dell, and John Michael Vlach. *Common Places: Readings in American Vernacular Architecture*. Athens: University of Georgia Press, 1986.

Vantine, A. A., and Co. *Vantine's: The Oriental Store*. New York: A. A. Vantine and Co., ca. 1910–15. Trade Catalog Collection, Hagley Museum and Library, Wilmington, DE.

———. *Vantine's: The Oriental Store*. New York: A. A. Vantine and Co., 1914. Printed Book and Periodical Collection, The Winterthur Library, Winterthur, DE.

———. *Vantine's: The Oriental Store*. New York: A. A. Vantine and Co., 1915. Printed Book and Periodical Collection, The Winterthur Library, Winterthur, DE.

———. *Vantine's: The Oriental Store*. New York: A. A. Vantine and Co., 1917. Printed Book and Periodical Collection, The Winterthur Library, Winterthur, DE.

Vaux, Calvert. *Villas and Cottages*. New York: Harper, 1857.

Vidler, Anthony. *The Architectural Uncanny: Essays in the Modern Unhomely*. Cambridge: MIT Press, 1992.

Villa, Raúl Homero. *Barrio-Logos: Space and Place in Urban Chicano Literature and Culture*. Austin: University of Texas Press, 2000.

Vlach, John Michael. *The Afro-American Tradition in Decorative Arts*. 2nd ed. Athens: University of Georgia Press, 1990.

———. *Back of the Big House: The Architecture of Plantation Slavery*. Chapel Hill: University of North Carolina Press, 1993.

———. *By the Work of Their Hands: Studies in Afro-American Folk Life*. Ann Arbor: University of Michigan Press, 1991.

West, Cornel. "A Note on Race and Architecture." *Keeping Faith: Philosophy and Race in America*. New York: Routledge, 1993. 45–54.

Westcott, Thompson. *Centennial Portfolio: A Souvenir of the International Exhibition at Philadelphia, Comprising Lithographic Views of Fifty of Its Principal Buildings, with Letter-Press Descriptions*. Philadelphia: Thomas Hunter, 1876.

Wheeler, Gervase. *Rural Homes; Or Sketches of Houses Suited to American Country Life with Original Plans, Designs, Etc*. New York: Scribner, 1851.

Wheeler, John Hill. *Library Catalogue*. John Hill Wheeler Papers No. 765. Southern Historical Collection. Wilson Library. University of North Carolina at Chapel Hill.

Whiffen, Marcus, and Frederick Koeper. *American Architecture*. Vol. 2, *1860–1976*. Cambridge: MIT Press, 1981.

White, David Manning. *Popular Culture*. New York: Hudson Group, 1975.

Wideman, John Edgar. "Charles Chesnutt and the WPA Narratives: The Oral and Literate Roots of Afro-American Literature." *The Slave's Narrative*. Ed. Charles T. Davis and Henry Louis Gates Jr. New York: Oxford University Press, 1985. 59–78.

Wiley, Hugh. *Jade: And Other Stories*. New York: Knopf, 1921.

Williams, Clara Andrews. *The House That Glue Built*. New York: Frederick A. Stokes, 1905.

Wilson, Edmund. "Vantine's in Five Floors." *The American Earthquake: A Documentary of the Twenties and Thirties*. 1958. Rpt. New York: Farrar, Straus and Giroux, 1979. 86.

Wong, K. Scott, "Chinatown: Conflicting Images, Contested Terrain." *MELUS* 20.1 (Spring 1995): 3–15.

Woods, Mary N. *From Craft to Profession: The Practice of Architecture in Nineteenth-Century America*. Berkeley: University of California Press, 1999.

Woodward, George E., and Edward G. Thompson. *A Victorian Housebuilder's Guide: "Woodward's National Architect" of 1869.* 1869. Rpt. New York: Dover, 1988.

Worden, Daniel. "Birth in the Briar Patch: Charles W. Chesnutt and the Problem of Racial Identity." *Southern Literary Journal* 41.2 (Spring 2009): 1–20.

Wright, Frank Lloyd. "Building the New House." *Frank Lloyd Wright: An Autobiography.* 1943. Rpt. Petaluma, CA: Pomegranate Communications, 2005. 141–44.

Wright, Gwendolyn. *Building the Dream: A Social History of Housing in America.* New York: Pantheon, 1981.

———. *USA: Modern Architectures in History.* Chicago: Reaktion Books, 2008.

Wu, William F. *The Yellow Peril: Chinese Americans in American Fiction 1850–1940.* Hamden, CT: Archon Books, 1982.

Yip, Christopher L. "California Chinatowns: Built Environments Expressing the Hybridized Culture of Chinese American." *Hybrid Urbanism: On the Identity Discourse and the Built Environment.* Ed. Nezar AlSayyad. Westport, CT: Praeger, 2001. 67–82.

Yoshihara, Mari. *Embracing the East: White Women and American Orientalism.* New York: Oxford University Press, 2003.

Index

Page numbers in italics refer to illustrations

abolition, 16, 51, 57, 213n14, 239n10
Absalom, Absalom! (Faulkner), 73
The Adventures of Huckleberry Finn
  (Twain), 72
Aesthetic Movement, 157
African Americans: and built environment,
  29, 35, 141–42; as carpenters and house
  builders, 215n33, 217n17; and memory,
  71, 100; in pattern books, 48–49, 190–94;
  as president, 195, 200, 203; shaping,
  mapping, and claiming ground, 71, 92,
  100–102. *See also* Historically Black Colleges and Universities; homeownership
Aladdin Company, 189; "Famous Board
  of Seven," 127–28; house models, 126,
  131, 226n28, 227n39; industrial housing,
  128–29, 226n37; marketing, 126, *127*, 129, *130*
American Agriculturalist, 11
American Institute of Architects, 128,
  211n36
"Am I Blue?" (Waters), 202
Andrews, William, 102, 217n18
anti-immigrationism, 69, 91. *See also*
  immigration
architects, 3, 8, 64, 128, 130; incorporation
  of Asian design, 150–51; professional
  consciousness of, 208n7
architectural revivals, 3. *See also* Classical
  Revival; Colonial Revival
architectural styles: Beaux Arts, 136; Queen
  Anne, 156, 189; Richardsonian Romanesque, 136; Romanesque, 189; shingle
  style, 156–57; stick style, 155; Venetian
  Gothic, 136

architectural tropes, 27, 52, 56, 203; of
  "Oriental" space, 162–65, 185; in *Uncle
  Tom's Cabin*, 55
architecture: African, 6, 89; "black," 193; in
  children's culture, 4–6, 18–25; Chinese,
  5, 8, 152; and class, 137–38; defined, 27;
  East Indian, 153; Egyptian, 153; and/
  of empire, 27, 29, 106–7, 114–15, 118,
  120–23, 125, 129–30, 134; English, 4, 7;
  fictionality of, 1; French, 4; and gender,
  27–28, 77; Gothic, 3, 153; homologies
  with narrative form, 26–27, 34–35; and
  interior decoration, 233n26; Italian,
  3; Japanese, 30, 151, 155–57; legibility
  of, 71–72, 216n8; and literature, 2–3,
  26, 30, 207n1; and material culture,
  18–25; modern, 193–94; Moorish, 153;
  and national "home," 8; and national
  identity, 167; and national morality, 8;
  nineteenth-century racial understanding of, 3–10, 20, 28, 45, 167, 191, 194; in
  North Carolina, 84–85, *87–88*; Persian,
  153; and popular culture, 6, 120, 123,
  125, 159, 193, 198, 202–4; and popular
  fiction, 30, 55–57, 69, 106, 151, 162–67,
  177, 184; professionalization of, 26–27,
  89, 128, 194, 211n36; racial politics of,
  17; Russian, 4; of slavery, 1, 17, 45–51,
  74, 193; southern, 8–10, 47–50, 76–78,
  83–89, 195–96, 212n5; Turkish, 4, 8.
  See also built environment; domestic
  architecture; domestic space; vernacular
  architecture; *and names of specific
  architectural structures*

Chase, Salmon P., 15
Chesnutt, Charles: ambivalence about
conjure genre, 67; interest in social
experience of architecture, 69, 78, 83,
93, 97, 101–104; literary blockage, 68;
and preferred fictions of white memory,
93–100; interest in public architecture,
220n46; revisionist historicism of,
70–71, 78–93, 99; vs. white amnesia, 71
—conjure tales, 1, 26, 28–29, 67–104,
216n5, 221–22n57; "The Conjurer's
Revenge," 70, 76, 77, 218n25; "Dave's
Neckliss," 76–78, 93; "A Deep Sleeper,"
78–82, 93, 99; "The Dumb Witness,"
70, 78, 82–93, 97–100; "The Goophered
Grapevine," 69–70, 71, 74, 78, 93–96,
98, 101; "The Gray Wolf's Ha'nt," 97–98;
"Hot-Foot Hannibal," 93, 97, 98–101;
"Lonesome Ben," 78, 82–83; "Po' Sandy,"
70, 75–76, 78, 79, 81, 83, 93; "Sis' Becky's
Pickaninny," 97; "Tobe's Tribulations,"
97; "A Victim of Heredity," 97. See also
The Conjure Woman
Chicago World's Fair, 30, 71, 91, 150, 156–57
See also Ho-o-den
China Retreat, 152
"The Chinaman" (Fiske), 5
Chinatown: in *The House without a Key*,
170–75, 177, 179–80, 184–85; popular
images of, 162–67; as socio-architectural
space, 167, 235–36n45. *See also* China-
town fiction; "Underground Chinatown"
Chinatown fiction: imagined buildingscape
of, 163–65, 167, 170–75, 177, 179–80, 184;
and national identity, 167; underground
passages in, 164–65; "Oriental" décor in,
165–67, 175, 184; violence of, 164–67
Chinese Exclusion Act, 163
O Choque das Raças (Lobato): election of
black president in, 202; republication
during 2008 U.S. presidential campaign,
240n27
Civil War, 35, 66, 84
Classical Revival, 3, 83–84; nostalgia of, 70;
in South, 84, 86
Cleveland News and Herald, 71

Clotel; or, The President's Daughter (Brown),
197, 199, 204
Cody, Jeffrey W., 129
collage albums. *See* scrapbook houses
Colonial Revival, 1, 89, 92, 167, 198, 211n40;
appeal of porches for, 91; consonance
with anti-immigrationism, 69, 91; and
neoclassicism, 91; nostalgia of, 26, 70,
123–24, 197; preservationist zeal of, 197;
and White House, 197
The Conjure Woman (Chesnutt), 68, 77, 93,
98, 102, 103. *See also* Chesnutt, Charles—
conjure tales
"Contrasted Architecture" (*Cottage
Souvenir No. 2*), 190–91, 192
cosey corner, 159, 234n31
The Cosmopolitan, 189
cottage, 12, 28; Downingesque, 41, 60,
62, 102, 201; respectability of, 39; West
Indian, 2
Cottage Residences (Downing), 39–41
Cottages and Cottage Life (Elliott), 13;
discussion of slavery in, 13, 16–17; idiosyncrasies of house plans in, 11–13; social
and political tensions in, 13–15; as pattern
book novel, 10–11, 14; reviews of, 11–12
Cottage Souvenir No. 2 (Barber): advertisements for, 189–190; architectural styles,
189; invocation of plantation fiction, 193;
"old folks cabin" trope in, 203; popularity of designs, 189–90; representation of
race in, 190–194
Country Gentleman, 129
The Crack in Space (Dick), 203
Crafts, Hannah: and Downing, 28, 35,
41–44, 51–54; as fugitive slave, 28, 33–34,
41, 43–45; interest in architectural space,
35, 38; narrative borrowings compared
to builder's treatment of pattern book,
64; use of Dickens by, 28, 35, 57–59,
61–62, 64–66
Craftsman, 139
Crook, J. Mordaunt, 67
Culbertson, Martha, 139
cultural geography, 2, 195
Curtis Publishing Company, 129

Davis, Alexander Jackson, 153
Davis, Richard Harding: admiration for
   William Walker, 117; on the architecture
   of empire, 114–15, 118, 120, 139; compared
   to Torres, 29, 106–10, 132–35, 141–42, 145,
   148; on intervention in Central America,
   107, 115–18; obsession with transit rights
   across Central America, 111. See also
   Soldiers of Fortune; *Three Gringos in
   Venezuela and Central America*
Davis, Jr., Sammy, 202
de Certeau, Michel, 105
Democratic Review, 117
dialect tales, 2. *See also* Chesnutt,
   Charles—conjure tales; *The Conjure
   Woman*
Díaz, Porfirio, 113, 136
Dick, Philip K., 203
Dickens, Charles, 28, 35, 57–59, 61, 63,
   64–66
The Domestic Architect (Smith), 7–8
domestic architecture: Downing's
   principles of, 39–40; Japanese, 151;
   midcentury reform movement in, 17;
   and national identity, 8; "Oriental"
   forms of, 153; polycultural evolution of,
   70; racial implications of, 25; relation
   to social issues, 14; stick style and, 155.
   See also bungalow; cottage; domesticity;
   domestic space; home
domesticity, 13: cosmopolitan, 167; Downing on, 43; and gender, 27; histories of,
   190; imperial, 107. *See also* bungalow;
   cottage; domestic architecture; domestic
   space; home
domestics, as euphemism for slaves, 9–10
domestic space, 27; African American,
   54–55; "cottage desire" and, 35; hierarchies of, in slavery, 46; women and, 28.
   See also bungalow; cottage; domestic
   architecture; domesticity; home
Dos Passos, John, 172
Douglass, Frederick: and African American memory, 69; attention to domestic
   space by, 214n22; barred from Lincoln's
   election reception, 197; on black home-

ownership, 63; "slave cabin" study of,
   204; Washington, D.C., home, 63, 204
Downing, Andrew Jackson, 15, 35, 56;
   discussion of slavery by, 45–51, 213n14;
   on importance of homeownership, 51,
   213n12; mentor to Elliott, 11; national
   influence, 40; pastoral cottage ideology
   of, 11, 17, 28, 39–41, 60, 102, 193, 201;
   racialized theory of architecture, 7, 45,
   153; on regional fitness in architecture,
   209n11; shocking death, 41; and stick
   style, 155
Dunn, Nathan, 153
Duchscherer, Paul, 121
Dutch East India Company, 152

Eastern State Penitentiary, 152
East India Company, 152
Eastman, Mary H., 56–57
Edwards, Jay, 86, 219n39
Egyptian Revival, 3
Eldridge, Michael, 126
Elliott, C. W., 10–17, 157, 233n26; and
   Downing, 10–12, 15; invention of pattern
   book novel, 10; member of Semi-Colon
   Club, 14; related to Stowe by marriage,
   14, 210n24
El México de Afuera, 142–43
El Paso del Norte, 106
Empress of China, 152
Encyclopaedia of Gardening (Loudon), 12
Erbe, Scott, 126
Everett, Marshall, 112
*Exciting Experiences in Our Wars with Spain
   and the Filipinos* (Everett), 112

Fair Housing Act, 205
Fairmount Park, 155
Fairmount Waterworks, 152
Faulkner, William, 73
Fiske, N. W., 4–6
Fletcher, Banister, 89
Fletcher, Banister F., 89
Foote, Elizabeth Elliott, 14
Foote, Samuel, 14–15
Fowler, Orson Squire, 6–7, 19, 45

Melville, Herman, 216n8

Memorias de mi viaje (Torres), 29; architectural epistemology, 134–35; bird's-eye-view, 142–46; bungalow form in, 138–40; class hierarchies in, 142–46; as "Gulf" narrative, 106–9; incorporation of English words, 134–35; publishing history of, 106, 108, 228n48, 228–29n52; racial hierarchies in, 140–42, 148; representation of built environment in, 113, 131–46; and *Soldiers of Fortune*, 132–34, 145–48; spatio-political awareness, 145–48; and *Three Gringos*, 107–8, 132–35, 141–42, 145–48; travel route, 108

memory, 53–54; Chesnutt and, 68–69, 71, 76, 78, 93; validation of, for African Americans, 100–101. See also *lieux de mémoire*

Merchants' Magazine and Commercial Review, 11

Mexican Revolution, 29, 105, 113, 133

Mexico City, 133; architecture of, 136; Torres's flight from, 105, 107–8, 113, 142, 148

minstrelsy, 191

The Model Architect (Sloan), 8–9, 49, 153

Modern Houses (Shoppell), 191

Moddelmog, William E., 222n66

Monroe Doctrine, 118

Montgomery Ward, 175

Monticello, construction pattern of, 212n5

Morrison, Toni, 193

Mount Vernon, 197

Murphy, Gretchen, 118, 124–25

My Bondage and My Freedom (Douglass), 214n22

National Era, 11

neocolonialism. *See* Colonial Revival

New Englander, 11

New Yorker, 203

New York Times, 150

New York Tribune, 132

Nicaragua Canal, 111, *112*

Nora, Pierre, 103–4

Norris, Frank, 163–64, 172

Nute, Kevin, 156–57, 178

Nutt, Haller, 153

Obama, Barack, 195, 203; moving into the White House, 204–5

Obama, Michelle, 203–5

"Old Cabin Home" (*Cottage Souvenir No. 2*), 190–94

"The Old Cabin Home" (song), 191, 193

"Old Kentucky Home" (Semple), 95–96, 221n53

Olmsted, Frederick Law, interest in slave housing, 214n21

"Oriental Articles for Occidental Men" (Vantine's), 175–76

Orientalism: architectural, 3, 29–30, 152–58, 160–62, 185; commercial, 175–76; decorative, 21, 26, 29–30, 150–52, 157, 159–62; narrative, 151, 162

O'Sullivan, John L., 117

Overland Monthly, 67

"Ozymandias" (Shelley), 75, 218n20

Page, J. W., 55

Page, Thomas Nelson, 95

Page, Walter Hines, 68, 78, 83, 93, 96, 98

pagoda, 5–6

Pagoda and Labyrinth Garden, 152, 155

Palumbo-Liu, David, 167

Panama Canal, 132

Panama-Pacific International Exposition, 167, 177

paper doll houses. *See* scrapbook houses

pattern books, 18–19, 26, 27, 30, 52, 64, 201; bungalow in, 121; cultural influence of, 6, 20; depiction of female slave in, 48–49; discussion of cottages in, 39–40; evasion of slavery and other social and political tensions in, 8–10, 13, 17, 45–51, 54, 195, 209n13; as guides for living, 11; heyday of, 3, 208n7; ideology shaped and consumed by women, 28; merged with fiction, 10, 14; "Oriental" building motifs in, 150, 153, *154*; possible satire of, 12; racial assumptions of, 3–4, 6–8, 21, 191–94; stick style in, 155; visual idiom of, 56. *See also* builders' guides; *and individual pattern books by name*

Perkins, James Handasyd, 14–15

Perkins, Sarah Elliott, 14
Philadelphia Centennial Exposition, 150, 156, 157, 159; Japanese pavilion, 155, 187
phrenology, 19–20
piazza, 12; central imaginative space for Chesnutt, 69–78, 83–86, 97–99, 103–4; as differentiated from porch, 216–217n9; polycultural origins of, 29, 86–91, 196, 219n39; site of interracial conflict, 85–86; as zone of surveillance, 77. *See also* porch; portico; veranda
The Piazza Tales (Melville), 216n8
Pitcher, J. R., 121, 122, 125
place: desire for, 65; meaning of, during Jim Crow, 68–69; and memory, 101; mixed-race Americans and, 82–83; permanence of, through possession of a home, 51; and plantation genre, 193; politics of place construction, 70, 81; public segregation of, 142; sense of, for slaves, 80
place attachment theory, 211–212n2
plantation fiction, 67–69, 75, 94–95, 100, 193
plantation landscape: big house/slaveo-wner's mansion, 73, 76, 84, 86, 204; big house quarters, 219n34; hierarchy of forms on, 73–73, 76; physical approach to, 94–97; slave's landscape, 96; threshold devices of, 95–96. *See also* slave cabin
plaza, 2, 118, 225n22
Poe, Edgar Allan, 89
"The Politics of Fear" (Blitt), 203–204
porch: and architecture of segregation, 74; Caribbean, 121; in Chesnutt, 1, 28, 195; Colonial Revival nostalgia and, 91, 103; as differentiated from piazza, 216–17n9; and Indian *bangla*, 120; as narrative framing device, 1, 26, 69; as physical and social space, 1; of plantation mansion, 1, 26, 76, 84; racially amalgamated, 91, 196; screened-in, 187; as site of communitas, 77; of southern country house, 46; symbol of order and authority, 84; as threshold device, 95. *See also* piazza; portico; veranda

portico, 83–84, 137, 196–97, 201, 216–17n9. *See also* piazza; porch; veranda
The Practice of Everyday Life (de Certeau), 105
Putnam, George P., 41

race: and architectural profession, 31; and built environment, popular interest in, 195; complexly intertwined with architecture, 2–3, 4, 7, 25–26, 205; importance for study of architecture, 1–3, 25–26, 30–31, 194–95, 205, 208nn2, 4; and memory, 68, 78, 101; role in establishment of national architecture, 7; and southern landscape, 70, 74; and U.S. housing crisis, 205
A Rapid Tour Around the World (Fiske), 4–6
Reconstruction, 1, 28, 66, 70, 72, 76, 101–2, 170; architecture of segregation during, 74
regionalism (southern), 95
Reiff, Daniel Drake, 209n7
"Rena Walden" (Chesnutt), 68, 82, 101. See also *The House Behind the Cedars*
Rising Sun Stove Polish, 23–24
Robbins, Hollis, 57, 58, 61, 215n27
Rock, Chris, 203
Rohmer, Sax, 30, 165, 169, 180. *See also* Fu-Manchu
Roosevelt, Theodore, 197–98
Rosaldo, Renato, 231n85
Roth, Rodris, 210n28
Rufus Jones for President, 202–3
Rural Essays (Downing), 41
Rural Homes (Wheeler), 9–10
Rural Residences (Davis), 153
Rydell, Robert W., 236n48
Rzepka, Charles J., 171, 174–75

Saturday Evening Post, 129, 169, 178, *179*
Schuyler, David, 209n13
scrapbook houses: commercial versions of, 21, 25, 210–11n35; common pattern and decorative ethic of, 20–21; depic-

tions of servants in, 21–25; possible class empathies of, 24–25; and race, 20–25, 210–11n35; use of clippings from trade catalogs in, 20–21, 210n28; and women's periodicals, 20

Scully, Jr., Vincent J., 232n21

Seale, William, 196–97

Secret Service, 164–65

segregation: built environment of, 29, 46, 54, 74, 144; Chinatown and, 163, 167; on plantation, 9; racial, 74, 76, 102–3, 141–42, 199

Seelye, John, 112, 115, 224n14, 225n23

Selinger, Eric, 218n25

Semi-Colon Club, 14–15

Semple, Patty B., 95–96

A Sense of Things (Brown), 25

Shaw, Richard Norman, 156

Shelley, Percy Bysshe, 75

Shoppell, Robert, 191

skyscraper, 89, 125, 194

slave cabin, 2, 30, 55–57, 61, 73–75, 79; exported to West Indies, 129; in pattern book, 191; refashioned by Douglass into study, 63, 204–5. *See also* plantation landscape

slave narratives, 54

slavery, 10, 13, 15–16, 28–29, 39, 42–45, 94, 195, 20; built environment of, 1, 8–9, 17, 34–35, 45–51, 74, 75–76, 103; economics of, 9, 49; literature of, representations of built space in, 54–57; sexual violation of, 27, 44, 85; slave resistance to, 78–81; socio-spatial complexities of, 8; white nostalgia for, 191–93

slaves, 10, 14, 16, 33, 46, 74, 129, 195; psychology of place attachment among, 211–12n2; returning to former plantations, 81–82, 92; territorial appropriation by, 79–82, 92–93, 96–97; vernacular building traditions of, 70

Sloan, Samuel, 8–9, 49, 153–54

Sloan's Homestead Architecture, 153, *154*

Smeins, Linda E., 191

Smith, Jeff, 196

Smith, Oliver P., 7–8, 10

Smith, Valerie, 17

Smith's Pictorial Parlor Oracle, 18–20, 197

Soldiers of Fortune (Davis), 29, 129; as "Gulf" narrative, 111–13; imperial drama of, 113, 120, 122–23, 146, 147, 231n85; and *Memorias de mi viaje*, 132–34, 145; popularity of, 106; racialized space in, 122, 146; representation of built environment in, 113, 118–25, 138, 146–48; romantic racialism of, 147; and *Three Gringos*, 109, 118–20, 147; transnational bungalow in, 119–25, 138–39

space: architectural, 25–26, 35, 42, 60, 101, 185, 197, 235–36n45; colonial, 114–15; "cottage," 38–39; liminal, 77, 218n25; "Oriental," 29–30, 150–51, 160, 163; politics of, 35; racialized, 20, 104, 174; resistance to planter-controlled, in slavery 79–81, 85, 93, 99; and social order, 71; urban, 27, 194. *See also* domestic space

Stepto, Robert, 69–70, 75

Stickley, Gustav, 139

Stowe, Harriet Beecher, 14–15, 18, 55, 193

Sullivan, Louis, 229n58

Sundquist, Eric, 76, 82, 102

Sweeting, Adam, 47, 208n7

Taft, Helen Herron, 198–99

Taft, William Howard, 198

Tatum, George B., 154

Taylor, Yuval, 202–3

Tchen, John Kuo Wei, 152, 162–63, 232n10

Teng, Emma J., 235–36n45

Three Gringos in Venezuela and Central America (Davis), 29; architectural tropes in, 117; attitude toward imperialism in, 114–18; built environment in, 110, 113–20, 147; as "Gulf" narrative, 109–11; and *Memorias de mi viaje*, 107–8, 132–35, 141–42, 145; preference for cleanliness and order in, 114–16; and *Soldiers of Fortune*, 109, 118–20, 147; travel route, 110–11

Thurston, William W., 121

Wright, Frank Lloyd, structures designed by: Francis W. Little House, 160; Hanna House, 183; Imperial Hotel, 187–88; Martin House, 183; Northome parlor, 160, *162*; Roberts House, 183; Robie House, 183; Ward W. Willits House, 157, *158, 182, 183*
Wright, Gwendolyn, 125, 217n16

Wu, William, 149, 165, 234n36
Wyeth, Nathan C., 198

"Yellow peril" fiction, 150. *See also* Chinatown fiction
Yip, Christopher L., 234n36
Yoshihara, Mari, 27, 159, 185, 233–34n30

About the Author

WILLIAM GLEASON is Professor of English at Princeton University, where he also teaches for the Program in American Studies and is Associate Faculty in the Center for African American Studies. He is the author of *The Leisure Ethic: Work and Play in American Literature, 1840–1940*.